Electric Energy: its ge

McGRAW-HILL Electrical Engineering Series

Consulting Editor
Richard G. Meadows
The Polytechnic of North London

Electric Energy:
its generation, transmission
and use

E. R. LAITHWAITE, DSc, PhD, CEng, FIEE, FIEEE
Professor of Heavy Electrical Engineering
Imperial College of Science and Technology, London

and

L. L. FRERIS, MSc(Eng), PhD, DIC, CEng, MIEE
Reader in Power Systems
Imperial College of Science and Technology, London

McGRAW-HILL Book Company (UK) Limited

London · New York · St Louis · San Francisco · Auckland
Bogotá · Guatemala · Hamburg · Johannesburg · Lisbon · Madrid
Mexico · Montreal · New Delhi · Panama · Paris · San Juan
São Paulo · Singapore · Sydney · Tokyo · Toronto

Published by
McGRAW-HILL BOOK COMPANY (UK) LIMITED
MAIDENHEAD · BERKSHIRE · ENGLAND

British Library Cataloguing in Publication Data

Laithwaite, Eric Roberts
Electric energy.
1. Electric power systems
I. Title   II. Freris, L L
621.31   TK1001   79-42872

ISBN 0-07-084109-8

1 2 3 4 5 M & G 83 21 0

PRINTED AND BOUND IN GREAT BRITAIN

To Sheila and Delphine

CONTENTS

PREFACE

Following the pioneering years of the late nineteenth century when the foundations of electric power systems were being laid, the early part of this century saw engineers exploiting electrical power in a great diversity of applications. The advent of the thermionic valve and its successors, the products of solid state physics, saw a falling off of interest in heavy electrical engineering in academic circles. The industry, of course, continued to expand, but the bright young men and women of the years after the Second World War were attracted by the bright lights of electronics, in both academic and industrial spheres.

It took a major breakdown of a very large power network in the northeast of the American continent in 1965 to put the spotlight back on to the heavier side of the profession. Some thirty million people living within an area of around eighty thousand square miles lost their supplies and it took up to twelve hours before complete restoration was made. In the nineteen-seventies other major blackouts followed. These events, together with a general concern about the world's impending 'energy crisis', have been major factors in throwing up the power aspects of the electrical profession into sharp relief. The problems of the power engineer of today are seen to be at least as complex and demanding for the student of the subject as are any that the electronics industry has to offer.

We have compiled this text in the belief that young engineers will take up this challenge. They will need both the experience of past generations and a new and enlightened approach to the theory and practice of power generation, transmission, distribution, and utilization, taking into account some of the techniques that have evolved in the light current field and applying them in the large scale projects. The use of computers has made a vast difference to the control of power networks.

We see generators, transmission lines, transformers, and rotating machinery used as motive power as an integrated whole subject of which all facets are interdependent. We have endeavoured to convey our own enthusiasm for a subject that is full of possibilities for innovation. 'If I can see farther than others,' said Isaac Newton, 'it is because I stand on the shoulders of giants.' Never has the world had so many giants as in the contemporary scene, almost by definition. New discoveries, far from convincing the engineer that now 'it has all been done', show just how much further there is to go.

We do not take the reader's previous knowledge for granted. We have included data and answers to some basic questions in power systems. This is the kind of information not found in many other textbooks on the subject. Yet we do not have the space to include stock items such as the derivation of transmission line parameters, basic network and matrix theory, field theory, and basic mathematical analysis. Such topics are well covered in classic textbooks and in courses specifically designed for the purpose. But we do introduce new topics such as integrated control of power systems, security analysis, and economic dispatch. Elements of mathematical programming—not easily found at such a basic level—are included and used as a tool to formulate and solve optimum dispatch problems. Load flow analysis and particularly the Newton–Raphson method, usually treated superficially in elementary books, are covered in sufficient detail for students to be able to write their own programs.

There is a new look about the treatment of electromechanical energy converters too. The basic building block, the Goodness Factor, is used to separate what is vital from what is design detail in the elements of machines. Nowhere else is the theory of machines divided as between those types that carry current on *both* sides of the airgap and those that carry it only on one. The importance of this division is that the former become easier to design, more cost effective, *better* in every way, the *bigger* they are. The latter improve the *smaller* they are.

We have tried to write a book that departs from the 'run of the mill', to include topics that we ourselves find exciting. A new concept of magnetic equivalent circuits, including new components corresponding to inductance, capacitance, reactance, and impedance in a *magnetic* sense, is shown to reduce the degree of difficulty of problems involving parallel magnetic circuits or series electric circuits by a whole order of magnitude. There is a section on linear electrical machines that includes such new concepts as the use of transverse flux paths, a technique not readily applicable to rotary machines. The fundamental changes that enable linear machines to be designed to have high performance characteristics—a great stumbling block to linear machines for over a century—are clearly laid out.

Finally we have tried to introduce social, environmental, and economic aspects of power systems in general and nuclear energy generation in particular. This follows the general public concern about such matters.

The first author wishes to record his tremendous indebtedness to the late Professor Sir Frederic Williams, FRS, for showing him how to look at machines from an entirely new angle, and for teaching him to invent. In addition, the seventeen years that he spent in machines research with Professor J. F. Eastham (University of Bath) made possible many inventions, discoveries, and techniques that he could never have achieved working alone. In earlier days this author was first fired with enthusiasm for machines by the late H. P. Young at The Polytechnic, Regent Street, London, during the tough years of 1943–4. He is also indebted to his industrial colleagues at Linear Motors Limited, Loughborough, England.

The second author wishes to acknowledge the following in particular: Her Majesty's Stationery Office for permission to use freely in Chapter 1 text and diagrams from the report of the Royal Commission on Environmental Pollution; the late Professor G. Th. Kakrides of Athens Polytechnic whose book *The Theory of Alternating Currents* inspired Chapter 4; Mr P. H. Ashmole and Dr G. Shackshaft of the CEGB for assistance with Chapter 8; Drs E. Arriola-Valdes and N. Nabona and Mr Cheng Yu Teo, all past students of Imperial College, and Professor J. Meisel of Wayne State University, Detroit, USA, for their many stimulating discussions and ideas that helped to crystallize the content of Chapter 9.

We are both deeply indebted to our colleagues at Imperial College, London, for many valuable and stimulating discussions, and especially to Elizabeth Boden for a great deal of work both in preparing the manuscript and in reading the proofs.

E. R. Laithwaite
L. L. Freris

ONE

INTRODUCTION

1.1 THE FUNCTION OF A POWER SYSTEM

The function of a power system is to generate electric energy economically and with the minimum ecological disturbance and to transfer this energy over transmission lines and distribution networks with the maximum efficiency and reliability for delivery to consumers at virtually fixed voltage and frequency.

Electric power systems, in comparison with other manmade systems, e.g., communication, gas, water, sewage, etc., are the most expensive in terms of capital invested, the most influential in terms of seriousness of disruption of our mode of life in case of breakdown, the most visually intrusive in terms of the impact on the landscape of power stations, cooling towers, and transmission lines, and the most ecologically intrusive in terms of thermal, chemical, and potential radiological pollution.

Electrical engineering in its infancy was basically electric power engineering which, because of its long history, has not been attracting the publicity of the more recent branches of the profession devoted to communication, computing, and control. This in spite of the fact that our modern industrial society's muscle power is provided by electricity and that a host of challenging problems in power demand keen minds for their solution. But since the USA East Coast electric power failure, the 1973 oil crisis, and the demand for more efficient use of electricity at home, in industry, and in transport, there has been a resurgence of interest in power engineering. New renewable non-polluting resources will be brought increasingly into play and their incorporation into the present system will present some challenging problems.

Power system engineering is a discipline rooted in electrical engineering, but as a power system consists of electrical, mechanical, electronic, and control hardware, the engineer dealing with it should have a broad technological knowledge if he is to plan, design, and operate the system as a whole. In addition, he should be aware of the impact of his decisions on society and on the environment.

In fact, the power systems engineer, because of his pervading influence, should strive perhaps more than any other technologist to fulfil the aims of engineering, i.e., through applied science and practical ingenuity to alleviate the material problems of humanity and to arrive at minimum cost solutions that do damage neither to people nor to the environment.

1.2 WORLD ENERGY SUPPLY AND DEMAND

Power system engineering deals with energy transfer and utilization; a brief review of the world energy situation will therefore provide a background against which the technological information in following chapters can be seen in perspective.

World energy resources can be divided into the two categories of non-renewable, e.g., fossil and nuclear fuels, and renewable, e.g., solar energy. Early

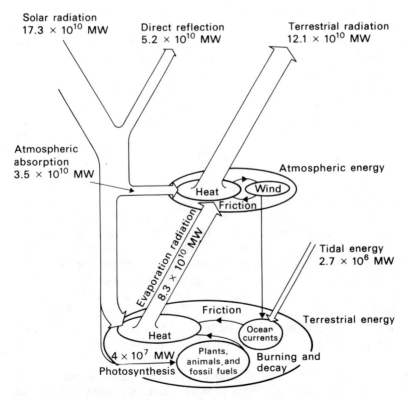

Figure 1.1 Energy flow diagram for the earth. (*Permission of the Open University*)

man was, and to a large extent the population of the poor countries of the world at present is, dependent on solar energy to meet their energy needs. This is done indirectly through the use of plants and animals to provide food, shelter, and heat. Industrialized man however depends to a much greater extent on fossil and nuclear fuels.

In 1975 the world use of primary energy was about 75 000 TW h—one terawatt hour is 10^{12} W h—of which 3.3 per cent was used by the UK and over 30 per cent by the USA. If the entire world population had the same energy per person year requirement as the USA, the whole world's fossil fuel resources would disappear in less than thirty years. The world of tomorrow may have to face considerable restrictions with respect to energy use.

Figure 1.1 shows the energy flow balance of the earth: the input of solar and gravitational energy, the storage and transformation of energy within the

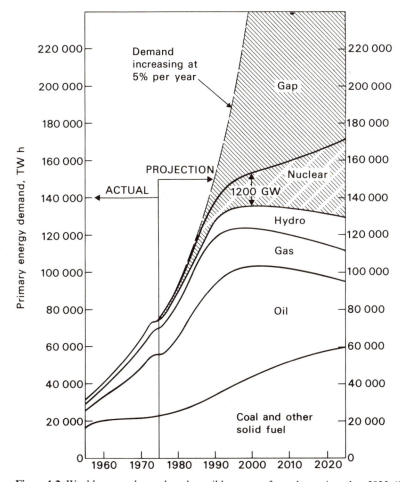

Figure 1.2 World energy demand, and possible means of supply, projected to 2025. (*HMSO*)

earthly system, and the radiation of degraded energy from the earth. It should be remembered that energy is not consumed but simply transformed from one form to another, during which process its quality is continuously downgraded. In other words its capability to perform useful work becomes progressively limited following each transformation; finally in its most degraded form it is radiated from earth into space.

The expansion of world demand for energy over the past thirty years has been met by ever increasing exploitation of fossil fuels, mainly oil and natural gas. The recoverable world oil reserves are estimated to be 2.8 million TW h. This represented eighty years' supply at the 1977 rate of oil consumption but if the recent trend of seven per cent increase per annum is assumed, the reserves will last only until the end of the century. The picture with natural gas is very similar. In the case of coal, the reserves are much less defined. At the current rate of consumption the ultimate resources might last several thousand years, though currently available reserves would suffice for only about two hundred years. However, as oil and gas are depleted, more coal will be needed to make portable fuel, especially for transport use, and to replace feedstock in industry, therefore its future consumption may be expected to increase rapidly.

Figure 1.2 illustrates that if world demand were to increase at a rate of five per cent per year, an enormous energy gap would result in the next few decades. There are claims that nuclear fission power is the only energy source which could close the gap. A programme of such magnitude, however, will require the commissioning throughout the world of three 1000 MW reactors each week for the rest of the century. This programme, if based on conventional reactors, would exhaust the world uranium reserves in about twelve years. The same quantity of uranium used in fast breeder reactors

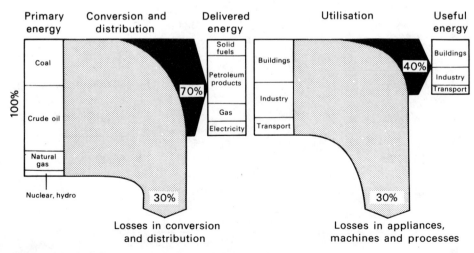

Figure 1.3 United Kingdom energy flow (1975). (*Dept of Energy*)

(FBRs) will produce an amount of energy many times as great as that available from all fossil reserves; however, FBRs depend on an initial supply of plutonium that has to be created in conventional reactors. There are also many misgivings, which will be dealt with later, associated with the extensive use of FBRs. In any case, studies show that with the most optimistic assumptions only about one-sixth of the gap could be filled by nuclear power.

Figure 1.3 shows the energy flow in the UK, a typical situation in an industrialized nation, where the average losses associated with conversion, distribution, and utilization are such that no more than 40 per cent of the primary energy consumed ends up as 'useful' energy to satisfy customer needs.

1.3 PROGRAMME OF ACTION

The conclusion that can be drawn from the world energy picture is that the energy problems that mankind will soon be facing should be urgently attacked now, as new developments and strategies take considerable time from conception to implementation.

The following programme of action is at present under way and its intensity will be increasing.

(1) *Constraint on energy demand.* In the world of tomorrow, there will be constraints on expansion of demand through government legislation. World energy prices will rise steadily in real terms to enforce economies. Expansion of energy demand will also be constrained by ecological considerations such as limits to available sites for power stations, heat and water disposal, water availability, air pollution, and possible effects on weather. Energy from non-renewable sources eventually appears as extra heat in the environment and this could have noticeable effects on local weather pattern and climate. The average solar power density on the earth's surface is $100\,W/m^2$. Manmade global average power densities are less than $0.1\,W/m^2$; however, in areas of dense population such as New York the figure is $300\,W/m^2$.

(2) *Improved efficiency.* In an industrialized society, energy is needed for (a) heating of buildings (low temperature), (b) industrial processes (high temperature), (c) mechanical power, and (d) electric lighting and operation of electronic equipment. Owing to fundamental thermodynamic laws and restrictions to maximum temperatures set by available materials, heat engines that convert thermal to mechanical energy have poor efficiency. The overall efficiency of even the most efficient power station is barely 35 per cent, the average for a power system being nearer 30 per cent. Two-thirds of the heat energy is lost to the environment as low-grade heat through the cooling water used in power stations. Further losses are involved in the transportation of electric energy from generators to consumers.

Internal combustion petrol engines have efficiencies of 25 per cent, i.e., comparable to the overall efficiency of a power system. However, industrial and domestic boilers have efficiencies in the 70s and 80s and it therefore seems

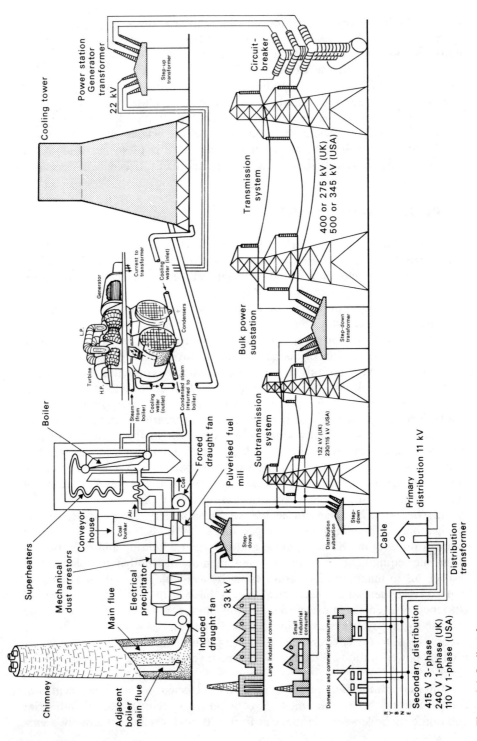

Figure 1.4 Outline of power system structure.

6

absurd to use electricity as a source of heat except for a few special applications.

A sensible approach to efficient use of energy would be to match the type of energy source to different user needs. An example of such an integrated approach is the combined heat and electrical power system alternatively known as a 'total energy' system. In such a scheme the waste heat from a generating plant is supplied through pipes carrying hot water to domestic and other consumers. The overall efficiency of such systems is in the region of 70 to 80 per cent, but they are only possible if power stations are sited within 30 km of urban areas. Total energy schemes are widespread in the continent of Europe as a whole but have not found favour in the UK.

Insulation of buildings to high standards can provide dramatic reduction in energy consumption for space heating. Future government policies are certain to encourage improvements in efficient use of energy. With a concerted effort, total energy savings as high as 25 to 30 per cent are technically and economically feasible.

(3) *Renewable energy sources.* The years to come will see an explosive development in methods to harness economically the renewable energy sources. These 'natural' sources include direct sunlight and its indirect effects of wind and waves and temperature difference with depth in the oceans. Other possibilities are exploitation of tidal and geothermal energy. An account of the efforts made to harness these sources is given in Chapter 10.

Renewable sources of energy have obvious advantages in that they are inexhaustible and their exploitation does not result in chemical or thermal pollution.

Power engineers will play a major role in this programme of action and the challenge offered is at least as exciting as that faced by Edison, Ferranti, and Westinghouse at the end of the last century when the first steps were taken in the creation of electric power systems.

1.4 THE STRUCTURE OF A POWER SYSTEM

Figure 1.4 gives a pictorial outline of a power system. As the large majority of power stations throughout the world are fossil fuel fired, such a power station is depicted. Nuclear and hydropower stations will be dealt with later.

Coal is fed to the coal bunkers by means of a conveyor belt from a large open-air coal store adjacent to the boiler house. The coal is pulverized in the mill and the very fine coal powder is mixed with preheated air and blown into the furnaces where it burns like a gas. Alternatively, the furnace could be oil fired in which case the preheated heavy fuel oil is fed into the furnace through burners.

The walls of the furnace are lined with tubes containing water. A typical boiler supplying a 500 MW turboalternator would consume approximately 200 tons of coal or 100 tons of oil per hour. The heat energy input is so great that nearly 100 gallons of water are boiled and turned into high-pressure, high-temperature steam every second.

In Fig. 1.4 the bare minimum of detail is shown. In practice, boilers have preheaters for both air and water, economizers, reheaters, superheaters, forced and induced draught fans to provide finely controlled air supply, and other refinements to extract the maximum heat from the fuel used. The flue gases are forced through mechanical dust extractors and parallel plate electrostatic precipitators before being allowed to go up the chimney stack. A dust collecting efficiency of 99.3 per cent is usual in modern power stations.

Power stations can burn low quality coal containing a high percentage of ash. This is recovered in the form of a fine powder and has found many uses including road foundations, manufacture of lightweight building blocks, and as a fill in old gravel pits and land reclaimed for agriculture.

The steam raised by the boiler is supplied to the turbine driving a generator. Typical steam inlet conditions to a standard 500 MW set in the UK are 538 °C and 2300 lb/in^2 (160 bar). The steam first passes through the high-pressure (h.p.) turbine, in the process expanding and giving up some of its energy. It then passes through a double-flow intermediate-pressure (i.p.) turbine and finally—not shown in Fig. 1.4—through as many as three double-flow low-pressure (l.p.) turbines. With each passage the steam expands and the l.p. turbine blades in the final stage are typically 0.94 m long on a base diameter of 1.52 m.

The amount of energy that can be extracted from the steam that drives the turbine depends on the differences between the input and output temperatures. The input steam temperature is of course confined by the limitation imposed by materials. The output temperature can be kept low by rapidly condensing under vacuum the exhaust steam from the l.p. turbine. Large quantities of cooling water are needed for this, e.g., 50 million gallons (230 000 cubic metres) per hour for a 2000 MW station. If the power station is built on a river estuary, the river would supply this water, otherwise the same cooling water has to be recycled. Cooling towers enable this to be done by getting rid of the low-grade waste heat in the atmosphere. Only relatively small amounts of make-up water are required to supplement that lost through evaporation.

The electrical machine driven by the turbine generates, for reasons to be explained in the next chapter, three-phase voltage at 22 kV between lines. This voltage, as will again be explained later, is too low for transmission over long distances; it is therefore stepped up to 275 kV or 400 kV in the UK, 345 kV or 500 kV in the USA, by means of transformers. At that voltage, it is transmitted to a bulk power substation where lines from other parts of the network converge. Bulk power substations are big junction points in a network—not unlike junctions in a railway system—where power is fed in from several power stations for distribution to towns and industrial complexes. The voltage at these stations is stepped down to 132 kV in the UK and fed to the subtransmission system for shorter transmission runs to distribution substations in the vicinity of the load centres. In these stations the voltage is further reduced to 33 kV and 11 kV for distribution by underground cable to consumers. Large industrial consumers are supplied at the 'primary distribution' level of 33 kV while smaller industrial consumers are supplied at 11 kV. Finally, the voltage is stepped down further by small transformer stations located in residential and commercial areas where it is supplied to these consumers at the secondary distribution level of 440 V three-phase, 240 V one-phase. The three-phase supply, consisting of the three lines red (R), yellow (Y), and blue (B), plus neutral (N), is fed through underground cable to urban and suburban areas and domestic consumers are supplied from one phase (known as 'line') and neutral, plus an earth. The intention of the electricity supply authority is to distribute consumers evenly on the three phases, and due to load diversity among a large number of consumers this is achieved to a good approximation. However, as perfect balance cannot be achieved, the neutral conductor carries the out-of-balance current and although it is earthed at the distribution transformer end it may not be at earth potential at the consumer terminals. A third wire which is truly at earth potential is also supplied to all consumers for protection purposes. The earth is connected to the outer metal casing of electrical appliances; thus if a breakdown of insulation takes place and the casing becomes 'live', the fuse connected in series with the line blows and the consumer is protected.

For protection purposes, circuitbreakers are interposed in many points on the electric network, although only one is shown in Fig. 1.4. As the fuses afford protection to consumers, circuitbreakers are the means by which the transmission, subtransmission, and distribution systems are protected from faults and malfunctioning of equipment. More will be said on protection in the next chapter.

1.5 NUCLEAR POWER STATIONS

Nuclear power stations use the heat from nuclear energy instead of that generated from the burning of coal or oil to raise steam. Having raised the steam the rest of the station follows the conventional pattern shown in Fig. 1.4.

Einstein's famous equation $E = mc^2$ shows that there is an equivalence between mass m and energy E, the constant of proportionality c being the speed of light. Physicists have shown that if a very heavy nucleus could be made to divide or 'fission' into parts then the sum of the masses of the resulting nuclei would be somewhat less than the mass of the original nucleus. This mass difference is released as energy. In nuclear reaction the fission process is controlled so that the energy release takes place steadily and continuously.

The released energy due to the annihilation of a small amount of mass is enormous. The complete fission of 1 g of uranium-235 produces an energy of 22 800 kW h; in contrast, the combustion of 1 g of carbon produces 0.01 kW h.

Some substances called fissile have the property that their nuclei may be induced to fission if they first capture neutrons. One such substance is uranium-235, which is present in natural uranium—mostly U-238—in seven parts per thousand. If U-235 is struck and captures a neutron and then fissions, it will form fission products together with two or three surplus neutrons. If one of these neutrons is in turn captured by another fissile nucleus, the process can become self-sustaining. In a nuclear reactor the reactivity is controlled so that the assembly of fissile material is just critical, i.e., the energy is released at a steady rate and in an orderly manner. The principle of the atomic bomb is based on an assembly which is supercritical.

Criticality depends upon a number of factors such as the concentration of fissile nuclei in the assembly, its size and shape, and whether the neutrons are travelling at the right speed. Capturing of neutrons by fissile nuclei is much more likely to happen if the neutrons have a relatively low velocity. Neutrons can be slowed down through collisions with a variety of light elements such as hydrogen, oxygen, and carbon. Such materials are called moderators and their presence enables a critical assembly to be achieved with a smaller concentration of fissile material.

In a nuclear reactor heat is generated in the assembly owing to the breakdown of the fissionable material, this heat being carried away by a coolant that is then used to raise steam. Figure 1.5 shows the main parts of a Magnox reactor, the first commercially successful design. The fuel elements are contained in metallic cans, in this case magnesium alloy. Surrounding the fuel elements is a graphite moderator. The heat generated is extracted by carbon

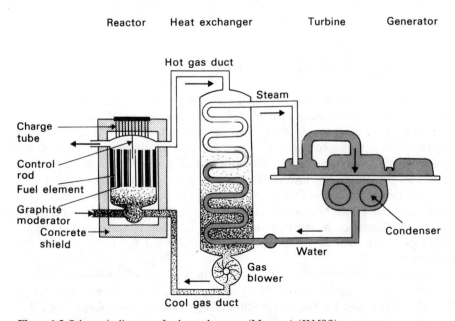

Figure 1.5 Schematic diagram of a thermal reactor (Magnox). (*HMSO*)

Table 1.1 Major reactor types

Reactor	Magnox	AGR	CANDU	LWR	SGHWR	HTR
Meaning of acronym	Magnesium alloy fuel cans	Advanced gas cooled reactor	Canadian deuterium natural uranium	Light water reactor	Steam generating heavy water reactor	High temperature gas cooled reactor
Moderator	Graphite	Graphite	Heavy water	Water	Heavy water	Graphite
Coolant	Carbon dioxide	Carbon dioxide	Heavy water	Water	Water	Helium

dioxide which in turn is transferred to water in a heat exchanger to raise steam for the turbines. The criticality is controlled by a set of boron steel rods that absorb neutrons. These rods can be quickly lowered into the assembly to shut the reactor down in emergencies. A 'biological shield' consisting of concrete several metres thick surrounds the reactor to protect operators from the core, which is intensely radioactive.

A considerable number of different reactor designs have been developed over the years and although their detailed description is out of place here, Table 1.1 summarizes their salient characteristics and explains the rather confusing acronyms devised to label them.

In conventional reactors, owing to the neutron bombardment, uranium-238, which plays little part in the fission process, is converted into plutonium-239 which is fissile. In such a process the number of plutonium-239 nuclei created are fewer than the number of U-235 nuclei destroyed, i.e., the 'breeding' ratio in less than unity. If it were possible to operate with a breeding ratio above unity then more fissile material would be created than destroyed, thus enabling the exploitation of the very large percentage of non-fissionable U-238. This would have a tremendous impact on the availability of fissionable material, multiplying by a factor of about sixty the yield of available supplies.

For a breeding ratio appreciably above unity to be achieved, the reactor should be unmoderated, the reactivity being sustained by fast neutrons alone. For this to be achieved, the fuel must contain a large proportion of plutonium mixed with the uranium fuel and the geometry of the core must be compact. This creates problems on the extraction of the generated heat from a small volume and liquid sodium is used for this process. In such a reactor the core is surrounded by a blanket of depleted U-238 (from which the useful U-235 has been previously utilized in conventional reactors), which absorbs neutrons and is converted to plutonium-239. Such an arrangement can breed enough plutonium to keep itself fuelled and have some 10 to 20 per cent to spare, hence its name 'fast breeder reactor' (FBR). Figure 1.6 shows a simplified outline of the 250 MW prototype FBR at Dounreay, UK.

Reactor   Heat exchanger   Turbine   Generator

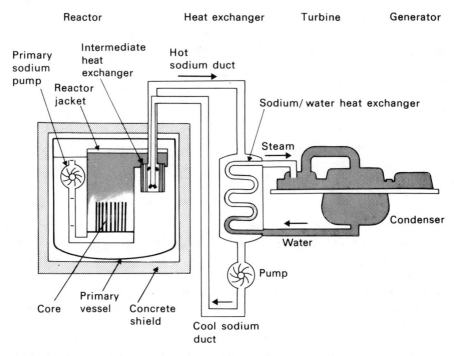

Figure 1.6 Schematic diagram of the prototype fast reactor (PFR). (*HMSO*)

An FBR requires an initial fuelling with plutonium, a manmade element that can only be supplied from a conventional reactor. An FBR therefore presupposes the running of a conventional reactor of equivalent capacity for many years for the production of plutonium.

1.6 THE NUCLEAR POWER CONTROVERSY

There are a number of major safety and ethical issues raised by the proposed extensive use of nuclear power to meet our future growing energy demand and to replace the depletion of oil and to a lesser extent coal. The decisions are particularly crucial in the case of the extensive development of FBRs, as plutonium is highly toxic and is the stuff that nuclear bombs are made of. Power system engineers should appreciate and be familiar with the issues involved, and a summary of the arguments for and against nuclear power is given below. These arguments are taken from reference 1, where the whole issue is treated in great detail and clarity.

It is worth stressing again that engineering is to do with people and their needs. Therefore technological choices are inextricably enmeshed with political and ethical issues.

(1) *The arguments for:*

(a) Nuclear power offers the only hope for meeting the future world energy demand and the world faces the choice between a nuclear future or decline. The decline may result in political instability and wars between nations for the control of the few remaining fossil fuel deposits.

(b) The environmental effects of nuclear power may be less damaging than those of fossil fuel power stations from which the amount of sulphur dioxide emitted will increase if the nuclear power programme is not established. Eventually, the carbon dioxide in the atmosphere may reach such concentrations that it may substantially modify the climate in some areas.

(c) Nuclear power stations use much smaller quantities of fuel than do fossil fuel stations. For example, one AGR station of 1000 MW output requires 50 tonnes of fuel a year compared with the oil contained in twenty tanker ships the size of *Torrey Canyon* for an oil-fired station. The transportation of large quantities of oil poses considerable environmental hazards, particularly with regard to possible collisions at sea.

(d) The risk of serious accident in any single reactor is extremely small; the hazards posed by reactor accidents are not unique in scale nor of such a kind as to suggest that nuclear power should be abandoned for this reason alone.

(2) *The arguments against:*

(a) If nuclear power were to be the main source of world electrical energy in the year 2000 and beyond then FBRs would have to be extensively used as such a programme could not be sustained on the limited quantities of naturally available U-235. A situation would therefore be developed in which plutonium, notwithstanding its dangers, would be in widespread use as a basic fuel of energy supply. This would lead to what has been called 'the plutonium economy'.

(b) With respect to reactor accidents, although the risks are very small, one can argue that man is unable to foresee reliably all the failure mechanisms that could lead to serious accidents and therefore to introduce appropriate safeguards. Nuclear industry is not alone in presenting the risk of major accidents that could lead to the deaths of many people, though it appears to be unique in the persistence of the contamination that such accidents would cause.

(c) The spread of FBRs among many nations poses serious dangers of proliferation of nuclear weapons and a high probability of a nuclear war.

(d) The quantity of highly radioactive wastes produced would increase in rough proportion to the growth in generating capacity, though the cumulative total of waste would grow much more rapidly because of the slow decay of the fission products. The creation of wastes that will have to be contained for many centuries is an unfair legacy of risk to our descendants.

(e) There could be substantial movement of plutonium between different facilities. This would create the danger of the capture of plutonium by terrorist groups for threat and blackmail against society because of its great radiotoxicity and the potential it offers to illicit groups to construct a crude nuclear weapon.

(f) The problem of safeguarding society from plutonium hazards would require the establishment of special security organizations that, because of the vast potential consequences of plutonium loss, would need to exercise unprecedented toughness and vigilance. There is therefore the fear that adequate security could be attained only at the price of gradual infringement of democratic freedom.

1.7 HYDRO AND PUMPED STORAGE

In world terms hydro resources represent a minute percentage of available natural energy; however in some countries blessed with large rivers they still play a major role. In developed countries most of the easily available hydro potential has been already exploited and it is in developing countries that it could still exercise a considerable impact.

The running costs of hydroelectric stations are very low indeed as energy is free but the civil engineering component of the capital cost is very high. The type of turbine used to drive the electric generators depends on the head of water available. As energy is extracted from water falling through the available head, the lower the head the larger the quantity of water necessary for a given turbine rating. High-head turbines therefore operate inherently with low water volumes while the opposite is true with low-head turbines.

Figure 1.7 shows the three basic types of water turbines. The Kaplan turbine has variable pitch blades that, together with the wicket gates, can be adjusted for optimum regulation. This type of turbine has been built for heads up to 60 m and is used for run of river and pondage stations. In the Francis turbines the guide and runner blades are designed for higher heads—up to 500 m—regulation being provided by adjustment of the guide vanes. Finally, the impulse turbine or Pelton wheel is suitable for high heads—up to 1800 m—and small quantities of water. In this turbine the water is injected through one or more nozzles on to buckets arranged around the wheel circumference. Regulation is by means of needle valves on the nozzles and jet deflectors.

All turbines are fitted with servomotors operated by oil under pressure for movement of the regulating devices. In the event of the load being thrown off and the regulating devices failing to operate, the turbine and generator are designed to withstand the forces arising from runaway speeds of twice normal.

Hydro plant has the advantage in comparison with steam-driven plant of quick starting and can therefore effectively meet the abrupt increases in load demand when working in conjunction with thermal stations. The advantages of hydro plant in meeting peak demand on the system when water supplies are not available can be provided from a pumped storage scheme. This consists of two reservoirs at different heights, with the hydro plant situated at the level of

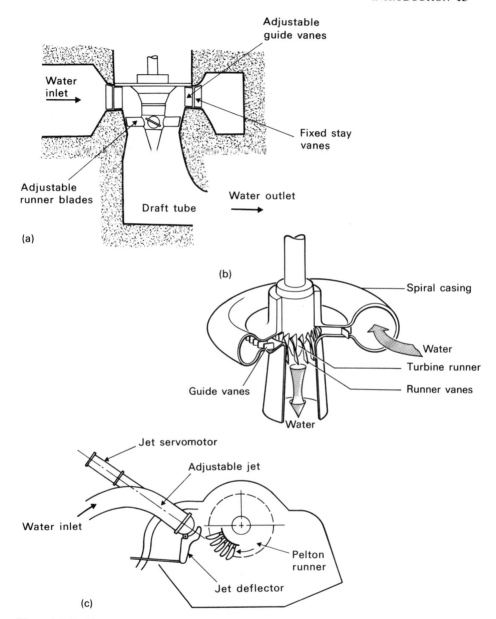

Figure 1.7 Turbine types: (a) Kaplan turbine; (b) Francis turbine (*permission of the Open University*); (c) impulse turbine (Pelton wheel).

the lower reservoir. During periods of low demand on the system, e.g., late at night, the 'generators' act as motors and drive the turbines, which act as pumps. Water is then transferred from the lower to the higher reservoir using cheap electricity from efficient thermal stations. During periods of peak

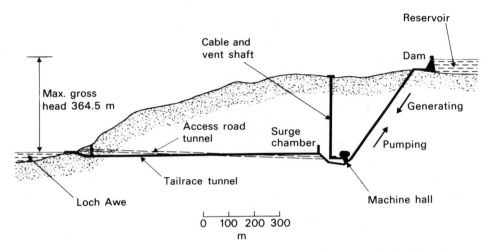

Figure 1.8 Loch Awe pumped storage scheme. (*Permission of North Scotland Hydro-Electric Board*)

demand in day time, the water flow is reversed, with the turbine now driving the generator in the normal manner. The overall efficiency of the operation is about 65 per cent; nevertheless, the advantages of quick response to load demand, and the fact that under peak demand old power stations with high running costs would otherwise have had to be utilized, make pumped storage schemes operationally attractive.

The variation of load demand and how this is met in practice is described in detail in the following chapters.

Figure 1.8 shows an outline section of the Loch Awe pumped storage scheme in Scotland. The reservoir was created by a buttress type dam 316 m long and it provides a usable storage of 9.9 million cubic metres, equivalent to 8.3 million kWh of electricity. Two inclined shafts supply water to four reversible Francis pump–turbines driving four 100 MW generators.

1.8 GAS TURBINES

Gas turbines are continuous-flow internal-combustion engines. Air is drawn from the atmosphere, compressed, mixed with fuel, and burned to form a high-temperature, high-pressure gas. This gas is then expanded through a turbine coupled to a generator and finally discharged to atmosphere or to a heat recovery plant. The advantages of gas turbine plant are:

(1) It is capable of starting and taking up load quickly, within two minutes; it is therefore invaluable for dealing with the peaks of the system load. It is less economical, however, to operate under normal running in comparison with modern steam plant.

(2) As its working medium is air, it is independent of water supplies for either operation or cooling, an important factor where water supplies are limited.

(3) Its capital cost per kilowatt installed is low and it can be erected and commissioned in very short times compared with those for conventional steam plant.

1.9 STATISTICS OF A POWER SYSTEM

It is instructive to examine in some detail the statistics of a particular power system because of the insight this will provide on the complexity and size of the enterprise. The public electricity supply of England and Wales will be taken as an example.[2] Its statistics are not untypical of power systems of other

Figure 1.9 The 400/275 kV grid system in England and Wales. (*Permission of Electrical Times*)

Table 1.2 Declared net capability by type of plant in the CEGB system at 1 January 1979

Type of plant		Number of stations	Declared net capability at 1 January 1979 MW	Proportion of total DNC %
Steam	Coal fired	79	36 004	64.4
	Oil fired	18	8 683	15.5
	Coal and oil fired	3	840	1.5
	Coal/oil fired	1	1 920	3.4
	Coal/gas fired	2	1 606	2.9
Steam sub-total		103	49 053	87.7
Nuclear		9	4 232	7.6
Diesel		1	10	–
Gas turbines		10	2 143	3.8
Hydro		7	112	0.2
Pumped storage		1	360	0.7
Total		131	55 910	100.0
Total declared gross capability, MW			59 662	

(*Permission of CEGB Operations Department*)

industrial nations, although the figures vary in detail. For example, the percentage contribution to generation of hydropower is very small in the UK compared with, say, Norway or France. In many other respects similarities are strong and the UK data provide information that characterizes power systems in general.

Figure 1.9 shows the geographical disposition of the British 400/275 kV grid system. Only power stations of more than 1000 MW rating are shown. Note that this complex network includes neither the lower-voltage transmission lines nor the primary or secondary distribution.

Table 1.2 gives information on the capability by type of plant in the CEGB (Central Electricity Generating Board) system. The net capability is the rated installed capacity less normal plant power consumption.

Table 1.3 gives information on the UK national grid and distribution system in service at 31 May 1976.

Finally, Fig. 1.10 shows the flow of primary energy in the UK. The diagram reveals that the electricity industry absorbs about one-third of all the primary energy used in the UK though it provides only about one-eighth of the energy used by the final consumer, the losses amounting to about one-quarter of the total primary energy used. These losses incurred must of course be seen in perspective. Electrical energy used in industry for a flexible motor

Table 1.3 UK transmission and distribution system

Transmission system	
400 kV lines	8 417 c.k.*
275 kV lines	4 386 c.k.
No. of towers	21 021
No. of transformers	531
No. of substations	194
Subtransmission and distribution	
132 kV lines	18 373 c.k.
33 kV lines	34 466 c.k.
11 kV lines	209 514 c.k.
650 V and under	282 955 c.k.
Total below 132 kV	581 059 c.k.
No. of distribution system transformers	404 098

   *c.k. = circuit kilometer.

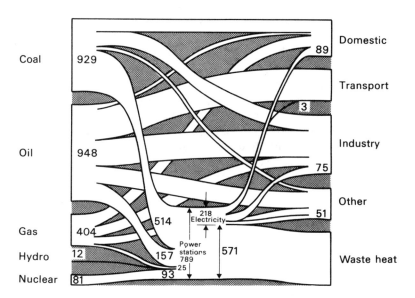

Figure 1.10 Energy flow in the UK in 1975. Figures in TW h.

		TW h	%
Use of electrical energy:	Generation loss	534	67.7
	Transmission loss	19	2.4
	Power station use	18	2.3
	Sales	218	27.6
	Total	789	

drive is utilized at an efficiency of 85 per cent, while an internal-combustion engine for the same drive would have an efficiency in the low twenties. This last efficiency would be comparable to the overall efficiency of the electric system from the fuel at the power station to the mechanical power output at the shaft. There is no doubt, however, of the advantages with respect to reliability, controllability, low servicing costs, cleanliness, and quietness of the electric drive compared with its alternatives.

At the other extreme, electricity used for low-temperature space heating and water heating incurs heavy losses of primary energy in comparison with fuel utilized locally in a boiler with efficiency between 70 and 80 per cent. For the national primary energy consumption to be minimized in the future, loads will have to be appropriately matched to types of energy supply.

1.10 CONCLUSIONS

Hopefully this chapter should have made clear that there is nothing obsolescent about power engineering. The two great challenges ahead are the gradual integration of nuclear and renewable energy sources into the network to replace the fossil-based ones and the development of more efficient methods of energy utilization ranging from total energy schemes to new types of machinery for drives and transport.

There is a large number of other challenging problems dealing with improvements in present methods with respect to economic operation and standards of reliability and the use of computers to achieve these ends. In fact at the end of the book a short speculative chapter has been specially devoted to the problems in power systems that require solution urgently. In this way the authors hope to convey the excitement and sense of adventure in power system engineering research.

REFERENCES

1. Royal Commission on Environmental Pollution, *Nuclear Power and the Environment*, HMSO, London, Sept. 1976.
2. The Electricity Council, *Handbook of Electricity Supply Statistics*, London, 1976.

TWO

ANSWERS TO SIMPLE QUESTIONS ON POWER SYSTEMS

2.1 WHY A.C. RATHER THAN D.C.?

Michael Faraday, perhaps the greatest experimenter of all time, demonstrated all the fundamentals of electromagnetism in a single year, the year 1831. These included the invention of the disk dynamo for the generation of direct current and the transformer for the voltage conversion of alternating current. History records that in the same year an Italian, Hippolyte Pixii, using Faraday's results, built a simple two-pole alternator, in which he rotated a horseshoe (permanent) magnet so that the north and south poles passed alternately beneath a pair of iron-cored coils.

Today the word 'alternator' is considered oldfashioned and has been replaced by the term 'a.c. generator'. Readers may judge for themselves the merits of this nomenclature, for a box of electronic equipment, deriving its energy directly from the sun and delivering output in the form of electric currents that alternate, plus and minus, in a sinusoidal manner could also be described as an 'a.c. generator', but it would have little in common with a rotating machine. The description of all rotating electrical machinery as 'electromechanical energy converters' is surely the means of resolving the difference, and since many older reference books that describe the generators of alternating current as 'alternators' are still of great value to the modern student, it is important at the outset that this latter term should contain no mystery.

The subject of electromagnetism is bound to be difficult, since it deals with phenomena that we do not 'understand', in the strict sense of that word. We have invented imaginary substances in which imaginary lines of force can exist in order to 'explain' the various phenomena of magnetism and electricity in terms of visual ideas, but even this can be done only within certain rules. For example, the physics book will often describe a *line of magnetic force* as 'the direction in which a free north pole will move' but will forget to add that since there can be only *one* such direction for any given position, lines of force can never merge or intersect, nor can they terminate abruptly. In fact, they have *no meaning unless they close on themselves to make loops.* Lines of force from permanent magnets should not terminate at the surface but continue through the magnet itself, just as an electric current flows through a chemical battery that drives it as well as in the circuit external to the battery. What one is even less likely to find in a physics textbook is the parallel statement that electric current and voltage have no *meaning* in the absence of a closed loop. Evidence hurled against this concept consists almost entirely of electrostatics, whose relationship to electromagnetics is, to say the least, remote in power engineering (see pages 65–72) and the man who uses a capacitor in this aspect of the subject does so because it appears to 'conduct a.c.'.

During the Second World War the armed services were geared to high technology and conscripted men of a variety of trades and professions were thrown together and taught to service such complex devices as automatic pilots and radar sets. To do this some of the traditional scientific 'corners' had to be cut and drastically so. How shall you differentiate between the capacitor used as an energy store on the one hand and as a conductor of alternating current on the other for a man whose life's work to date has consisted of selling fruit and vegetables?

One answer (which is not to be taken as a general guide to obtaining good answers!) is shown in Fig. 2.1. The military trainee was simply told as a fact of life that, 'A condenser [in the 'old days' this was the word used for a capacitor] is represented by a pair of parallel lines.' [As in (a).] 'Now d.c. is represented by a straight line.' (Fact of life again!) 'So when d.c. comes along it can't pass

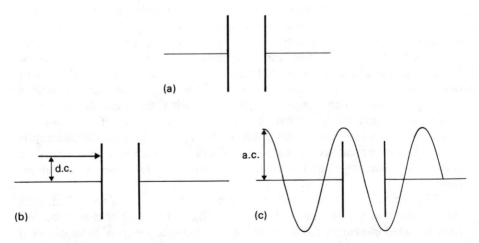

Figure 2.1 An analogy bordering on the ridiculous.

through the condenser, as you see. [In (b).] But a.c. is a wave and so it can pass between the plates of the condenser.' [As in (c).] And that was that. There were to be no arguments; that was what a condenser did!

Now if this analogy, crude as it is, is guilty of knowing the answer and building up a plausible story just to *get* that answer and is therefore to be deplored, *so also is the whole of science,* as revealed by its history. 'Light is a stream of corpuscles—no it isn't, it is simply waves—no, it isn't one or the other; sometimes it is one, at other times it is the other,' is an example of the way that scientific concepts, each of which is as illegitimate in its own way as that in Fig. 2.1, have been built up. It is merely a question of fixing the degree or level of sophistication at which it is done. The engineer should be ever aware that the concept illustrated in Fig. 2.1 helped to win a world war, and similar concepts are not to be despised.

Well then, if we are to believe in lines of force as closed loops that can never be 'opened' to allow conductors to link with them unnoticed, the basic principle of all generation of electricity by relative movement becomes clear at once. *What went in must come out,* and if the electric circuit remains closed, no net linkages can ever occur and we will be forever restricted to generating current that flows first one way and then the other—'alternating current'. To make d.c. in an electromechanical converter we must, in effect, continually make and break the electric circuits to allow lines of force to be wrapped around them continuously. The problem in its simplest form is illustrated in Fig. 2.2, in which 'generation' is represented by wrapping string (the electric circuit) on to the closed metal ring (magnetic circuit). If the string remains a

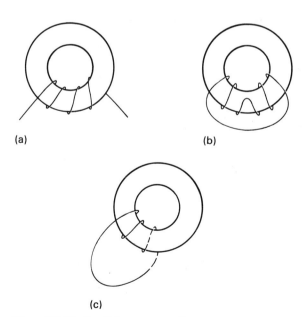

(a)   (b)

(c)

Figure 2.2 The line linkage concept illustrated using string and a wire ring.

closed loop, it can only be wrapped as shown in (b), where there are exactly as many left handed loops as there are right handed loops following them. This corresponds to a.c. generation. But if the string can be cut and rejoined once per turn, as in (c), permanent linkages (d.c. generation) are possible.

In school books, the d.c. machine is not usually taught as a special case of a.c. generation, even though it should be obvious that the flux in the rotating part changes direction twice per revolution. The output of a d.c. generator is confused with that from a chemical battery and the commutator is seen (without actually saying so) as a necessary and integral part of the process of generation. This of course is not so. (Nor is the commutator and brush mechanism to be seen as merely a rotary switch. It is, in more sophisticated studies, to be seen as a frequency changer.) The fact that almost all the electric motors that one encounters in early life, from battery driven toys to vacuum cleaner motors and 'do-it-yourself' power drill motors, have brushes and commutators, coupled with the school teaching of d.c. machines on the grounds that they are 'easier' to understand than are a.c. machines, leaves the majority of mankind (whom we students in a common cause may term 'laymen') convinced that *all* electric motors have brushes and commutators.

This mistake began historically with Pixii's machine and no less an authority than Ampère himself fell into the trap, for virtually the only principal uses of electricity at that time were in arc lamps and electroplating—another Faraday invention—and before 1831 the power source was always a battery. Electric filament lamps were several decades away, and the flow of electric current was detected by a galvanometer or compass needle. Pixii's machine was seen to cause a needle to *vibrate* rather than to deflect it permanently. Pixii showed his machine to Ampère who at once declared that what was

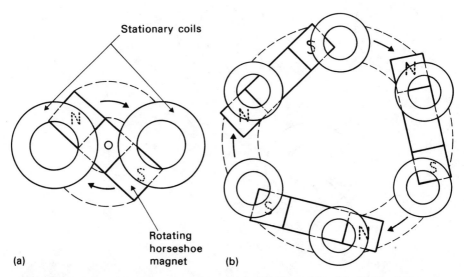

Figure 2.3 Plan view of the pole and coil layouts (a) of Pixii's machine, (b) of Stöhrer's generator.

really needed was 'battery-like current' (i.e., d.c.). Ampère showed Pixii how to fit a two-pole changeover switch that was geared to the main driving shaft so that reversal of current direction was achieved synchronously. Thus did Ampère invent the commutator and set back the progress of electrical engineering by nearly sixty years!

We must note that Pixii's machine was basically identical in principle to the modern alternator. True, the field magnet was a permanent magnet, but this was the *rotating* part of the machine and it did generate a.c. directly into *static* coils. Another inventor of the eighteen-forties, Emile Stöhrer of Leipzig, developed Pixii's machine by using three horseshoe magnets and making a six-pole alternator. Looking at his pole system in plan, and comparing it with Pixii's, as in Fig. 2.3, an important relationship for all a.c. machines is immediately to be seen: in one revolution of the two-pole system each coil is passed by one N-pole and one S-pole. The output voltage wave goes through one complete *cycle* of events. In one revolution of the six-pole magnet system, each coil is passed by three N-poles and three S-poles and the voltage wave completes three cycles for every revolution of the magnet system. So if both machines are driven at the *same speed* the output frequency from the six-pole generator will be three times that from the two-pole generator.

The theme that runs throughout this book is that of integrated *systems* where many generators are feeding into a common distribution network. Such a system is essentially one of constant frequency and therefore the appropriate comparison between the two primitive generators shown in Fig. 2.3 is that the six-pole machine will generate the same frequency as will the two-pole machine when driven at *one-third* the speed.

The reason why this fact is introduced early in the text in discussing an 'antique' machine of the eighteen-forties is that in later discussions of modern a.c. machines the location of 'poles' is much less obvious and yet the fundamental relationship of speed and frequency will always involve us in a *pole concept*. The relationship between angular speed and frequency could not be more simple. A two-pole machine produces *one* cycle of electrical events for *one* cycle of mechanical events. Thus if the machine makes one revolution per

Table 2.1

No. of poles	Speeds for 50 Hz		Speeds for 60 Hz	
	rev/min	rad/s	rev/min	rad/s
2	3 000	100π	3 600	120π
4	1 500	50π	1 800	60π
6	1 000	$100\pi/3$	1 200	40π
8	750	25π	900	30π
10	600	20π	720	24π
12	500	$100\pi/6$	600	20π
20	300	10π	360	12π
100	60	2π	72	2.4π

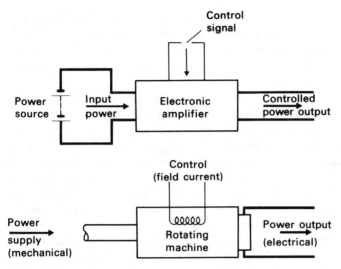

Figure 2.4 A rotating machine seen as an amplifier.

second, its output frequency is one cycle per second (1 Hz). Rotary speeds are often quoted in revolutions per minute (rev/min) or in radians per second (rad/s), the former usually by mechanical engineers and the latter by physicists. A table of speeds in either system, for both 50 Hz and 60 Hz for various pole numbers, is given in Table 2.1. There is obviously no need to commit this to memory as its derivation is obvious from what has just been discussed. The table's impact of the 'easy numbers' in rev/min for a 50 Hz system is helpful in reading section 2.3, which is why we reproduce it at some length.

Stöhrer's six-pole machine (Fig. 2.3(b)) makes a second fundamental point that is more easily discussed here than in relation to sophisticated modern machines. Six magnet poles could be matched to six output coils and the output from such a machine would be greatly increased compared with a two-pole version, for the heating of the coils due to the passage of current would be *distributed*.

Alas for Emile Stöhrer; he found that his field system was now a very heavy thing to rotate, so he fixed the magnets and rotated the coils. If commutation was needed, this mattered little, but if the machine was ever to evolve into an alternator, then slip rings and brushes would be needed to collect the huge amounts of generated power. This was backward step number two, *away from* the alternators of the great power stations of the world today.

It is no bad thing, even at such an early stage in the study of electrical machines, to compare a generator (either a.c. or d.c.) with an electronic amplifier (see Fig. 2.4). A small amount of power is fed in, in order to regulate the conversion of power input to power output. The only differences are:

(1) In the case of the amplifier, the power input is already electrical (the battery). In the rotating machine the input is *mechanical*, and therefore:

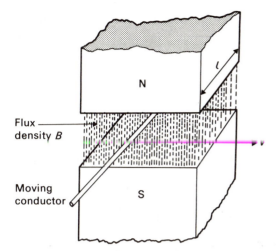

Flux density B

Moving conductor

Figure 2.5 Primitive generation system illustrating the 'flux-cutting' rule.

(2) The main purpose of the amplifier is to effect *control*. The main purpose of the machine is to effect *conversion*, although the control aspect is also useful.

In either case the main power flow may be hundreds of times the control power and if, therefore, the field magnets of a generator are made the stationary part of the machine, then the main power flow must pass through rubbing contacts (a commutator in the case of d.c. or 'slip rings' in the case of an a.c. generator), and at megawatt level such a concept becomes untenable. Thus most a.c. machines (motors or generators) are to be seen basically as d.c. machines turned 'inside-out' as regards the functions of the stationary and moving members, reversing therefore some of the work of Stöhrer.

Faraday knew that, having taken the concept of lines of force on board, *line linkages* were the only things that mattered in electromagnetic phenomena, and that it was immaterial whether the number of linkages changed through actual *movement* of the electric circuit through the field, or by means of a reduction in the magnetic field strength (and therefore the number of lines of force). Written mathematically, Faraday's law of electromagnetic induction is not simply

$$\text{e.m.f.} = \text{rate of cutting lines of force} = Blv$$

a phenomenon illustrated in Fig. 2.5, for this is only one part of the effect. If the number of lines of force (which from here on we shall call the 'magnetic flux') is ϕ and the number of turns of wire in the electric circuit that are linked by this flux is N, then Faraday's law is to be written

$$\text{e.m.f.} = \text{rate of change of line linkages}$$

$$= \frac{\mathrm{d}}{\mathrm{d}t}(N\phi) = \frac{\mathrm{d}}{\mathrm{d}t}(NBA)$$

where B is the line or flux density and A is the area contained by the turns N. If the latter remain unchanged, then

$$\text{e.m.f.} = N\frac{\text{d}}{\text{d}t}BA = N\left(B\frac{\text{d}A}{\text{d}t} + A\frac{\text{d}B}{\text{d}t}\right) \tag{2.1}$$

Figure 2.6 Allan's electric 'engine' (1852) based on the piston and cylinder principle. (*Crown Copyright. Science Museum, London*)

The first term is readily translatable into Blv by reference to Fig. 2.5 and is often known as the 'flux cutting' effect. The term $NA(dB/dt)$ is, by contrast, known as the 'flux linking' e.m.f., which is unfortunate, for both phenomena are the result of a change in line linkages. In transformers, only the second term of Eq. (2.1) is relevant, for the number of lines of flux increases as the result of a change in magnetizing current and not as the result of the physical movement of conductors. In d.c. machines, only the former term is needed. In a.c. rotating machines (as opposed to transformers) *both* terms are, in general, required.

There was a third retrograde step away from the modern alternator in the eighteen-fifties when it was declared that 'an engine should look like an engine' and the beam engine was well established as a prime mover. Allan's engine of 1852 used four 'cylinders', each of which consisted of a set of electromagnets in tandem. Conscious of the inability of an electromagnet to attract an iron core from much more than a centimetre distant, the first magnet was 'fired', attracting not only its own armature but the armatures of the other magnets also, which were connected to it by a one-way coupling, so that having fired magnet No. 1, No. 2 armature was now 'within range' of magnet No. 2, which was then energized, and so on, so as to achieve a stroke greater than one inch. Allan's engine, complete with overhead crankshaft, is shown in Fig. 2.6.

What was difficult to foresee in the period 1840–60 was the future generation of electricity in a few huge power stations situated hundreds of miles apart, yet supplying millions of separate customers. Such a system would require a distribution network in which the efficiency and cost of the transmission lines would be of vital importance. To transmit 10 MW as 100 000 A at 100 V would require the use of *very* thick copper cables and, even so, the ohmic losses would be a substantial fraction of the power transmitted, but to transmit the same amount of power as 100 A at 100 000 V is far more economical in cost and efficiency. Yet to use 100 000 V in a factory or private house is unthinkable because of the danger.

The fact that Faraday had demonstrated the transformer, also in 1831, and that this was the ideal mechanism for the transmission and distribution of electric power, cheaply and safely, did not prevent the development of d.c. machines from proceeding at speed in the middle of the nineteenth century. The electrical engineers of that time were just not thinking 'big enough'—and no one had seriously contemplated a.c. machines without brushes and rubbing contacts. The world still waited for Tesla and his invention of the brushless induction motor in 1888.

In the eighteen-nineties, men in Britain were putting together the idea of a distribution network that was spread all over the country. Surprisingly, there was much argument concerning whether a.c. or d.c. was to be preferred. The man whose arguments in favour of a.c. finally prevailed was Sebastian de Ferranti (grandfather of the present industrialist of that name) and he declared that we *must* use a.c., and not merely a.c. but three-phase a.c., 'in order to make best use of Tesla's remarkable invention'. Both Ferranti and Tesla himself knew that the induction motor was to dominate the world of industrial drives—to the extent, we now know, of over 95 per cent of the total power of electrical drives. It was the induction motor, as well as the ability to transform voltages easily, that set the pattern of distribution networks at the turn of the century.

A transformer of large capacity is expected to have an efficiency in the 98 to 99 per cent region and no mechanical devices before the days of gas bearings and superfluids could approach such a figure. Generators were limited in the voltage that could be produced before sparks ran around the commutator in a continuous band of fire. Even with a.c. generation, there was, and still is, a maximum alternator voltage that does not create vast insulation problems. Alternating current was obviously 'right' for a distribution network such as we have today, where one million volts is not considered impossible as a transmission voltage.

2.2 WHY A SINE WAVE?

Let us restrict our discussion about the shape of the waves of alternating current to the transformer in order to keep the arguments simple. Among the many erroneous answers to this question produced from time to time, many of which seem very plausible at first, are

(1) It is the easiest shape to generate.
(2) It makes the mathematics easy.
(3) It enables a designer to use Fourier series.
(4) It makes rotating fields 'perfect'.

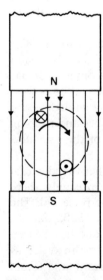

Figure 2.7 The simplest concept of generating a sine wave of voltage, never used commercially.

The first undoubtedly has its origins in school physics teaching where a simple rectangular coil is shown rotating in a uniform field, as shown in Fig. 2.7. The magnetic circuit is not closed, and often the rotating coil is shown with no iron core. Notice also again that the main power is handled by the moving member and this is done merely to be consistent with the d.c. machine explanation. What the reader is not told is that as soon as current is drawn from the coil, the flux pattern is distorted and the waveform of generated e.m.f. is no longer sinusoidal.

Up to a point, there may be some justification for arguments (2) and (4), but the advent of solid-state devices soon showed that machines fed from inverters, incapable of producing good sine waves, suffered little from loss of performance. As for Fourier series, any repetitive wave can be represented mathematically as an infinite series of Bessel functions (the Fourier–Bessel expansion) or a series of square waves, or indeed any of a whole range of mathematical abstractions.

The uniqueness of the sine wave is that it is the only wave shape whose differential curve is of the same *shape*. In transformers, if one starts with a sinusoidal input voltage, and does not involve the magnetic circuit in saturation, the magnetizing current will be non-sinusoidal, but of course the output voltage will reflect the input voltage and hence be sinusoidal. In electromechanical energy converters any voltage generated by rotation is necessarily a repetitive process, and the designer strives to shape the flux so that the wave shape is sinusoidal. The advantage of using Fourier series for the analysis of non-sinusoidal waveforms is that repetitiveness is assured because of the rotary nature of generators and because it helps us appreciate *why* as well as *by how much* non-sinusoids lower the economic effectiveness of machines.

It is a good engineering principle that when faced with an obscure problem, the process known as *reductio ad absurdum* often helps the explanation of phenomena that make their presence felt in only small doses. Let us therefore make use of this idea and consider a waveform as remote as possible from a sine wave—a *rectangular* waveform in fact. Figure 2.8 shows the effect of applying such a wave of e.m.f. to an ideal transformer. Since $e = \mathrm{d}/\mathrm{d}t(N\phi)$, it follows that $N\phi = \int e\,\mathrm{d}t$, and the flux wave, in the absence of magnetizing current, saturation, or magnetic leakage, will be triangular as in (b), but it must be remembered that in a *real* machine, the straight portions of the triangular wave are to become portions of exponential curves, as shown dotted, and as the result of winding resistance and magnetizing current in particular, the flux wave becomes more rectangular than triangular, as shown in (c). The output voltage wave is then the differential of this, as in (d), and application of such a waveform to the next transformer in the distribution network increases the complexity still further.

It is at this point that we may apply Fourier analysis quite properly, reducing our square wave to a series of waves of increasing frequency. We then find that increased frequency produces not only hysteresis loss rising in

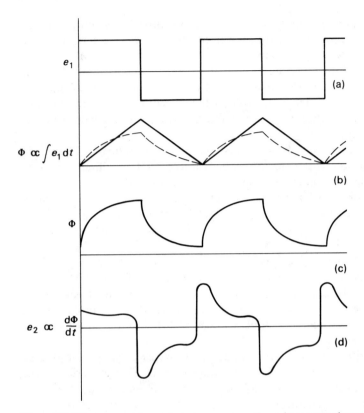

Figure 2.8 Effect on waveform of passing a rectangular voltage wave through a transformer.

proportion to frequency but also losses due to induced currents that rise in proportion to the *square* of frequency. Even the *noise* produced by a machine is multiplied by a large factor as the result of the higher harmonics. In transmission lines, all the arguments against the use of a much higher frequency enumerated in the previous paragraph apply, and in addition a long pair of transmission lines has a considerable capacitance between lines so that high frequencies result in lossy capacitive currents between lines and in some circumstances disastrous resonance effects may occur. Interference with neighbouring telephone lines is yet another hazard. It will be seen later (Chapter 7) that harmonics also reduce the efficiency of a.c. machines.

The cost of ensuring sine wave generation, however, is very high, and if departures of only two or three per cent are required at any point in the waveform, the cost of an alternator to meet such requirements may be many times that of an acceptable commercial machine. One of the reasons why meticulous design in this respect is seldom required is that the same design rules are applied to both generator and motor alike. Let us consider therefore a simple system in which two synchronous machines are connected so that the one can be driven by a prime mover and act as alternator to supply the second machine. If *both* machines have the same ill-formed waveform of induced e.m.f. due to, possibly, a badly shaped iron profile, will they not, as a pair of identical twins, find a sympathetic wave of flux existing as a matched pair, with self-compensation for the abnormal losses that would occur if either were to be used as motor and fed from a sinusoidal supply? Even if the answer to this question were an unqualified 'Yes', one must be wary of taking this argument too far, for it suggests that if only we could persuade all designers to make the same mistakes to the same degree, all would be well in an entire network of machines! The fallacy here lies in assuming that transformers behave like rotating machines and like transmission lines. The latter, having no iron cores, do not produce saturation effects. As in the previous section, the answer to an apparently simple question involves such complexities as will occupy our attention for the entire length of the book.

2.3 WHY 50 OR 60 HZ?

This question differs from those of sections 2.1, 2.2, or 2.4 in that the use of an exact decimal number was *chosen* by a group of men sitting around a table, rather than that it was inherent in the physics of the system. Fifty was chosen in preference to 51, and 60 was to be preferred to 60.3, only in that they simplified design calculations as explained in section 2.2. The meaning behind this question asks rather why 50 was to be preferred to 40 or to 60 by the Europeans while 60 was preferred to 50 or to 70 in America. One may go further and ask whether, if the whole of the British grid system were now to be scrapped and rebuilt, the designers of the new system would opt for 60 Hz, or raise the frequency still further to 70 Hz or 75 Hz?

First, simple arguments may be advanced to 'bracket' the likely range of possible values. For example, 10 Hz would be quite useless for lighting purposes because of the flicker detectable by the human eye. At once we can see how the lower end of the range has been raised by developments in other branches of the technology. 50 Hz is a sufficiently high frequency to be smoothed out by the thermal capacity of the filaments of filament lamps (which quantity, incidentally, can be regarded as the 'thermal inductance' of a thermal circuit and therefore acts as a smoothing 'choke').[1] But neither 50 Hz nor 60 Hz is sufficiently high to exploit the 'persistence of vision' of the human eye if rapid movement of objects is to be observed in the light of fluorescent (discharge) lamps. Indeed, legislation has been necessary for safety in factories where synchronized machines might appear stationary in fluorescent lighting, causing employees to come into contact with shafts and wheels revolving at 3000 rev/min (50 Hz) or 3600 rev/min (60 Hz). In such legislation use is made of the fact that other phases are available that effectively mix a higher frequency into the light effect from two lamps that are connected into different supply phases, giving a synchronous shaft an unmistakable blurred or 'misty' appearance.

The upper limit on frequency can be appreciated by consideration of a whole list of undesirable effects resulting from too high a frequency:

(1) Iron losses increase partly in proportion to frequency (hysteresis), partly to the *square* of frequency (eddy current).
(2) Leakage reactances in both machines and transmission lines increase in proportion to frequency.
(3) Capacitive reactance between transmission lines *reduces* in proportion to increase in frequency.
(4) As the result of (2) and (3), therefore, *resonance* effects may occur in long transmission lines.
(5) Radiation will affect neighbouring telephone lines to an increasing extent as frequency is increased.

While there are few attractive aspects of the use of low frequencies, there are nevertheless many benefits that accrue from frequency increase above those currently used, provided problems (1) to (5) above can be contained. The major benefit from the use of increased frequency is the overall increase in power/weight ratio. The output power P of a machine is often stated as being equal to KD^2ln where D is the machine diameter, l its axial length, and n its rotational speed. This simple concept is based on the idea that because of magnetic saturation there is a maximum economic value of the airgap flux density. Because of heating effects due to ohmic (I^2R) losses there is a maximum value of current around the machine periphery. The tangential force from unit pole area of a machine is the product of flux density and current loading and hence the total force is proportional to the *area* of the pole faces, i.e., to the area of a cylinder of length l and diameter D ($=\pi Dl$). The torque available is then this figure multiplied by $D/2$ and the *power* is the product of torque and angular speed. K is termed the 'output coefficient', which is clearly not constant as between one *type* of machine and another, between machines of the same type with different *cooling* systems, and so on. K also varies as between a small machine of a particular design and a scaled-up version of the same design. The equation $P = KD^2ln$ is therefore only useful in generalizations of the kind now here proposed. In consideration of linear machines (Chapter 10), n obviously has no meaning and it is through a study of such machines that it emerges that the *surface speed* of the magnetic field, rather than its revolutions per minute, is the fundamental quantity in the calculation of machine performance. The relationship between n and the surface speed v_s is a simple one, namely $\pi Dn = v_s$, and was disguised in the formula $P = KD^2ln$ by the use of D^2. A more useful interpretation is therefore obtained by adjusting the value of K to K' and writing $P = K'Dlv_s$.

Apart from the general benefits that accrue from the increase in frequency at fixed pole pitch, there are 'user' benefits that may be entirely dependent on the apparatus to be served by a machine. This is particularly true where induction or synchronous motors are used to drive equipment such as mechanical pumps. The efficiency and capacity of a particular type of pump are much greater at 3600 rev/min than at 3000 rev/min. The smallest number of poles that can be used in an a.c. machine is two; these are the maximum speeds attainable from 60 Hz and 50 Hz supplies, respectively. What is true for the user is also true for the generator prime movers, and steam turbines are also more efficient at higher speed.

This feature often demands a higher frequency than would be suitable for long line transmission, and it is interesting to note that where a purely 'local' system of machines and transmission lines is concerned, as in an aircraft, the choice of frequency is usually 400 Hz but can rise to 1000 Hz in specific instances. In large aircraft the increased frequency makes the problems of transmission of electric power from end to end at least begin to resemble those of an overland 50 Hz line.

In general, however, scaling techniques involve the law that a reduction in linear dimension by a factor N involves an increase in frequency of N^2 and therefore an overall increase in linear speed, v_s, of N.

2.4 WHY THREE-PHASE?

The answer to this question, like those to the earlier ones, is somewhat complicated and certainly not obvious. A summary answer might state that there were two distinct reasons for the use of more than one phase, the one concerned with raising the rating of a.c. generators and the other with the use of a.c. for conversion to mechanical motion, as opposed to its use for lighting and heating. It is proposed to deal with each argument separately.

As already stated, the tangential thrust is dependent on the product of the radial magnetic field, or 'flux' density, B_g, in the airgap and the 'current loading', J (that is, the number of amps flowing in unit peripheral distance around the stator surface). Now B_g is related to the saturation level B_{sat} of the steel of which the rotor and stator are made, and to the design geometry, which can be assumed to have been optimized, so that $B_g = kB_{sat}$ and B_{sat} has a maximum value for the best steel available at any time. J, however, depends not only on the property of the electric circuits, i.e., the copper wires in the slots, but on how effectively the I^2R losses in the copper can be extracted from the machine. The improvement in power/weight ratio, not only of alternators, but of all electromagnetic machines, that has occurred in over seventy years of research can therefore be credited basically to scientists of three disciplines:

(1) Metallurgists who created new alloys of steel that could contain greater flux densities (i.e., increasing B_{sat}).
(2) Chemists who invented better insulating varnishes that allowed a larger proportion of the cross-sectional area of each slot to be filled with copper, rather than insulator, but, more important, insulators that would not fail until they had reached a higher temperature than that which would have burnt out their predecessors. This allows a greater I^2R loss to be tolerated and hence an increased value of J.

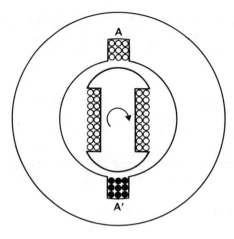

Figure 2.9 Primitive, two-pole alternator with a single stator coil.

(3) Aerodynamicists and mechanical engineers who designed better means of blowing air, or in some cases other gases, on to the windings in order to remove heat loss at a greater rate. Again this allows J to be increased. This research was made possible by acceptance of the use of perhaps 5 per cent of the machine's output to drive its own ventilating system so that output could be perhaps doubled, for a fall in efficiency from 90 to 85 per cent.

Of the three classes, the last had by far the greatest effect. Today it is recognized that the output of a machine is dependent almost entirely on the temperature of the hottest spot in the machine. Let us examine where this spot is located.

Figure 2.9 shows a cross section through a two-pole a.c. generator of rather obvious and naive design, where a single coil in the stator slots receives

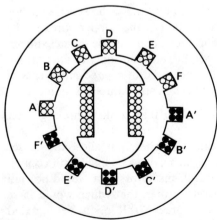

Figure 2.10 First stage of development—the stator winding is distributed into six slots per pole.

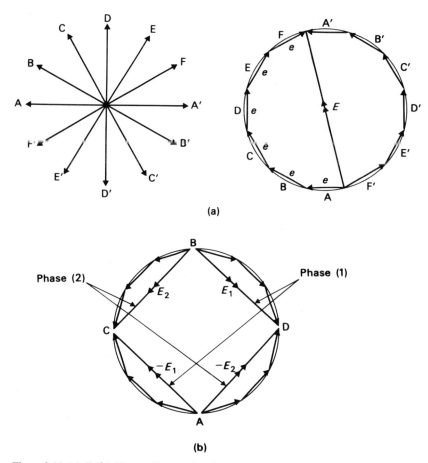

Figure 2.11 (a) (Left) Phasor diagram for the slots of the alternator shown in Fig. 2.10. (Right) Connection as a two-pole, single-phase machine with output voltage E. (b) Connection as a two-phase machine.

induced voltage by the rotation of the electromagnet rotor. Materials that insulate electrically generally do so thermally also, so the I^2R loss in the stator coil is contained by the slot liner and can only escape longitudinally (perpendicular to the plane of the diagram) along the wires to the end windings outside the slots. The hottest spots will tend to be at the bottom of the slots as indicated at A, A'.

A *better* machine from a cooling point of view would result if the bunch of conductors in a single slot could be spread out around the periphery as shown in Fig. 2.10, for each slot is less deep and end windings are spread over a larger area. But the e.m.f. induced in the conductors in slot A is not in phase with that in slot B, and so on, the relative phases for the various slots being shown in Fig. 2.11(a). If now all the conductors are to be connected in *series* (as they must, for parallel connection of out-of-phase e.m.f.s constitutes short circuit), some output potential is lost as shown in Fig. 2.11(a), for the phasor sum is E, which is clearly less than the sum of the n voltages e, i.e.,

$$E < ne \qquad (2.2)$$

Where does one stop? To use the full periphery and to go to the 'ideal' of using an infinite number of slots is to accept the diameter of a circle as 'output voltage', when the semicircumference was available, a loss of $2/\pi$. In a two-phase machine, as in Fig. 2.11(b), windings between A and C, and B and D, are in series and the 'waste' of e.m.f. due to distribution is less serious, the ratio of arithmetic to phasor sum being merely the ratio of arc to chord as between A and C, a factor of $\pi/2\sqrt{2}$, or $\sqrt{2}$ times that for a single-phase machine. However, the extra circuit introduced for two phase, as compared with single phase, requires an extra supply wire, one wire being common to both phases. Assuming a fixed current (set by heating) and a fixed consumer power factor, the output capacity of a machine becomes effectively the e.m.f. potential. At the same time the number of feed lines of a transmission system depends on the number of phases, for even if the polyphase system is slightly unbalanced, the common (neutral) wire of systems with three phases or more need carry but a small fraction of the line current.

Table 2.2 lists the comparative capacities of machines of the same size designed for various numbers of phases, and also the effective number of terminals and transmission lines corresponding. The answer to the question of why three was chosen should now be fairly obvious. Power gains beyond three are trivial, yet three is the only gain that involves no increase in the number of lines.

The second aspect of polyphase systems is that they can be arranged to produce 'rotating magnetic fields', and *all* a.c. machines operate on this principle. While philosophers may argue that a magnetic field exists only in the mind and physicists may attempt to 'explain' electromagnetic induction in terms of the modifications of the forces between electrostatic charges imposed by the Special and General Theories of Relativity, the engineer is concerned only with pursuing the profitable and argues that, while individual molecules of water near the surface of a liquid that carries moving ripples only pursue a

Table 2.2

No. of phases	Capacity figure	No. of lines
1	1.000	2
2	1.414	3
3	1.500	3
4	1.531	4
...	...	...
∞	1.570	∞

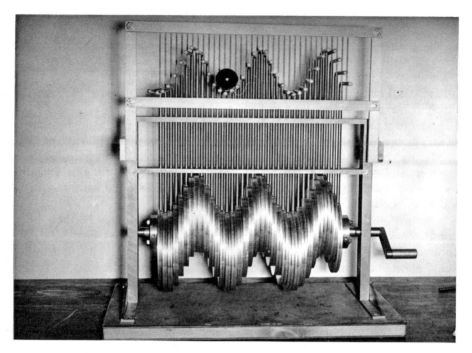

Figure 2.12 Travelling wave demonstrated mechanically by a row of rods lifted by a cam system.

motion that consists of a narrow ellipse with its major axis vertical, a surfrider is successfully propelled shorewards continuously by a collection of such molecules, each of which remains virtually in the same location. He then goes on to liken a wave of magnetic flux to a viscous fluid in this respect, and proceeds to get a remarkable number of correct answers from such a concept, as we shall see in later chapters.

How then does a polyphase system produce a travelling magnetic field (in the case of linear motors) or a rotating magnetic field (for rotary machines)? Perhaps the linear array is the easier to appreciate at this stage. If a row of coils P, Q, R, etc. is fed with an alternating current system such that coil P at the end of the row carries current $I \sin \omega t$, while Q carries $I \sin (\omega t + \phi)$, R carries $I \sin (\omega t + 2\phi)$, etc., and the distance between P and Q is a, that between P and R is $2a$, and so on, then it is not difficult to see that the whole array produces the effect that can be seen when a row of vertical rods is arranged as shown in Fig. 2.12. The first rod is moved vertically according to the formula $y = A \sin \omega t$ by means of a cam rotated at velocity ω. The cam moving the next rod is displaced by angle ϕ and its vertical displacement y is $A \sin (\omega t + \phi)$, but it is displaced *horizontally* by distance a, as in the case of the row of magnets. The effect seen as a pattern of rod tops when the common camshaft is rotated is a travelling wave whose equation is

$$y = A \sin \left(\omega t - \frac{\pi x}{p} \right) \qquad (2.3)$$

where x is the horizontal distance measured from one end of the array and p is a half-wavelength given by $na = p$ if there are n rods in half a wave. If the array is then imagined to be capable of being 'rolled up' into a circular array, a 'rotating wave' is produced, be it of rod tops or of magnetic field.

As one example of the use of such a field, a bar of iron or a compass needle pivoted in the centre of such an array would 'keep in step' with the field, producing, respectively, a reluctance motor and a synchronous motor. Or, as another, if a copper cylinder is pivoted in the centre, the rotating field, acting like the ripples in a viscous fluid, will drag the cylinder around with it, as in an induction motor.

A three-phase arrangement, as shown in Fig. 2.13(a), may be thought to constitute a very crude substitute for the multi-rod system (and, by comparison, multi-phase system) of Fig. 2.12, but in practice each coil does not stand alone, but consists of a distribution of coils represented diagrammatically as in Fig. 2.13(b) and the overlap of one phase with another results in each slot of the machine containing a mixture of two phases in different proportions, producing a gradual phase change from slot to slot rather than the 120° 'jump' suggested by the simple system shown in (a).

The nature of electromagnetic induction is such that a single-phase induction motor is capable of producing its own imperfect but nevertheless workable rotating field, *once it is running*, but it cannot start itself from rest. The theory of single-phase induction motors is, oddly enough, more complex than that of a polyphase machine and is dealt with more fully in Chapter 7.

It should also be noted that a two-phase system is, strictly speaking, 'two

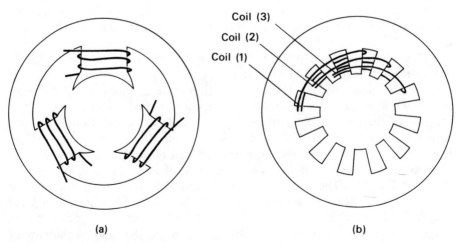

(a)   (b)

Figure 2.13 (a) Primitive three-phase stator arrangement. (b) Distributed coil system for three-phase alternator.

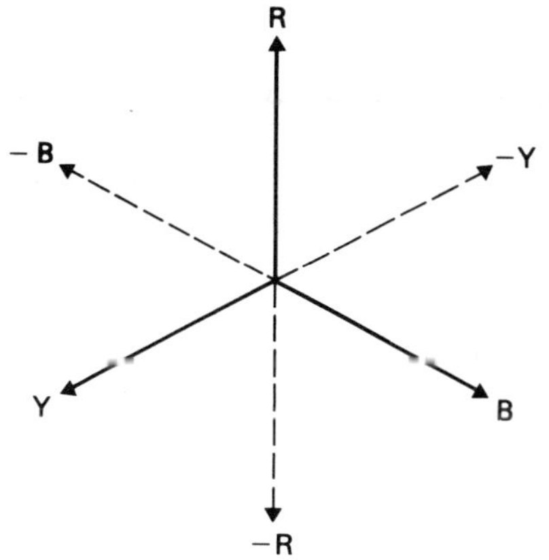

Figure 2.14 Phasor diagram showing how a three-phase system can be made into a six-phase system by reverse connection.

phases of a four-phase system', a three-phase system is similarly three phases of a six-phase system, and so on, and the additional benefits of the extra phases are to be seen in the connections of coils in the same phase as alternately positive and negative. Thus, according to the phasor diagram of Fig. 2.14, it is beneficial and therefore more usual to connect a coil sequence as R, −Y, B, −R, Y, −B, R, −Y, etc., rather than simply, R, Y, B, R, etc. (see also Chapter 7). A well known authority once declared that a statue should be erected to the man who first showed how to incorporate the back-connected windings into the system but doubted whether this would ever be realized since it would be more remote than a memorial 'to an unknown warrior'. It is one of those events that was not invented—it just happened!

2.5 WHY CONSTANT VOLTAGE RATHER THAN CONSTANT CURRENT?

The use of a constant voltage system is so familiar to most of us that contemplation of an alternative seems unthinkable. The power engineer has tended to leave the study of constant current systems to his electronically minded colleagues who dealt in pentodes and more recently in solid state devices. The idea of series and parallel connection is almost inseparable from that of current and voltage feeding, respectively, and therefore it is only necessary to contemplate the idea of a whole nation of consumers' apparatus connected in *series* to be ready to declare such a system 'impossible'.

Yet it is not so. The choice was open to us from the beginnings of systems. In the following question-and-answer series it is hoped to convey two distinct ideas:

(1) Only economic reasons justify the parallel world.
(2) Within a local system (which can include a single electrical machine) series connection can be profitable.

The first question is perhaps the obvious one:

Q: If all the houses in a whole country are connected in series, what happens if some idiot cuts the supply wire?

A: Much the same as if the same idiot drops a spanner across the main inlet cables of a parallel system—protective devices would isolate it from the system before any damage was done.

Q: How can you protect a series system?

A: In the same comparable way. In a parallel circuit, an *open* circuit isolates one consumer. In a series circuit a *short* circuit isolates one consumer. Any attempt to introduce excessive impedance into a series circuit results in a high voltage at the supply terminals. Overvoltage can be made to strike an arc, melt metal, and short circuit the system. This is the equivalent of a fuse. On the other hand the overvoltage can be made to *close* a breaker. In the parallel system overcurrent *opens* a breaker.

Q: How do you introduce a new appliance? Can it simply be plugged into a socket?

A: Yes, the kind of socket already used in certain applications. The principle is illustrated in Figs. 2.15(a) and (b). In (a) the incoming plug makes contact with each side of the spring clip. Having done this, the shape of the plug causes the socket clip to open, and the new appliance takes its place in the circuit. Light switches are placed in parallel with the lights they control and are closed when the light is off.

Q: Is everything, so to speak, the 'opposite way around'?

A: Yes, the dual is complete. For 'series' substitute 'parallel', for 'on' substitute 'off', for 'short circuit' substitute 'open circuit', and even for 'flux' substitute 'current', and all of the above also apply vice versa.

Q: The association of 'current' and 'series connection' is fairly obvious, but why is voltage similarly connected with magnetic flux?

A: Most of the highly effective electric machines (having a high value of *G*) are magnetized by a 90° lagging current, often referred to as the

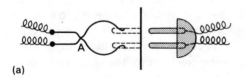

(a)

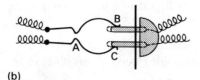

(b)

Figure 2.15 Plug and socket arrangement for a series system.

'magnetizing' current. In the absence of series resistance the only way the system can oppose the applied e.m.f. is by the rate of change of flux, $d\phi/dt$, produced by the magnetizing current. For a constant frequency supply $d\phi/dt$ is proportional to the peak value of ϕ. The magnetizing current will adjust itself to give the same value of ϕ for the same applied voltage, no matter how the shape of the magnetic circuit is changed. Thus defining flux is another way of defining supply voltage.

Q: An electric cooker alone may need as much as 10 kW. To run lamps connected in the same series circuit demands either (1) a very high voltage across the cooker or (2) a most unusual design of lamp.

A: It would appear so, but more use would be made of current transformers than in a parallel system where *small* devices, such as doorbells, operate at *low voltage*. In a series system only *large* devices (the cooker) would be used in conjunction with current transformers to operate at *high current*. Thus we can add two more items to the list of duals given above. For 'small' read 'large' and for 'low' read 'high'.

Q: What machines are good examples of the 'series world'?

A: Machines that contain short circuited windings, i.e., windings that surround a magnetic circuit, or a part of it, and that are closed on themselves without being connected to an external supply, and machines that necessitate the use of parallel magnetic circuits. The moving coil regulator and the shaded pole induction motor are examples we shall discuss in detail in Chapters 6 and 7. The magnetic/electric circuit concept is yet another example of a dual. A parallel magnetic circuit can be treated as a series electric circuit, and vice versa.

Q: What economic factors finally settled the choice between series and parallel in distribution systems?

A: The relative cost of iron, copper, and insulating materials had a part to play that is complex to evaluate but it must be remembered that the choice was made before the age of automatic control and some idea of the difficulties of those times may be formed by imagining that all electric motors must be operated at constant current to be effective. If this is to be achieved in a constant voltage world, some continuously variable tapped choke or similar device, manually operated, would be needed in order to start up every motor.

Now the nature of most electric motors, especially that of the induction motor, is such that input impedance increases with increase in speed. On starting, impedance is low, and a motor consumes very little energy in a constant current system. Therefore starting performance would be inherently bad. This is not a question of design, it is *fundamental*, and the characteristics are therefore not compatible with a constant current. All the difficulties and expense we would encounter if we were to feed all machines at constant current would therefore have faced the engineer of three-quarters of a century ago. From a passive load (lighting and heating) point of view, there was not so much difference between the two systems as is generally thought, but for dynamic loads (moving machinery) the choice of a parallel world was a natural one, economically.

Furthermore, in a constant current system, the I^2R losses are the constant quantity and iron losses in machines, corona losses between lines, and insulation leakage in both together constitute the variable losses. It is due, as Sir William Bragg put it so beautifully, to 'the Nature of things' that the levels of voltage and current are such as to make the I^2R losses dominate, and working at fixed (and therefore peak at all times) I^2R loss is thus far less profitable than working at peak iron, corona, and insulation loss.

2.6 COULD MAGNETIC TRANSMISSION SYSTEMS BE VIABLE?

Most certainly, provided two conditions could be met:

(1) There exists a magnetic 'insulator' to compare with porcelain, varnishes, plastics, and other materials used to confine electric current inside a wire.
(2) There exists a magnetic conductor with the same relative 'conductivity' as that of the copper in the electric circuit.

The fact is that condition (1) still cannot be met, except by the use of superconductor that *behaves* as if it had zero permeability, but its cost is prohibitive. It should also be noted that air conducts magnetically but not electrically (until ionized). It is instructive, however, to examine condition (2) also, for we will find that the magnetic conductivity of the best ferromagnetic materials known falls far below the comparable electrical conductivities of copper and of aluminium. This result reinforces the condition that the windings of electrical machines are generally elaborate, multi-turn, and of relatively small cross section, while their magnetic circuits have remained short, fat, and single turn for over a century and are likely to remain so for as far ahead as we can see.

Both magnetic and electric circuit materials are limited in the amounts of flux and current they can carry in a given cross-sectional area. The former has its limit imposed by the saturation phenomenon. It is reasonable to consider this to become prohibitive beyond a flux density of 2 teslas for the purpose of this example. The electric circuit is limited by the rate at which ohmic loss can be dissipated. It could be argued that in an a.c. system the mean value of flux density is only $(2/\pi)$ times the saturation value and that iron losses may place a temperature limit similar to that in the case of the electric circuit unless the steel is laminated to a sufficient degree. But it can also be argued that 'skin effect' (see Chapter 7) in very thick copper or steel-cored aluminium cables may lower the cable rating. In other words, a magnetic circuit suffers from current based imperfections as does an electric circuit from magnetically based imperfections. In this simple example we will ignore these effects in order to bring out the more fundamental part of the argument.

The comparison to be made is between the volt drop per kilometre of single-line, copper conductor of circular cross section $1\,\text{cm}^2$ in area, expressed as a percentage of the working voltage at the end of the line, and the m.m.f. drop in a single steel cable of the same dimensions compared with the m.m.f. at the line termination, for the same kV A transmitted.

For the electric circuit it is possible to dissipate 1 watt per cm^2 of surface from a bare conductor of the given dimensions, that is to say that the I^2R loss per metre of cable might be as high as $200\sqrt{\pi}\,\text{W}$. The resistivity being assumed to be $2 \times 10^{-8}\,\Omega\,\text{m}$, the resistance per metre is $2 \times 10^{-4}\,\Omega$, whence $I = \sqrt{(\pi \times 10^6)}$ or about 1330 A. Covered cables cannot dissipate the heat so rapidly and underground cables are still further restricted in respect of maximum current density. In order deliberately to bias the argument in favour of the magnetic transmission line, the low figure of $150\,\text{A}/\text{cm}^2$ will be assumed. The volt drop per metre is then 0.03, which is of the order of 1 part in 10 million for a 300 kV line and the transmitted kV A is 45 000.

The reluctance of the magnetic circuit per metre is $10^4/(4\pi \times 10^{-7} \times 10^3)$ (for $\mu_r = 1000$) $\approx 0.8 \times 10^7$ ampere-turns/weber, and the m.m.f. drop per metre at 2 T is $10^4/2\pi \approx 16\,000$. The change of flux from $2 \times 10^{-4}\,\text{Wb}$ to $-2 \times 10^{-4}\,\text{Wb}$ (2 T in $1\,\text{cm}^2$) occurs in a half-cycle of the a.c. supply, that is in a time $1/2f$. The average rate of change of flux per turn is therefore $4 \times 10^{-4}(2f) = 8 \times 10^{-4}f\,\text{Wb/s}$ and in SI units this is the average e.m.f. induced. The effective or r.m.s. value is obtained by multiplying by $\pi/(2\sqrt{2})$, making the volts per turn $2\sqrt{(2)}\pi f \times 10^{-4}$ or 0.0444, requiring ampere-turns equal to $45 \times 10^6/0.0444$ to give the same kVA transmitted. The m.m.f. drop per metre is therefore $(16\,000 \times 0.0444)/45 \times 10^6$, i.e., one part in 60 000 compared with one part in 10 million for the electric line. In other words, the magnetic material is over 160 times worse as a conductor. It should also be noted that to contain $45 \times 10^6/0.0444 \approx 10^9$ ampere-turns in an electric circuit at the receiving end (since multiple turn magnetic circuits are excluded because air 'conducts' magnetism) at $150\,\text{A}/\text{cm}^2$ would require a total copper cross section of over 600 square metres.

Magnetic materials are quite unsuited for power transmission. More than that, the above example is extremely relevant to the design structure of all electrical *machines.* The student should be ever conscious of the fact that for well over a century, ingenious men have lavished their art upon the electric circuit and have produced such complex and yet vitally useful pieces of hardware as the windings of the modern three-phase commutator motors. Yet all the time the magnetic circuit—that other partner in the vital electro-magnetic duo—has been the weak link. It is as if the best physicists of the world had for years been expending their energies on treating the healthy, while the sick lay unattended!

2.7 WHAT FIXES THE NUMBER OF TURNS IN A MACHINE WINDING?

The simplest machine to consider for discussion of this question is the transformer. If such a machine is to be used to step down a 200 V supply to 100 V, for a 20 A secondary current, then it is obvious that the turns *ratio*, primary to secondary, will be 2:1. It is less obvious why the designer has chosen maybe an 840 turn primary and 420 turn secondary, as opposed to, for example, a 960 turn primary and 480 turn secondary. Indeed the uninitiated are entitled to ask: 'Why not have just two turns in the primary and one turn in the secondary?' If this question is put to the average undergraduate in electrical engineering he is likely to answer: 'The magnetizing current would be of enormous proportions,' and he might be surprised to be told that this is not necessarily so. A transformer having a two-turn primary can be designed to take only a modest magnetizing current compared with its 10 A load current, but the magnetic circuit must be capable of generating 100 V per turn. The value of volts per turn is proportional to the peak flux density, to the area of the core, and to the frequency, and for 50 Hz the core area required for 100 V per turn is of the order of 0.3 m². The thickness of wire required for the 20 A secondary is of the order of 0.004 m diameter. Figure 2.16(a) is an attempt to show the proportions of such a machine to scale. It is obviously a massive machine to handle a mere 2 kV A. The magnetic circuit is obviously far too big.

If we are so foolish, however, as to think that transformer size can be reduced *ad infinitum* by simply increasing the number of turns in each winding proportionately, let us rework the above example using two million primary turns and one million secondary turns. The 'holes', often referred to as the 'windows', in the magnetic circuit must now each contain three million wires of 0.1 cm² cross-sectional area, a total copper area of 30 m². The volts per turn

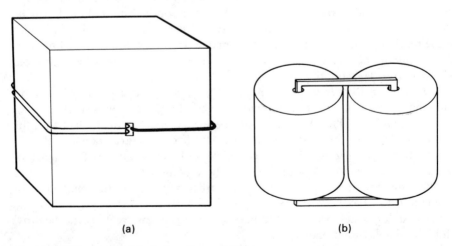

(a)   (b)

Figure 2.16 The two extremes in transformer design.

amount to 10^{-4} and the magnetic core section is $0.003\,\text{cm}^2$ in area. Figure 2.16(b) illustrates this equally ridiculous design, to scale.

This whole exercise has been carried out not only to enable us to discover just what numbers of turns *are* chosen by the experienced designer and why, but as an example of an engineer's method of containing a problem by *reductio ad absurdum*—going to extremes in both directions in order to highlight the limitations. Machines of more reasonable proportions but which are nevertheless biased towards the design of Fig. 2.16(a) are known as 'iron' machines; those tending slightly towards (b) are called 'copper' machines. The choice of the optimum numbers of turns must obviously lie between the limits of (a) and (b), and will be dealt with in full in Chapter 6.

2.8 WHY SUCH A VARIETY OF VOLTAGES?

As we saw in Chapter 1, a power network is divided by transformers into sections, each section operating at a different voltage.

The basic principle underlying the choice of voltage is illustrated by Fig. 2.17, in which R represents the resistance of a transmission line, V_g the generator voltage, and V_l the load voltage. The power received by a load of power factor $\cos\phi$ is $P = VI\cos\phi$ and the percentage transmission loss is $I^2R \times 100/P$. For efficient transmission it is necessary to keep the percentage loss within limits, somewhere in the region of 5 to 10 per cent. For this to be achieved, the resistance R and/or the current should be kept low. Large diameter conductors even at $50\,\text{Hz}$ suffer from skin effect, i.e., the tendency of the current to crowd itself near the periphery of the conductor, which causes poor utilization of the costly conductor material. Reduction of current necessitates an increase in transmission voltage V if P is to be kept constant. A high transmission voltage appears to be desirable, nevertheless this solution involves other problems. The higher the voltage adopted, the taller the towers that carry the line, the longer the insulator strings, the broader the right-of-way, all of which increase the cost of transmission. Added to that, transformer and substation equipment costs and corona loss, as well as radio interference, increase steeply with voltage. Here, as in all engineering problems, a

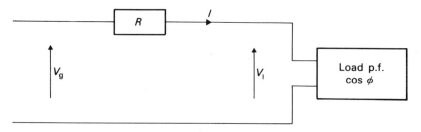

Figure 2.17 Circuit to determine transmission loss.

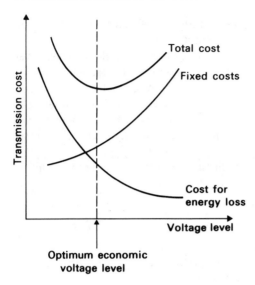

Figure 2.18 Optimum economic voltage level.

compromise has to be struck, in this case between the rising capital costs as the voltage increases against the rising losses as the voltage decreases. Figure 2.18 illustrates graphically this compromise and shows that an 'optimum' voltage level can be found that gives a minimum cost for a transmission line of a particular length and of a given cross-sectional area.

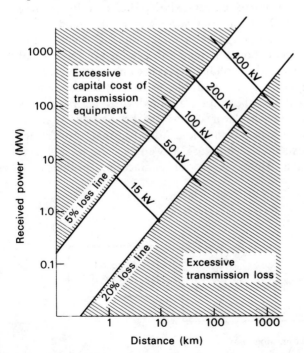

Figure 2.19 Relationship between power, distance, voltage, and loss.

The choice of voltage is complicated by several other factors that have to be satisfied, e.g., the voltage regulation at the receiving end of the line between no load and full load, the effect of the line reactance on the transmission line power transfer capability, and the stability performance of the line.

As in previous sections of this chapter, the answer to an apparently simple question turns out to be of such complexity that it cannot be given concisely at the beginning of the book. Most of the factors affecting power system choices that demand a compromise solution will be dealt with in later chapters.

A useful diagram due to Ailleret, that illustrates the constraints imposed on the voltage choice due to line length, line losses, and capital cost of equipment, is shown in Fig. 2.19. For long distance bulk power transfer the optimum voltage is high, in the region of several hundred kilovolts. At the other extreme, for secondary distribution to consumers where small powers are transferred over short distances, the optimum voltage is low.

2.9 WHY INTERCONNECTED?

Before answering this question we will have to look at some important characteristics of power systems:

(1) In contrast to other types of energy, electrical energy cannot be conveniently stored. Our attempts to store it, e.g., in pumped storage schemes, require its conversion into potential energy. The energy thus stored, although very useful, represents only a small fraction of the total daily energy consumption. The unavoidable fact is that in a power system a sudden demand by a consumer switching on a load has to be immediately supplied by an equal infeed of energy at generation points. It follows that the installed generation capacity should be at least equal to the maximum demand likely to occur on a very cold and windy winter day. For long periods of the year most of this capacity remains idle. This creates special problems in electric power systems that are not present, say, in gas systems where the generation of gas could be set at a more or less constant rate, the peaks and troughs of demand being 'smoothed out' by the gasometer.

A state of balance exists in a power system when the power infeed is equal to the power demand plus all the power losses. This could be likened to a car cruising at constant speed on the level. If the power demand increases but the infeed is unaltered the power system frequency starts running down in the same way that the car running on the level at constant throttle will slow down if an upwards incline is met. The frequency of the power system is in fact a sensitive indicator of how well the input matches the output plus losses.

Engineers in control centres endeavour to match input to output and keep the frequency constant to a tolerance, in the UK, of 50 Hz $\pm$ 0.5 Hz. More will be said on this very important topic in Chapter 8.

(2) The consumer demand on the system is not steady but varies considerably from hour to hour within a day, from day to day within a week,

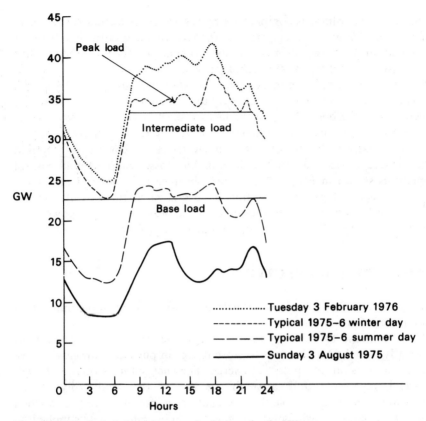

Figure 2.20 Typical winter and summer load curves for the UK system.

and from season to season. Typical winter and summer load curves for the UK system are shown in Fig. 2.20.

(3) In regions within large countries encompassing several time zones, e.g., USA and Russia, and between neighbouring small countries, e.g., Britain and France, there are time and habit differences that displace the peak demands.

(4) The fuel used for a power station plays an important part in the location of the station. Coal mines and hydroelectric potential may be in areas remote from the large load centres. In the case of nuclear power, the stations are located well away from load centres for reasons of safety and security.

(5) Generating sets are becoming increasingly large so that advantage is taken of the 'economies of scale'. It is a well known fact that often the larger the piece of equipment, the cheaper the service it provides. For example, it costs less to transport one tonne of crude oil in a supertanker than in a vessel of ordinary size. Similarly the capital, installation, and space costs per kW of installed capacity are lower with 500 MW turboalternator sets than with a smaller unit. An added bonus is that the efficiency of the larger units is substantially higher.

(6) The electricity supply authorities are, for obvious reasons, keen to run the most efficient modern power stations twenty-four hours a day even if these are not located near load centres, rather than use less efficient local stations. Even if a power station is not in the top efficiency league it is still highly desirable that it runs as long as possible as a revenue accrues from the sale of electricity to the public.

(7) The typical winter day load curve of Fig. 2.20 is shown subdivided into regions of base, intermediate, and peak load. It is self-evident that the base load is supplied by the most economic generating sets. As the intermediate load picks up at the early hours of the morning sets of lower and lower efficiency are brought in, with the least efficient sets supplying the peak load. Generating sets in an interconnected power system are listed in order of cost per unit generated; this list is known as the 'merit order'. The above picture of power system economic operation is rather rough but will be further refined in Chapter 9.

(8) In order to meet sudden increases in load demand and to forestall a loss of the larger generating set in the system, a certain amount of generating capacity known as 'spinning reserve' is required. This consists of one or more generators connected to the systems, but only partly loaded and therefore capable of picking up load in emergencies.

Bringing all these strands together we see that they either assume or point towards the desirability of an interconnected system for economic reasons.

Let us consider two isolated small power systems, each with its individual spinning reserve requirement. If the two systems are interconnected, the combined spinning reserve requirement will be considerably lower than the sum of the two original reserves, thus some generation capacity will have been released to supply future demand increases.

If networks in different time zones are interconnected, the peak demand of the joint system is likely to be less than the sum of the peak demands of the two individual systems. The joint power system will have a less peaky load curve and will be more economic to operate, as sets very low in the merit order will not be used.

The benefits of interconnection have been recognized many decades ago by power system engineers. In the USA the majority of the independent utilities are interconnected and in western and northern Europe all countries are transferring power over their national barriers through a labyrinth of interconnections. It is now possible to trace a continuous network from the north of Scotland through the Cross Channel d.c. link to the southernmost tip of Italy.

2.10 WHY NORMALIZATION?

Suppose we were told that the voltage drop over a transmission line carrying its rated current was 1.5 kV and, further, that the armature resistance of a d.c.

generator was $1\,\Omega$. What exactly do we learn from such statements? Surely they convey a minimum of information?

In the case of the transmission line we do not know whether the voltage drop is unacceptably high or ridiculously low because we were not told the voltage rating of the line. With a line rated at 3.3 kV such a voltage drop is of course enormous; however, with a rating of 400 kV the drop is much less than expected.

In the case of the d.c. machine, a large generator, e.g., 1 kV, 500 A, will experience an internal voltage drop of 500 V, about half of the machine rating being dissipated in the resistance. With a small d.c. machine rated at 100 V, 1 A, the internal voltage drop would be only 1 V, an unrealistically low value.

All this points to the importance of *normalizing* quantities so that data referring to volts, amps, and ohms, which by themselves convey very little, when divided by the *normal* or *base* values become very meaningful.

If we were originally told that the 1.5 kV voltage drop occurred in a fully loaded transmission line rated at 33 kV, the normalized drop being $1.5 \times 100/33 = 4.5$ per cent, we would know from engineering experience that this figure is reasonable. Similarly, if the $1\,\Omega$ armature resistance referred to a 200 V, 10 A, d.c. machine we could see that at full load current the internal voltage drop is 10 V, i.e., $10 \times 100/200 = 5$ per cent of the rated terminal voltage, a reasonable value.

An alternative way of getting the same answer is to divide the armature resistance R_a by the *normal* resistance R_n given by the ratio of rated voltage to rated current, i.e., $R_n = 200/10 = 20\,\Omega$. This results in $R_a \times 100/R_n = 1 \times 100/20 = 5$ per cent. This alternative approach tells us that with an armature resistance of $20\,\Omega$, all the generated e.m.f. is dropped across it with the machine supplying 10 A through, obviously, a short circuit. With $1\,\Omega$ resistance only, one-twentieth of the voltage is dropped.

Let us now go further to define normal values of voltage and current as $V_n = 200$ V and $I_n = 10$ A. With the machine supplying half full-load current, i.e., 50 per cent current, the voltage drop is $5 \times 50 = 250$. This figure does not represent 250 per cent voltage drop but should be divided by 100 for the right answer to be obtained.

The per unit (p.u.) system of normalization is used in power system engineering as it possesses all the advantages of the percentage system without the last mentioned disadvantage. In the p.u. system 100 per cent corresponds to 1 p.u., e.g., 5 A in the last example corresponds to 0.5 p.u., and the voltage drop calculation reads 0.5 (p.u. current) $\times$ 0.05 (p.u. resistance) $= 0.025$ (p.u. voltage). To convert the p.u. values into quantities possessing dimensions, we multiply by the relevant base quantity, e.g., 0.025 (p.u. voltage) $\times$ 200 $(V_b) = 5$ V.

The following advantages are gained through the use of the p.u. system.

(1) The p.u. values of impedance, voltage drops, losses, etc. of machines of like rating fall within a narrow range that is recognizable by a power systems engineer. In cases where data are unknown or difficult to determine, fair

estimates can be made with little loss of accuracy. Conversely, if p.u. values for equipment are given, gross errors are immediately obvious.

(2) For equipment of the same general type the p.u. volt drops and losses are of approximately the same order regardless of size.

(3) In three-phase power system studies involving complex networks, operating at different voltages and linked by transformers, the solution of the network is greatly facilitated by the use of the p.u. method.

At the outset, some base or normal quantities have to be chosen. In a power system the quantities of interest are volts, amps, ohms, and volt amperes (S), related by $S = VI$ and $Z = V/I$. Selecting two of these quantities as base defines the base value of the other two. Recalling now the constant voltage nature of power networks and the fact that equipment is rated in volt amperes, the two obvious base quantities to choose are S_b and V_b. The other two base quantities are then

$$I_b = \frac{S_b}{V_b} \text{ amperes} \tag{2.4}$$

and

$$Z_b = \frac{V_b}{I_b} = \frac{V_b}{S_b/V_b} = \frac{V_b^2}{S_b} \text{ ohms} \tag{2.5}$$

and base admittance is

$$Y_b = \frac{1}{Z_b} = \frac{S_b}{V_b^2} \text{ siemens} \tag{2.6}$$

Any voltage, current, volt amperes, impedance, or admittance can now be expressed as p.u. through division by the appropriate base, e.g.

$$Z_{pu} = \frac{Z_\Omega}{Z_b} = Z_\Omega \frac{S_b}{V_b^2} \tag{2.7}$$

To convert a p.u. impedance from an old base S_b', V_b' to a new base S_b'', V_b'' we write

$$Z_{pu}' = Z_\Omega \frac{S_b'}{V_b'} \quad \text{and} \quad Z_{pu}'' = Z_\Omega \frac{S_b''}{V_b''}$$

therefore

$$Z_{pu}'' = Z_{pu} \frac{S_b''}{S_b'} \left(\frac{V_b'}{V_b''}\right)^2 \tag{2.8}$$

Finally, the merits of the p.u. method when dealing with a transformer will be illustrated. In Fig. 2.21 an impedance Z_Ω ohms is shown connected to the h.v. side of a transformer rated at S_t MVA and V_l, V_h kV on the low and high voltage sides, respectively. The impedance could be any external impedance or the total transformer series impedance referred to the h.v. side (see Chapter 6).

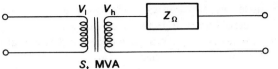

Figure 2.21 Per unit method applied to transformer.

Let the base voltage for the l.v. side $V_b = V_l$ and let a different base voltage $V_{bh} = V_h$ be specified for the h.v. side and let $S_b = S_t$ for both sides.

The base impedances at the two sides are

$$Z_{bh} = \frac{V_{bh}^2}{S_b} \quad \text{and} \quad Z_{bl} = \frac{V_b^2}{S_b}$$

Expressing Z_Ω in p.u. on the h.v. side

$$Z_{puh} = \frac{Z_\Omega}{Z_{bh}} = Z_\Omega \frac{S_b}{V_{bh}^2}$$

Transferring Z_Ω from the h.v. to the l.v. side using the square of the turns ratio (see Chapter 6), we get

$$Z'_\Omega = Z_\Omega \left(\frac{V_b}{V_{bh}} \right)^2$$

Determining now the p.u. value of Z'_Ω using the l.v. base quantities

$$Z_{pul} = Z'_\Omega \frac{S_b}{V_b^2} = Z_\Omega \left(\frac{V_b}{V_{bh}} \right)^2 \frac{S_b}{V_b^2} = Z_\Omega \frac{S_b}{V_{bh}^2} = Z_{puh}$$

To summarize, if the transformer MVA rating is chosen as base MVA and two separate base voltages are chosen for the l.v. and h.v. sides to coincide with the voltage ratings of the two sides, respectively, then an impedance has the same p.u. value no matter which side of the transformer it is placed.

As will be shown in the next section, this simplifies computation in power networks containing transformers and is equally applicable to single- or three-phase systems, in the latter case the transformer connection, e.g., star–star or delta–star, being immaterial.

Example 2.1

The list below gives information on power system components. It is required to express this data in p.u. using the following base values: $S_b = 100\,\text{MVA}$, $V_b = 220\,\text{kV}$.

(1) A voltage of 210 kV.
(2) A resistor of 500 Ω.
(3) A transmission line reactance of 100 Ω.
(4) The nameplate reactance of 0.1 p.u. of a transformer rated 50 MVA, 15 kV/220 kV.

(5) Using $S_b = 100\,\text{MVA}$, $V_b = 15\,\text{kV}$, the nameplate reactance of 0.75 of an alternator rated at 75 MVA, 15 kV.

First compute the base impedance

$$Z_b = \frac{V_b^2}{S_b} = \frac{220^2}{100} = 484\,\Omega$$

(1) $$V_{\text{pu}} = \frac{210}{220} = 0.955$$

(2) $$R_{\text{pu}} = \frac{500}{484} = 1.033$$

(3) $$X_{\text{pu}} = \frac{100}{484} = 0.2066$$

(4) Here we use the change of base Eq. (2.8)

$$X_{\text{tpu}} = 0.1 \times \frac{100}{50}\left(\frac{220}{220}\right)^2 = 0.2\,\text{p.u.}$$

(5) Using again Eq. (2.8)

$$X_{\text{apu}} = 0.75 \times \frac{100}{75}\left(\frac{15}{15}\right)^2 = 1\,\text{p.u.}$$

2.11 WHY ONE-LINE DIAGRAMS?

It is not the intention to give here an exposition of three-phase circuit theory but only a brief review to preserve continuity with the knowledge the reader should possess.

The voltages generated in the three phases of an alternator are equal in magnitude but phase shifted by 120°. The distribution of power to a balanced three-phase load can be visualized in Fig. 2.22 where the three-phase system has been split up into three separate single-phase systems. From the phasor diagram we gather that $\bar{I}_1 + \bar{I}_2 + \bar{I}_3 = 0$, with the consequence that if the three

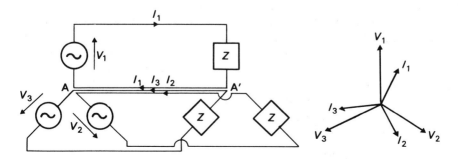

Figure 2.22 A balanced three-phase system.

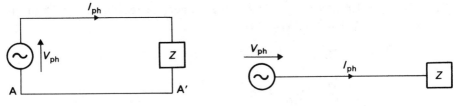

Figure 2.23 Single-phase equivalent.　　　**Figure 2.24** One-line diagram.

generators are connected at point A and the three loads at point A' then the conductors AA' are redundant and can be disposed of. A delta connected system poses no problem as it can be easily converted into an equivalent star.

Actual power networks are very close to this balanced condition. Industrial loads are invariably three-phase and therefore designed to be balanced. For single-phase commercial and domestic loads equal loading on all three phases is ensured by distributing the available load equally among the phases.

We are, therefore, perfectly justified in looking at only one phase of the system, as in Fig. 2.23, with the understanding that the impedance of conductor AA' is zero and that the other two phases carry currents of the same magnitude through identical impedances.

Figure 2.23 can be further simplified into the one-line diagram of Fig. 2.24 by omitting conductor AA'. All balanced power system networks are drawn in this shorthand style. Figure 2.25 shows a typical one-line diagram of a power network and indicates the symbols used to represent the network components.

Example 2.2

A one-line diagram of a simple three-phase power network is shown in Fig. 2.26. As will be shown in later chapters, the series impedance of most power system components, e.g., transmission lines, transformers, and alternators, is mostly inductive, therefore the resistive part is often neglected.

Here an alternator feeds a transmission line through a step-up transformer that in turn is supplying at 210 kV a resistive load of 500 Ω. We are required to find the alternator source voltage.

Let us choose an arbitrary 100 MVA as a common base MVA for the whole system. Next choose a base voltage of 15 kV for the system to the left and a base voltage of 220 kV for the system to the right of the transformer. The transformer can now be removed from the one-line diagram containing the p.u. values of impedance. The reader may have noticed that all the donkey work for this system has been done in Example 2.1.

The resulting one-line diagram is shown in Fig. 2.27.

The system current in p.u. is given by

$$I = \frac{0.955}{1.033} = 0.924 \,\text{p.u.}$$

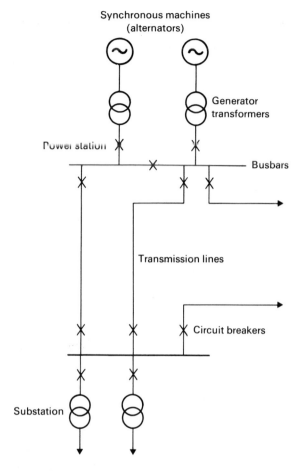

Figure 2.25 One-line diagram of a part of a power system.

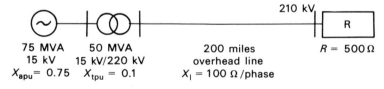

Figure 2.26 One-line diagram for Example 2.2.

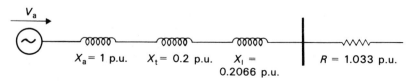

Figure 2.27 One-line diagram with p.u. values.

Applying Kirchhoff's voltage law to the phasor voltage drops in the network and using complex notation

$$\bar{V}_a = \bar{I}[1.003 + j(1 + 0.2 + 0.2066)]$$

Taking $\bar{I}$ as reference, i.e., $\bar{I} = 0.924 + j0$

$$\bar{V}_a = 0.924(1.033 + j1.4066) = 0.954 + j1.30$$

therefore

$$\bar{V}_a = \sqrt{(0.954^2 + 1.30^2)} = 1.612\,\text{p.u.}$$

The value of $\bar{V}_a$ in volts is given by

$$1.612 \times 15 = 24.18\,\text{kV line to line}$$

or

$$\frac{24.18}{\sqrt{3}} = 13.96\,\text{kV phase voltage}$$

2.12 WHY CIRCUITBREAKERS? WHY FUSES?

In Chapter 1 and in Fig. 2.25 mention was made of circuitbreakers, devices found in great numbers in power networks. The circuitbreaker is the most obvious component of a large number of complex but not so obvious networks that carry information on the health of the power network. These monitoring and overseeing networks constitute the protection system that takes action when the power network suffers a malfunction. The subject of protection is very wide in scope; the protection engineer is required to have knowledge of all the abnormal states of the power network and of the best possible action necessary to restore a faulty system back to normality. The principles and practice of protection are somewhat specialized for an elementary book on power systems; therefore very little of this interesting topic will be covered here. The subject will be given some further attention in section 8.5, which deals with system security.

No matter how well a power network is designed it is almost bound to suffer from malfunctions or faults that usually, but not always, result in overcurrents somewhere in the system. Let us look at a few typical situations that result in faults. The combined long term cyclic heating and mechanical stress on insulation in generators, motors, and transformers may result in its deterioration to such an extent that a low impedance path or 'short circuit' appears between points of high potential. The insulator string on a transmission line tower may fail mechanically owing to the combined load of ice and wind, the conductor touching the tower and causing a short circuit. Lightning may strike an overhead transmission line and produce such a surge of voltage that the insulation of components connected to the line may be irreparably damaged. A trawler dragging its anchor may accidentally damage an underwater power cable, again resulting in insulation failure. An industrial induction motor drives a mechanical load, the bearings of which overheat and jam, the consequences being that the motor current considerably exceeds the rated level. A householder incorrectly wires a three-pin plug causing a short circuit and an excessive current in the house wiring.

In all these examples, unless some protective action is taken there is likelihood of considerable damage to equipment, of fire, explosion, and perhaps loss of life. Electrical equipment is rated so that it can withstand the long term effects of (1) heating produced by internal electrical and mechanical losses, (2) mechanical forces produced by the interaction of current carrying conductors and magnetic fields, and (3) stressing of the insulation by the applied voltage. If the rated values of voltage and/or current are exceeded damage may or may not occur, depending on the magnitude and duration of the overvoltage or overcurrent. Obviously, the larger this magnitude, the quicker some protective action should be taken.

The function of the protection system is to detect the fault and take such discriminating action as to remove only the faulty part of the network, the healthy part being left intact and working. This action should be instantaneous if the fault is severe, but if the fault is mild, action should be appropriately delayed as it is the experience of power system engineers that a large proportion of power system faults are of a transient nature.

Domestic and commercial equipment and lighting and power circuits are usually protected by the simplest, cheapest, and most reliable protection device, the fuse. Figure 2.28 shows a typical fusing current–time characteristic for a cartridge fuse. The inverse time nature of the curve is very useful as it ensures that heavy overcurrents are cleared with a short time delay while with moderate overcurrents not likely to produce immediate damage a longer fusing time elapses. The fuse, therefore, mercifully, does not blow with small overcurrents of transient nature.

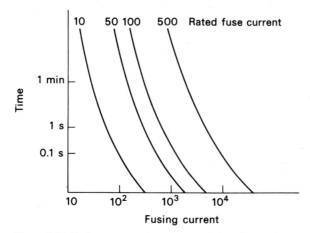

Figure 2.28 Fusing current–time characteristics of low voltage cartridge fuse links.

For the protection of industrial equipment and power network components at the transmission, subtransmission, and distribution level, circuitbreakers activated by relays are used.

Circuitbreakers operate on the principle of fast separating contacts. Owing to the inevitable inductance of the interrupted circuit, an arc is drawn which ionizes the medium in the vicinity of the contacts. In a.c. circuits the current passes naturally through zero and the arc is momentarily extinguished; however, a fast growing voltage appears across the parting contacts and the arc may be restruck through the ionized surrounding medium. The art of circuit breaking is to clear away the ionized medium and to establish 'insulation' at a rate faster than that of the rising restriking voltage. In the oil circuitbreaker, oil, and in the air-blast circuitbreaker, air, are injected between the parting contacts.

Figure 2.29 shows a section through an air blast circuitbreaker of the type used in high voltage substations. In this unit two interruptor heads are connected in series and followed by a series switch known as an isolator. With the two interruptor heads open but without air blasting, the insulation afforded by the heads is not enough to stop the restriking of an arc. The isolator opens immediately after successful interruption of the arc to ensure long term break of the circuit. Isolators by themselves can close a live circuit but not open one.

The signal that initiates the circuitbreaker action originates from a device known as a relay. Relays monitor appropriate system quantities, e.g., current and voltage derived from current and voltage transformers interspersed in the power network. If an abnormal condition is detected, a signal is sent to the circuitbreaker trip circuits.

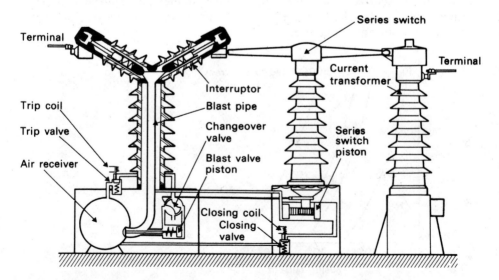

Figure 2.29 A typical air blast circuitbreaker. (*Permission of John Wiley & Sons Ltd*)

There exists a great diversity of relay types to cover a variety of applications. Relays operate electromagnetically, the most widely used type having induction disk elements, not unlike the household watt hour meter. Recently, solid state relays have been introduced and digital computers have been used in the complicated task of substation protection.

For protection purposes, the power network is divided into zones separated by circuitbreakers. During a fault, the zone that includes the faulted component is disconnected from the system. The problem of effective protection is to select a relay scheme that will recognize the existence of the fault within a given zone and initiate the appropriate circuitbreaker action. In the event of a failure of a protection circuit component the first line of defence will be inoperative, therefore some form of second line of defence or 'back-up' protection is provided to do the next best thing. This may require the disconnection of adjacent healthy zones, as well as the faulty one. The reader will appreciate that in a substation containing a large number of transformers, circuitbreakers, and busbars, into which a considerable number of transmission lines converge, it is not an easy task to determine the optimum protection policy. This requires the fast execution of complex logic, a task eminently suitable for digital computers.

Finally, the topic of protection coordination will be touched upon. Let us look at a secondary distribution system in which the distribution transformers are protected by fuses but the primary feeder supplying them is protected by a circuitbreaker. Frequent blowing of fuses with interruption of supply to consumers is clearly undesirable. The following protection scheme may be devised. When a fault occurs on any of the transformers, the feeder circuitbreaker is arranged to trip almost instantly before any fuse has time to blow. The circuitbreaker then recloses, say after one second's time delay, in the process modifying its relay control so that subsequent tripping takes place only after some delay. Now a large proportion of faults on power systems are temporary and self-clearing when the circuit has been de-energized. If the fault has not cleared itself on reclosing, the fuse adjacent to the fault will blow. It is worth noting that fuses are appropriately graded, so that on any current flowing to a fault, the fuse adjacent to the fault must blow before any other fuse that also carries the fault current.

References 2 to 5 cover the topic of protection in greater detail.

REFERENCES

1. E. R. Laithwaite, *Engineer Through the Looking-Glass*, BBC Publications, London, 1980.
2. A. R. van C. Warrington, *Protective Relays, Their Theory and Practice*, Chapman & Hall, London, 1962.
3. *Electrical Transmission and Distribution Reference Book*, Westinghouse Electric Corporation, East Pittsburgh, 1950.
4. B. M. Weedy, *Electric Power Systems*, 2nd edn, Wiley, London, 1972.
5. D. Jones, *Analysis and Protection of Electrical Power Systems*, Pitman, London, 1971.

THREE

ANALOGUES

3.1 SOME HISTORY AND SOME PHILOSOPHY

It is important for the scientist always to remember that the 'Laws of Physics' were written by men as the result of their experiences to date. All laws are therefore valid only until better laws are needed to replace them, or, what is more common, to be built on top of them, for many of the laws have withstood the test of time and are not likely to lead us vastly astray, until a new phenomenon demands the 'mixture as before' with a little addition to embrace the new information.

The history of science teaches us that greater knowledge can combine what have hitherto been seen as separate disciplines. In the sixteenth century electrostatics was one subject and magnetism was another. This belief was to last a couple of centuries or more before the 'greats' put the subject of electromagnetism in its place in a relatively few years, culminating in Faraday's incredible year of 1831, when he made so many discoveries in the new subject.

Another good example of the fact that the laws of physics can only ever be *partial* truths is that given in Chapter 2 (page 23) relating to the theories of light propagation. No amount of ingenuity could bend the corpuscular theory to make it fit the phenomena of diffraction and interference. When Thomas Young's wave theory was seen to answer all the questions posed by these two phenomena, it *replaced* the corpuscular theory rather than built upon it. The scientists of Young's time were prepared to throw the corpuscular theory out of the window. Then came Max Planck, Niels Bohr, and others who showed that light was to be regarded sometimes as particles, sometimes as waves. In other words both corpuscular and wave theories were but separate facets of a great whole, and we, in our time, would be foolish indeed to pretend that these are the *only* facets and therefore the truth. We personally have never seen the particle–wave complex set down more succinctly than in some unpublished notes by the late Sir Lawrence Bragg:

> Electrons scattered by matter exhibit interference patterns of a form which would be accounted for by their being waves. Particles behave like waves, and waves like particles.
>
> The relation is a subtle one. When we postulate an experimental set-up, and wish to prophesy the result, we must treat both light and matter as waves. The nature of physical reality is such that we can only calculate the relative probability of an effect in various places. On the other hand, when we write the history of what did actually happen in an experiment, it is a history of particles whether of matter or light. A wave-like uncertain future, only expressible in probabilities, forever streaming through the moment 'Now', is transformed into a definite past of particles. Determinism takes on a new meaning.

In science there is to be found, perhaps, the whole of knowledge, but there is no reason why the acquisition of it should ever contain one grain of wisdom. The Book of Proverbs instructs us: 'Wisdom is the principal thing; therefore get wisdom: And with all thy getting get understanding.' Almost every generation of pure scientists seems to have fallen into the trap of believing that it was close to knowing all there was to know in physics—'the Key to the Cosmos' was how Einstein interpreted it. The feeling of travelling along a twisted road in the belief that just around the next corner the Promised Land would all lie before us has been with us for a long time now. The latest arguments rage about the origin of the universe, which is foolish, for to argue about it implies that it *had* one, which is not necessarily true. We look at the universe through the five senses (some would claim six!), as if we are trapped in a box with five windows and could never be sure that what we saw through them were more than 3-D, holographic images bearing no relation to *reality* outside the box.

The engineer is less likely to fall foul of the temptation to claim that he seeks the truth. Rather he is concerned with sifting the profitable from the unprofitable, whether it be in concepts (as will the academic) or in hardware (as will the industrialist). The aim of the engineer is beautifully defined in the inscription around the edge of the Lamme Medal, awarded by the Institute of Electrical and Electronics Engineers, which reads: 'The engineer views hopefully the hitherto unattainable.'

We could, as engineers, claim St Anselm as our patron saint. He lived in the eleventh century and became Archbishop of Canterbury. After a lifetime of contemplation he declared a mighty philosophy in but three Latin words: '*Credo ut intellegam.*'—I believe, in order that I may understand.

Here, surely is the wisdom, here the definition of understanding as in the Book of Proverbs. We must first believe in *something*. Then we may deduce the rest by logic. The only question now to settle is where to begin. The alchemists began with 'earth, fire, air, and water'. Since their time there has been a continuous search to establish all matter as mixtures of sometimes three, sometimes four, 'fundamental' things. In the nineteen-twenties there were protons, neutrons, and electrons. Then the positron was identified. That was no major upset. A positive counterpart to the negative electron had a 'tidiness' so desirable in science up to that time. But then came others, neutrinos, mesons, π and k, until there were scores of 'fundamental particles' and the time was ripe for a new pronouncement that all of them were made up of three or four 'something else's'. The words 'up', 'down', 'quark', 'charm', 'beauty', 'taste', and 'flavour' are the fashionable words of our day in the higher strata of pure science.

Where does this leave the engineer? Quite simply, we believe that electric power engineers need go no further back than electrons. A good engineer knows just enough physics to accept the hydrogen atom as if it were an orange in New York and a pinhead in Boston, the pinhead's position being part of an orbit around the orange. He also knows that this model is not the whole truth, for example:

The pinhead is not solid.
The pinhead is not divisible so it cannot have a shape, yet:
The pinhead can be accredited with a spin and an angular momentum as *if* it were solid and had a shape.
The orange is not solid, either
—and many similar properties.

Most of all, the engineer knows that the model of an atom is itself but an analogue and an analogue is a sophisticated name for a parable, a fairy story, not to be taken as the truth, but used to establish a moral most forcibly.

There may be some engineers who can think about electric current without the model of water flowing in a pipe, but we would guess that they are in the minority in their profession. The engineer is a master of the art of analogue, knowing just where to use a particular model and where to discard it. If we take the electric current–water-in-a-pipe analogue, for example, it is an excellent model for giving school children a 'feel' for current flow in wires, for it reveals e.m.f. as 'electrical pressure' at once. Yet we must not pursue the analogue as far as trying to answer the question: 'Where, in the cross section of a wire, does the current flow fastest?' In a pipe, the water flows fastest in the centre. High frequency alternating current in a thick wire flows mostly in a thin 'skin' around the periphery. The water pipe analogue has broken down, but that failure is no reason for abandoning it in elementary teaching.

Let therefore our teaching be a succession of analogues and let the teacher make it known to his audience that any given analogue may not be as profitable for a particular member of his audience as it has been for him. In that way, we shall set the next generation on a firmer footing than perhaps the one which we were given. Gilbert Walton, in an essay on 'Facts and artefacts',[1] quotes Quintilian, who himself is quoted by Butler in the preface to *The*

Analogy of Religion to the Constitution and Course of Nature, on the subject of analogy: 'The force of analogy is this, that it refers what is doubtful to something like it which is not in question.'

3.2 ELECTROMAGNETISM AND RELATIVITY

The following analysis is carried out not so much as an aid to designing machines and power systems but as a reminder of a number of important facts that must never be out of our sights:

(1) Electromagnetism involves units and dimensions that cannot be expressed solely in terms of mass, length, and time. A fourth 'dimension'—not to be confused with Einstein's definition of a fourth dimension—is necessary, and it can be chosen from among all magnetic and electric quantities, charge, current, capacitance, permeability, flux density, etc. The choice is arbitrary. For many of us the choice of permeability is a good one, expressing as it does our total ignorance of the nature of free space, which can apparently be considered to be a 'conductor of magnetism', for its permeability is neither zero nor infinite.

In this context, we may recall how Faraday, having discovered that all substances exhibited small magnetic effects, some of which were 'paramagnetic' (producing a slightly higher conductivity than air) while others were 'diamagnetic' (slightly less conducting than air), examined pure gases enclosed in soap bubbles and found that gases also exhibited relative permeabilities. He also made magnetic liquids (particles of ferrous material in suspension) and showed that a less permeable piece of ferromagnetic metal immersed therein behaved as would a diamagnetic substance in air. John Tyndall (Faraday's successor at the Royal Institution) writes of him in his book, *Faraday as a Discoverer*:[2]

> And now theoretic questions rush in upon him. Is this new force (diamagnetism) a true repulsion, or is it merely a differential attraction? Might not the apparent repulsion of diamagnetic bodies be really due to the greater attraction of the medium by which they are surrounded? He tries the rarefaction of air, but finds the effect insensible. He is averse to ascribing a capacity of attraction to space, or to any hypothetical medium supposed to fill space. He therefore inclines, but still with caution, to the opinion that the action of a magnet upon bismuth is a true and absolute repulsion, and not merely the result of differential attraction.

But notice the 'with caution'. He went on, not satisfied with his own conclusions, as Tyndall describes in the same book:

> He next labours to establish the true magnetic zero, a problem not so easy as might at first sight be imagined. For the action of any magnet upon any gas, while surrounded by air, or any other gas, can only be

differential; and if the envelope were made in vacuo, the action of the envelope, in this case necessarily of a certain thickness, would trouble the result.

Tyndall then quotes Faraday's own writings, thus:

Perhaps it is hardly necessary for me to state that I find both iron and bismuth in such vacua perfectly obedient to the magnet. From such experiments, and also from general observations and knowledge, it seems manifest that the lines of magnetic force can traverse pure space, just as gravitating force does, and as statical electrical forces do, and therefore space has a magnetic relation of its own, and one that we shall probably find hereafter to be of utmost importance in experiments also; I will do myself the honour to bring them before the Royal Society.

He did so. The concept of μ_0 was born. It is possible that Faraday in his search for $\mu = 0$ conceived the possibility of another universe, in whose space a piece of *our* space would exhibit paramagnetism.

Later in life, Faraday was influenced by James Clerk Maxwell and was almost persuaded as to the reality of the ether, for he wrote:

I am more inclined to the notion that in the transmission of the [magnetic] force there is such an action [an intermediate agency] external to the magnet, than that the effects are merely attraction and repulsion at a distance. *Such an affection may be the function of the ether; for it is not at all unlikely that, if there be an ether, it should have other uses than simply the conveyance of radiations.*

Would that we could all keep our minds, at all times, as open to the possibilities propounded by others.

With the acceptance of SI units as the language of the learned societies, strengthened in Europe by the formation of the European Economic Community, the unit of current became preferred to permeability. So the SI system is the metre–kilogram–second–ampere system.

The use of a single quantity to bring the whole of electromagnetic theory within the dimensional analysis school of thought can itself be made the subject of a parable. To claim that such an adoption allows us to 'understand' electromagnetic theory is to be like an unworthy domestic servant who cleans a room by sweeping all the dust into a heap in one corner, then lifts the carpet and tucks the dust heap under it in the hope that no one will notice it. Upon the heap being discovered, the servant argues indignantly and, we are bound to admit, with a certain amount of justification, that 'at least the rest of the room is clean'!

In the days when even the writers of technical books wrote in elegant prose—a practice regrettably now fallen into disuse—E. G. Cullwick wrote delightfully on the subject of the fourth quantity needed for dimensional analysis:[3]

How confusing it must be for him (the student) if he is not told at once what this fourth physical concept is. If he is introduced to electric charges, magnetic poles, electric and magnetic fields as though they were all equal in the possession of physical reality, little wonder that they become in his mind all equal in mystery. And if he is then told, in dimensional formulae, that none of these is to be linked with mass, length and time in the quaternion of primary concepts, but that he must use *either* the 'permittivity' *or* the 'permeability' of free space, the race is indeed for the swift and the battle for the strong.

But these words were written at a time when electricity and magnetism were taught as separate subjects in school physics, and when permittivity was introduced as the constant required in the inverse square law for the force F between charges q_1 and q_2, thus

$$F_c = \frac{q_1 q_2}{\varepsilon d^2}$$

Permeability, on the other hand, was the corresponding constant for the inverse square law of force between 'magnetic poles', of strength m_1, m_2, thus

$$F_m = \frac{m_1 m_2}{\mu d^2}$$

It was then possible, by working out a quantity such as electric current on a dimensional basis from first one and then the other equation, and equating the answers, to show that

$$\frac{1}{\sqrt{(\mu\varepsilon)}} = [LT^{-1}]$$

—the dimensions of velocity.

Upon being told that the numerical value of this velocity in space was c, the velocity of light, the school pupils of that time were inclined to be struck with the thought that they had just been confronted with a revelation of God Himself, for 'light' was another subject in another book! The metre–kilogram–second (MKS) system of units, which preceded the 'Rationalized MKS' system, which in turn preceded the SI system, dug a hole for this startling revelation and buried it so deeply that it was never to rise again, but alas, along with it was buried an awareness, early in life, of the relationship between coils of wire, bar magnets, and radiation of a variety of kinds. This omission can, of course, be put right by the following analysis, using only the Special Theory of Relativity, in which the relationship $\mu_0 \varepsilon_0 = 1/c^2$ is built into the analysis from the start.

(2) The use of Relativistic mathematics brings us no nearer to an 'understanding' than did the old-fashioned analysis. It simply substitutes one analogue for another. Instead of 'believing' in μ_0 and ε_0 and deducing that they were related by c, you simply believe in c and its properties (such as that it is a

constant on any frame of reference) and deduce the force between currents that, if pursued further, would lead you back to the concept of poles, giving them a 'reality' to which they also are not entitled.

This part of the exercise is useful also in demolishing the idea that any given law of physics is ultimate truth and unbreakable. We have no proof that c is constant with time. A reduction of one per cent per 100 million years would give us at once the vision of an expanding universe when, in fact, the whole was one static set of masses. We are not suggesting that this makes a good working hypothesis. It merely plants doubt where doubt may be needed. In his excellent little book, *The Special Theory of Relativity*,[4] Herbert Dingle has this to say about the concept.

> The principle of relativity is a generalization from the fact that all known effects, apparently caused by the intrinsic motion of a single body, depend on the motion of that body with respect to another body. In this it resembles the second law of thermodynamics: the principle that heat cannot by itself pass from a cooler to a hotter body is likewise a generalization from the fact that in all our experience we have never observed such a thing to happen. Both principles are similarly vulnerable to observation: a single well-authenticated instance of a violation would suffice to overthrow either of them.

(3) Once having been satisfied about the 'proof' of the force between currents, one need no longer rely on such formulae as that accredited to Laplace or more commonly to Biot–Savart

$$F = \frac{idl \sin \theta}{r^2}$$

which is often introduced with such authority that the student is too awestruck to ask why the denominator was not r or r^3 or $r^{3/2}$.

(4) The use of Relativity settles once and for all what otherwise can lead to tedious arguments about the difference between 'flux cutting' and 'flux linking' phenomena, discussed briefly in Chapter 2 and often the cause of much confusion in the mind of the student. The analysis shows clearly that the effect of current upon current ('translated' by analogy into the 'field' due to one current reacting with the other) depends only on relative *velocities* between charges, and therefore Special Relativity suffices. Where changing fields involving e.m.f. generation by induction from static coils (the '$L(di/dt)$' kind of e.m.f.) are involved, rates of change of current mean accelerating electrons and any relativistic approach will require the General Theory, which is as different from Special Theory as power is from energy. It is unfortunate that the names imply that one is a special case of the other.

(5) In considering individual charges in wires one is spared the fear of being asked why uncharged wires affect each other at all, considering that lines of magnetic flux are mere inventions of the mind, why parallel beams of electrons in a cathode ray vacuum tube repel, but attract if the tube is gas

filled, or whether the electrons actually flow in wires. The relativity approach teaches us to appreciate the strange similarity between several physical phenomena where one captures but the merest fraction of what was apparently available.

The analysis below will have considerable appeal to some readers, may leave others totally unmoved. If you take your place with the latter you have no cause to worry. You can survive the rigours of a career in power engineering without ever knowing about Einstein, or even about c. The procedure follows closely that of Cullwick.[3] (See also page 72.)

Relativity tells us first that if an observer is at rest in a field that he measures as E (electric) or B (magnetic), another observer, travelling *perpendicularly* to that field at velocity v, measures it as $E/\sqrt{[1-(v/c)^2]}$ or $B/\sqrt{[1-(v/c)^2]}$, respectively. If his motion is *parallel* to the field, he measures it simply as E or B. Secondly, if a charge q is moving through a field with velocity v relative to an observer at rest in the field, the physical phenomena measured by that observer are consistent with the assumption that the force experienced by the charge is given simply by Eq or by Bqv, as appropriate.

We can now build on these new 'beliefs', beginning with the simple case of parallel beams of electrons in a vacuum. We may consider two charges of value q_1 and q_2 moving side by side in parallel paths distant r apart, each having the same velocity v. The charge q_1, as observed by a stationary observer at the position occupied by q_2, will be credited with exerting an electric field E, given by

$$E = \frac{q_1}{4\pi\varepsilon_0 r^2} \{1/\sqrt{[1-(v/c)^2]}\}$$

(q_1 considered as a current element idl in the Biot–Savart formula) and a magnetic field B, of value

$$B = \frac{\mu_0(q_1 v)}{4\pi r^2} \{1/\sqrt{[1-(v/c)^2]}\}$$

where ε_0 and μ_0 are the free space permittivity and permeability, respectively. Now, charge q_2 moving in these fields experiences forces due to two causes

(1) an electrostatic repulsion force

$$F_s = \frac{q_1 q_2}{4\pi\varepsilon_0 r^2} \{1/\sqrt{[1-(v/c)^2]}\}$$

(2) an electromagnetic attraction force

$$F_m = \frac{\mu_0 q_1 q_2 v^2}{4\pi r^2} \{1/\sqrt{[1-(v/c)^2]}\}$$

There is thus a net repulsive force given by

$$F_s - F_m = \frac{q_1 q_2}{4\pi r^2} \{1/\varepsilon_0 \sqrt{[1-(v/c)^2]} - v^2\mu_0/\sqrt{[1-(v/c)^2]}\}$$

Writing $1/\sqrt{(\varepsilon_0 \mu_0)} = c$

$$F_s - F_m = \frac{q_1 q_2}{4\pi\varepsilon_0 r^2} \left\{ 1/\sqrt{[1-(v/c)^2]} - \frac{v^2}{c^2} \Big/ \sqrt{[1-(v/c)^2]} \right\}$$

$$= \frac{q_1 q_2}{4\pi\varepsilon_0 r^2} \sqrt{[1-(v/c)^2]} = F_s [1-(v/c)^2]$$

This exercise is useful in that it can give an immediate physical picture of the nature of, and relationship between, electrostatic and electromagnetic forces. The latter, often considered to be the result of magnetic fields acting on electric currents, can now be seen as the result of relative movement between electrons and the observer of the forces. The electromagnetic force is seen to oppose electrostatic repulsion between beams of electrons, the amount subtracted being negligible for $v < 0.1c$ but rising rapidly as $v \to c$ and eliminating F_s entirely at $v = c$, which is elegantly tidy but of course takes no account of random velocities of billions of different electrons in an electron beam. Nevertheless, as an *aide-mémoire*, it will be of use to those whose inclinations lie in the direction of completeness.

3.3 CURRENTS IN WIRES

Again our starting point will be a single positive ion A (Fig. 3.1) and its loosely bound conduction electron B, the latter moving at velocity v_1, as shown, and the former, being some 1845 times more massive, being assumed to be at rest. In the second wire, a positive ion C and free electron D are momentarily situated, not necessarily immediately opposite A and B, but distant r from them, with r inclined at angle α to the direction of flow. Electron D moves at velocity v_2, generally different from v_1. In this more complex case it is necessary to use binomial expand and neglect techniques, but the mathematics is still only of elementary level.

The pair AB can be considered, when necessary, to be a current element $I_1 dl_1 = qv_1$ in wire (1) where dl is an elementary length of the conductor. Likewise the pair CD may be qv_2 or $I_2 dl_2$ as required. The force on the fixed charge C arises from both A and B. From A it is a repulsive force

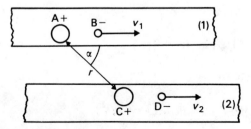

Figure 3.1 Consideration of forces between a pair of atoms in neighbouring wires.

$$F_s = \frac{q^2}{4\pi\varepsilon_0 r^2}$$

having components $F_1 = F_s \cos\alpha$ along the wire and $F_2 = F_s \sin\alpha$ perpendicular to the wire.

No relativistic correction is necessary.

From B, the force is attractive, but since B is moving it is necessary to split the electric field of B into components

$$\frac{q \cos\alpha}{4\pi\varepsilon_0 r^2} \quad \text{in the direction of current flow}$$

and

$$\frac{q \sin\alpha}{4\pi\varepsilon_0 r^2 \sqrt{[1-(v_1/c)^2]}} \quad \text{perpendicular to the wires.}$$

Since C is at rest relative to the observer, the force components are

$$F_3 = F_s \cos\alpha \qquad \text{parallel to the wires}$$

and

$$F_4 = \frac{F_s \sin\alpha}{\sqrt{[1-(v_1/c)^2]}} \quad \text{perpendicularly.}$$

The net force on C due to the pair AB is one of attraction since $1/\sqrt{[1-(v_1/c)^2]} > 1$.

This net force is perpendicular to the wires and of value

$$F_C = F_s \sin\alpha(\{1/\sqrt{[1-(v_1/c)^2]}\} - 1)$$

and for $v \ll c$ this reduces to

$$F_C = \tfrac{1}{2}F_s \sin\alpha(v_1/c)^2$$

since $v_1 \ll c$ generally.

The force on the moving charge D is first calculated as though the observer were moving *with* D. Relative to D, A moves at velocity v_2 and the force due to A therefore has attractive components

$$F_5 = F_s \cos\alpha \qquad \text{along the wire}$$

and

$$F_6 = \frac{F_s \sin\alpha}{\sqrt{[1-(v_2/c)^2]}} \quad \text{perpendicularly.}$$

Relative to D, B moves at velocity $(v_1 - v_2)$ and the appropriate force components are

$$F_7 = F_s \cos\alpha \qquad \text{along the wire}$$

and

$$F_8 = \frac{F_s \sin\alpha}{\sqrt{[1-(v_1-v_2)^2/c^2]}} \quad \text{perpendicularly.}$$

F_5 and F_7 cancel as before and the net force is again an attraction perpendicular to the wires of value

$$F_D = F_s \sin \alpha \{1/\sqrt{[1-(v_2/c)^2]} - 1/\sqrt{[1-(v_1-v_2)^2/c^2]}\}$$

$$= F_s \sin \alpha \left\{ \tfrac{1}{2}(v_2/c)^2 - \tfrac{1}{2}\left(\frac{v_1^2 - 2v_1 v_2 - v_2^2}{c^2}\right)\right\}$$

$$= F_s \sin \alpha \left\{ \frac{v_1 v_2}{c^2} - \tfrac{1}{2}(v_1/c)^2 \right\}$$

To an observer at rest with respect to C, the force F_D appears to be

$$F'_D = F_D \sqrt{[1-(v_2/c)^2]}$$

(see page 69).

The total force on C and D due to A and B is therefore attractive and perpendicular to the wires, and given by

$$F = F_C + F'_D$$
$$= F_s \sin \alpha \{\tfrac{1}{2}(v_1/c)^2 + \sqrt{[1-(v_2/c)^2]}[v_1 v_2/c^2 - \tfrac{1}{2}(v_1/c)^2]\}$$

Neglecting all higher powers of v/c beyond the second

$$F = F_s \sin \alpha (v_1 v_2/c^2)$$

But

$$F_s = \frac{q^2}{4\pi\varepsilon_0 r^2} \quad \text{and} \quad \frac{1}{\varepsilon_0 \mu_0} = c^2$$

Thus

$$F = \mu_0 \frac{(qv_1)(qv_2)}{r^2} \sin \alpha$$

$$= \mu_0 \frac{I_1 I_2 dl_1 dl_2}{r^2} \sin \alpha$$

which is the classical formula from which the Biot–Savart (Laplace) law is readily deducible. Cullwick concludes:

> It thus appears that the magnetic forces between conductors carrying electric currents may be explained by the extremely small modification of electrostatic forces due to the small drift velocities of the moving electrons in the conductor. It is true that we have neglected the unknown random velocities of the conduction electrons, but we can consider the moving charge to be that in an elementary volume of the conductor, large enough to contain a very great quantity of conduction electrons, whose velocities may then be assumed to cancel. That the resultant 'magnetic' forces should be of practical magnitudes is due to the almost inconceivably large density of charge in metallic conductors.

Let us quantify these comments, that we may marvel even more at the delicate balance of the physical world. Let us evaluate $1/\sqrt{[1-(v/c)^2]}$ for electrons moving at $0.1c$ (a mere $30\,000\,000$ metres per second): $(v/c)^2 = 0.01$,

$1 - (v/c)^2 = 0.99$, $\sqrt{0.99} = 0.995$, $1/0.995 = 1.005$; i.e., there is a one-half per cent increase in electrostatic force. Now it only remains for us to calculate the drift velocity of the conduction electrons in copper.

There are approximately 5×10^{22} free electrons per cm^3 of copper. Each carries a charge of 1.602×10^{-19} coulomb. A current of 1 ampere involves the passage of $10^{19}/1.602$ electrons past any given point in one second of time. Thus the volume in which the electrons passing a given point in one second are contained (for a current I) is

$$\frac{10^{19}I}{1.602 \times 5 \times 10^{22}} \approx \frac{I}{8000} \ cm^3$$

For a wire section of area A, the effective length of column that passes per second, i.e., the drift velocity, is

$$\frac{I}{8000A} = \frac{J}{8000} \ cm/s$$

where J is the current density in amperes per square centimetre.

Domestic electricity supplies are generally rated at approximately $150 \, A/cm^2$, in which case the drift velocity is of the order of a fraction of a millimetre per second, or $c/10^{12}$. Try squaring 10^{-12}, subtracting it from unity, taking the square root of the answer and then the reciprocal of that—you will conclude perhaps that 'magnetic' forces are of no consequence, BUT—since one cubic centimetre of copper contains 8000 coulombs of charge in the form of conduction electrons, let us calculate F_s on the assumption that we could collect all the free electrons from $10 \, cm^3$ of copper and set them one metre apart from a similar heap of electrons from a second $10 \, cm^3$ of copper; between the collections the force F_s would be

$$\frac{(8 \times 10^6)^2}{4\pi \times \varepsilon_0} = 64 \times 10^{12} \times 9 \times 10^9 \ newtons$$

which is of the order of 6×10^{19} tonnes-force, and that is the order of magnitude of force required to split the earth in half!

Yet the electrostatic forces that we can harness are of the weakest kind. Usable electromagnetic forces are considerably bigger, inertial and gravitational forces bigger still, and atomic forces a whole order of magnitude greater. This 'skimming of the cream', an expression we might use in relation to the $\{1/\sqrt{[1-(v/c)^2]} - 1\}$ operation, happens at all levels. An atomic bomb is one order of things, a hydrogen bomb far more powerful. Yet the energy so released is only the conversion by the formula $E = mc^2$ of the *difference* in mass between two hydrogen nuclei and one helium nucleus, which is an apparently trivial fraction.

This rather long, specialized digression in the more general subject of analogy has led the reader, we hope, to an appreciation of the phenomena that, as a power engineer, he seeks to exploit. We consider this to be important as a foundation, for later we shall become involved with fundamentally important questions such as 'What is denied to us because we, and the earth on which we live, are (1) too small, (2) too large, compared with the size of a proton, an electron, and like particles?' Likewise it is interesting and instructive to try to design a power station on the understanding that humans are reduced to an average height of five centimetres; and what then would be the approximate cost of electricity per kilowatt hour? An interesting debating point is whether the fact that a two-horsepower petrol engine is of the same overall dimensions and weight as a two-horsepower electric motor is an accident or whether the sizes can be related by equations. The scope for such questions is very large. This whole section on relativity has been included to prepare the mind for the more ready absorption of new and easier concepts, such as magnetic circuits that contain reactive components as well as reluctance.

We shall now continue with the study of analogy, beginning with one of the most commonly used.

3.4 MAGNETIC FLUX

Action at a distance is a phenomenon we have never been able to 'translate' into simpler terms. In the case of electrostatic forces, magnetic and electromagnetic forces, and gravitation, the '*Credo ut intellegam*' doctrine has begun with belief in an experimentally established inverse square law, which is interpreted in terms of 'field' theory. Some students whose teachers were more bold than the rest were, in the last century, taught field theory on the basis that the field actually consisted of 'lines of flux' that behaved in every way like strands of elastic material in tension, each of which tried at all times to reduce its length. Those who used the concept for gravitational fields were in the minority. There were obvious difficulties for all in this simple concept. For example, if the phenomena were those of *repulsion*, as in like magnetic poles or like charges, the 'pieces of elastic' idea could scarcely be defended. Michelson and Morley's failure to detect 'ether drift' added weight to the argument that action at a distance occurred across pure emptiness.

Had the forces between permanent magnets of moderate sizes been as small as those occurring when one such magnet is swept across the surface of a coin lying on a table, there can be little doubt that ferromagnetism would not yet have found its way into school textbooks of physics for children of twelve to sixteen years. But magnets can be bought in toyshops and they are full of wonder and the children have a right to demand an explanation of their behaviour, so the whole process of plotting 'lines of force' developed. The physicists who wrote the books were always careful not to commit heresy by giving 'reality' to these lines, yet were unwilling to admit openly that the lines were 'just not there'. So a *definition* of a line of force was agreed. It was to be 'the direction in which a free north pole would move'. When you contemplate this definition for a moment, it is a beautiful compromise between heaven and

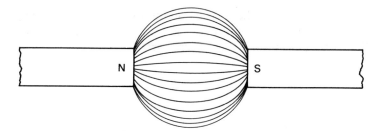

Figure 3.2 'Lines of elastic' would not remain in the positions shown.

earth. It is real and unreal at the same time. 'Direction' has a real meaning for all of us, whether we are aware of relativity or not, but there is no mention of chemistry. *The only substance you will find in the airgap of an induction motor at any time is air*!

But an engineering approach demands something more tangible, more physically identifiable than lines of force. The engineer is prepared to 'bend the rules' to get quick, accurate answers. 'If you can tell one lie you can tell another to cover it,' is almost his argument. The man who brought together the pure and the profane to sit at the same table, who gave the engineer the *reality* he wanted, yet also gave a *respectability* to the strands of elastic, was undoubtedly James Clerk Maxwell. Mathematically unshakable, he translated the findings of Ampère, Gauss, and Faraday into four basic equations that now bear his name. But, more than that, he catered for the less mathematically skilled in giving a simple 'magic' second property to the lines of elastic.

It is easily appreciated from a glance at Fig. 3.2 that if the lines of force were really physical springs in tension they would not be content to bulge out sideways and remain in the positions shown. In theory, in the example used here, only the line in the very centre is straight. What is worse, if the energy stored in such a system be calculated on the basis that it is an elastic material of coefficient λ, natural length l, and extended by x, so that the stored energy is $\lambda x^2/2l$, the result will be exactly *one-half* the energy actually measured in practice. Maxwell therefore credited the lines of force with a second property in addition to their tensile ability. 'All lines repel each other with a constant force per unit length for no good reason we need to consider,' would be a loose translation of his more elegant findings. (There *has* to be a 'magic' somewhere. We are dealing with a four-dimensional (in the Relativistic sense) phenomenon that we cannot hope to understand in terms of three-dimensional concepts.) Now the reason for the bulging lines is clear. Now you can find a 'reason' for repulsion between like poles. Now you can integrate the compressive energy and discover the half that was missing. The 'respectability' referred to above came when the scientific hierarchy was prepared to accept the tensile property of lines of force as 'Maxwell's first stress' and the compressive property as his 'second stress'. We have included these advanced concepts early in the book for we have seen many an industrialist occupying a top post in management silenced when in full spate by a new honours graduate who began a sentence: 'But sir, if you would consider Maxwell's second stress...'. Readers of this book need never fall foul of this ploy in their riper years!

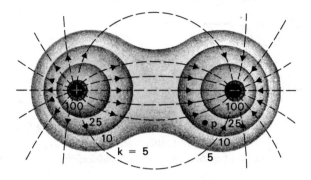

Figure 3.3 Three-dimensional field effect produced by degrees of shading. (*Permission of John Wiley & Sons, Inc.*)

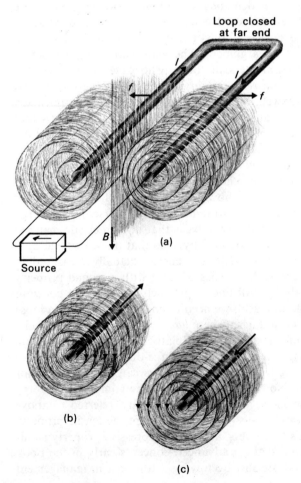

Figure 3.4 A splendid representation of equipotential surfaces that helps the student a great deal in forming such a concept. (*Permission of John Wiley & Sons, Inc.*)

The engineer was now ready to quantify lines of force like bunches of grass and to call it 'flux'. Physicists generally disapproved heartily, for the word means literally 'that which flows'. Magnetic flux is not like electric current, we were told. 'It does not flow.' In *our* riper years we would reply with authority, 'If *we* say it flows, it *flows!*'—meaning that it flows for us; it may not do so for you. It all depends on what we regard as being a profitable concept for the individual. In the days before SI units the quantification was simple and yet perhaps misleading. One gauss was equated to 'one line per square centimetre'. The confusion is nicely typified by a lecture at Manchester University to first-year undergraduates of the nineteen-fifties by the great Professor Sir Frederic Williams, master builder of electronic circuits. He was asked by a student whereabouts in the 'square centimetre' that could be drawn on a blackboard the 'one' line was to be located. Instantly the Professor replied, 'In such cases, I should have told you, you have to draw in all the "microlines".'

We can think of no finer compromise between the reality and the myth that is called 'field' than this concept of the infinite subdivision of a line of force to express uniformity of magnetic flux density.

A great deal can be expressed in diagrams when it comes to getting a physical 'feel' for field theory. The figures in the book *Scientific Basis of Electrical Engineering* by J. M. Ham and G. R. Slemon[5] are superb in this respect and some are reproduced here (Figs. 3.3 and 3.4) by kind permission of the publishers, John Wiley and Sons, Inc.

3.5 MAGNETIC CIRCUITS

Despite the fact that Faraday used the concept of magnetic circuits frequently well over a century ago, the idea is still not commonly used in textbooks, especially *physics* textbooks. The main reason for this is undoubtedly the extent of present day knowledge on ferromagnetism which includes the following phenomena.

(1) The relationship between the magnetizing force H, and the flux density B is non-linear so that $\mu(= B/H)$ varies with B.
(2) Ferromagnetic substances, once magnetized by an applied H, retain a certain value of B when H is removed ('residual' magnetism).
(3) The magnetic state of any specimen is influenced by the whole of its previous magnetic 'experience' (its magnetic 'history').

The whole subject of ferromagnetism is so complex that it is our view that its treatment in school physics and even in basic university undergraduate courses should be minimal. Only in such courses as materials science, where it can be given a comprehensive treatment, should it be attempted at undergraduate level, otherwise it stifles a most useful concept, the analogy with the electric circuit.

In this concept, the textbook tells the student that $B = \mu H$ and μ is a constant, just as $E = RI$ in an electric circuit and R is constant. Yet even ordinary metals, such as copper, change their conductivity with changes in temperature. What is more, the resistance of a wire itself is responsible for the generation of heat and the resultant temperature rise then produces more heat, at a constant current, and the situation has all the ingredients of an unstable system. Were it not for the laws governing the convection and radiation of heat, the passage of a constant electric current would always result in a 'burnout'. (Even at constant voltage, where increase in resistance tends to limit the rate of production of heat, we must always ensure that such heat can get away from the source, as a former undergraduate reading history, known to one of us, discovered when he tried to dry out a damp hostel bed by stuffing a 60 watt electric light bulb between the sheets and going off to have dinner! The bed did not catch fire until his return. There was not enough oxygen trapped inside to support total combustion. The situation was analogous to the heating of coal in a gasworks in order to drive off coal gas without burning either gas or solid residue. But the bed smoked, and when the student tore the covers off, the whole bed instantly became a sheet of flame.) The engineer knows full well that in practice, neither μ nor R need necessarily be constant, depending on the material concerned.

In order to make the analogy between electric and magnetic circuits more complete, we use magnetomotive force (m.m.f.) rather than H. The relationship between m.m.f. and H is simple

$$\text{m.m.f.} = Hl$$

where l is the length of the magnetic circuit or part of such circuit. We may then write the analogue as follows

$$\text{electric circuit:} \quad \text{e.m.f.} = \text{current} \times \text{resistance} \tag{3.1}$$

$$\text{magnetic circuit:} \quad \text{m.m.f.} = \text{flux} \times \text{reluctance} \tag{3.2}$$

What is more

$$\text{resistance} = \frac{\text{electric length } l_e}{\text{conductivity } \sigma \times \text{electric area } A_e} \tag{3.3}$$

while

$$\text{reluctance} = \frac{\text{magnetic length } l_m}{\text{magnetic conductivity } \mu \times \text{magnetic area } A_m} \tag{3.4}$$

The use of the words 'magnetic conductivity' to describe μ has, in our experience, raised a lot of eyebrows, even in the nineteen-seventies, for μ is usually defined by the force F between magnetic poles situated in a medium of 'permeability' μ, thus

$$F = \frac{m_1 m_2}{\mu d^2}$$

But the concept of a magnetic pole can be a very false friend whose limitations are more obscure and therefore more dangerous than those of the circuit concept. Besides, the circuit concept can take magnetic poles into account, as it were, 'in its stride', as described on pages 95–103. But to justify the idea of μ as an expression of magnetic conductivity we need only write the magnetic circuit equation as follows

$$\text{m.m.f. } (= \text{current } I \times \text{No. of turns } N) = \text{flux } \Phi \times \text{reluctance} \left(\frac{l_m}{\mu A_m}\right)$$

and then manipulate a little, thus

$$NI = \frac{\Phi l_m}{\mu A_m}$$

Therefore

$$\frac{NI}{l_m} = H = \frac{\Phi}{\mu A_m} = \frac{B}{\mu}$$

giving the well known relation $B = \mu H$ at once.

A further simplification of school physics based on the same analogue can be used in connection with heat transfer where it is generally taught that quantity of heat flowing, Q, produced by a temperature difference T is related to length l_T, area A_T and thermal conductivity K by the equation $Q = K A_T T s / l_T$ where s is time. Consider instead the simplification by use of the 'Ohm's law' analogue

temperature difference = heat flow rate × thermal resistance

i.e.

$$T = \left(\frac{Q}{s}\right) \times \frac{l_T}{K A_T}$$

for is not electric current also quantity of electricity (charge) per unit time? For those whose curiosity takes them further, a similar analogue exists in connection with gyroscopic theory whereby

torque = angular velocity of precession × wheel momentum

Now let us examine the extent to which the magnetic circuit analogy can be taken. Let us, for example, set down the two 'Ohm's laws' as shown in Fig. 3.5. This arrangement is a total expression of all the mystery we call 'electromagnetism', for the cross-coupled quantities, m.m.f. and current on the

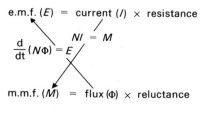

Figure 3.5 A visual analogue of the process of electromagnetism.

one hand and e.m.f. and flux on the other, are mutually self-generating, since m.m.f. is simply NI, while e.m.f. is $d/dt \cdot N\Phi$. In the language of the Bible: e.m.f. begat current, begat m.m.f., begat flux, begat e.m.f.... etc. This continuous interchange of energy between electric and magnetic circuits is as basic to the theory of electromagnetic radiation as it is to the passage of energy from stator to rotor of an electric motor, and the only point to note in this respect is that, in the case of radiation, the electric vector E (derived from e.m.f.), the magnetic vector H (from m.m.f.), and the power flow (Poynting's vector) exist in mutually perpendicular planes. In the case of an electrical machine, Maxwell's 'displacement current' can be neglected and the radiation from stator to rotor can be assumed to cross the airgap in zero time. (A few millimetres at the speed of light is certainly negligible in relation to $1/f$ at power frequencies (f)!)

But how much simpler are Eqs. (3.1) to (3.4), and what a great help are they in establishing that bedrock of machine theory, the Goodness Factor (see Chapter 5). More than that, they can steer us away from a fallacious way of thinking, whereby H is seen always as *cause* and B as *effect*, just as e.m.f. is often taught as if it were always the *source* of a current. Students of electronics are less prone to this 'disease', for current forcing is as much a way of life in electronics as is voltage forcing. (Likewise, in gyroscopes, precession can be seen as the cause of torque, if the experimenter so wishes.) But perhaps, most of all, is the magnetic circuit concept useful when it is extended to include terms comparable to self- and mutual inductance and to capacitance in electric circuits, for then we can establish a perfect 'dual' between the electric and magnetic circuits, enabling us to combine considerations of series and parallel connection, inductance and capacitance, short and open circuits, and many other pairs of 'opposites' in a single exercise (see pages 93–95). But first, let us devote a paragraph or two to the use of equivalent circuit techniques.

3.6 EQUIVALENT CIRCUITS

The simplest example to consider in this context is the single-phase transformer, for having no mechanical output, it lends itself at once to the idea of representing it as a 'black box' with a pair of input terminals and a pair of output terminals. Inside the box is a passive network consisting of resistors and inductors only. The essential feature is that the terminals of the box shall give every appearance of there being a real transformer within.

An easy way of discovering what network is to be drawn is to begin with the concept of a 'perfect' transformer, whose magnetic circuit consists of material which never saturates, carries no eddy currents, has a B–H loop of zero area, has a value of μ which is infinitely large (in terms of a B–H diagram its loop is simply the B-axis itself), and whose electric circuits each have zero resistance. Such a transformer only carries primary current (I_1) when secondary current (I_2) is demanded. In terms of the numbers of turns N_1, N_2

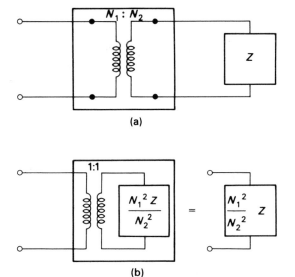

Figure 3.6 The concept of lumping impedances.

in the primary and secondary coils, respectively, the e.m.f. and current ratios are $E_1/E_2 = N_1/N_2$ and $N_1 I_1 = N_2 I_2$. Such a transformer may be drawn as shown in Fig. 3.6(a), but if the load impedance Z be multiplied by the square of the turns ratio, i.e., $(N_1/N_2)^2$ then the load impedance can be taken inside the black box and the need for the perfect transformer element disappears. This is apparent from Fig. 3.6(b), where application of an e.m.f., E_1, to the input terminals draws a current $E_1/[(N_1/N_2)^2 Z]$, as does the box in (a) where

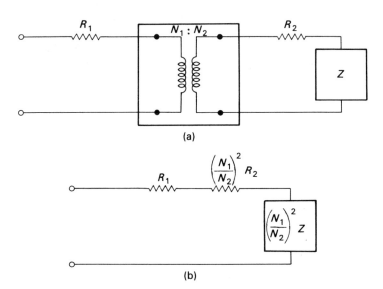

Figure 3.7 The introduction of imperfections (resistances only).

$E_2 = (N_2/N_1)E_1,\ \ I_2 = E_2/Z = (N_2/N_1)E_1/Z\ \ \text{and}\ \ I_1 = N_2 I_2/N_1 = (N_2/N_1)^2 E_1/Z,$
which is the value given for circuit (b).

This process of eliminating the perfect transformer is often known as the 'lumping' of impedances and can now be applied to some of the imperfections of the real transformer. For example, as a first step, consider a transformer that is imperfect only to the extent that its windings have resistances R_1 and R_2 respectively. Its equivalent box may show the perfect transformer with the imperfections brought out as separate items, as in Fig. 3.7(a), but since R_2 is bound to be in series with any load impedance the circuit reduces to that of Fig. 3.7(b), with load included, by the lumping technique.

We can now treat leakage reactances in a similar manner, but there is a complication ahead. There is one fundamental difference between the materials available to the designer of magnetic circuits and those available to those who design merely electric circuits. There is no magnetic insulator (see section 2.5). At first sight, therefore, an equivalent circuit that takes into account both primary and secondary leakage reactances is as simple as that shown in Fig. 3.8, where the X's are simply added in series with the R's. The reasons for including this intermediate stage are twofold. First it illustrates that it is convenient to represent both R and X as elements in *series* with the load, since neither has any effect unless load current is drawn. But the other imperfections we are yet to introduce, i.e., iron losses and magnetizing current, occur whether secondary load current is drawn or not, and can be represented more conveniently as *parallel* components.

Secondly, the idea of leakage reactances specifically ascribed to the primary and secondary sides of the real transformer is to be seen as the analogue of an analogue and since analogues are seldom wholly true, there is a real danger here of oversimplification of what actually takes place. We have found this stated no more clearly than in Behrend's book *The Induction Motor*,[6] written in 1921. Taking the more complicated example of the flux patterns in a rotating machine, Behrend produces diagrams similar to Fig. 3.9(a) and (b). Diagram (a) is consistent with the belief that each set of

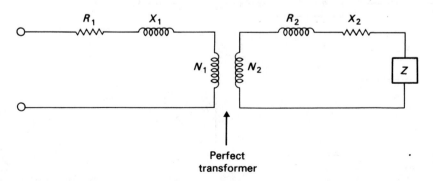

Figure 3.8 A simple treatment of leakage reactances.

conductors (stator and rotor) has its own appropriate leakage reactance, representable in an equivalent circuit such as that shown in Fig. 3.8. The student at this point is entitled to ask: 'Is not every reactance to be seen as the result of a magnetic flux? In which case, where are the fluxes ϕ_1 and ϕ_2 responsible for X_1 and X_2, respectively, to be drawn?' Behrend insists quite rightly that the interpretation *must* be as in Fig. 3.9(a). But he then points out the inconsistency of such a figure with the procedure adopted by the designer of a transformer in calculating the flux in the core. Paraphrasing Behrend's remarks, this argument amounts to the following.

In the part of the magnetic circuit ringed and labelled 'A' in Fig. 3.9(a) we see two fluxes whose instantaneous directions oppose each other. That this must be correct is easily seen from the fact that leakage reactance produces a voltage *drop* on load and in the absence of winding resistances such drop could be obtained by arithmetical subtraction of ϕ_2 from the useful flux ϕ_m, and by appropriate proportioning of the applied voltage and the voltage drop. But if that were so then there can be only a *single* flux existing through the loop A whose value is $\phi_m - \phi_2$, and the existence of flux across the slot opening is to be drawn more properly as completing its circuit through the primary, as shown in Fig. 3.9(b). Now there is no disagreement between (a) and (b) in Fig. 3.9. It is merely a question of notation, of interpretation, of telling a fairy story in which the knight killed the dragon by an aggressive sword thrust, as opposed to a defensive sword play in which the dragon ran on to the blade. In Fig. 3.9(a) the applied voltage has to account for only $(\phi_m + \phi_1)$, but the output voltage is the result of $(\phi_m - \phi_2)$. In Fig. 3.9(b), the

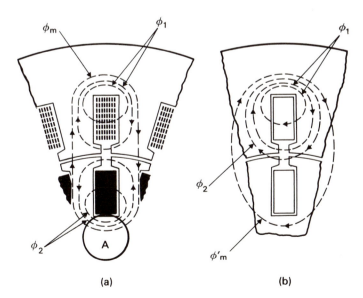

(a)   (b)

Figure 3.9 Secondary leakage flux: (a) the generally accepted interpretation; (b) Behrend's alternative outlook.

applied voltage accounts for $\phi'_m + \phi_1 + \phi_2$ while the output voltage is produced by ϕ'_m alone. Thus it must be that

$$\frac{\phi_m + \phi_1}{\phi_m - \phi_2} = \frac{\phi'_m + \phi_1 + \phi_2}{\phi'_m}$$

for the real transformer yields always a unique answer to the question: 'What is the voltage ratio?' It is seen at once that the 'useful' flux ϕ'_m in (b) is equal to the apparently 'main' flux ϕ_m less ϕ_2.

If this seems a trivial argument it must be seen in the context of the 'explanation' of the action of a loaded transformer. Does the designer argue that the whole of the input m.m.f. produces a core flux equal to that m.m.f. divided by the core reluctance, then go on to credit the total secondary current with producing an opposite core flux and subtract the two to get the resultant flux? The answer is that he *could* do so, but elects not to, because he knows that the two fluxes so treated would each correspond to core flux densities of the order of hundreds of teslas, whereas it is known that the core saturates between two and three teslas, so quite properly he subtracts the two m.m.f.s and uses this as the driving function for the main flux. But if we follow the procedure for Fig. 3.9(a), we take the opposite view!

Why is all this important? The answer is to be found when the transformer core is considered to have a finite permeability and therefore a reluctance greater than zero. The philosophy of using Fig. 3.9(b) is surely sound. It merely states that the secondary coil draws all its excitation from the primary, which in this context is truly to be seen as the ultimate *cause* of any action that takes place. So the secondary is quite incapable of 'setting up shop' on its own and producing leakage flux that can be 'thrown back in the face' of the primary. *But this is not necessarily so.* Consider Fig. 3.10. This is another

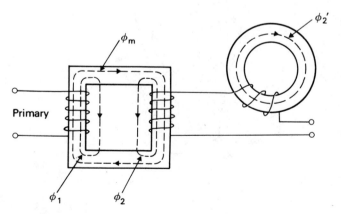

Figure 3.10 It can be argued that the origin of ϕ_2 should properly be the primary. But the same cannot be said of ϕ'_2.

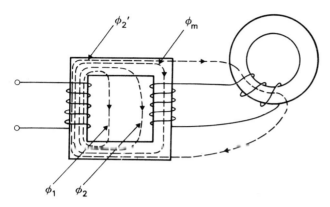

Figure 3.11 The alternative outlook is not always acceptable.

example of '*reductio ad absurdum*'. The separate iron ring is clearly capable of producing a flux loop of its own, completely disconnected from the transformer core. To argue in favour of Fig. 3.9(b) must be to draw the ridiculous flux diagram shown in Fig. 3.11, which even the most imaginative mind could not see as a reasonable flux analogue. So it appears that we have argued successfully against both the techniques of Fig. 3.9(a) *and* (b). What are we to do?

Alas, in practice, there are always some fluxes (if there are to be fluxes at all) that are clearly to be treated by the one technique and other fluxes by the other. Figure 3.12 illustrates one of the simpler cases, a transformer. In (a) the flux is clearly a separate flux outside the secondary coil, but a part of it could be said to be eliminated inside the coil by a part of the flux set up by the primary. Yet, while it could be argued in this way that it then lines up with the Fig. 3.9(b) philosophy, it would need a flux path as in Fig. 3.12(b), that could not possibly have emanated from the primary.

Now all this arises because we need to incorporate in our equivalent circuit the second and third imperfections of the magnetic circuit, i.e., the fact that μ is finite and that both hysteresis and eddy current losses in the iron

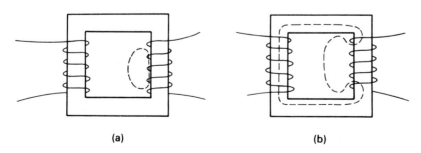

(a)   (b)

Figure 3.12 The borderline case.

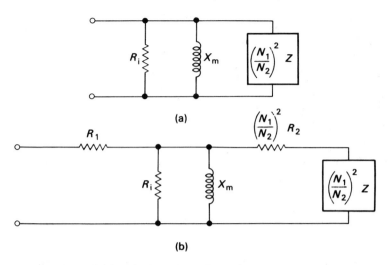

Figure 3.13 The division of primary/secondary resistances.

will occur. Since the voltage sets up the flux, it is convenient to ascribe a component X_m to be the result of the useful flux and to put it in parallel with the load impedance. This is simple and clearly correct if $R_1 = R_2 = X_1 = X_2 = 0$ (Fig. 3.13(a)), only slightly less simple and equally correct if R_1 and R_2 are finite (Fig. 3.13(b)) but what of Fig. 3.14? Either technique illustrated in Fig. 3.9 will give the correct answer for the total lumped reactance, but where are we to split X_1 and X_2 with X_m? Fortunately, in most machines with high Goodness Factor and low leakage, $X_m > R_2$ and $X_m > X_1$ or X_2, and very little error is incurred in making X_1 and $(N_1/N_2)^2 X_2$ equal.

But in the final reckoning it is a seldom made but very profound statement that no measurements made on the machine from its primary and secondary terminals can reveal the *ratio* of X_1 to $(N_1/N_2)^2 X_2$. Only by the presence of a *third* circuit can such division properly be made. A moment's thought will suffice to see that the most convenient form of third circuit will always be an isolated search coil connected to a voltmeter.

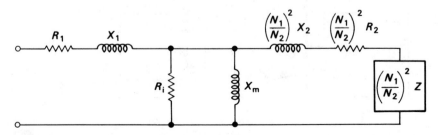

Figure 3.14 Usually accepted complete equivalent circuit.

If we accept a position at which X_m divides X_1 and X_2 it is not then unreasonable to ascribe a fictitious resistor R_i across the same points to account for the (largely constant for constant supply voltage) iron losses. The final equivalent circuit is then as shown in Fig. 3.14.

Before we pass on to the next area of our discussion, let us just consider a simple problem that is easily solved by the formidable technique of 'reductio ad absurdum' mentioned in connection with Fig. 3.10. The following problem can be resolved mentally once it is revealed that the information is both sufficient and necessary to provide a unique solution:

A sphere of homogeneous material has an axial, cylindrical hole drilled through it (like coring an apple), such that the length of the hole is 2 cm. Calculate the volume of material remaining as a function of π.

One of our former colleagues provided the answer mentally in less than twenty seconds! A good engineer should certainly manage it in about one minute. The solution is given at the end of the chapter.

3.7 AN ALTERNATIVE APPROACH

Equivalent circuits, as just described, make use of what are called 'lumped parameters', that is to say, the whole of each imperfection is represented as a single resistor and reactor. That this is permissible is due to the fact that the electric circuits are fully insulated and that the magnetic circuit has been designed to be a single turn, short and fat, so that, in the main, the designer knows to a fair degree of accuracy where the flux is being threaded, for flux is usually loath to leave the sanctuary of the highly permeable steel unless the area out of which it may emerge is very large.

But there are many occasions where the bulk of the flux may be compelled to find paths largely restricted to permeability μ_0 (for example, the leakage flux from primary end windings in rotating machinery) and in such situations there is no alternative to either a long computer program based on the skilful application of boundary conditions to Maxwell's four vector equations or an electrolytic tank model (itself an analogue where current flow models flux) to enable the field pattern to be determined.

In some cases transformers and other kinds of machinery, such as machines with superconducting windings, may be constructed without the use of any ferromagnetic material. Such machines (the transformer type) made their appearance early in the days of radio and other vacuum tube electronic developments, that of course preceded the computer age by several decades. Prediction of the performance of such transformers was difficult and a technique was developed aimed at burying the magnetic circuit (undoubtedly the villain of the piece). The concept was that of *mutual inductance*. The primary and secondary coils were each known to exhibit *self*-inductance provided the unused coil was left on open circuit. Let us ascribe the quantities L_1 and L_2 to these inductances (see Fig. 3.15). Their values can be calculated

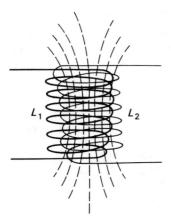

Figure 3.15 Two coils sharing the same magnetic circuit.

theoretically only if the details of the magnetic circuit can be identified, for each inductance is defined as the flux linkages per unit current or $L = \phi N/I$ where ϕ is given by the magnetic circuit equation

$$NI = \phi \times \text{reluctance} = \phi \mathscr{R} \text{ (say)}$$

whence

$$L_1 = N_1^2/\mathscr{R}, \quad L_2 = N_2^2/\mathscr{R}$$

The differential equation for each coil separately is then

$$e_1 = R_1 i_1 + (N_1^2/\mathscr{R})\frac{di_1}{dt}$$

and

$$e_2 = R_2 i_2 + (N_2^2/\mathscr{R})\frac{di_2}{dt}$$

Now if all the flux from one coil threads the other coil and vice versa, $\mathscr{R}$ is the same for each and the flux developed by the primary m.m.f. $(N_1 I_1)$ is seen to be given by $N_1 i_1 = \phi_m \mathscr{R}$. The voltage induced in the secondary is therefore

$$\frac{d}{dt}(N_2 \phi_m) = \frac{N_1 N_2}{\mathscr{R}}\frac{di_1}{dt}$$

which is written $M(di_1/dt)$, where M is called the 'mutual inductance'. Repeating the calculation from the secondary's point of view clearly gives the same result, i.e., if

$$e_2 = M\frac{di_1}{dt} = \frac{N_1 N_2}{\mathscr{R}}\frac{di_1}{dt}$$

then

$$e_1 = M\frac{di_2}{dt} = \frac{N_1 N_2}{\mathscr{R}}\frac{di_2}{dt}$$

hence the correct use of the word 'mutual' to describe the effect.

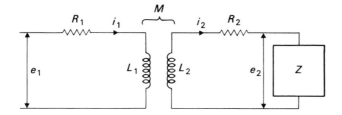

Figure 3.16 A transformer equivalent circuit using the concept of mutual inductance.

Since the self induced voltages e'_1 and e'_2 can be similarly evaluated to give

$$e'_1 = L_1 \frac{di_1}{dt} = \frac{N_1^2}{\mathcal{R}} \frac{di_1}{dt}$$

$$e'_2 = L_2 \frac{di_2}{dt} = \frac{N_2^2}{\mathcal{R}} \frac{di_2}{dt}$$

it follows at once that $M = \sqrt{(L_1 L_2)}$.

Such a situation, unattainable in a practical world, is known as 'perfect coupling'. Where only a fraction k of the flux from one coil links with the other, k is called the 'coupling factor' and is seen to be equal to $M/\sqrt{(L_1 L_2)}$.

An equivalent circuit may now be drawn as in Fig. 3.16 in which M is usually obtained by measurement in the first instance, after which the equations governing the behaviour of this circuit are as follows

$$e_1 = R_1 i_1 + L_1 \frac{di_1}{dt} + M \frac{di_2}{dt}$$

$$e_2 = R_2 i_2 + L_2 \frac{di_2}{dt} + M \frac{di_1}{dt}$$

(Note the interchange of the suffixes (1) and (2) in the last two terms of each of the above equations.)

Few writers ever set down clearly the relationship between the reactive components of the equivalent circuit of a transformer, as expressed in Fig. 3.14, and those of the mutual inductance analogue, $L_1 \omega$, $L_2 \omega$ and $M\omega$. At first sight there might appear to be a direct connection between $M\omega$ and X_m, since both depend on the useful flux. The fact is that there is *no* connection whatever between the two, *per se*, for each describes a quite different facet of the magnetic circuit, thus:

X_m indicates how much m.m.f. is required to set up the useful flux.
M, on the other hand, simply tells you what proportion of the total flux set up by either coil also threads the other coil.

Thus X_m cares neither for what happens to the flux nor where it goes, while M never asks the 'price' (in ampere-turns) of setting up the useful flux.

But of course there is a relationship between $M\omega$ and the relative values of X_m, X_1 and X_2', for these last two are a statement of the 'leakage' or 'failure to link' flux $(X_2' = (N_1/N_2)^2 X_2)$. Likewise, L_1 and L_2 must be related to X_m, for they, together with the usually small winding resistances, determine the magnetizing current drawn by whichever side is chosen to be the primary in the absence of current in the secondary, but the relationships are not straightforward. They are recorded here as an example of the complexity of trying to 'marry' two different analogues.

$$\left.\begin{aligned} X_1 + X_m &= L_1\omega \\ X_2' + X_m &= L_2\omega \\ \frac{X_m}{X_1 + X_m} &= k \end{aligned}\right\}\quad \begin{aligned} &\text{which express the components of} \\ &\text{the mutual inductance circuit in} \\ &\text{terms of the equivalent circuit} \end{aligned}$$

Conversely:

$$\left.\begin{aligned} X_1 &= L_1\omega(1-k) \\ X_2' &= L_2\omega - kL_1\omega \\ X_m &= kL_1\omega \end{aligned}\right\}\quad \begin{aligned} &\text{expressing the equivalent circuit} \\ &\text{components explicitly} \end{aligned}$$

But note the flaw in the argument. X_2' need not be equal to X_1, in which case we could write $X_m/(X_2' + X_m) = k$ by the interchange of primary and secondary. So apparently X_2' is equal to X_1, for mutual inductance is said to be the same when viewed from either pair of terminals! What is fact is that the magnetic circuit that links both windings will, of necessity, induce the same *volts per turn*, whether it be in the excited or the open circuit winding. But the existence of primary resistance in appreciable amounts will upset the tidy concept of mutual inductance, as it will the simple rule that the voltage ratio is exactly equal to the turns ratio.

But such effects become trivial as soon as we make big machines of superior 'quality' (high Goodness Factor: see pages 131–135). It is a strange irony that the design of a 'bad' machine is far less easy to achieve (and in this context the word 'achieve' really means to optimize) than that of a good one. Indeed it was in this cause that one of us wrote a book *Induction Machines for Special Purposes*[7] which, but for the fear of bad publicity and low sales, might well have been called 'The Design of Bad Induction Motors'!

3.8 THE TRANSFORMATION OF MECHANICAL WORK INTO AN EQUIVALENT CIRCUIT

It is a natural consequence of the concept of expressing hysteresis loss in an electrical machine by means of a parallel resistor (see Fig. 3.14), as if it were the result of a current flowing in a wire, which in reality it certainly is not, that we should contemplate the further development of this idea to embrace the mechanical power delivered by a machine, even to the extent of considering its operation as a generator to demand the inclusion of a *negative* resistor in the equivalent circuit.

We have often marvelled at the fact that a picture of forked lightning can hardly be distinguished from that of a young tree in winter if the negative of the photograph of the tree is used in place of a print and then inverted. Likewise it is not easy to distinguish either of these from a map of the Mississippi river and its tributaries. Nature makes her own analogues and often we cannot answer the question, 'Why?' All we know as engineers is that the same concepts, often the same formulae or even the same numbers recur in the oddest way. Maximum power flows from a battery when the external circuit's resistance is equal to the internal resistance of the battery—a condition of operation corresponding to only a fifty per cent efficiency. If an induction motor be run up from rest to synchronous speed ω_s against nothing but an inertial load of moment I, the heat loss in the rotor is equal to $\frac{1}{2}I\omega_s^2$, a condition corresponding to a fifty per cent energy efficiency. There are many other similar situations. Once he is aware of this the skilled engineer will 'cash in' even more on the power of analogue. Our favourite example is that of the operation of the induction motor which may be explained—more than that, *evaluated*—without recourse to an ampere, a volt, a watt, or an ohm! This approach follows next *both* as a substitute for the conventional textbook treatment, where it would properly be found in an appropriate chapter or book on induction machines, *and* as an easy introduction to the incorporation of mechanical quantities into equivalent circuits.

The argument is slightly easier to follow if one compares the mechanical system chosen with a *linear* induction motor (see Chapter 10), but a rotary equivalent can be substituted if desired. The analogue is based on the idea that the rotor of an induction motor behaves as if it were immersed in a fluid whose viscosity is such as to impart torque from the outer walls of a spinning vessel.

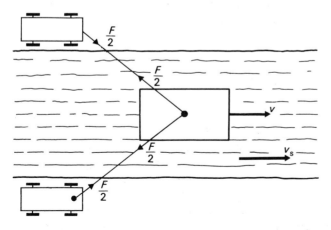

Figure 3.17 An analogue of a linear induction motor.

In the case of a linear induction motor its stator field becomes a flowing river, its moving secondary is a piece of wood floating on the surface (see Fig. 3.17). When we load the secondary, we attach carts to the wooden block by means of ropes as shown. The block pulls the carts along the river banks.

In the absence of the loads, the block would soon approach the speed of the water, v_s, but when loaded, the speed of the block falls to speed v and some of the water 'slips' past the block at relative speed $(v_s - v)$. Let us assume that the system has reached a steady state where v_s and v are constant. The force F produced by the water on the block must now be equal in magnitude to the force produced by the block on the load—or the block would be accelerating, which we have agreed it is not. 'Personalizing' the water for a moment, what does it experience? It says effectively, 'I, the water, am moving at speed v_s and applying force F to the block. I am giving up power at the value Fv_s.' This is then the power *input* to the system. Looking at the situation from the carts' point of view, they would declare that they were travelling at speed v, pulled by a force F. They receive power to the value of Fv. This is the power *output* of the system and we may write

$$\underset{\text{(input)}}{Fv_s} - \underset{\text{(output)}}{Fv} = \text{power loss} \qquad (3.5)$$

'Where does this power loss manifest itself?' is a non-obvious question but the answer is that the water temperature around it and the block temperature itself have increased owing to 'eddy current' (viscous friction) caused by the 'slip' phenomenon.

Let us now divide each side of Eq. (3.5) by Fv_s, leaving it as Fv_s on the left and replacing it by the words 'power input' on the right, thus

$$\frac{Fv_s - Fv}{Fv_s} = \frac{\text{loss}}{\text{input}} = \frac{v_s - v}{v_s}$$

Now $v_s - v$ is the slip velocity. We will call this a proportion of v_s and the quantity $(v_s - v)/v_s$ is then the 'fractional slip', s. Now we are in a position to calculate the efficiency of the energy transfer, for

$$\text{efficiency} = \frac{\text{output}}{\text{input}} = \frac{\text{input} - \text{loss}}{\text{input}} = 1 - \frac{\text{loss}}{\text{input}} = (1 - s)$$

It is the same result for an induction motor, by that unwritten law that tells us almost instinctively that things that 'look' alike often 'behave' alike.

The quantity Fv_s is often called the 'synchronous' power in induction motor theory. In the river analogue it was the input, but in the whole system it must have added to it the frictional losses of water on the river bed (corresponding in the real motor to the stator winding resistive losses and the stator iron losses) before we can account for the *total* input. It is only necessary to substitute torque T for force F and angular velocities ω_s and ω for v_s and v, respectively, to adapt this procedure to rotating machines.

The concept of synchronous power, Fv_s or $T\omega_s$, has shown us the way to include output as a resistive loss in an equivalent circuit, for the true ohmic

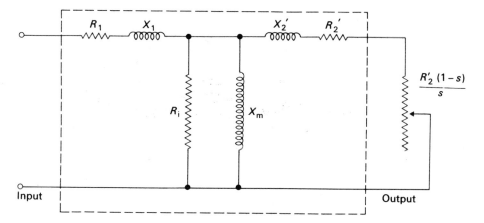

Figure 3.18 Equivalent circuit of an induction motor including output expressed as a variable resistor.

losses are seen at once as $sT\omega_s$ (since s is virtually defined as loss/$T\omega_s$). So instead of the actual secondary winding resistor R_2, which becomes $(N_1/N_2)^2 R_2$ after lumping, we have only to substitute R_2/s for R_2 and the 'loss' in $(N_1/N_2)^2(R_2/s)$ will include *both* the actual electrical loss $(N_1/N_2)^2 R_2$ *and* the mechanical output $(N_1/N_2)^2 R_2[(1-s)/s]$. If preferred, the mechanical output can be taken outside the black box, as shown in Fig. 3.18. Perhaps the most important part of the concept is that the total power crossing the airgap is represented by the loss in $R_2/s(N_1/N_2)^2$, and since this is equal to $T\omega_s$, the torque T follows directly.

One other very important concept is revealed by the electro/mechanical analogue of R_2/s. Since torque is proportional to the total loss in $(N_1/N_2)^2 R_2/s$, torque is, as it were, generated by the real loss in the secondary circuits, including therefore eddy current losses in the secondary core. Likewise, since the torque in a hysteresis motor is seen to arise as the result of the hysteresis loss in the rotor steel (see pages 249–252), a process not unlike that occurring in the induction motor, the resistor R_i in the equivalent circuit of Fig. 3.18 can now be seen to represent the *stator iron losses only*. This point is not often brought out in elementary textbooks on machines, perhaps because it is inclined to raise the question, 'Why not make the rotor just a cylinder of solid steel?' The answer to this question does not properly belong in a chapter on analogues, but it will be dealt with fully in Chapter 7, pages 213–220.

3.9 MIRRORS AND DUALS

Mirrors are common in everyday life and the idea of 'reflection' in its broadest sense implies 'where left becomes right and right becomes left'. But the concept of reflection goes far beyond the limitations of a mirror when we examine it in a metaphorical sense and see how often it arises in scientific theory.

One of the commonest left–right analogues is that of the left and right hand rules credited to Fleming in regard to the relationship between the directions of field, current, and motion or force in electromagnetic situations. The 'magic' of the three mutually orthogonal directions is that when thumbs and forefingers point in the same direction in pairs, second fingers point oppositely. But if forefingers and second fingers agree in pairs, thumbs oppose each other, and finally, if thumbs and second fingers are aligned, forefingers oppose. This phenomenon is expressed in the negative sign in the equation

$$\frac{\partial y}{\partial x} \cdot \frac{\partial x}{\partial z} \cdot \frac{\partial z}{\partial y} = -1$$

relating to a Cartesian coordinate system. 'Translated' into real terms it means that if any three-dimensional object be formed from plastic material, with the only limitation that it have no infinitely sharp corners or edges, and a point be marked on its surface, then sections can be cut in the x–y plane, the y–z plane, and the z–x plane and plotted in systematic order as shown in Fig. 3.19. In each case the section is made to pass through the chosen surface point. It will *always* emerge that the chosen point lies on two upward slopes and one

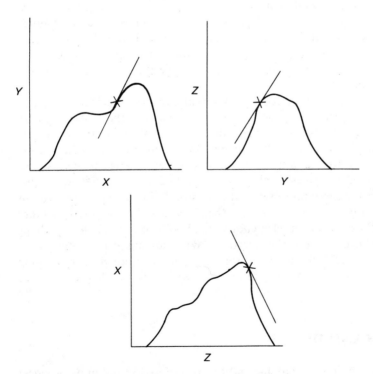

Figure 3.19 The human concept of three-dimensional space.

downward, as in the example shown, or on two downward slopes and one upward. There is no three-dimensional solid that will not conform to this rule. (Zero and infinite slopes must be treated consistently as slightly plus or minus the true value.) It is a limitation of the human mind that will go with man though he learn to travel to the furthest galaxy. It is the reason we shall never 'understand' electromagnetism. That we can nevertheless exploit, without understanding, is the purpose of this book and many that have gone before. The use of reflections or 'duals', as they are usually called in conceptual contexts, is almost as potent a tool for the engineer as is analogy itself. Series is to parallel as black is to white, as inductance is to capacitance, as nodal analysis is to mesh analysis, as night is to day, as magnetic circuit is to electric, and therefore as flux is to current.

We saw the beginnings of this in the expression of Ohm's law for both electric and magnetic circuits. Where e.m.f. becomes m.m.f., current must become flux to maintain the balance. Then the restraint terms remain of the same kind, i.e., both prohibitive, both proportional to length and inversely proportional to area and to conductivity. Now if the concept of mutual inductance appears, as suggested on page 87, to have been invented to 'bury' the magnetic circuit, there must inevitably exist a dual concept in which all quantities are expressed in magnetic terms, as if the electric circuit concept never existed.

3.10 MAGNETIC EQUIVALENT CIRCUITS

The first question that the student might ask with good reason, on being shown the latter concept, is: 'What *use* is it?'—and the answer is strange indeed, for it reveals a feature of power systems so common that the majority of engineers simply assume that there is no other alternative. It is simply this. We have elected to connect all consumers of electrical power from a national or state network in parallel. Parallel systems cry out for an electric equivalent circuit treatment. Series systems, if similarly treated, become undesirably complex to analyse. The fact that we shall consider, in later chapters, the theory of machines whose operation involves series electric circuits—or parallel magnetic circuits, for the two are later to be identified as the result of a dual—is justification enough for including the concept of magnetic equivalent circuits here, as well as merely for the sake of completeness or for academic 'tidiness'. Machines particularly singled out for such treatment include the shaded pole induction motor, the moving coil regulator, the amplidyne, and the metadyne. The order of the differential equations needed for the analysis of these machines is reduced by at least *one* by the use of the magnetic equivalent circuit concept.

In the beginning, the idea of an equivalent circuit is a device that will remove entirely the necessity for solving differential equations. It is assumed at this point that the reader is already familiar with the complete solution for the current in a circuit containing resistance, inductance, and capacitance that is voltage driven from a source of e.m.f. varying in time t, according to the law $e = \hat{E} \sin \omega t$, where e is the instantaneous value, $\hat{E}$ its maximum value, and ω the angular frequency of variation. Although we know that the formal solution lies in discovering a particular integral and solving for the complementary function of the equation

$$L\frac{d^2q}{dt^2} + R\frac{dq}{dt} + \frac{1}{C}q = \hat{E}\sin\omega t$$

we solve it by a simple phasor diagram that shows us that the impedance Z is simply written in the complex notation

$$Z = R + j\left(L\omega - \frac{1}{C\omega}\right)$$

and by the foreknowledge that the particular integral is therefore

$$e = \left\{\hat{E}\bigg/\sqrt{\left[R^2 + \left(L\omega - \frac{1}{C\omega}\right)^2\right]}\right\}\sin\left[\omega t - \arctan\left(\frac{L\omega - 1/C\omega}{R}\right)\right]$$

which gives us the 'steady state' solution. The complementary function is simply the solution of

$$\left(LD^2 + RD + \frac{1}{C}\right)q = 0$$

with D as operator and initial conditions being inserted after integration. We also know that this solution is always concerned with transient conditions depending on the application of a step function, as at the instant of switch-on, and therefore usually of no consequence a short time thereafter.

To approach the solution of a.c. networks by the differential equation approach is called 'deductive teaching'. To study first Ohm's law for a purely resistive circuit, then to add the $L(di/dt)$ term and so on, increasing the complexity at each step, is by contrast 'inductive teaching' and in our experience the method preferred by the vast majority of engineers. Accordingly this is the method we shall adopt here for the introduction of the magnetic equivalent circuit, first published in 1967,[8] and never before in any textbook on a.c. machines.

Beginning, therefore, with a simple transformer example as shown in Fig.

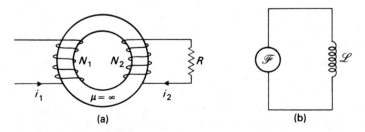

(a)　　　　　　　　　　　　(b)

Figure 3.20 Simple example of a perfect transformer: (a) electric; (b) equivalent magnetic.

3.20, we assume that the magnetic circuit has infinite permeability, and therefore there is no magnetizing current and no leakage flux. Likewise, we shall consider there to be no iron loss and the differential equations governing the performance are simply

$$N_1 i_1 + N_2 i_2 = 0 \quad \text{(ampere-turn balance)}$$

$$N_2 \frac{d\phi}{dt} + R i_2 = 0 \quad \text{(Faraday's and Kirchhoff's laws)}$$

Substituting for i_2 in the first equation from the second gives

$$N_1 i_1 = \frac{N_2^2}{R} \frac{d\phi}{dt}$$

If we now ascribe a symbol $\mathscr{F}$ for m.m.f., we may rewrite this equation as

$$\mathscr{F} = \left(\frac{N_2^2}{R} \right) \frac{d\phi}{dt}$$

It is at this point that the memory conjures up a similar relationship

$$e = L \frac{di}{dt}$$

where e and i were quantities known from our Ohm's law days and L was once something new. Expressed in this equation is the idea that to isolate the 'new' concept, we assume a perfect electric circuit and discover that such a circuit of zero resistance would by no means pass infinite current when connected to a voltage source, if the value were such that $e = \hat{E} \sin \omega t$.

Could it be that $\mathscr{F} = (N_2^2/R) \, d\phi/dt$ is an analogue in which we could write

$$\mathscr{F} = \mathscr{L} \frac{d\phi}{dt}$$

and $\mathscr{L}$ is a new quantity corresponding with inductance? The answer to any such question, of course, is 'Yes'. But the test is whether it can be extended to cover many aspects of the subject—to be an analogue 'in depth'.

The first encouragement comes with the realization that an evaluation of electrical inductance in terms of magnetic and electric circuit constants is to the effect that $L = N^2/\mathscr{R}$ where N is the number of turns in the electric circuit and $\mathscr{R}$ is the reluctance of the magnetic. Certainly this idea goes well with the dual concept that 'magnetic inductance' $\mathscr{L} = N^2/R$. (It is extremely convenient in this treatment to ascribe italic capital letters to electrical quantities and script letters to corresponding magnetic concepts.)

But now other manifestations begin to appear like shapes out of a mist, first in blurred outline, suggesting that the analogue may soon be dashed to pieces on some obvious contradiction, but then, as we progress, becoming sharp edged until we have a whole new picture with all the elegance that a good analogue demands. We step tentatively forward by ascribing the imperfection of reluctance into the magnetic circuit to replace Fig. 3.20 by

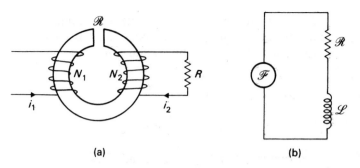

Figure 3.21 Introduction of the first imperfection, reluctance.

Fig. 3.21. At once we see that the only addition needed to the basic equations is that the ampere-turn balance is no longer true but now

$$N_1 i_1 + N_2 i_2 = \phi \mathscr{R}$$

where $\mathscr{R}$ is regarded as the reluctance of the gap while the permeability is still regarded as infinite. After the substitution from the second equation as before, we have simply

$$\mathscr{F} = \left(\frac{N_2^2}{R}\right)\frac{d\phi}{dt} + \phi \mathscr{R}$$

as for the electric equivalent where

$$e = \left(\frac{N^2}{\mathscr{R}}\right)\frac{di}{dt} + iR$$

The perfect dual persists.

Let us take yet another situation (still academic but essential to the understanding) and replace R in Fig. 3.21 by a pure inductance L. The first of the two equations remains unaltered. The second now reads

$$N_2 \frac{d\phi}{dt} + L \frac{di_2}{dt} = 0$$

which, upon substitution, gives the result

$$N_1 \frac{di_1}{dt} = \frac{N_2^2}{L}\frac{d\phi}{dt} + \mathscr{R}\frac{d\phi}{dt} = \left(\frac{N_2^2}{L} + \mathscr{R}\right)\frac{d\phi}{dt}$$

From dimensions alone, N_2^2/L has the dimensions of reluctance and can be so indicated by $\mathscr{R}'$, making the basic equation

$$\frac{d\mathscr{F}}{dt} = (\mathscr{R}' + \mathscr{R})\frac{d\phi}{dt}$$

or

$$\mathscr{F} = (\mathscr{R}' + \mathscr{R})\phi$$

Thus electric inductance transforms into magnetic reluctance just as magnetic inductance is the transform of electric resistance. But there is more.

The coil producing the inductance L must have a magnetic circuit of its own. Let this circuit have reluctance $\mathscr{R}''$, and let the number of turns on the coil be N_3.

Then, since

$$L = \frac{N_3^2}{R''} \quad \text{and} \quad \mathscr{R}' = \frac{N_2^2}{L}$$

$$\mathscr{R}' = \left(\frac{N_2}{N_3}\right)^2 \mathscr{R}''$$

proving that the rule of lumping of impedance applies to the magnetic circuit discipline also.

It is now time to ascribe an appropriate name to the quantity $\mathscr{L}$, for 'magnetic inductance' is not only cumbersome but inaccurate, since it suggests that it has the mechanism of an inductance insofar as it can store energy. In fact the opposite is true. $\mathscr{L}$ is derived from R, and R absorbs energy. In magnetic circuits it is $\mathscr{R}$ that stores, $\mathscr{L}$ that dissipates. We might give the name 'absorbance' to $\mathscr{L}$, but two things suggest that this is not the best choice. First, we are surely going to look now for the alternative magnetic circuit involving the concept of 'mutual magnetic inductance', $\mathscr{M}$, and since the latter will involve transfers of energy, the name 'mutual transferance' would be appropriate, in which case $\mathscr{L}$ becomes a 'self transferance' or merely a 'transferance'. Second, nothing in the treatment of magnetic circuits so far has placed any restriction on the variations of $\mathscr{F}$ or ϕ which could be sinusoidal, impulsive, or otherwise, and therefore the concepts of $j\omega\mathscr{L} = j\mathscr{X}$ and of $\mathscr{Z} = \sqrt{(\mathscr{L}^2\omega^2 + \mathscr{R}^2)}$ will need names, since sinusoidal variation occurs most commonly in the study of machines. The fact that operators such as the Laplacian p (as in $\mathscr{L}(p)$) are not specifically named is also in accordance with electric circuit practice. We shall use 'absorbance' as the name for $\mathscr{L}\omega$ (magnetic reactance), and 'concedance' for $\mathscr{Z}$ as indicative of the fact that it is the opposite of that which impedes ('impedance'), while words such as 'admittance' have already been used in electric circuit techniques. The table below shows the correspondence between electric and magnetic circuit nomenclature and the transformations that may be performed between the two:

Electric	*Magnetic*
(1) Resistance, $R(= l_e/\sigma A_e)$	Reluctance, $\mathscr{R}(= l_m/\mu A_m)$
(2) Inductance, $L(= N^2/\mathscr{R})$	Transferance, $\mathscr{L}(= N^2/R)$
(3) Reactance, $X(= L\omega)$	Absorbance, $\mathscr{X}(= \mathscr{L}\omega)$
(4) Impedance, $Z(= R + jX,$ whose modulus is $\sqrt{(R^2 + Z^2)})$	Concedance, $\mathscr{Z}$ $(\mathscr{R} + j\mathscr{X},$ whose modulus is $\sqrt{(\mathscr{R}^2 + \mathscr{X}^2)})$
(5) Mutual inductance, $M(= N_1 N_2/\mathscr{R})$	Mutual transferance, $\mathscr{M}(= N_1 N_2/R)$
(6) Capacitance, C (often regarded as $-1/L$)	Mechanical input, $\mathscr{C}$ (may be regarded as $-1/\mathscr{R}$)

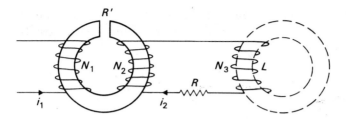

Figure 3.22 The magnetic treatment of R and L in series.

So far we have tested the concepts (1) and (2) separately. It remains to test them in combination, which will make (3) and (4) valid, and then to discover the nature of situations that can be handled by (5) and (6).

Let us begin with a real-life pair of circuits as shown in Fig. 3.22. Now this will be a difficult task unless we first establish a rule for transformations between series and parallel circuits. Hence we will first examine the arrangement shown in Fig. 3.23(a) in which resistors R_1 and R_2 are connected in parallel across the secondary. The equivalent resistance R is given by

$$\frac{1}{R} = \frac{1}{R_1} + \frac{1}{R_2}$$

Hence

$$\mathscr{F} = \left(\frac{N_2^2}{R}\right)\frac{\mathrm{d}\phi}{\mathrm{d}t} + \phi\mathscr{R}$$

that is

$$\mathscr{F} = \left[\left(\frac{N_2^2}{R_1}\right) + \left(\frac{N_2^2}{R_2}\right)\right]\frac{\mathrm{d}\phi}{\mathrm{d}t} + \phi\mathscr{R}$$

and the circuit corresponds to that shown in Fig. 3.23(b) where

$$\mathscr{F} = (\mathscr{L}_1 + \mathscr{L}_2)\frac{\mathrm{d}\phi}{\mathrm{d}t} + \phi\mathscr{R}$$

—a *series* circuit where both R_1 and R_2 are treated as before, i.e., they convert

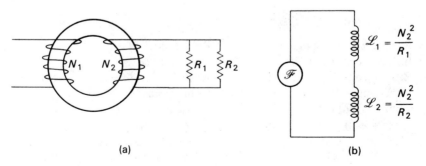

(a)   (b)

Figure 3.23 Electric/magnetic interchange changes series/parallel also.

into magnetic inductances each of which obeys the same rule for the calculation of its value, i.e., (turns)^2/resistance. Similarly it can be shown that series resistances transform into parallel components of $\mathscr{L}$ form. We shall not therefore be surprised if the circuit of Fig. 3.22 transforms into a parallel magnetic circuit, but the acid test will be whether the components retain their identity, for if the resulting $\mathscr{L}$ and $\mathscr{R}$ equivalents are complex compounds of L and R, the elegance will be lost.

We must therefore return to first principles and write

$$N_1 i_1 + N_2 i_2 = \phi \mathscr{R}' \tag{3.6}$$

$$N_2 \frac{d\phi}{dt} + i_2 R + L \frac{di_2}{dt} = 0 \tag{3.7}$$

Substituting for i_2 in Eq. (3.7) from Eq. (3.6) gives

$$\frac{d\phi}{dt} = N_1 \frac{R}{N_2^2} i_1 - \phi \mathscr{R}' \frac{R}{N_2^2} + \frac{L}{N_2^2} N_1 \frac{di_1}{dt} - \frac{L}{N_2^2} \mathscr{R}' \frac{d\phi}{dt} \tag{3.8}$$

If we now draw the magnetic equivalent circuit of Fig. 3.22, using the rule that we make a model of the circuit in which magnetic components such as reluctance are drawn as they appear in the actual situation, i.e., as series or parallel components, then wherever an electromagnetic transformation takes place we replace resistive components by transferances of value N^2/resistance and inductive components by reluctances of value N^2/inductance, exchanging series for parallel and vice versa as the transformation is made. It will suffice if, in the relationship between i_1 and ϕ, the individual terms can be identified.

The magnetic equivalent circuit will appear as shown in Fig. 3.24 and the relevant equations are

$$\mathscr{F} = N_1 I_1 = \phi \mathscr{R}' + \mathscr{L} \frac{d\phi_1}{dt} \tag{3.9}$$

$$\mathscr{F} = N_1 I_1 = \phi \mathscr{R}' + \phi_2 \mathscr{R} \tag{3.10}$$

$$\phi = \phi_1 + \phi_2 \tag{3.11}$$

From Eq. (3.11)

$$\frac{d\phi}{dt} = \frac{d\phi_1}{dt} + \frac{d\phi_2}{dt} \tag{3.12}$$

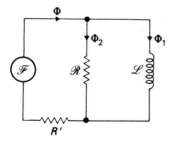

Figure 3.24 Magnetic equivalent of the circuit shown in Fig. 3.22.

Substituting from Eq. (3.9), differentiating Eq. (3.10) and substituting into Eq. (3.12) gives

$$\frac{d\phi}{dt} = \frac{N_1 i_1}{\mathscr{L}} - \phi \frac{\mathscr{R}'}{\mathscr{L}} + \frac{N_1}{\mathscr{R}} \frac{di_1}{dt} - \frac{\mathscr{R}'}{\mathscr{R}} \frac{d\phi}{dt}$$

Each term on the right hand side can now be identified with a term on the right hand side of Eq. (3.8) with the proviso that, taking the terms in order

(1) and (2)

$$\mathscr{L} = \frac{N_2^2}{R}$$

(3) and (4)

$$\mathscr{R} = \frac{N_2^2}{L}$$

The first relationship is already established, hence the elegance is retained. The second is a new relationship which is incredibly simple, being the perfect dual of the first. Among the many things implied is that when mathematical operators ($j\omega$, p, etc.) are applied, the Q-factor or Goodness Factor ($L\omega/R$) comes through the transformation unchanged since $\mathscr{L}\omega/\mathscr{R} = L\omega/R$.

There is no need to repeat the detailed analysis to realize that 'magnetic capacitance' ($\mathscr{C}$) can be seen as a negative transferance ($-\mathscr{L}$) and hence as a negative resistance in an electrical network or as power fed in mechanically to a machine (such as an induction machine used as a generator where the slip and hence R_2/s is negative).

It only remains to investigate the dual of the mutual inductance concept. In the world of electric equivalent circuits this concept is essentially born of a pair of coils linking a single magnetic circuit. The magnetic dual must therefore consist essentially of a pair of magnetic circuits linked by a common electric circuit. However, since the usual excitation in machines of medium and large sizes is a current-carrying coil (as opposed to a permanent magnet or mechanically generated, changing m.m.f.) the system we shall examine is that shown in Fig. 3.25 in which the two outer coils merely act as sources of m.m.f. The magnetic circuits have airgap reluctances $\mathscr{R}_1$ and $\mathscr{R}_2$, respectively, the numbers of turns on each coil being indicated on the diagram.

For the left hand magnetic circuit

$$N_1 i_1 + N_3 i_3 = \phi_1 \mathscr{R}_1 \tag{3.13}$$

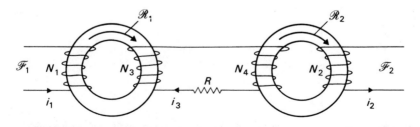

Figure 3.25 An electromagnetic arrangement that introduces the concept of magnetic mutual inductance.

and for the other circuit

$$N_2 i_2 + N_4 i_3 = \phi_2 \mathcal{R}_2 \tag{3.14}$$

For the common electric circuit

$$N_3 \frac{d\phi_1}{dt} + i_3 R + N_4 \frac{d\phi_2}{dt} = 0 \tag{3.15}$$

Substituting for i_3 from Eq. (3.15) into Eqs. (3.13) and (3.14) gives

$$N_1 i_1 = \frac{N_3^2}{R} \cdot \frac{d\phi_1}{dt} + \frac{N_3 N_4}{R} \cdot \frac{d\phi_2}{dt} + \phi_1 \mathcal{R}_1 \tag{3.16}$$

$$N_2 i_2 = \frac{N_4^2}{R} \cdot \frac{d\phi_2}{dt} + \frac{N_3 N_4}{R} \cdot \frac{d\phi_1}{dt} + \phi_2 \mathcal{R}_2 \tag{3.17}$$

Using the previously obtained conversions $N_3^2/R = \mathcal{L}_1$, $N_4^2/R = \mathcal{L}_2$, Eqs. (3.16) and (3.17) can be rewritten

$$\mathcal{F}_1 = \mathcal{L}_1 \frac{d\phi_1}{dt} + \mathcal{M} \frac{d\phi_2}{dt} + \phi_1 \mathcal{R}_1$$

$$\mathcal{F}_2 = \mathcal{L}_2 \frac{d\phi_2}{dt} + \mathcal{M} \frac{d\phi_1}{dt} + \phi_2 \mathcal{R}_2$$

when $\mathcal{M}$ is the 'mutual transferance' whose value is $N_3 N_4/R$, and the magnetic equivalent circuit is as shown in Fig. 3.26. It is to be noted at once that just as the electric mutual inductance concept gives

$$M = \sqrt{(L_1 L_2)} = \frac{N_1' N_2'}{\mathcal{R}} \quad \text{where} \quad L_1 = \frac{N_1'^2}{\mathcal{R}}, \quad L_2 = \frac{N_2'^2}{\mathcal{R}}$$

so

$$\mathcal{M} = \sqrt{(\mathcal{L}_1 \mathcal{L}_2)} = \frac{N_3 N_4}{R} \quad \text{and} \quad \mathcal{L}_1 = \frac{N_3^2}{R}, \quad \mathcal{L}_2 = \frac{N_4^2}{R}$$

The story is complete. The dual is flawless to the extent of the premises so far invoked. The limitation of this particular analogue lies in that it is only able to deal with lumped parameters, i.e., it is not directly applicable to distributed circuits where neither currents nor fluxes are constrained within coils of wire on the one hand and single ferrous loops of high permeability on the other. Students who would seek to develop magnetic equivalent circuits

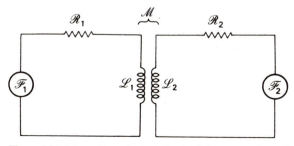

Figure 3.26 Magnetic equivalent circuit of the system shown in Fig. 3.25.

further to the stage of deriving such quantities as a magnetic Poynting vector and similar concepts are recommended to consult a paper by one of our colleagues.[9]

This chapter would not be complete without returning once more to Cullwick's book.[3]

> The known facts of electricity and magnetism form an exact and coherent body of knowledge of surprising beauty and symmetry, and the unravelling of this beauty by patient thought and experiment forms one of the most fascinating stories of all time. From small and disjointed beginnings, from lodestone and amber, this most incorporeal of nature's secrets gradually capitulated to the restless mind of man, until at last the knowledge handed on by Oersted and Faraday, by Ampère and Maxwell, bids fair to embrace the whole of the physical universe.

May your minds be ever restless, may you view the incorporeal in a new light, through the power of analogy, which gives substance to those things that rightfully have none.

Solution to Problem on page 87

The first thing to note is that the radius of the sphere is not given. It follows at once that the radius cannot matter, for the information given was 'sufficient'. By the *reductio ad absurdum* principle the engineer takes the extreme cases of a very large and a very small sphere, for example, first, the earth itself. The hole cut would have to be almost the same diameter as the earth, leaving an annulus 2 cm high and of almost zero thickness, almost infinitely long. This is unhelpful—discard it at once! What of smaller and smaller spheres? The least size that makes the hole 'necessary' is a sphere of 2 cm diameter, when the hole has shrunk to zero diameter. There is the solution! The volume remaining must be that of a sphere of radius 1 cm, i.e., $\frac{4}{3}\pi r^3$ with $r = 1$, giving $\frac{4}{3}\pi$ cubic centimetres.

REFERENCES

1. G. Walton, 'Facts and artefacts', *The Modern Churchman*, **7**, 233, 8 July 1964.
2. John Tyndall, *Faraday as a Discoverer*, Longmans, London, 1870.
3. E. G. Cullwick, *The Fundamentals of Electromagnetism*, 1st edn, Cambridge University Press, 1939.
4. H. Dingle, *The Special Theory of Relativity*, 4th edn, Methuen, London, 1961.
5. J. M. Ham and G. R. Slemon, *Scientific Basis of Electrical Engineering*, Wiley, New York, 1961.
6. B. A. Behrend, *The Induction Motor and Other Alternating Current Motors*, McGraw-Hill, New York, 1921.
7. E. R. Laithwaite, *Induction Machines for Special Purposes*, Newnes, London, and Chemical Publishing Company, New York, 1966.
8. E. R. Laithwaite, 'Magnetic equivalent circuits for electrical machines', *Proc. IEE*, **114**(11), 1805–9, 1967.
9. C. J. Carpenter, 'Magnetic equivalent circuits', *Proc. IEE*, **115**(10), 1503–11, 1968.

FOUR

THE TRANSFER OF ENERGY IN A POWER SYSTEM

4.1 INTRODUCTION

For a power system to be an efficient channel of energy flow it should accomplish this task with the minimum of loss. To this end, power system equipment, like generators, transformers, and transmission lines, is designed to operate at very high efficiencies. Recalling also the constant voltage nature of power systems, it is necessary that the desirable energy transfers are achieved with the voltage at consumer terminals neither exceeding the voltage rating of appliances nor slumping below statutory levels.

The study of energy transportation in networks leads to certain concepts peculiar to power systems that have been developed to enable the engineer to handle this problem with ease and elegance.

In this chapter the topic of energy transfer is tackled from first principles and in the process the basic conventions followed in this book are laid down.

4.2 GENERATORS AND CONSUMERS OF ENERGY

We start with the very simple notion of power associated with the circuit element of Fig. 4.1, in which the block may represent any piece of equipment

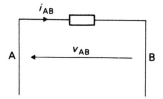

Figure 4.1 Circuit element.

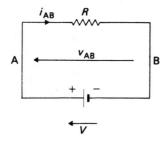

Figure 4.2 Simple d.c. circuit.

found in a power system network. The terminals of the element are labelled A and B. Let us now define i_{AB} as the current flowing from terminal A to terminal B *through* the element at a particular instant. The direction of current flow from A to B is denoted by the sequence of the subscripts. If positive charge is transferred from terminal A to terminal B through the element, then we choose to assign a positive sign to i_{AB}. If the positive charge transfer is from B to A, then i_{AB} is negative. At any instant, therefore, $i_{AB} = -i_{BA}$.

We can then agree to denote the potential difference of terminal A with respect to terminal B by v_{AB}. If the potential of A is higher, i.e., more positive, than that of B, then v_{AB} is positive. From this follows that at any instant $v_{AB} = -v_{BA}$.

After having settled these 'reference' directions of voltage and current, it is worth stressing there is nothing really new in all this but a precise statement of the conventions the reader already implicitly knows with respect to d.c. circuits. In the simple d.c. circuit of Fig. 4.2, consisting of a resistor and a battery, $v_{AB} = V$, $i_{AB} = V/R$, both being positive. With the connections to the battery reversed, $v_{AB} = -V$ and $i_{AB} = -V/R$.

At any instant, the power p in watts associated with the element of Fig. 4.1 is, by definition, the product of the instantaneous potential difference and the instantaneous current, i.e.,

$$p = v_{AB} \cdot i_{AB} \tag{4.1}$$

If the sign of p is positive, then, as the circuit of Fig. 4.2 confirms, the element is consuming power at that instant. If, however, the sign of p is negative, the element is generating power. This can be clearly seen in Fig. 4.3

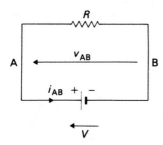

Figure 4.3 Simple d.c. circuit.

where the notation of Fig. 4.1 is now applied to the *battery* rather than the resistor. Here $i_{AB} = -V/R$ and $p = v_{AB} \cdot i_{AB} = V(-V/R)$, i.e., the power is negative.

To sum up, the power in an element is taken as positive and therefore consumed, when the current is flowing through the element from higher to lower potentials. If the reverse were true then the power would be negative and the element would be a generator.

4.3 THE A.C. CASE

We are now ready to ask an interesting question. What is the power associated with an element if v_{AB} and i_{AB} are sinusoidal quantities of the same frequency?

In Fig. 4.4 a plot against time is shown of v_{AB} and i_{AB} lagging v_{AB} by an interval t_ϕ. A point by point plot of $v_{AB} \cdot i_{AB}$ results in the waveform p. We can, therefore, say that, in general, with v and i sinusoidal, p will take both positive and negative values, i.e., during parts of the cycle the element will be acting as a consumer and during other parts as a generator of power.

What decides whether the element is consuming or generating power is the *sign* of the average power P over a period T. In other words, a positive integral

$$\frac{1}{T} \int_t^{t+T} p \, dt$$

indicates that the element is, on average, a consumer; a negative integral that it is, on average, a generator. In Fig. 4.4, P is positive and the element is a consumer.

Let $v_{AB} = V_m \sin \omega t$ and $i_{AB} = I_m \sin(\omega t - \phi)$, where ϕ is the phase angle between v_{AB} and i_{AB}, and $\omega = 2\pi f$ is the angular velocity of the sinusoids.

We can then write

$$p = v_{AB} \cdot i_{AB} = V_m I_m \sin \omega t \sin(\omega t + \phi)$$

Using a trigonometric identity we get

$$p = \tfrac{1}{2} V_m I_m \cos \phi - \tfrac{1}{2} V_m I_m \cos(2\omega t - \phi)$$

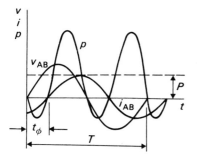

Figure 4.4 Power in an a.c. circuit.

and if r.m.s. quantities are introduced then

$$p = VI\cos\phi - VI\cos(2\omega t - \phi) \tag{4.2}$$

The average power is given by

$$P = \frac{1}{T}\int_t^{t+T} p\,dt = VI\cos\phi - \frac{1}{T}\int_t^{t+T} VI\cos(2\omega t - \phi)\,dt$$

The second term has an average value of zero, therefore

$$P = VI\cos\phi \tag{4.3}$$

As the r.m.s. values of V and I are always positive, the product VI is also always positive and gives no information either of the power or of its sign. This product is known as 'volt amperes' or occasionally as 'apparent power'. For the power to be obtained, the volt amperes must be multiplied by the 'power factor' $\cos\phi$, a very important quantity in power systems. Furthermore, it is the sign of $\cos\phi$ that determines whether an element is a generator or a consumer of power.

Using now the convenient shorthand notation of phasors instead of time varying sinusoids, and representing v_{AB} and i_{AB} by $\bar{V}$ and $\bar{I}$, we arrive at the phasor diagram of Fig. 4.5. In Fig. 4.5(a) the voltage, and in 4.5(b) the current, are taken as reference phasors and set along the x-axis. In both cases, the y-axis represents the boundary between generators and consumers.

Let us look more closely at Fig. 4.5(b), using the convention that positive ϕ corresponds to counterclockwise rotation from the reference axis.

The position of $\bar{V}$ in the diagram is very significant. The element is a consumer when $\bar{V}$ falls within the right hand shaded area in which $-\pi/2 < \phi < \pi/2$ and $\cos\phi$ is positive. The element is a generator when $\bar{V}$ falls within the left hand shaded area in which $\pi/2 < \phi < 3\pi/2$ and $\cos\phi$ is

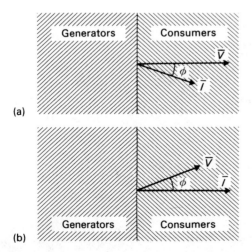

(a)

(b)

Figure 4.5 Phasor diagrams.

negative. If $\bar{V}$ were to coincide with the y-axis, the element would be acting as neither a generator nor a consumer of power.

4.4 REACTIVE POWER

The average power given by Eq. (4.3) can be looked at as being the product of V and $I \cos \phi$. This idea is illustrated in Fig. 4.6 through phasors by resolving the current into an 'in-phase' component I_p and a 'quadrature' component I_q. Clearly, $P = VI_p$, but the question now arises whether any meaning can be attached to VI_q. In fact, this quantity is known as 'reactive power' and is used extensively in power systems engineering. For the uninitiated the whole concept is mysterious and obscure; a close look at the underlying ideas is therefore necessary.

The sinewaves $v = V_m \sin \omega t$ and $i = I_m \sin(\omega t - \phi)$ are shown in Fig. 4.7(a). Current i is split into its in-phase and quadrature components, $i_p = I_m \cos \phi \sin \omega t = I'_m \sin \omega t$, and $i_q = -I_m \sin \phi \cos \omega t = I''_m \cos \omega t$ and these are plotted in Fig. 4.7(b).

From $p = vi$ we can write

$$p = v(i_p + i_q)$$
$$= V_m \sin \omega t I'_m \sin \omega t - V_m \sin \omega t I''_m \cos \omega t$$
$$= V_m I'_m \sin^2 \omega t - \frac{V_m I''_m}{2} \sin 2\omega t$$
$$= \frac{V_m I'_m}{2}(1 - \cos 2\omega t) - \frac{V_m I''_m}{2} \sin 2\omega t$$

Let us now define p_p and p_q as

$$p_p = \frac{V_m I'_m}{2}(1 - \cos 2\omega t)$$

$$p_q = \frac{V_m I''_m}{2} \sin 2\omega t$$

and plot these two power components in Fig. 4.7(c).

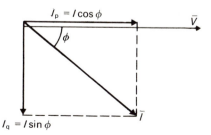

$I_p = I \cos \phi$

$\bar{V}$

ϕ

$\bar{I}$

$I_q = I \sin \phi$

Figure 4.6 In-phase and quadrature components of current.

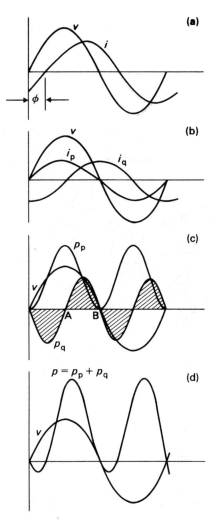

Figure 4.7 Active and reactive components of power.

Component p_p contains a sinusoidally varying double-frequency term that has a zero average value. The average value of p_p is

$$P = \frac{V_m I'_m}{2} = VI \cos \phi$$

Component p_q has zero average value and a peak of

$$\left| \frac{V_m I''_m}{2} \right| = VI \sin \phi$$

The total power p is plotted in Fig. 4.7(d). The intention has been to show that of the power p consumed by an element at any instant, a part p_p is utilized for permanent irreversible consumption, e.g., conversion into heat. This part *always* has positive values, i.e., it cannot be recovered and returned to the rest of the circuit. In contrast, the remainder p_q is utilized in establishing either a magnetic or an electrostatic field, i.e., it is stored and eventually returned to the circuit. This is illustrated by the successive positive and negative shaded areas of Fig. 4.7(c).

The energy $\int_A^B p_q \, dt$ oscillates between the element and the rest of the circuit at the rate of two reversals per period T.

It is important to appreciate that as far as the instantaneous value of p is concerned, its two components p_p and p_q represent at times truly consumed power, notwithstanding the fact that p_q will shortly be returned to the circuit. Although p_q has a zero average value, it does nevertheless represent real reciprocating energy that must be present by virtue of the inductance or capacitance of the network.

4.5 THE QUADRANT DIAGRAM

The quantity $VI_q = VI \sin \phi = Q$ corresponds to the peak value of the oscillating energy and is referred to as 'reactive volt amperes' or 'reactive power'. Although the average value of p_q is nil, Q has to be present and, as will be shown later, the oscillatory transfer of p_q between points in a power system results in voltage drops and losses in generation and transmission equipment. As both the efficiency and the voltage regulation of a power system are very important, the transfer of Q over the system is also of prime interest.

The mathematical concept which is about to be described was evolved to help with the handling of Q. Although there is no real physical justification behind this concept, it is of great use to power systems engineers. This should not perplex the reader. Both physicists and particularly engineers have often used concepts that have no real physical existence or justification but are most effective tools for problem solving.

Let us now look at the concept of the reactive power

$$Q = VI \sin \phi \tag{4.4}$$

By analogy to the active power of Eq. (4.3) we could imagine that there are generators and consumers of Q and that the element of Fig. 4.1 is a consumer of Q if Eq. (4.4) has a positive sign and a generator of Q if its sign is negative.

The phasor diagram of Fig. 4.8 can therefore be drawn as a counterpart of Fig. 4.5(b). If $\bar{V}$ in Fig. 4.8 falls within the upper shaded area, i.e., $0 < \phi < \pi$, $\sin \phi$ is positive and the element is said to be a consumer of Q. In contrast, the element is said to be a generator of Q if $\pi < \phi < 2\pi$.

The statement about the sign of Q, although devoid of physical meaning, imparts some useful information on the phase relationship between $\bar{V}$ and $\bar{I}$.

Before going any further, let us first adopt some conventions with respect to phase relationships. In Fig. 4.8, if $\bar{V}$ is in any position between $\phi > 0$ and

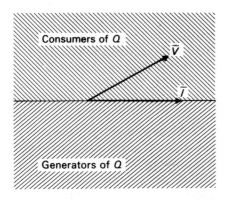

Figure 4.8 Phasor diagram.

$\phi < \pi/2$ we say that the voltage leads the current or the current lags the voltage; in other words it is the *smallest* angle between the two phasors that determines the lead–lag relationship. In the extremes of $\phi = 0$ or $\phi = \pi$, the phasors are in-phase or antiphase, respectively, and no statement can be made about lead or lag.

Returning now to the sign of Q, irrespective of whether the element is a generator or consumer of active power, if Q is positive the current lags the voltage, and if Q is negative the current leads the voltage. If $Q = 0$, then $\phi = 0$ or $\phi = \pi$, in which case the element is a resistor or a pure source of active power, respectively.

Squaring Eqs. (4.3) and (4.4) and adding,

$$(VI \sin \phi)^2 + (VI \cos \phi)^2 = (VI)^2$$

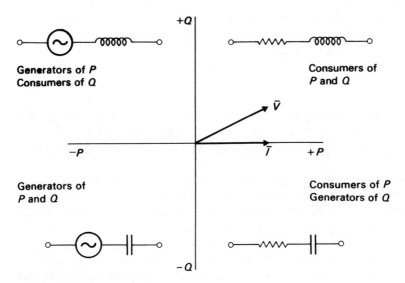

Figure 4.9 Quadrant diagram.

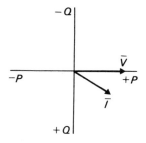

Figure 4.10 Quadrant diagram with voltage phasor as reference.

therefore

$$VI = \sqrt{(P^2 + Q^2)} \tag{4.5}$$

The superposition of Figs. 4.5 and 4.8 results in the 'quadrant' diagram of Fig. 4.9.

With $\bar{I}$ as reference phasor, the position of $\bar{V}$ on the diagram defines the mode of operation of the element in terms of P and Q. As illustrated in Fig. 4.9, a resistive–inductive element consumes P and Q while a resistive–capacitive element consumes P but generates Q. Quadrants 2 and 3 require generation of active power and are occupied by 'active' elements such as alternators. As will be shown in Chapter 5, a synchronous machine can operate in any of the four quadrants. With the voltage phasor as reference, the quadrant diagram takes the form of Fig. 4.10. In Fig. 4.9 the active and reactive powers can be found by resolving $\bar{V}$ along the P- and Q-axes to get $P = VI \cos \phi$ and $Q = VI \sin \phi$.

4.6 THE BALANCE OF ACTIVE AND REACTIVE POWER

At this point the reader may be justly wondering why all this trouble has been taken with no apparent returns! This section should dispel these doubts.

Let us look at the principles regulating the P and Q transfer within a power system. A single-phase system consisting of generation, transmission lines, and consumers could be divided into two subsystems X and Y interconnected by two conductors A and B, as shown in Fig. 4.11. Let the voltage between lines A and B be denoted by v_{AB} and the reference current

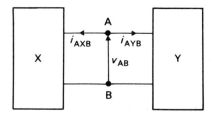

Figure 4.11 Power system subdivided into two subsystems.

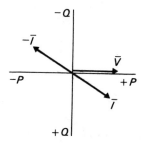

Figure 4.12 Quadrant diagram to illustrate the conservation of real and reactive power.

directions by i_{AXB} and i_{AYB} in accordance with the convention of Fig. 4.1. Here, clearly, $i_{AXB} = -i_{AYB}$. With v_{AB} represented in the quadrant diagram of Fig. 4.12 by $\bar{V}$ and i_{AYB} by $\bar{I}$, then i_{AXB} is represented by $-\bar{I}$. We can now arrive at the obvious but important conclusion that if a part of a system consumes power P at terminals AB, the remaining system generates P at these terminals. A further, but not so obvious, conclusion is that if a part of the system consumes reactive power Q at terminals AB, the remaining system generates Q at these terminals.

The principle of conservation of energy demands that a balance exists between generated and consumed active power. By analogy, a similar statement can be made about reactive power, although in truth it is neither consumed nor generated.

Figure 4.13 shows a one-line diagram of one junction of a power system. At this junction an alternator is feeding active power P_g and reactive power Q_g, a load is consuming P_l and Q_l, and transmission lines transfer P and Q towards or away from the node. As P and Q are *scalar* quantities, and using the P and Q conservation law, we can write

$$\Sigma P \text{ leaving junction} = 0$$
$$\Sigma Q \text{ leaving junction} = 0 \qquad (4.6)$$

Therefore

$$P_l + P_2 - P_1 - P_g = 0 \qquad \text{or} \qquad P_l + P_g = P_1 + P_2$$

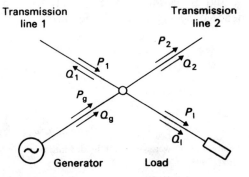

Transmission line 1

Transmission line 2

Generator   Load

Figure 4.13 A power system node.

and

$$Q_1 + Q_2 + Q_l - Q_g = 0 \quad \text{or} \quad Q_g = Q_1 + Q_2 + Q_l$$

It is clear that P and Q are of considerable value as working quantities as they can be added and subtracted arithmetically at power system junctions. This is in contrast to currents that are phasors and have to be added phasorially.

Furthermore, a 'balance sheet' for active and reactive power can be drawn for a power system, the total injected P and Q being equal to the total extracted P and Q plus any P and Q losses in the system, respectively.

In the following sections, it will be shown that the P and Q flows over a network are fairly independent of each other and are influenced by different control actions. This further justifies the use of P and Q as working quantities.

Finally, electrical machinery can be looked at very usefully in terms of P and Q when a range of operating conditions is to be examined and the limits of their performance are to be assessed.

4.7 COMPLEX POWER

Before dealing in greater detail with the transfer of P and Q in a power system, it is advisable to examine whether the complex representation of the voltage and current phasors could be used to provide us with values for P and Q.

In Fig. 4.14, $\bar{V}$ and $\bar{I}$ are drawn at angles ϕ_v and ϕ_i, respectively, with regard to the real axis. Resolving $\bar{I}$ along and at right angles to $\bar{V}$ we get

$$P = VI \cos(\phi_v - \phi_i)$$

and

$$Q = VI \sin(\phi_v - \phi_i)$$

The intention now is to see whether the above two quantities could be derived from the multiplication of the complex numbers $\bar{V}$ and $\bar{I}$. From Fig. 4.14

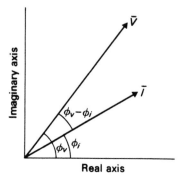

Figure 4.14 Phasor diagram.

$$\bar{V} = V(\cos \phi_v + j \sin \phi_v)$$

and

$$\bar{I} = I(\cos \phi_i + j \sin \phi_i)$$

Our natural tendency would be to evaluate $\bar{V}\bar{I}$ hoping that something useful might emerge. In fact, for reasons that will be clear shortly, let us evaluate $\bar{V}\bar{I}^*$ where

$$\bar{I}^* = I(\cos \phi_i - j \sin \phi_i), \text{ the conjugate of } \bar{I}$$

This gives

$$\bar{V}\bar{I}^* = VI(\cos \phi_v + j \sin \phi_v)(\cos \phi_i - j \sin \phi_i)$$
$$= VI[\cos \phi_v \cos \phi_i + \sin \phi_v \sin \phi_i + j(\sin \phi_v \cos \phi_i - \cos \phi_v \sin \phi_i)]$$

Thus

$$\bar{V}\bar{I}^* = VI[\cos(\phi_v - \phi_i) + j \sin(\phi_v - \phi_i)] = P + jQ \qquad (4.7)$$

We have established that to arrive at P and Q and to satisfy the agreed sign convention, it is necessary to use the conjugate of the current in the complex multiplication.

Equation (4.7) can be rewritten as

$$\bar{S} = P + jQ \qquad (4.8)$$

where $\bar{S}$ is, with good justification, known as 'complex volt amperes' because the magnitude of $\bar{S}$ is given by $S = \sqrt{(P^2 + Q^2)}$, which is indeed the value of volt amperes. In fact, the whole concept of complex power fits very neatly into the quadrant diagram as shown in Fig. 4.15 in which the axes are labelled $\pm P$ and $\pm jQ$.

To recapitulate, our conventions for the reference and therefore positive directions of voltage, current, and real and reactive power are summarized in Fig. 4.16. The element in the block is a consumer of real and reactive power and is therefore equivalent to a resistive–inductive impedance.

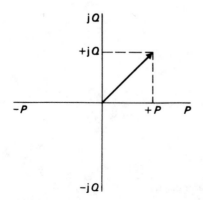

Figure 4.15 Quadrant diagram.

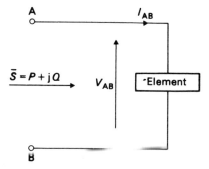

Figure 4.16 Reference directions.

Positive or consumed P and Q are active and reactive power, respectively, directed into the element terminals.

Negative or generated P and Q are active and reactive powers, respectively, directed out of the element terminals.

4.8 TRANSFER OF P AND Q TO SIMPLE LOADS

We will now deal with the intricacies of power supply to a simple consumer, i.e., a plain impedance. Such consumers are connected to feeders at the very extremities of the distribution network. As far as such consumers are concerned, the feeder and whatever complex network lies behind it can be replaced, according to Thévenin, by one source voltage $\bar{V}_A$ behind a source impedance $\bar{Z}_S$, as shown in Fig. 4.17. Here, any shunt impedance present, such as the transmission system capacitive reactance, may be very large, in which case it could be neglected or, if its effect is not negligible, it could be lumped with the load impedance Z_B.

In a power system, both $\bar{Z}_S$ and $\bar{Z}_B$ are likely to be resistive–inductive. This is because both the impedances of alternators and the series impedance of transmission lines, as well as the majority of consumer loads, are inductive–resistive. For reasons mentioned earlier, it is very appropriate to examine the power–voltage relationship at the load terminals. To do this, let

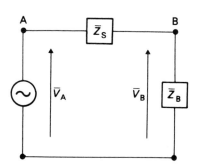

Figure 4.17 Power system supplying a passive load.

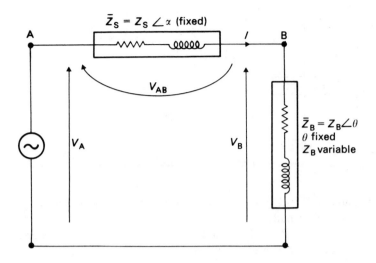

Figure 4.18 Power system supplying a passive load.

us assume a power system with fixed characteristics, in other words constant values for $\bar{V}_A$ and $\bar{Z}_S$. Next, consider a variable load impedance Z_B but of fixed power factor angle θ, a realistic enough assumption, as a typical group of loads connected to the end of a feeder, e.g., domestic consumers, are of similar power factors but the current they absorb depends on the number of such loads switched on at each instant. The power circuit to be examined is shown in Fig. 4.18.

The current and voltages are depicted by the phasor diagram of Fig. 4.19 in which $\bar{V}_B$ is drawn as reference phasor and two values of Z_B, and therefore I, are considered. From this diagram it should be clear that as Z_B and therefore I vary, the locus of point A is a circle of radius V_A.

From the triangle OAB and using the cosine formula,

$$V_A^2 = V_B^2 + (IZ_S)^2 + 2V_B(IZ_S)\cos(\alpha - \theta) \tag{4.9}$$

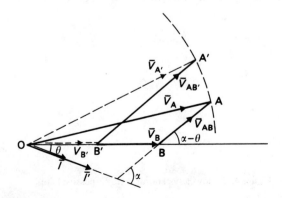

Figure 4.19 Phasor diagram.

Letting $\alpha - \theta = \psi$ and solving the quadratic Eq. (4.9) for IZ_S, we get

$$IZ_S = -V_B \cos \psi \pm \sqrt{(V_A^2 - V_B^2 \sin \psi)} \qquad (4.10)$$

The active power supplied to the load is given by

$$P_B = V_B I \cos \theta \qquad (4.11)$$

Substituting I from Eq. (4.10) into Eq. (4.11) we get

$$P_B = -\frac{V_B^2}{Z_S} \cos \theta \cos \psi + \frac{V_B}{Z_S} \cos \theta \sqrt{(V_A^2 - V_B^2 \sin^2 \psi)} \qquad (4.12)$$

Recalling the advantages of normalized quantities described in Chapter 2, Eq. (4.12) can be normalized using an arbitrary but sensible normal load power, say $P_n = V_A^2/10Z_S$, in which case Eq. (4.12) becomes

$$\frac{P_B}{P_n} = 10 \left\{ -\left(\frac{V_B}{V_A}\right)^2 \cos \psi \pm \frac{V_B}{V_A} \sqrt{\left[1 - \left(\frac{V_B}{V_A}\right)^2 \sin^2 \psi\right]} \right\} \cos \theta \qquad (4.13)$$

This somewhat complicated expression can be simplified if Z_S is assumed to be purely reactive, in which case $\alpha = \pi/2$ and $\psi = \pi/2 - \theta$. This is not an

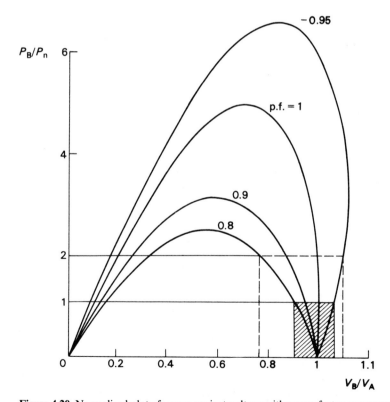

Figure 4.20 Normalized plot of power against voltage with power factor as a parameter.

unrealistic assumption, for at 50 Hz the reactance to resistance ratio of generator and transmission line impedances ranges from 5 to 20. With this simplification, the curves of Fig. 4.20 were plotted for two lagging, one leading, and unity load power factors.

Several lessons can be learned from these curves:

(1) A given power transfer can be achieved with two alternative values of load voltage. As power systems are run on a constant voltage basis, it is obvious that only the solution with the high voltage is acceptable.

(2) For a given power transfer, the voltage regulation deteriorates with decrease in the lagging power factor. Low power factor inductive–resistive loads have a detrimental effect on load voltage. Alternatively, such loads can be described as heavy consumers of reactive power. It naturally ensues that transfer of reactive power from generators to consumers over transmission lines is undesirable because of the severe voltage regulation effect.

(3) For leading power factor loads, the voltage at the load terminals may exceed the no-load value. With low leading power factors, a dangerous situation could occur where power system equipment may be damaged because of too high a voltage at the consumer terminals.

(4) The connection of a capacitor across an inductive–resistive consumer, so that the power factor of the combination is near unity, results in a consumer voltage that remains practically level for a wide range of power variation. This procedure is known as 'power factor correction or improvement', and is widely used in industry and encouraged by power supply authorities through tariffs that penalize poor power factor loads. An alternative way of looking at the power factor correction idea is to appreciate that the reactive power demanded by the load is generated locally by the capacitor rather than transferred over the transmission system.

(5) The maximum power transfer capability of the system is diminished as the lagging power factor decreases.

(6) Power systems are never run at peak power transfer conditions because these require an unacceptably low voltage at the consumer terminals and because the resistive part of Z_s present in practical systems dissipates too much energy. Such high losses result in unacceptably low efficiencies.

(7) The choice of $V_A^2/10Z_s$ as normal power was earlier referred to as arbitrary but sensible. This requires some further explanation. For most power systems under normal operating conditions the load voltage V_B remains roughly the same from no load to full or normal load. The value chosen for normal power implies that the normal load impedance is approximately equal to ten times the transmission system impedance Z_s. For working conditions up to full load and for power factors between 0.8 lag and 0.95 lead operation is confined within the shaded area of Fig. 4.20. With Z_s one-fifth of the load normal impedance the operating area is depicted by the dashed rectangle. Here the voltage regulation is severe.

We can conclude that for acceptable operating conditions the transmission

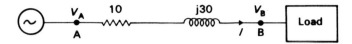

Figure 4.21 Circuit of Example 4.1.

system impedance should be about one order of magnitude lower than the load impedance.

Example 4.1

The simple transmission system of Fig. 4.21 consists of a fixed voltage generator of 11 kV, a transmission system impedance $\bar{Z}_s = 10 + j30\,\Omega$, and a load.

(1) With a load of unity power factor, evaluate the load power if V_B is kept at 10 kV.
(2) An inductor is connected in parallel with the load in (1) so that the overall power factor is reduced to 0.9. Evaluate the new load voltage and power.

(1) $\theta = 0°, \psi = \alpha - \theta = \alpha = \tan^{-1}\frac{30}{10} = 71.56°$
$\cos\psi = 0.316, \sin\psi = 0.949, Z_S = \sqrt{(10^2 + 30^2)} = 31.62$
Applying directly Eq. (4.12),

$$P_B = -\frac{(10 \times 10^3)^2}{31.62} \times 0.316 + \frac{10 \times 10^3}{31.62}\sqrt{[(11 \times 10^3)^2 - (10 \times 10^3)^2 0.949^2]}$$

$$= (-0.999 + 1.759) \times 10^6 = 0.76\,\text{MW}$$

Alternatively, the phasor diagram of Fig. 4.22 can be used:

$$11^2 = 10^2 + (IZ)^2 + 2 \times 10 \times IZ \times 0.316$$

Solving the quadratic equation,

$$IZ = \frac{-6.32 + \sqrt{(6.32^2 + 4 \times 21)}}{2} = 2.4\,\text{kV}$$

therefore

$$I = \frac{2.4 \times 10^3}{31.62} = 76\,\text{A}$$

$$P_B = 10 \times 10^3 \times 76 = 0.76\,\text{MW}$$

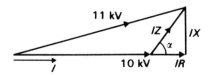

Figure 4.22 Phasor diagram.

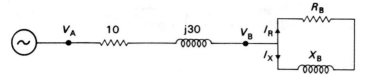

Figure 4.23 Circuit of Example 4.1(2).

(2) Equation (4.12) is not useful here. A solution can be found from the circuit of Fig. 4.23

$$\theta = \cos^{-1} 0.9 = 25.84°$$

From (1) the purely resistive load is

$$R_B = \frac{10 \times 10^3}{76} = 131.57\,\Omega$$

but

$$\frac{I_X}{I_R} = \frac{V_B/X_B}{V_B/R_B} = \frac{R_B}{X_B} = \tan 25.84°$$

therefore

$$X_B = \frac{131.57}{0.484} = 271.68\,\Omega$$

Total impedance seen by generator is

$$Z_A = 10 + j30 + \frac{j131.57 \times 271.68}{131.57 + j271.68}$$
$$= (10 + 106.55) + j(30 + 51.60) = (116.55 + j81.60)\,\Omega$$
$$I = \frac{11 \times 10^3}{\sqrt{(116.55^2 + 81.6^2)}} = 77.31\,A$$

therefore

$$V_B = 77.31 \times \sqrt{(106.55^2 + 51.6^2)}$$
$$= 77.31 \times 118.4 = 9.15\,kV$$

and

$$P_B = 9.15^2/131.57 = 0.636\,MW$$

4.9 PASSIVE AND ACTIVE ELEMENTS IN POWER SYSTEMS

In the previous section we looked at a generator supplying a load through a source impedance and we drew some very important conclusions about the relationship between the real and reactive power transfer and the voltage at the load terminals. In this simple system, the power transfer to the load and the voltage across the load terminals depend on the value of the load impedance. The former quantities can be said to be 'dependent' variables. Elements in a power system, such as impedances consisting of resistance, and inductive or capacitive reactance, are known as 'passive' and form the main bulk of power system loads. All heating and lighting elements and the majority of motors fall in this category. Such passive elements exhibit this inter dependence between changes in impedance and resulting changes in power and terminal voltage.

Another class of power system elements, known as 'active', do not suffer from this dependence syndrome. Typical active elements are all synchronous machines, irrespective of whether they operate as generators or as motors. The property of these elements that distinguishes them from passive elements is that they contain internally an induced voltage by virtue of their rotation and the presence of an independent magnetic field. This internal voltage is adjustable and not dependent on the power transfer. The generator in the circuit of Fig. 4.18 is such an active element. The analysis was applied on the assumption that V_A remained constant irrespective of the changes in Z_B.

At the transmission level of interconnected power systems, power is transferred between sections of the power system itself, these sections containing generators. For example, several interconnected generators in a power station may be supplying power over a transmission line to an extensive, interconnected network containing a large number of other generators and loads. Because of the relative size of the interconnected network, the P and Q injected by the transmission line will produce virtually no change of voltage at the point of connection or of system frequency, i.e., the 'load' in this case is an 'active' element. Such an interconnected constant voltage, constant frequency system is referred to as an 'infinite bus'.

A simpler system consisting of two active elements linked by a transmission line impedance is shown in Fig. 4.24. M_A and M_B are two synchronous machines, one acting as a generator and the other as a motor.

As will be shown in Chapter 5, $\bar{V}_A$ and $\bar{V}_B$ are adjustable in both magnitude and phase. It should now be clear that the study of P and Q transfer as affected by $\bar{V}_A$ and $\bar{V}_B$ is of vital interest in power system analysis.

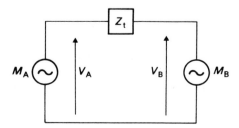

Figure 4.24 Power system consisting of two active elements.

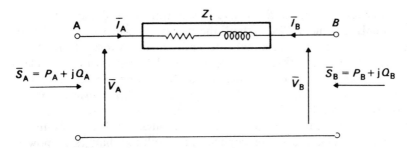

Figure 4.25 Reference directions of a two active element system.

4.10 TRANSFER OF POWER BETWEEN ACTIVE ELEMENTS

The system to be investigated is shown in Fig. 4.25. The transmission system impedance is again taken as resistive–reactive for reasons explained earlier. Both ends of this system are treated identically and in conformity with the convention developed earlier and illustrated in Fig. 4.16.

Let $\bar{Z}_t = R_t + jX_t = Z_t e^{j\alpha}$ and let $\bar{V}_B$ be the reference voltage, i.e., $\bar{V}_B = V_B e^{j0}$. Let $\bar{V}_A = V_A e^{j\delta}$, leading $\bar{V}_B$ by an angle δ, usually referred to as the 'load angle'.

The currents are given by

$$\bar{I}_A = \frac{\bar{V}_A - \bar{V}_B}{\bar{Z}_t} \quad \text{and} \quad \bar{I}_B = \frac{\bar{V}_B - \bar{V}_A}{\bar{Z}_t} = -\bar{I}_A$$

The complex volt amperes at terminals A are given by

$$\bar{S}_A = \bar{V}_A \bar{I}_A^* = \bar{V}_A \left(\frac{\bar{V}_A - \bar{V}_B}{\bar{Z}_t} \right)^* = V_A e^{j\delta} \left(\frac{V_A e^{-j\delta} - V_B}{Z_t e^{-j\alpha}} \right)$$

therefore

$$\bar{S}_A = P_A + jQ_A = \frac{V_A^2}{Z_t} e^{j\alpha} - \frac{V_A V_B}{Z_t} e^{j(\alpha + \delta)} \tag{4.14}$$

Similarly, at terminals B,

$$\bar{S}_B = \bar{V}_B \bar{I}_B^* = \bar{V}_B \left(\frac{\bar{V}_B - \bar{V}_A}{\bar{Z}_t} \right)^* = V_B e^{j\delta} \left(\frac{V_B - V_A e^{-j\delta}}{Z_t e^{-j\alpha}} \right)$$

$$\bar{S}_B = P_B + jQ_B = \frac{V_B^2}{Z_t} e^{j\alpha} - \frac{V_A V_B}{Z_t} e^{j(\alpha - \delta)} \tag{4.15}$$

Equations (4.14) and (4.15) describe the way in which the complex power is transferred between active parts of a power network.

To explore the implications of these two equations it is helpful to again assume that impedance Z_t is predominantly reactive, with the consequence that $\alpha = \pi/2$ and $\bar{Z}_t = X_t e^{j(\pi/2)} = jX_t$.

Equations (4.14) and (4.15) now become

$$\bar{S}_A = j\frac{V_A^2}{X_t} - j\frac{V_A V_B}{X_t}e^{j\delta} = j\frac{V_A}{X_t}(V_A - V_B e^{j\delta}) \tag{4.16}$$

and

$$\bar{S}_B = j\frac{V_B}{X_t}(V_B - V_A e^{-j\delta}) \tag{4.17}$$

To discern clearly the dependence of P and Q on the terminal voltages we will examine separately the influence of differences in terminal voltage magnitude and angle.

(1) Let us look first at the situation with $\bar{V}_A$ and $\bar{V}_B$ in phase, i.e., $\delta = 0$, and $V_A > V_B$.

Equations (4.16) and (4.17) become

$$\bar{S}_A = j\frac{V_A}{X_t}(V_A - V_B) \quad \text{and} \quad \bar{S}_B = -j\frac{V_B}{X_t}(V_A - V_B) \tag{4.18}$$

The network, phasor, and quadrant diagrams for this condition are shown in Fig. 4.26. Current $\bar{I}_A$ lags by $\pi/2$ voltage $\bar{V}_{AB}$, therefore terminals A are associated with positive and terminals B with negative reactive power. As a consequence there is an overall transfer of Q from A to B through the system.

The following conclusion can now be drawn: with a purely inductive transmission system impedance and with the terminal voltages in phase but differing in magnitude, reactive power only is transmitted from terminals of higher to terminals of lower potential.

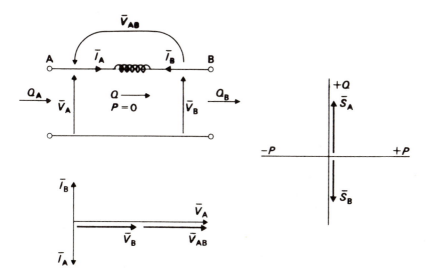

Figure 4.26 P and Q transfers caused by voltage magnitude differences.

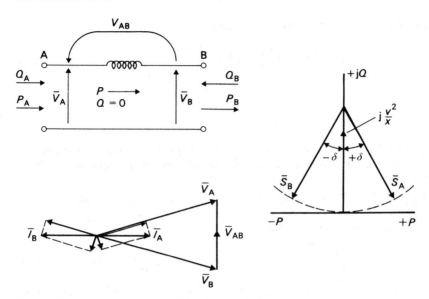

Figure 4.27 P and Q transfers caused by phase angle differences.

The sum of the infeeds of complex power at A and B from Eq. (4.18) gives

$$\bar{S}_A + \bar{S}_B = j\frac{(V_A - V_B)^2}{X_t} = j\frac{V_{AB}^2}{X_t} = jX_t I_A^2 \qquad (4.19)$$

i.e., the difference between the infeed of Q at A and the outfeed of Q at B is the loss of Q in Z_t. The reactive power consumed by a reactor is XI^2, a companion expression to RI^2, the active power consumed by a resistor.

(2) Next, let us look at the situation with $V_A = V_B = V$, but $\delta > 0$. Equations (4.16) and (4.17) become

$$\bar{S}_A = j\frac{V^2}{X_t} - j\frac{V^2}{X_t}e^{j\delta} \qquad \text{and} \qquad \bar{S}_B = j\frac{V^2}{X_t} - j\frac{V^2}{X_t}e^{-j\delta} \qquad (4.20)$$

The network, phasor, and quadrant diagrams for this condition are shown in Fig. 4.27.

In the phasor diagram, $\bar{I}_A$ is again drawn lagging $\bar{V}_{AB}$ by $\pi/2$. Both $\bar{I}_A$ and $\bar{I}_B$ are resolved into in-phase and quadrature components with respect to the relevant voltages. From the phasor diagram, it should be clear that terminals A are absorbing and terminals B supplying active power and that both ends are absorbing reactive power. These results are confirmed by the quadrant diagram that illustrates Eq. (4.20). As Z_t is purely inductive, P_A(consumed) = P_B(generated); both ends, though, absorb half the $Q = I_A^2 X_t$ consumed by X_t. Another conclusion can therefore be drawn: with a purely inductive transmission system impedance and with the terminal voltages of the same magnitude but out of phase, active power is transmitted from points of leading to points of lagging voltage.

In practical systems Z_t, although mainly inductive, possesses some resistance. This however does not invalidate the general conclusions about the mechanism of P and Q transfer in power systems.

4.11 THE SCALAR POWER EQUATIONS

From Eqs. (4.14) and (4.15), expressions for the scalar quantities P and Q at the two ends of the line can be derived. The real and imaginary parts of S_A correspond to P_A and Q_A, i.e.,

$$P_A = \text{Re}\,(\bar{S}_A) = \frac{V_A^2}{Z_t}\cos\alpha - \frac{V_A V_B}{Z_t}\cos(\alpha+\delta) \tag{4.21}$$

$$Q_A = \text{Im}\,(\bar{S}_A) = \frac{V_A^2}{Z_t}\sin\alpha - \frac{V_A V_B}{Z_t}\sin(\alpha+\delta) \tag{4.22}$$

Similarly, for end B of the system,

$$P_B = \text{Re}\,(\bar{S}_B) = \frac{V_B^2}{Z_t}\cos\alpha - \frac{V_A V_B}{Z_t}\cos(\alpha-\delta) \tag{4.23}$$

$$Q_B = \text{Im}\,(\bar{S}_B) = \frac{V_B^2}{Z_t}\sin\alpha - \frac{V_A V_B}{Z_t}\sin(\alpha-\delta) \tag{4.24}$$

On the assumption that δ is positive, i.e., $\bar{V}_A$ leads $\bar{V}_B$, the useful active power transfer is the power delivered at terminals B. If V_A and V_B were kept constant and δ were allowed to vary, Eq. (4.23) tells us that maximum P_B (this is negative, as it is 'generated' at terminals B) occurs when the second term is a maximum, i.e., when $\cos(\alpha-\delta) = 1$, i.e., $\alpha-\delta = 0$, $\delta = \alpha$.

Again, using the approximation $Z_t = X_t$ and $\alpha = \pi/2$, Eqs. (4.21) to (4.24) become

$$P_A = -P_B = \frac{V_A V_B}{X_t}\sin\delta \tag{4.25}$$

$$Q_A = \frac{V_A}{X_t}(V_A - V_B\cos\delta) \tag{4.26}$$

$$Q_B = \frac{V_B}{X_t}(V_B - V_A\cos\delta) \tag{4.27}$$

Equation (4.25) states that the power transfer over a reactive transmission system is related to the sine of the power angle, maximum power occurring when $\delta = \pi/2$. As will be shown in Chapter 8, this condition is not realizable in practice because of limitations imposed by stability.

While all the equations in this chapter were derived on the basis of a single-phase system, they are all perfectly applicable to a three-phase system if line voltages are used in the expressions. For example, in Eq. (4.25) with V_A and V_B as phase voltages, P_A gives the power in one phase. Three-phase power is given by

$$P_A(\text{three-phase}) = \frac{3V_A V_B}{X_t} \sin\delta = \frac{\sqrt{3}V_A\sqrt{3}V_B}{X_t} \sin\delta = \frac{V_{A1}V_{B1}}{X_t} \sin\delta$$

where V_{A1} and V_{B1} are line voltages. Finally, with V_A and V_B in kV, the VA, P, and Q from the expressions are in MVA, MW and M VAR

Example 4.2

It is required to supply a load consuming 60 MW and 20 M VAR over a 60 mile, 132 kV, three-phase transmission line that has a reactance of 0.8 Ω per mile and negligible resistance. The load voltage is to be kept at 130 kV. Determine the voltage at the generator end of the line and the load angle.

Here $Z_t = X_t$, therefore Eqs. (4.25) and (4.27) can be used. The line reactance is $X_t = 60 \times 0.8 = 48\,\Omega$.

From Eq. (4.25),

$$P_A = \frac{130V_A}{48} \sin\delta = 60$$

therefore

$$V_A \sin\delta = \frac{60 \times 48}{130}$$

From Eq. (4.27),

$$-20 = \frac{130}{48}(130 - V_A \cos\delta)$$

therefore

$$V_A \cos\delta = \frac{130^2 + 20 \times 48}{130}$$

and

$$\tan\delta = \frac{60 \times 48}{(130^2 + 20 \times 48)} = 0.1612$$

Therefore

$$\delta = 9.16°$$

and

$$V_A = \frac{60 \times 48}{130 \times \sin 9.16} = 139.16\,\text{kV}$$

4.12 THE CONTROL OF ACTIVE AND REACTIVE POWER

Power systems are designed to meet the requirements of active as well as reactive power transfer. Example 4.1(2) illustrates that with consumers demanding reactive as well as active power, the voltage regulation is increased with a reduction in the active power transfer capability of the line.

With the reactive power demand of consumers met at the consumer terminals, the power authorities have to provide only the reactive power loss in the transmission system. In practice, this condition is not realized and the authorities enforce on industrial consumers special tariffs that encourage them to supply their own reactive power or in other words to install power factor correction equipment. The topic of reactive power compensation will be dealt with more fully in Chapter 8. Here some general remarks will be made on the control of active and reactive power in power systems.

Whereas active power is only supplied by generators, reactive power may be supplied from several sources. A list of generators and consumers of reactive power follows:

(1) *Generators of Q*
Synchronous machines (generators and motors)
Static capacitors
Distributed capacitance of transmission lines and cables
A.C. commutator motors
Phase advancers (rotary)
(2) *Consumers of Q*
Synchronous machines (generators and motors)
Inductive static loads
Induction motors
Distributed inductance of transmission lines and cables
Transformer inductance
D.C. to a.c. and a.c. to d.c. converters
A.C. commutator motors
Reluctance and hysteresis motors

In a purely inductive transmission system, active power flow depends almost entirely on the power angle δ between terminal voltages and reactive power flow on magnitude differences between terminal voltages. Practical high voltage systems behave more or less in accordance with the pure reactance concept, therefore the flow of active power through a power system and the flow of reactive power are approximately independent of each other.

Figure 4.28 is a pictorial illustration of the flow of P and Q in a simple transmission system. These flows involve P consumption in the resistance and Q consumption in the reactance of the lines; thus the active and reactive flows are not entirely independent.

The desired division among the generators of the overall active and

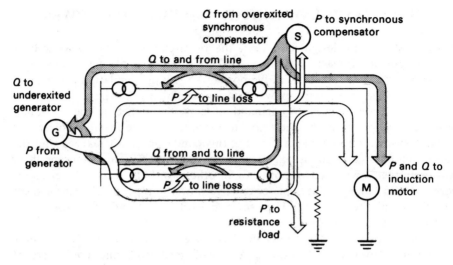

Figure 4.28 Flow of P and Q over a power system. (*From 'Electric Transmission Lines' by H. H. Skilling, McGraw-Hill, New York, 1951.*)

reactive power demand of the loads and the transmission system is achieved by control of two parameters. Increasing the mechanical torque on a rotating generator shaft effectively advances the generator internal voltage with respect to the other system voltages. This results in increased power angle and increased active power injection by this generator.

Increasing the generator excitation increases the internal voltage magnitude with respect to other system voltages and this results in increased reactive power injection by this generator.

These aspects of synchronous machine operation will be treated in greater length in Chapter 5.

The determination of the active and reactive power distribution in a complex interconnected power network is a daunting task and only very simple networks can be tackled using a sliderule or a pocket calculator. In most cases digital computers are used for this purpose. Such a study based on a digital computer programme is described in Chapter 8.

THE GENERATION OF ELECTRICITY

5.1 PRELUDE TO THE STUDY OF ELECTRICAL MACHINES

Most electrical machines have a structure so complex that no formal treatment *ab initio* is possible. Many 'design' formulae are empirical and the rise of resistivity in the electric circuits with rise in temperature, together with the non-linear relationship between m.m.f. and flux in the electric circuit, would make formal analysis impossible, even if the geometry were simple, which it most certainly is not. Engineers other than those of the electric discipline (and this includes 'light current' electrical engineers), physicists, chemists, and laymen alike probably believe that the electric motors and generators that they buy and use actually were 'designed' by industrialists. This is seldom the case. Each 'design' is based on a machine supplied earlier to some other customer, with just slight modification to the dimensions to meet the requirements of the new situation. In biology this process is known as evolution and it is most effective. Many designers themselves are not sure which of the formulae they use are empirical, yet all of them know, almost by mere inspection of the finished article, whether it is 'right' for the job or not.

How is this knowledge acquired? 'Experience' is the usual unhelpful answer. The uninitiated, however, are entitled to ask what are, at first sight, naive questions but which may be aimed at much deeper roots than are any questions about slot sizes, airgap clearance, and numbers of turns. In particular, it is fair to ask what factors make a machine 'acceptable' to the customer.

5.1.1 The Quality of a Machine

The desirability of one particular design over another will be different for different customers. It appears that there may be as little agreement about the qualities of a particular design as there is about a work of art, and the pure scientist may declare the quality of a machine to be·solely 'in the eye of the beholder'.

But it is not so. Every electrical machine is composed of electric and magnetic circuits. By theoretical techniques such as the 'lumping of impedances' (pages 176, 177) these can be reduced to a single loop of conductor interlinked with a single loop of ferromagnetic. This simple structure is as fundamental to electromagnetic performance as the much more complex DNA molecule is to living tissue. In machines with moving parts (as opposed to transformers; although this does not imply that the subsequent analysis does not apply to transformers also) the requirement of all customers is *power*. Power is the product of *force* and velocity. Force is the product of flux density B, and current loading J, per unit pole area. Thus it follows that the 'best' machine will have circuits that can produce the highest current for a fixed e.m.f. (in the case of the electric) and the highest flux for a fixed m.m.f. (in the case of the magnetic). The designer's tasks consist, in the main, of shifting the emphasis of one particular property to another to please the customer. The latter, for example, can always have a machine of higher efficiency than that of any previous machine made, provided he will accept a higher cost, or a larger weight, or a lower power factor, or a combination of these quantities.

But there will always come a time when the engineer will have to answer the question, 'What designs will be *impossible* within the constraints of present day materials and of the accountants?' In other words, what makes a 'Good' machine where the interpretation of the word can be almost anything?

5.1.2 A Factor of Goodness

From here on we shall regard the word 'Goodness' as a scientific quantity (for we shall be able to calculate it) and shall ascribe to it the symbol 'G'. (It is interesting to note that at the time G was being formulated in the UK, a similar quantity was being worked out by Russian engineers who also wished to give it a name to stress its fundamental importance. They chose the name 'magnetic Reynolds number' by comparison with the Reynolds number of fluid flow theory.)

The first step is to appreciate that resistance and reluctance are the two quantities that prevent the designer from having, respectively, as much current and flux as he requires from the most minute quantities of e.m.f. and m.m.f. In some way, therefore, the *product* (because force is $B \times J$) of resistance and reluctance must represent the 'Badness' (or reciprocal of Goodness), but not necessarily quantitatively. In other words, we can at least say of G that

$$G \propto \frac{1}{\text{resistance} \times \text{reluctance}}$$

Now each of the quantities in the denominator of the right hand side can be expressed in terms of the lengths l, the conductivities σ and μ, and the areas

A of the electric and magnetic circuits, thus:

$$G \propto 1 \bigg/ \left(\frac{l_e}{\sigma A_e} \times \frac{l_m}{\mu A_m} \right)$$

or

$$G \propto \sigma \mu \left(\frac{A_e A_m}{l_e l_m} \right)$$

If we examine the right hand side dimensionally, it carries the dimensions of time. The basic reason for this is to be found in Eqs. (3.1) and (3.2), where e.m.f. is seen to have the same dimensions as current, but e.m.f. is the *rate of change* (with time) of flux. It can easily be shown[1] that for an a.c. machine the constant of proportionality in the expression for G is the angular frequency ω of the supply, whence

$$G = (\omega \mu \sigma) \left(\frac{A_e A_m}{l_e l_m} \right) \tag{5.1}$$

The right hand side of Eq. (5.1) has been grouped into two brackets because the terms ω, μ, and σ are usually fixed by the available materials and by the need to use mains frequency. Where any of these quantities can be relaxed (as is most common in the case of ω, where motors are fed from thyristor inverters, but now also if superconducting material is used as electric circuit), the designer has a freedom not accorded to most. The second bracket contains, in the four symbols, every shape and size that has been used by inventor and designer to try to maximize the value of G.

What is most important in Eq. (5.1) is the fact that if a motor of Goodness Factor X is scaled up in every linear dimension by a factor of 2, the Goodness of the resulting design is $4X$. In other words, machines that are subject to Eq. (5.1), that is those that have been annotated 'electromagnetic' in this text, become 'better' as they are made *bigger*, by the very nature of electromagnetism.

There are two types of machine that do not come within the scope of Eq. (5.1), for they produce tangential thrust by purely 'magnetic forces', i.e., the kind of force that causes a bar magnet to attract an unmagnetized piece of iron. The secondary members of such machines contain no conductor. Where relative velocity between primary field and secondary is concerned, the latter may be laminated to prevent conduction, although this is not usually necessary, as iron is a poor conductor of electricity.

These machines, here annotated 'magnetic machines', produce force proportional to pole area (L^2) (for B has a maximum value set by saturation and magnetic forces are calculable as $B^2/2\mu_0$ per unit area of pole face). The weight rises as L^3 and hence magnetic machines get better as they are made smaller. The two types involved are usually called 'reluctance machines' and 'hysteresis motors', the latter hardly ever being used as generators. An elaboration of 'the smaller the better' rule follows the specific treatment of the reluctance machines in section 7.4.5. (pages 247–254).

5.1.3 Evaluation and Effects of G

Many rotary machines are basically of the same topology as that of a transformer, i.e., *two* electric circuits interlinked with a magnetic circuit but not with each other. In such an arrangement it is clearly possible to identify a Goodness Factor G_1 by considering only the imperfections of the primary electric circuit and those of the magnetic and to distinguish it from a factor G_2 that depends only on the magnetic–secondary electric combination. The relationship between G_1 and the parameters of an equivalent circuit is readily obtainable, for G_1 is defined as the quantity $\omega/R\mathcal{R}$ with the resistance R being that of a single loop of copper of sectional area equal to the total area of all the conductors in the primary, i.e., $R = R_1/N_1^2$. Hence

$$G_1 = \frac{\omega}{R\mathcal{R}} = \frac{\omega N_1^2}{R_1 \mathcal{R}}$$

where $\mathcal{R}$ is the equivalent reluctance of the magnetic circuit. Now the latter is *always* a single loop, so that $\mathcal{R}$ is also the *actual* reluctance. When viewed from the primary side the reactance

$$X_m = L_m \omega = \frac{N_1^2 \omega}{\mathcal{R}}$$

Hence

$$G_1 = \frac{\omega N_1^2}{R_1 \mathcal{R}} = \frac{X_m}{R_1}$$

and, similarly,

$$G_2 = \frac{X_m}{R_2}$$

The process of lumping of impedances has shown us that R_2 can be brought into the primary circuit by multiplying its actual value by the square of the turns ratio, so that the total resistance, viewed from the primary, is $R_1 + (N_1/N_2)^2 R_2$. If both windings are then to be replaced by a single loop, its effective resistance is

$$\left[R_1 + \left(\frac{N_1}{N_2}\right)^2 R_2 \right] \Big/ N_1^2 = \frac{R_1}{N_1^2} + \frac{R_2}{N_2^2}$$

and the value of G for the whole machine is given by

$$\frac{\omega}{\mathcal{R}\left(\dfrac{R_1}{N_1^2} + \dfrac{R_2}{N_2^2} \right)}$$

Thus

$$\frac{1}{G} = \frac{R_1 \mathcal{R}}{\omega N_1^2} + \frac{R_2 \mathcal{R}}{\omega N_2^2} = \frac{1}{G_1} + \frac{1}{G_2}$$

Some idea of the potency of G can be obtained from Fig. 5.1, where the efficiency of a machine is plotted against G (to a log scale). In this exercise it is

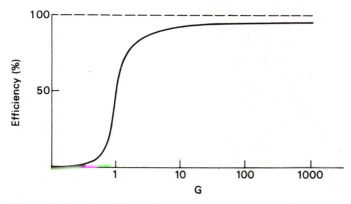

Figure 5.1 The effect of G on efficiency.

assumed that G is changed merely by changing the resistivity of the secondary, and that such quantities as pole pitch, synchronous speed, and all dimensions of length remain fixed. Most commercial machines have a value of G greater than 20, beyond which it may simply be regarded as 'adequate' and other requirements dictate the detailed design parameters, but where other considerations, such as the demand for a large airgap induction motor (as in some linear motors described in Chapter 10) demand a value of G in the region of 0.5 to 1.5, the effect of a small change in G can make the difference between success and disaster. Nowhere is this concept more important than in the study of single-phase induction motors (pages 221–230).

5.2 THE ALTERNATOR

Every electrical machine can be used to convert energy from a mechanical form to an electrical one, or vice versa. Moreover, the power flow can be reversed without alteration of the connections to the source or the load. In this it can be distinguished from an electronic device, where reconnection is essential. An electrical machine is more correctly described as an *electromechanical energy converter*. An alternator is given its name on the understanding that it is an a.c. machine that will always be used to produce an *electrical* output—an 'alternating' output. If the same machine were used to reverse the power flow we would call it a 'synchronous motor'. The proper name for the apparatus is therefore a 'synchronous machine', without specifying how it will be used.

Although Faraday's disk dynamo of 1831 was the world's first generator, it was a d.c. machine and could even be identified as an 'ideal' d.c. machine in that it effectively had an infinite number of commutator segments and an infinite number of rotor circuits. As outlined in Chapter 2, the features of Pixii's machine that withstood the test of time became the very bedrock of modern power station generator design. But in the 'lean years' between 1831 and 1900, Pixii's design was mutilated.

The three features mentioned were:

(1) By generating into stationary coils, the massive power output need not be collected through rubbing contacts.

(2) By allowing the current to alternate, no mechanical rectifier was needed. Later this advantage was expanded to make full use of transformers in power systems. Transformers have no moving parts and are therefore extremely reliable. (Note that there was a period of several decades spanning the turn of the century when 'rotary converters' were fashionable. These were, in effect, d.c. machines with fixed, outer, d.c.-fed magnets and d.c. windings on the rotor. At one end of the rotor the winding was tapped, d.c. fashion, and brought out to a commutator. At the other end it was tapped at three points only 120° apart in time and the tappings connected to three slip rings. The machine was self propelled, as a d.c. motor, but as it had no mechanical load other than friction and windage, this required a mere one or two per cent of the power input. The rotor was to be seen as the 'power house' proper where three-phase a.c. at one end was converted to d.c. at the other, or vice versa. The rotary converter prolonged discussions as to whether the British grid should be an a.c. or a d.c. network. Nowadays it is obvious that severe limitations would have been imposed on transmission lines, for the very nature of rotating machines is such that insulated windings housed in slots could not be used with voltages much beyond 33 000 without danger of insulation breakdown. Transformers with their simpler coils can be designed for millions of volts.)

(3) By generating into the outer member it was easier to spread the secondary conductors and to cool them more effectively. The rotating magnets are but the catalysts that enable the power to flow. The output winding of an alternator is one huge member of the system. The turbine, or other prime mover that drives it, is the other. The magnets are *vital* but are not, as it were, situated in the main stream of the power flow.

5.2.1 Principle of Operation, Constructional Details

There are two quite distinct forms of modern alternator. While the principle of operation of each is the same, i.e., the movement of magnetic poles past stationary coils, their constructions are very different. The reason for this is that each has been designed to 'match' its prime mover, i.e., to suit the mechanical device that is to tap the two principal natural power resources—falling water, on the one hand, and steam, generated by heat from fossil fuels or nuclear fuels, on the other. The water power is harnessed by the water wheel (water turbine) which spins relatively slowly (hundreds of revolutions per minute rather than thousands). Steam is used in a steam turbine at as high a speed as can be accommodated by the power system it is to feed. The 'turboalternator', as the steam user is called, has therefore the

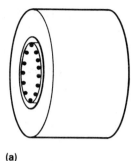

(a)

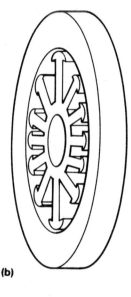

(b)

Figure 5.2 Basic topology and excitation systems of (a) a turbo-alternator (distributed m.m.f.), (b) a water wheel alternator (variable gap).

minimum number of poles possible—two. The speed of the drive is therefore set by the frequency of the transmission system which dominates any mechanical urge to use faster turbines (see Section 2.3).

To match the output of the turboalternators, the water wheel generators must therefore be multi-polar and hence of large diameter and small axial length. The contrast in basic geometry is illustrated in Fig. 5.2. There is a limit to the length of a turboalternator, based largely on the mechanical considerations involved in supporting a large rotor mass between a bearing at each end. At 3000 or 3600 rev/min (50 or 60 Hz) the rotor must be extremely well balanced and its surface smooth. With the lower speed water powered machine, such precautions can be relaxed with a view to making the larger rotor cheaper to make.

The fundamental difference in shape between the rotors of the two types of machine is consequent upon the above considerations, but now a secondary difference is introduced by what could be termed the experience and skill of the designer. It is necessary to produce a sine wave of induced e.m.f. The factors that affect the instantaneous value e of this are the flux density b, the length l of the conductor, and the velocity v (the use of small letters indicating the instantaneous values). Thus:

$$e = blv$$

The only reasonable quantity to vary sinusoidally at 50 or 60 periods per second is b, although in a linear alternator[2] in which oscillation of the secondary replaces rotation of the primary, b can remain constant and v be made to vary as $v = V \sin \omega t$, but such machines are beyond the scope of this book.

Now b is the result of an m.m.f. $\mathcal{M}$ acting against a reluctance $\mathcal{R}$ or $b = \mathcal{M}/\mathcal{R}A$, and it is this relationship that enables the designer to choose a topology for a water driven alternator different from that of a turboalternator. In the latter he causes $\mathcal{M}$ to vary, in the former $\mathcal{R}$ varies. Figures 5.3(a) and (b) show the two basic rotor topologies, each of which requires further explanation. In the first case, the rotor is not solid but built on a 'spider' of spokes. The main core of the d.c.-fed magnets (the 'yoke') is of solid iron, as are the poles. Only the pole shoes need be laminated. The pole shoes are shaped to produce a variable gap so that the flux distribution is sinusoidal as shown. An old and well used rule of thumb in such designs was to make the surface of each pole an arc of a circle whose radius was 0.6 times that of the stator bore.

In the case of the turboalternator the rotor carries a distributed winding of the same kind as those used both in the stator of the same machine and in

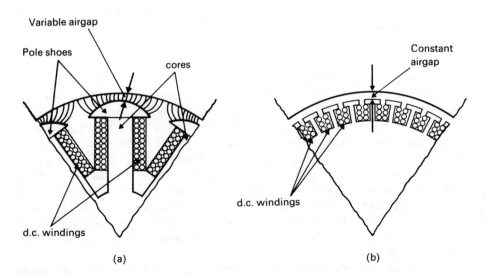

Figure 5.3 Methods of obtaining sinusoidal flux distribution: (a) a water wheel alternator; (b) a turboalternator.

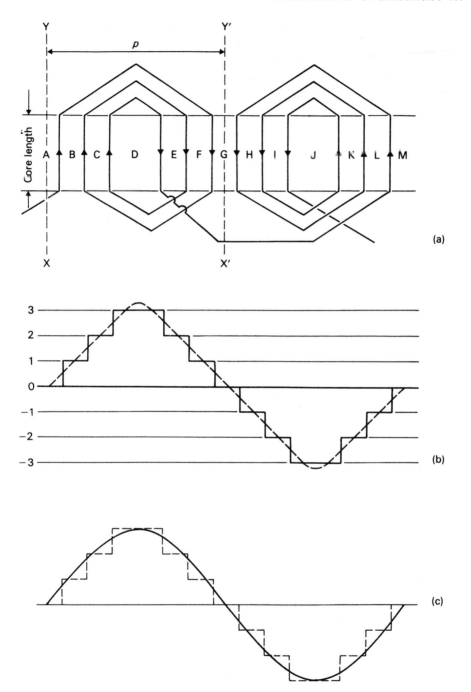

Figure 5.4 Generation of a sine wave of flux by distributing the winding: (a) developed diagram of coil layout; (b) m.m.f. diagram; (c) flux distribution.

induction motor primaries. In each case the philosophy is the same: shape the m.m.f. by a series of steps that 'fit' a sine curve, albeit somewhat crudely. Then rely on a large gap to allow the flux to spread and 'iron out the creases' (to use a tailor's analogy). Figure 5.4 illustrates how this is done by means of a linearized diagram of the airgap periphery (often known as a 'developed' diagram).

It is at this point that we can look back at Chapter 2 in order to decide what constitutes 'a pole' in the case of a turboalternator in which both the inner bore of the stator and the surface of the rotor are virtually smooth, cylindrical surfaces. Distribution of the windings as shown in Fig. 2.4 does not alter the pole number, as evidenced by the rotor, which still has its salient poles as real things that project above the windings. We must conclude that the distributed windings of Figs. 2.4 and 5.4(a) must constitute a two-pole system, the latter without reference to the salient nature of the rotor (in Fig. 5.2(a) both rotor and stator surfaces are smooth).

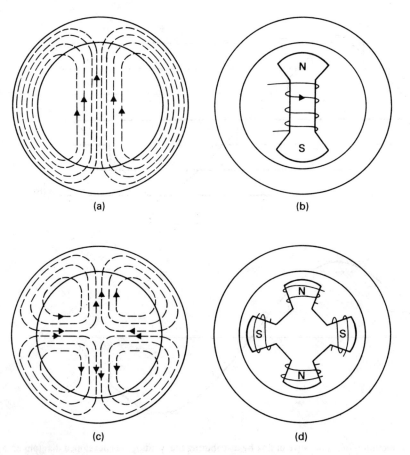

Figure 5.5 Flux patterns as a guide to pole numbers in machines with distributed windings.

A reasonably clear definition of what constitutes a 'pole' can be given by defining a *pole pitch* rather than a pole *per se*. A pole pitch is the distance (p) between points where the current flow is a maximum (as at XY, X'Y' in Fig. 5.4(a)). The number of poles in the machine is then the periphery ($2\pi r$) divided by p. This definition fits easily into linear motor technology (as in Chapter 10), where the number of poles need be neither even nor an integer. The speed of rotation expressed in Table 2.1 as $2f/n$ rev/sec, where n was the number of poles, can always be converted to a linear speed, for the periphery $2\pi r$ contains n pole pitches each of length p so that $2\pi r = np$. Hence the rotational speed $2f/n$ rev/sec 'translates' into a linear speed, v_s, such that

$$v_s = (2f/n)(2\pi r) = (2f/n)(np) = 2pf$$

which is simply the 'common sense' statement that a travelling wave moves two pole pitches (= one wavelength, λ) each cycle of events. (This corresponds to the well known formula $v = f\lambda$ for all wave motions.)

An alternative way of assessing pole number in a distributed winding machine is to study the main flux paths. If the flux peaks are 180° apart, as in Fig. 5.5(a), the system clearly corresponds to that in (b) and the system has two poles. But if the flux is as shown in (c) then it corresponds to the four-pole arrangement in (d)—so where is the difficulty?

The same rules for pole numbers with distributed windings apply equally well to the excitation windings of turbo-driven rotors and to the output (stator windings). The latter are basically the same as those of the stator windings of induction motors, commutator motors, indeed of all a.c. machines whose stators operate in rotating field systems, and the problems in thinking about pole numbers arise whenever the designer uses short chorded windings or where the machine is a polyphase motor or generator, for Figs. 2.9 *et seq.* illustrate that one dare use the coil pitch as the measure of pole pitch no longer. The best way to appreciate the difficulty is to look at nothing more complicated than the very primitive three-phase machine stator shown in Fig. 5.6(a). It does not, as it appears at first sight, have six poles, even though it has six obvious 'polar projections'. These are to be seen as six 'teeth' in a slotted stator with a three-phase 'distributed' winding, except that the distribution has virtually disappeared except insofar as there are three phases. Unless such a diagram makes clear how the two coils in each phase are *connected*, no one can say whether it has two poles or four. It is worth studying Fig. 5.6 carefully, first to appreciate the differences between (b) and (c), hence to 'see' the kind of difficulty that can arise in the mind of the student being confronted with the problem for the first time, and finally to demolish the problem so that it never arises in the future. For the connections shown at (b), both red-phase coils *assist* each other in driving flux diametrically across the machine. So do both yellow-phase coils and both blue-phase coils. So, whatever instantaneous currents flow in the system as a whole, the resultant flux will be the vector sum of three diametral fluxes which therefore is itself diametral and the machine corresponds to the two-pole system of Fig. 5.5(a). But if opposite pairs send

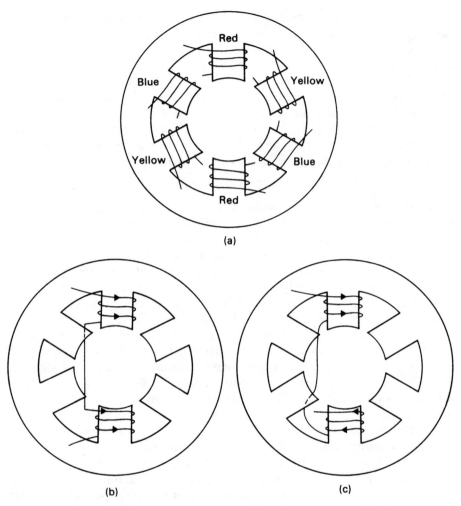

Figure 5.6 How pole number depends on connections between coils of the same phase. (Only the red phase is shown for clarity.)

opposing fluxes into the rotor then the only possible resultant flux pattern corresponds to that of Fig. 5.5(c) and the machine has four poles.

In this crude example the lack of winding 'distribution' is now obvious, since a two-pole, three-phase machine with only six slots has one slot per pole per phase, or, as is now more 'fashionably' written, one slot per pole *and* phase. The four-pole version has only half a slot per pole and phase, which gives a very 'lumpy' kind of travelling field, to be avoided in practice if at all possible by having a larger number of slots. The reader will appreciate, however, that if a more realistic example of two- and four-pole machines with, say, twenty-four slots each had been chosen, the diagrams might have become too obscure to make the point about 'pole counting'.

5.2.2 Windings, Generated E.M.F.

In Fig. 5.4(a) three concentric coils per pole are shown connected in series. The m.m.f. surrounding areas B, F, H, and L can be taken to be one unit each. The m.m.f. operating on areas C, E, I, and K is therefore two units each, while areas D and J are each subjected to three units. Areas A, G, and M have zero m.m.f. The distribution of diagram (b) shows the m.m.f. plot, superimposed on the dotted sine curve that is to be the final shape of the flux density distribution. In diagram (c) we see how the flux from the actual rotor teeth spreads according to Maxwell's Second Stress to produce the desired distribution $b - B \sin(\pi x/p)$, where x is the peripheral distance measured from a point midway between a pair of poles and p is the peripheral pole pitch.

The simplest form of stator winding for a two-pole alternator consists of a single coil located in two slots 180° apart, as shown in Fig. 2.5. This would undoubtedly experience induced e.m.f. of the form $e = E \sin \omega t$, where $E = NBlv = NBlr\omega$ and N is the number of turns in the coil. The fact that we do not use such an arrangement is due to considerations of usefulness of material. The power output of an alternator (or of any electromagnetic machine) is the product of tangential force F_T and surface speed $v(= r\omega)$. F_T is equal to the tangential force, F, per unit area, multiplied by the area of pole face acting on the stator, i.e., $F_T = 2\pi r l F$ where l is the active, axial length of the stator conductors. F_T itself is the product of the airgap flux density B_g multiplied by the current loading J in the stator. J is the current contained in unit length measured peripherally (and, in general, is sinusoidally distributed as $J = J_m \sin(\pi x/p)$, as we shall see in a moment).

The question now posed is how to obtain maximum output from a given size of machine. Efficiency is also a consideration but is relegated to second

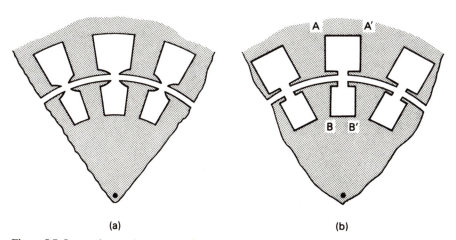

| (a) | (b) |

Figure 5.7 Stator slots and teeth have the advantage of an expanding geometry. Rotor slots and teeth are constricted. (a) The expansion–contraction is shared equally between teeth and slots. (b) Parallel sided stator slots allow space for extra leakage flux at A, A', but note the 'bottlenecks' in the rotor at B, B'.

place against power/weight ratio in a modern machine, provided it is not reduced by more than a few per cent by an all-out attack on power/weight ratio. B_g depends on how much flux can be pushed through the magnetic circuit, whose 'bottleneck' is the stator teeth. If a stator slot is of width w_s and a tooth of width w_t, then, assuming the tooth tips to be saturated to a value B_s, to a first approximation,

$$B_g = B_s \left(\frac{w_t}{w_t + w_s} \right)$$

Ultimately, then, B_g has a ceiling fixed by saturation of the magnetic material. Figure 5.7 shows how the use of the stator as output winding has yet another advantage over the primitive machines of the last century. Stator slots and teeth are the subject of an *expanding* geometry whereby either slots or teeth can be tapered. In the example shown, a parallel sided slot allows slot leakage flux to be accommodated in the ever widening tooth in approximately the right amount to ensure most economical use of magnetic material (entire tooth saturated simultaneously at full load). The use of bigger and bigger values of J means the production of more and more heat in the stator (proportional to J^2). The limit is not simply the maximum temperature rise that the insulation will withstand, regarding the copper simply as a heat sink, but on how much heat can be dispersed by almost any known means (ultimately, this implies the use of hollow conductors with gas or water pumped through them and the use of 'cooling fin technology' as used on the cylinders of motorcycles or in domestic 'radiator' designs). Unfortunately, materials that are good electrical insulators are usually good thermal insulators also, which means that the heat generated in the centre of the slot-housed stator conductors can be dispersed only from the end windings and must flow outwards from the centre, along the conductors, to allow this to happen. In such cases the central part of the machine is the hottest spot and this point, and this alone, sets the ultimate maximum value of J.

Now there are two methods of alleviating this problem: the first is pure mechanical engineering, the second is chemistry. In long machines, the stator

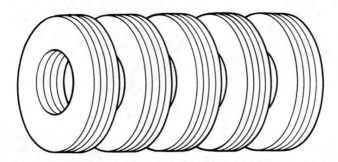

Figure 5.8 The formation of radial cooling ducts by assembling stator punchings in packets.

laminations are pressed together in tight slabs and the slabs are spaced apart on their holding bolts to form annular ducts in radial planes, as shown in Fig. 5.8. Air can now be blown through these ducts to impinge directly on the stator conductors.

In the second case, the apparent 'law' that good insulators of electricity are bad conductors of heat has been broken by the development of epoxy resins that can be cast into any spaces to fill them completely. These substances provide quite a measure of thermal conduction while being very effective electrical insulators capable of withstanding high temperatures.

But, without any doubt whatever, the biggest step in the cooling of windings was made very many decades ago when the single stator coil shown in Fig. 2.5 was distributed all around the periphery, as shown in Fig. 2.6. This arrangement is not without penalty, for the peak of the flux wave passes the slot A before it passes B, and so on. In other words, the e.m.f.s induced in the conductors of any pair of slots are not in phase. The total e.m.f. obtained when all such coils are connected in series is the phasor sum, which for a single-phase machine approximates (for a large number of slots) to the diameter of a

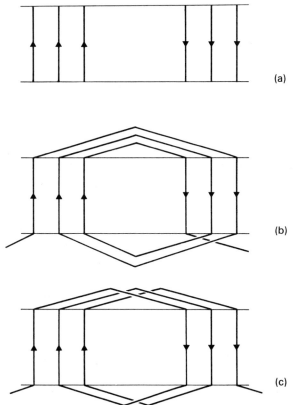

(a)

(b)

(c)

Figure 5.9 End connections for stator windings. (a) Only demand for current distribution. (b) Demand met by concentric coils (three shapes). (c) Overlapped coils (only *one* shape) give shorter end windings.

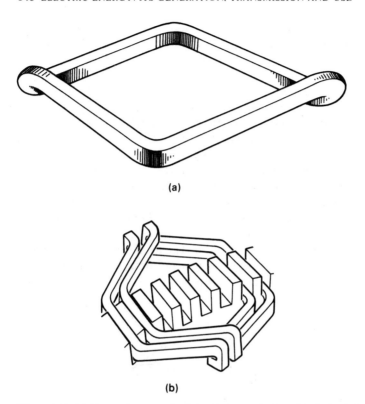

(a)

(b)

Figure 5.10 (a) Shape of stator coil of double-layer winding. (b) Method of overlapping successive coils.

circle whose semicircumference is the 'potential' e.m.f. Thus a factor of $2/\pi$ is sacrificed in order to gain the maximum permissible value of J. This effect is a contributor to the advantages of a polyphase system as opposed to single phase (see section 2.4).

What has been said earlier in explanation of the distributed magnetizing winding of the rotors of alternators might give the impression that a system of concentric coils such as that shown in Fig. 5.4(a) might accommodate the distribution demands of Fig. 2.6 and indeed it will, but concentric coils are oldfashioned and are seldom now used. There are two reasons, viz.:

(1) Any one machine requires several different sizes of coil and does not therefore lend itself to mass production methods so well as would a complete set of identical coils.

(2) With identical coils, it is possible to pack the end windings into a smaller space than is the case with concentric coils and any such reduction in turn reduces shaft length, danger of shaft 'whirling' (and therefore in the design, a smaller shaft diameter), and so on. Let us study Figs. 5.9 and 5.10. The only thing of which the rotor is 'conscious', so far as electromagnetic

action is concerned, is the stator pole area that it faces and the conductors embedded therein. It demands only currents that effectively stop at the boundaries of the stator core, as shown in Fig. 5.9(a) and it cares not whether we connect them as a concentric system, as in (b), or as a set of overlapping coils, as shown in (c). If, therefore, it is decided to build in the stator coils in two layers (a very popular technique but one that is by no means essential to exploit the idea), each coil can be bent into the shape shown in Fig. 5.10(a) with what are called winding 'noses' that stack together like certain shapes of tubular framed stacking chairs, as shown in (b).

5.2.3 Space Harmonics and Chording

It is difficult to generate a pure sine wave. It *costs* a great deal to generate such a waveform. To settle for less is to present a transmission system with the opportunity to radiate at harmonic frequencies, and this in turn will cause interference with telephone circuits and produce excess losses in transformers and similar undesirable phenomena. So we must try to minimize voltage time harmonics and to do this we need to examine their cause.

In a turboalternator, one set of conductor filled slots passes another set at high speed, perhaps as many as two thousand slots in one member passing any given point on the other in one second. In theory, a perfectly distributed winding should be housed in an infinite number of infinitely small slots. Anything less perfect introduces the discontinuities that are the source of harmonics. Now, in order to effect a cure (for 'cure' it is rather than 'prevention', since all *real* windings will produce harmonic voltages) it is necessary to appreciate at least the rudiments of the Fourier series. Any shape of repetitive wave can be seen to be made up of a fundamental frequency, together with a series of harmonic frequencies, possibly extending to infinity, thus:

$$f(t) = a_1 \sin \omega t + a_2 \sin 2\omega t + a_3 \sin 3\omega t + \ldots$$

but if the wave is symmetrical, no 'even' harmonics are possible, i.e., $a_2 = a_4 = a_6 \ldots = 0$. One of the several advantages of a three-phase system (other than those listed on pages 35–41) is that an alternator that is star connected may generate in each of its phase windings a third harmonic voltage, none of which appears in the line-to-line voltage. If the output of such an alternator is passed through a transformer, as is usual in any case, a star connected secondary may then have its star point earthed without taking the third harmonic into the phase windings of the transformer secondary. Indeed, every transformer virtually allows the designer to 'start a clean sheet' so far as voltage to earth is concerned.

The mechanism of third harmonic elimination in star connected alternators is not obvious. Figure 5.11 shows the three-phase voltages drawn as fundamental and third harmonic voltage waves separately. It can be seen that all three third harmonic voltages are in phase with each other (since

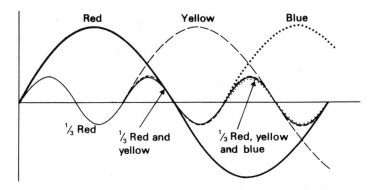

Figure 5.11 Third harmonic waves are in phase in a three-phase system.

$3 \times 120° = 360°$) and one can now draw, as it were, a phasor diagram *on* a phasor diagram as shown in Fig. 5.12. The three fundamental phasors rotate at ω, the three additional arrows at 3ω. But since the latter are always in step, the triangle RYB simply appears to rotate, its centre tracing out a circle as shown dotted. Its sides (which means the line-to-line voltage) remain of constant length and at 120° to each other. So far as the primary of the ensuing transformer is concerned, it is as if its terminal points are fed from a harmonic-free source but its neutral point is rotating in a circle, as shown in Fig. 5.13, at a speed 2ω.

The remaining harmonics from an alternator are now the following multiples of the fundamental frequency ω: (5, 7), (11, 13), (17, 19), (23, 25), (29, 31), (35, 37), etc. The purpose of grouping these in pairs is that each pair can be seen as

$$(6n \pm 1) \tag{5.2}$$

where n is an integer. The technique known as 'chording' exploits this feature. In a 'full pitch' winding, every stator coil of an alternator is such that opposite

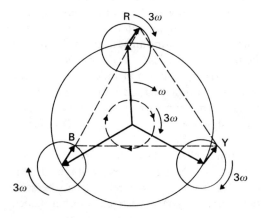

Figure 5.12 A phasor diagram for fundamental and third harmonics.

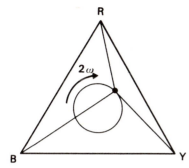

Figure 5.13 Third harmonics seen as a rotating neutral.

sides span a full 180 electrical degrees, as shown in Fig. 5.14(a). The contributions from the e.m.f. generated in each side are therefore arithmetically added, fundamental and harmonics alike. But suppose the winding could be shortened by one-fifth, as shown in Fig. 5.14(b). See how the fifth harmonics generated in opposite sides of the winding are now 180° opposed and the output of the winding freed from fifth harmonic (Fig. 5.15). The output from that coil is now, in effect, the chord of a circle, rather than the diameter, as is the case with full-pitched coils (see Fig. 5.16), hence the name of the technique. From harmonic considerations, only a coil of one and one-fifth times the span

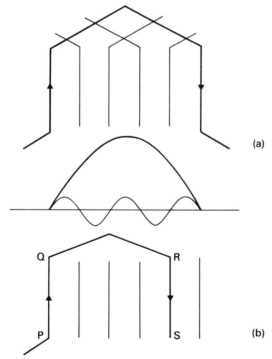

Figure 5.14 Elimination of harmonic by short chording.

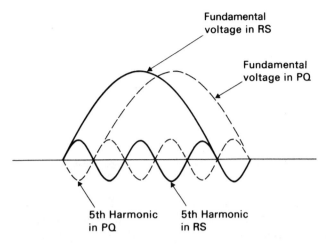

Figure 5.15 Addition of fundamental waves reduces amplitude to $\cos(180/10)^\circ = 0.951$, addition of fifth harmonics reduces amplitude to zero.

is equally effective to one of four-fifths the span, but the latter is almost invariably chosen because it shortens the end windings rather than lengthens them, as does over- or long chording. Shorter end windings usually bring benefits in lower I^2R loss and lower leakage flux. Often, the technique of short chording is used *primarily* for these purposes rather than for harmonic suppression.

It is usually impossible to chord a winding specifically against one particular harmonic, for the very nature of a three-phase winding suggests that unless one is prepared to try to balance a fractional slot winding (a balanced output is one for which all three output voltages are equal in magnitude and equally spaced in phase), the number of slots per pole will be a multiple of three. Therefore short chording will usually be $m/6n$, where n is the integer in expression $(6n \pm 1)$ and m is another integer, usually less than six, unless the total number of slots per pole is very large. Let us see the effect that one-sixth chord has on a winding generating fifth and seventh harmonics. The fundamental and fifth harmonic waveforms are shown separately in Fig. 5.17, the full lines representing the voltages from one side of a coil and the dotted

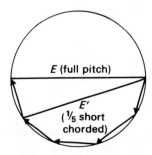

Figure 5.16 Phasor diagram for Fig. 5.14.

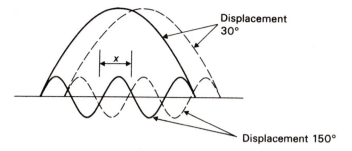

Figure 5.17 Wave displacements for one-sixth chording.

lines representing those from the other. Adding $\sin \omega t$ and $\sin(\omega t - \pi/6)$ reduces the amplitude of the fundamental by only $\cos(\pi/12)$ i.e., by 3 per cent, but the addition of $\sin 5\omega t$ and $\sin(5\omega t - 5\pi/6)$ reduces the amplitude of the fifth harmonic by a factor $\cos(5\pi/12)$, or 74 per cent. Similarly, the seventh harmonic is reduced to 74 per cent. By pitching the winding to split the number $(6n \pm 1)$, the designer can reduce any pair of the remaining harmonics in the list considerably.

In terms of double-layer windings, chording is an extremely simple process, as shown in Fig. 5.18. In (a) a full-pitch winding with two slots per

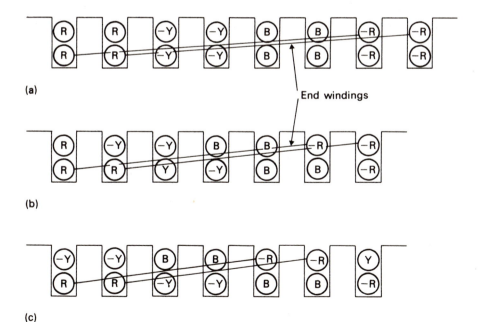

Figure 5.18 Cross section through slots to show that effect of chording is to shift top layer to the left shortening end windings.

pole and phase has blocks of four coil sides in two adjacent slots. The thin oblique lines are representative of the end windings joining opposite pairs of conductors. In (b) the top layer is simply shifted one slot pitch to the left and is thus five-sixths chorded. In (c) the shift is two slot pitches, for two-thirds chording, and so on.

5.2.4 Armature Reaction, Synchronous Impedance

The word 'armature' was being used to describe one member of an electrical machine decades before alternators and induction motors were ever exploited. In those days it meant the *rotor* of a d.c. machine. Since d.c. machines are not dependent on transformer action the words 'primary' and 'secondary' applied to such machines would be confusing, to say the least. In a d.c. machine the 'field' is usually stationary, the armature rotating. In a d.c. machine the field current is relatively small, the mere catalyst that makes things happen. It could, after all, be no more than a permanent magnet. The d.c. machine can be, and often is, both described and used as an amplifier, in which the throughput of large power (electrical to mechanical or vice versa) is monitored by a tiny amount of power in the field windings, and this is precisely the philosophy of the electronic amplifier. Later in this chapter we shall discuss the amplidyne in purely electronic terminology.

Now, by the same process, an alternator is a synchronous machine that does a similar job, but its catalytic field winding (usually known as the 'excitation') is on the rotating member, so, by inference and only by inference, the stator becomes the 'armature'. Given the choice, we will always elect to call the output winding of an alternator the 'stator winding', but for purposes of examining the particular phenomenon that appears in the heading of this and similar sections in other standard works it is necessary to identify the phenomenon by comparison with d.c. machine 'armature reaction'.

Put into its most fundamental terms the phenomenon may be stated thus: when setting up a magnetic flux in the airgap of a rotating machine by means of a primary winding, the size and distribution of that flux will depend entirely on the arrangement of the primary winding and the geometry of the magnetic circuit; but if further current then flows in the secondary winding, the airgap flux that then exists will be the result of *all* the m.m.f. in both primary and secondary. Any modification from the original flux pattern as the result of secondary current flow is called the armature reaction. You can see at once that such definition immediately relegates the rotor of a d.c. machine to the role of 'secondary' winding, even though when used as a motor it is quite clearly the main power *input* to the machine. Such are the hazards of trying to make a nomenclature fit all types of machine.

In d.c. machines, the main effect of rotor current is to, as it were, *drag* the flux around the gap in the direction of motion. This enables the flux to be considered as having a 'quadrature component' in space, often known as a cross field and being exploited enormously in the amplidyne generator (page

165). If reduction of flux on load occurs in a d.c. machine it is because the flux shift has increased the reluctance of the flux path, through the field pole geometry, or (more commonly) by the saturation of parts of the magnetic circuit.

In alternators, such a flux shift manifests itself as a change of phase that may itself therefore involve voltage reduction or voltage increase, depending on the nature of the load impedance. Figure 5.19 is a developed diagram of the airgap of a turboalternator under (a) a resistive load, (b) an inductive load,

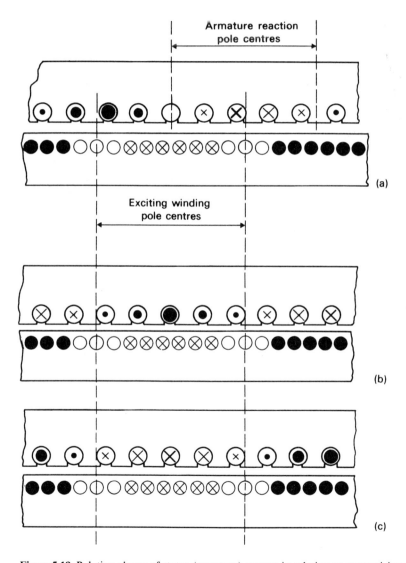

Figure 5.19 Relative phases of stator (armature) current in relation to magnetizing poles; (a) for resistive load, (b) for 90° lagging load, (c) for 90° leading load.

and (c) a capacitive load. The phase of the load currents in (b) is clearly such as to have a component tending to demagnetize the airgap and hence produce 'arithmetical' volt drop at the terminals. In (c) the load m.m.f. has a component in phase with the moving primary excitation, increasing the flux by an amount depending on the degree of saturation built into the machine by the designer on the assumption of the load being only resistive or resistive–inductive, as is usually the case. A resistive load on an alternator has the effect of cross-magnetization virtually as in a d.c. machine, but whereas in the latter no one questions the shape of the rotor waveform, since it is immediately rectified by a mechanical rectifier with a large number of 'anodes' (commutator bars), the waveform of the stator e.m.f. in an alternator goes out, as it were, 'raw' to the terminals. The effect of armature reaction on resistive load is therefore mainly one of waveform distortion, with an increasing tendency also to involve volt drop, especially in water wheel alternators, owing to magnetic circuit geometry.

Having thus established, on a qualitative basis, the effects of load current (armature reaction) as those shown in Fig. 5.20, we can now attempt to represent an alternator by an equivalent circuit with the usual technique of representing the machine as a 'perfect' device connected to a network that represents all the imperfections of the machine appearing as passive elements. For simplicity, let us first assume that armature reaction effects could be ignored and that a magnetic flux distribution unaffected by load current always threads the stator winding in the same way so far as calculating the generated e.m.f. is concerned. The imperfections of the stator winding are then fairly simply extracted. There is an ohmic resistance per phase in series with a leakage reactance per phase, the result of not all of the stator m.m.f. successfully adding or subtracting to or from the main flux, but driving fluxes around what might be described as its own 'private' magnetic circuits, such as across the stator slots or around the stator end windings. (The calculation of

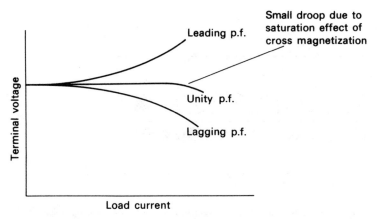

Figure 5.20 Effects of armature reaction on terminal voltage.

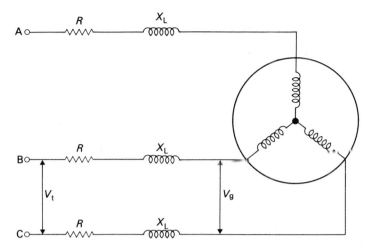

Figure 5.21 Simple model of an alternator ignoring armature reaction.

the latter has probably provided material for more doctorate theses than any other single topic in the whole of machine theory!)

Let us now therefore examine the effect of different types of load on a constant voltage generator feeding an R and an X_L in series, in each

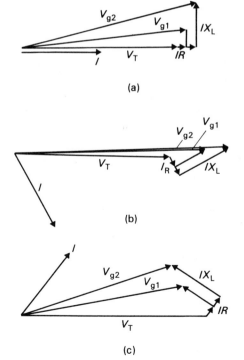

Figure 5.22 Phasor diagram for voltage modifications effected by different types of increasing load; (a) resistive, (b) resistive–inductive, (c) resistive–capacitive.

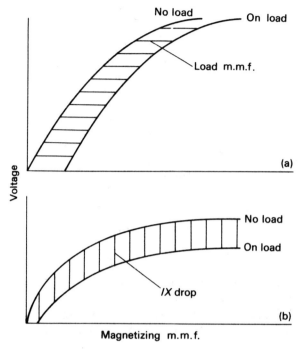

Figure 5.23 Approximate methods of predicting alternator regulation on load: (a) assumes it all to be due to armature reaction; (b) assumes it all to be due to leakage reactance.

phase, on the generation side of the terminals ABC (Fig. 5.21). The three phasor diagrams of Fig. 5.22(a), (b), and (c) are typical of the effect of resistive, resistive–inductive and resistive–capacitive loads, and at once it is clear that if specific values are inserted and curves of terminal voltage against load current are plotted, they will be virtually indistinguishable in form from those of Fig. 5.20, which were seen to arise purely as the result of armature reaction, an entirely different phenomenon.

This double mechanism of voltage change on load was recognized by the engineers of the late nineteenth and early twentieth centuries and formed the basis of much argument and publication as to just how the load characteristics of an alternator should be presented. One authoritative method, attributed to Rothert, supposed that leakage reactance effects should be regarded as extra m.m.f. due to armature reaction; another, credited to Behn–Eschenberg, supposed armature reaction to be an extra leakage effect. Figure 5.23 shows the first to be an optimistic method and the second to be a pessimistic method, for the one subtracted vertically, the other horizontally. The truth lay somewhere between the two. Various methods were adopted for splitting the effect by the use of extraordinary specified conditions such as a test run on zero power factor load, a test with a fixed load at various frequencies, finally predicting the characteristic on load by subtracting a triangle (of constant size

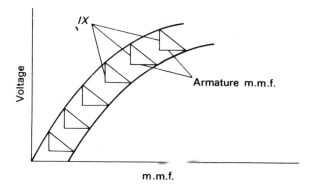

Figure 5.24 More accurate prediction in which armature reaction and leakage reactance voltages are subtracted separately.

for constant load) from the open circuit characteristic (Fig. 5.24) in which a vertical and a horizontal portion were effectively being extracted to represent leakage reactance and armature reaction effects in their own right.

Modern methods are based on the concept of considering the alternator to consist of two separate sets of effects. The one concerns an axis of the machine in line with the axis of the exciting poles—the *direct* axis—and the other the axis at right angles to this—the *quadrature* axis. (In multipolar machines the expression 'at right angles' implies 90 *electrical* degrees.) This 'two-axis theory', first conceived by Blondel *c.* 1921, was developed in classic papers by R. H. Park[3] and then by other authors, notably Adkins[4] and Gibbs,[5] until it could be applied to all electromagnetic machines and became known as the 'generalized machine theory'. Its main advantage is that the study of commercial machines involves distributed windings, various magnetic circuit geometries, and both flux cutting (Special Relativity) and flux linking (i.e.) transformer (General Relativity) effects, so that ordinary analysis becomes too complicated. Only one thing is certain. Coils, or sets of coils, that are at right angles are incapable of passing energy to each other by transformer action. Thus by concentrating attention into two perpendicular axes, transformer considerations are eliminated and the machine can be considered almost as if it existed in two different worlds.

Be assured, therefore, that when any modern author refers to the 'synchronous reactance' on the direct axis, he refers to the combined effects of leakage reactance and armature reaction, as they affect events in line with the poles. Combination of synchronous reactance X_s with resistance R in the usual manner leads to the 'synchronous impedance', Z_s, where $Z_s^2 = R^2 + X_s^2$.

If there is one most significant difference between the design of an alternator (the world's main generator of electric power) and that of an induction motor, certainly the world's biggest utilizer of electrical energy, it is in the sizes of the airgaps. Induction motor gaps are restricted to 1–3 mm, those of alternators may be as great as 20 cm. Now there has to be something very dramatic to account for such an apparent lack of agreement between the designers of what are, after all, at opposite ends of a transmission line. Many books on machines have dealt with each machine effectively, yet never wrestled with the underlying philosophy. Of *course* one can regard an induction motor as a synchronous machine and take it under the umbrella of the Generalized Machine (we ourselves do so in Chapter 7). But it is a very different 'animal' in that, as a generator, it belongs to that rarely encountered 'series world' where current faces current across the airgap in as nearly equal and opposite sizes as the designer can make them. The stator of an induction machine must carry both excitation and load current and the two cannot therefore be separated. This is necessary because the induction motor is a *transformer* and inherently so. The synchronous machine is a d.c. generator at heart, but a d.c. machine turned inside out and stripped of its commutator. In d.c. machines as in alternators, d.c. ampere-turns are cheap ('cheap' in pounds sterling or US dollars!) and generators have to operate in the parallel world that men *chose*, where you expect to put a plug in a socket and not change the voltage by so doing. By using a massive airgap, and a massive number of exciting ampere-turns to go with it, the result is a 'stiff' machine (a term often used within the industry) in which armature reaction effects are not too drastic.

On the other hand, with large airgaps, the designer virtually 'invites' leakage flux from the stator, but engineering is always a compromise and there is a second reason for accepting a high leakage reactance in an alternator. We have seen examination questions set that require the candidate to comment on the statement that, 'an alternator is designed for its misuse, rather than for its use.' A large modern alternator is almost inevitably coupled into a complex power network in which every precaution must be taken against the direct fault—a short circuit that can spell disaster in a parallel world. Older networks employed chokes (inductors) in series with alternators. The modern machine has the reactance built into it. Just how large are such reactances will become apparent from the next section in which the alternator phasor diagram (derived from an equivalent circuit concept) has reactive components larger than those of a transmission line or of a small laboratory machine.

5.2.5 The Synchronous Machine Operation and Phasor Diagram

We will now look more closely at the relationships between the electric circuit quantities in a synchronous machine (s.m.), i.e., armature voltage and current, and the space–time-varying quantities, i.e., m.m.f.s in the machine airgap.

Instead of using the developed diagram of Fig. 5.19, we will consider the machine in its original circular form as in Fig. 5.25, where a two-pole rotor is depicted. For simplicity it is assumed that the rotor winding carrying the exciting current I_f produces a sinusoidal m.m.f. distribution in the airgap that can be represented by the rotating space phasor M_f. At the instant shown, we can take it that i_A, the current in phase A, is a maximum. Owing therefore to the expected balance of the three-phase system, i_B and i_C have a value of

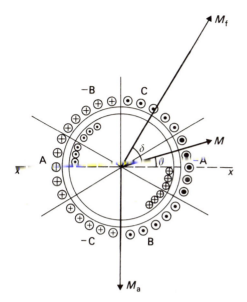

Figure 5.25 Synchronous machine m.m.f.s.

minus one-half maximum. The dots and crosses on the conductor sections indicate that with i_A maximum, the rotating m.m.f. M_a produced by the combined effect of the armature currents is in line with the axis of winding A.

The phasoidal summation of M_f and M_a gives the resultant m.m.f. M, which is truly the only m.m.f. present in the airgap. This resultant m.m.f. is in advance of the axis xx, which implies that the current in phase A exhibits a phase relationship of θ with respect to the induced voltage.

Space and circuit phasor diagrams for the s.m. operating as a generator are shown in Fig. 5.26. Diagram (a) shows the phasor addition of the m.m.f.s in the airgap and (b) the companion diagram of the voltage and current in one phase of the alternator. Voltage V_f corresponds to the e.m.f. that would have been induced if M_f were acting alone; similarly, V_a would have been induced if

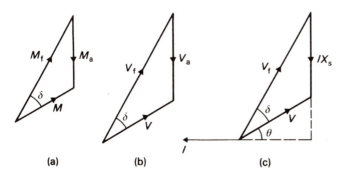

Figure 5.26 Synchronous machine phasor diagrams.

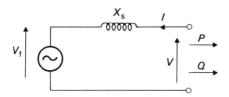

Figure 5.27 Simplified equivalent circuit of synchronous machine.

only M_a were present; and finally V is the voltage induced by M and is therefore the only truly existing voltage in the machine.

The m.m.f. and voltage triangles are similar, but there is no good justification in showing them with corresponding sides parallel. We can now, if we wish, assume that the voltage V_a due to the armature reaction is an internal voltage drop caused by the current flowing through the synchronous reactance X_s. This way of looking at things gives us Fig. 5.26(c) in which the phase current is also shown.

The conventions developed in Chapter 4 indicate that the phasor diagram (Fig. 5.26(c)) describes the behaviour of the circuit of Fig. 5.27 in which active and reactive powers are generated at the terminals. In such an equivalent circuit representation of the synchronous machine, the fictitious induced voltage V_f is known as the voltage *behind* the synchronous reactance.

It is easy now to appreciate that the 'load' or 'torque' angle δ between M_f and M or V_f and V is of great significance. It is the magnitude and sign of this angle that determines the active power transfer and its direction, i.e., whether the s.m. is generating or motoring. We can conclude that the s.m. is generating when V_f and M_f lead V and M, respectively, and that it is motoring if the converse is true.

For the sake of simplicity we can assume that the armature resistance and leakage reactance are negligible compared with the synchronous reactance and that the s.m. is connected to a constant voltage supply. In Fig. 5.28 a number of phasor diagrams are drawn on the quadrant diagram of Fig. 4.9 with a fixed s.m. current as a reference phasor. With the s.m. motoring, phasor V should lie in the first or fourth quadrant and should lead V_f. With low excitation (i.e., machine underexcited), V_t is less than V and the s.m. is associated with $+P$ and $+Q$, i.e., the first quadrant. In other words, the machine is motoring and absorbs reactive power. With the s.m. overexcited, V_t is larger than V and operation falls in the fourth quadrant $(+P, -Q)$ with the machine motoring but supplying reactive power. In quadrants two and three the s.m. is generating with underexcitation $(-P, +Q)$ and overexcitation $(-P, -Q)$, respectively. As s.m.s are the major sources of reactive power in power systems, they are, with few exceptions, run in overexcited mode.

The active power per phase is given, in all phasor diagrams of Fig. 5.28, by $VI\cos\phi$. Therefore the active power is provided with a smaller value of δ when the s.m. is over- rather than underexcited. In Chapter 8 where the stability of s.m.s is discussed, it is shown that the larger is δ, the more vulnerable is the s.m. to instability when sudden load changes take place. We

Generating
underexcited

Motoring
underexcited

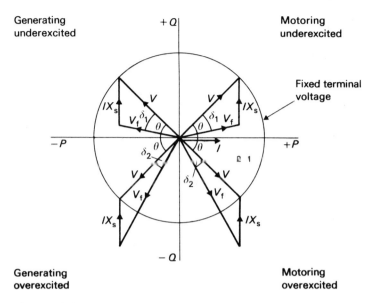

Figure 5.28 Quadrant diagram of a synchronous machine.

conclude that for a given active power transfer an s.m. is more likely to go unstable when under- than when overexcited.

The relationship governing active power transfer in an s.m. is described by Eq. (4.25), which is plotted in Fig. 5.29. At $\delta = \pm 90°$ the active power transfer is a maximum. If δ is gradually made to exceed $\pm 90°$ the s.m. will lose synchronism.

In order to connect an s.m. to the mains, it is necessary to make sure that there is compatibility between the mains and the s.m. induced voltages; otherwise, on connection, a considerable surge of current will result that is likely to trip circuit breakers or blow fuses.

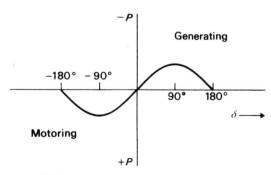

$$P = -\frac{VV_f}{X_s} \sin \delta$$

Figure 5.29 Synchronous machine power angle characteristic.

For the purpose of synchronization the following conditions must be fulfilled.

(1) The voltage magnitude V_t of the s.m. must be very close to the voltage V of the mains.
(2) The frequency of the s.m. voltage must be very close to that of the mains.
(3) The sequence with which the three voltages of the mains reach their peaks should be matched by the corresponding sequence of the s.m. voltages.
(4) At the instant of switching, the voltages of the s.m. must be in phase with the corresponding mains voltages.

In power station control rooms synchronization of s.m.s with the grid is performed by means of special instruments known as synchroscopes.

Example 5.1

A turboalternator having a synchronous reactance of 1.0 p.u. is connected to infinite busbars of one p.u. voltage and is supplying 0.75 p.u. of full load at unity power factor.

If the steam supply to the turbine is unchanged but the excitation is adjusted so that the voltage behind the synchronous reactance is increased by 40 per cent, determine the new value of the p.u. current and the new power factor.

With this higher value of excitation kept constant and the steam supply gradually increased, at what p.u. current and power factor would the machine lose synchronism?

The phasor diagram (a) of Fig. 5.30 illustrates the initial operating conditions of the alternator. Operation at three-quarters full load implies a current of 0.75 p.u., therefore the p.u. voltage drop in a synchronous reactance of 1 p.u. is also 0.75.

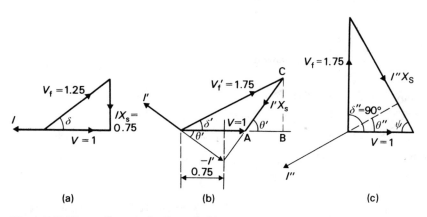

Figure 5.30 Phasor diagrams for Example 5.1.

We can calculate V_f from

$$V_f = \sqrt{[V^2 + (IX_s)^2]} = \sqrt{[1 + 0.75^2]} = 1.25 \text{ p.u.}$$

and

$$\sin \delta = \frac{0.75}{1.25} = 0.6$$

The increase in excitation results in the new V_f given by $V_f' = 1.25 \times 1.4 = 1.75 \text{ p.u.}$ and the new phasor diagram (b). Note that as the mechanical power input and therefore the electrical active power output have not changed, the in-phase component of the new current I' is the same as previously.

Equating active powers before and after the change,

$$\frac{V V_f}{X_s} \sin \delta = \frac{V V_f'}{X_s} \sin \delta'$$

therefore

$$\sin \delta' = \frac{V_f}{V_f'} \sin \delta = \frac{1.25}{1.75} \times 0.6 = 0.4286$$

and

$$\delta' = 25.377°$$

From triangle ABC we can determine

$$I'X_s = \sqrt{[(AB)^2 + (BC)^2]}$$
$$= \sqrt{[(1.75 \cos \delta' - 1)^2 + (1.75 \sin \delta')^2]} = 0.949 \text{ p.u.}$$

therefore

$$I' = \frac{0.949}{0.75} = 1.265 \text{ p.u.}$$

and

$$\cos \theta' = \frac{0.75}{1.265} = 0.593$$

The machine will lose synchronism when $\delta = 90°$, as shown in phasor diagram (c).

The voltage drop $I''X_s$ is given by

$$I''X_s = \sqrt{(1.75^2 + 1^2)} = 2.015 \text{ p.u.}$$

and

$$I'' = \frac{2.015}{0.75} = 2.687 \text{ p.u.}$$

therefore

$$\psi = \tan^{-1} \frac{1.75}{1} = 60.255°$$

$$\theta'' = 90 - 60.255 = 29.745°$$

and

$$\cos \theta'' = 0.868$$

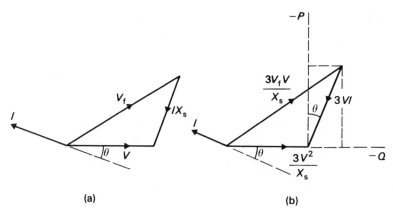

Figure 5.31 Synchronous generator phasor diagrams.

Note that in (b) the alternator is supplying Q to the system and $\theta' + 90°$ is the angle by which the current leads the voltage V, while in (c) Q is absorbed from the system and the current lags V by $\theta'' + 90°$.

5.2.6 Synchronous Machine Capability Chart

It is desirable to define the permissible or safe region of operation of s.m.s. A capability chart is a diagram delineating this region.

Figure 5.31(a) shows the phasor diagram of an s.m. when it is injecting active and reactive power into an infinite bus system. Multiplying the sides of the triangle by the constant $3V/X_s$, we arrive at triangle (b). The projection of the side $3VI$ on the vertical axis represents active power and on the horizontal axis reactive power generated by the s.m.

The triangle in (b) enables us to construct the capability chart of Fig. 5.32.

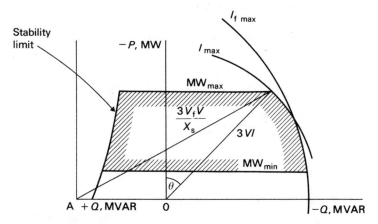

Figure 5.32 Capability chart of alternator.

The feasible operating region is bounded by a number of limits. First, there is the maximum MW limit imposed by the power rating of the prime mover. Second, there is a maximum MVA limit imposed by the maximum permissible armature current in $3VI$, this being a circle with centre O. Thirdly, there is a maximum $3V_f V/X_s$ limit imposed by the maximum permissible rotor current I_f, this being a circle with centre A. Fourthly, there is a stability limit in the region of underexcited operation that ensures that the load angle is not allowed to approach 90°. The dangers of such operation are described in section 8.5.4.

Finally, there is a minimum MW limit imposed by thermodynamic considerations of the boiler–turbine system in the case of a turboalternator.

The feasible region of operation is within the shaded area of the chart.

5.3 ASYNCHRONOUS GENERATION

Although the induction machine is easily the most popular type of motor for large power, it is only occasionally employed as a generator. When connected into a power network it can generally be treated as a synchronous machine whose power output is adjustable by controlling the prime mover. There is, however, the one difference that its excitation must be drawn from the a.c. network side as absorption of reactive power. To attempt to describe the operation of this machine when run in isolation from a system before having dealt with its operation as a motor is virtually impossible. Nevertheless, since few authors treat this topic and still fewer treat it with authority, its unusual characteristics are dealt with in Chapter 7, for its properties as a generator are called into play whenever rapid braking from the motoring condition is required, and this involves such possible applications as the use of linear induction motors in high speed transport systems.

When induction machines are designed as network feeders they are usually driven by water power and as such they resemble the existent salient pole synchronous machines of large diameter (5 metres is not uncommon) and multi-polar (of the order of 150 poles).

5.4 THE AMPLIDYNE

Although we expect readers to be sufficiently familiar with d.c. machine theory for it not to require a detailed treatment in this book, there is one embodiment that is unusual and that these machines share with alternators, induction machines, and others—the concept of two non-coupled axes. It was suggested in section 5.2.4 that a d.c. machine can be described in terms of an electronic 'amplifier'. If this concept is combined with that of direct and quadrature axes, then it becomes possible to build a two-stage rotary amplifier in one and the same machine.

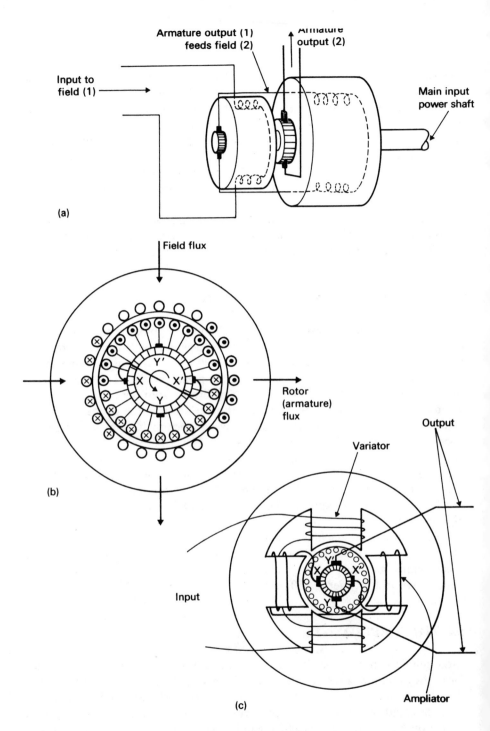

Figure 5.33 (a) Two d.c. generators, mechanically coupled to a common shaft, act like a two-stage electronic amplifier. (b) Armature reaction exploited to the state where primary and secondary currents are balanced and a large current can be drawn from quadrature brushes YY'. (c) Schematic diagram of an amplidyne with ampliators.

Figure 5.33(a) shows how two machines on a common shaft may be so regarded. The armature of the first machine is connected directly across the field winding of the second. Both machines draw the bulk of their power from the shaft. But now consider the system shown in Fig. 5.33(b). Armature reaction is generally regarded as a hindrance to the designer of a d.c. generator, producing distortion of flux, leading to partial saturation, voltage drop on load, and commutation problems. But suppose we were to take an opposite view and try to *increase* armature reaction and to *use* it. (This process of taking an opposite view of things out of sheer curiosity has recently been the subject of much formal writing, in which names such as 'lateral thinking' have been coined to identify it as a discipline in inventive processes.) Then the non-salient machine with small airgap becomes a constant current device, since in good machines equal and opposite currents should largely face each other across such an airgap. Thus the field current proper of the machine demands armature current to match, but armature current directions effectively make it into a magnetizing current for cross axis flux, and with a small airgap a large quadrature axis e.m.f. is developed.

The inventive part of the amplidyne was the realization that if the brushes XX' of the machine were short circuited, a very large armature current would result in the quadrature axis and a large voltage would appear across a pair of brushes YY' at right angles to the brush axis XX'. If the output from YY' were fed to a load circuit (which could be another machine), a huge current would be forced through the latter, whose magnitude was almost entirely dependent on the very small control current in the original field winding.

The system is comparable to a pentode in tube electronics or to a transistor. The gain of the amplidyne can be, and sometimes is, further increased by the addition of quadrature axis field coils in series with the brushes XX', as shown in the schematic diagram of Fig. 5.33(c). Such coils are sometimes known as 'ampliators' to distinguish them from the field winding of the first stage, which is then known as the 'variator'.

Amplidynes are used extensively in the London Underground Railways ('Tubes') feeding d.c. motors. When used in such large applications they are known as 'Metadynes'. The authors have traced the origin of this word and found it to mean, when first coined, 'an amplidyne manufactured by the Metropolitan–Vickers Company in Manchester, England'. Since that company was combined with the British Thomson–Houston Company in the late nineteen-fifties to become Associated Electrical Industries, and the latter company itself was annexed to the General Electric Company (UK), the original name for the 'Metadyne' now occurs in literature even though its derivation has sunk into obscurity!

REFERENCES

1. E. R. Laithwaite, *Induction Machines for Special Purposes*, Newnes, London, and Chemical Publishing Company, New York, 1966.

2. E. R. Laithwaite and R. S. Mamak, 'An oscillating synchronous linear machine', *Proc. IEE*, **109A**(47), 415–26, 1962.
3. R. H. Park, 'Two-reaction theory of synchronous machines—Parts I and II', *Trans. AIEE*, **48**, 716–30, 1929, and **52**, 352–4, 1933.
4. B. Adkins, *The General Theory of Electrical Machines*, Chapman & Hall, London, 1957.
5. W. J. Gibbs, *Tensors in Electrical Machine Theory*, Chapman & Hall, London, 1952.

THE TRANSMISSION OF ELECTRIC ENERGY

6.1 THE TRANSFORMER

6.1.1 Some Topology

Unlike the history of rotating machines, that of transformers has never contained a large amount of topological change. Faraday's original model was a simple ring, as shown in Fig. 6.1(a). For simplicity of core lamination this soon became a square, as shown in (b). Isolated primary and secondary coils give the flux many alternative paths that do not embrace both windings, and a square core in which primary and secondary coils lie on top of each other, as in (c), is an arrangement of lower leakage. It can easily be shown also, that if one coil be divided into two parts that sandwich the other, as shown in (d), then the leakage flux is still lower, and this technique is often used in transformer design. It is, after all, but one step towards the multi-division of the windings of one phase of the stator of rotating a.c. machines, and although the principal reason for such division was seen as the dispersal of heat, nonetheless it also reduces the stator leakage reactance. The magnetic circuit of (d) can be seen to be asymmetric with nearly all the leakage flux occurring on the open side. The 'shell' type of construction shown in (e) is clearly to be preferred. Since the flux along the centre core divides equally at each end, the cross-sectional area of each side limb need only be of the order of one-half that of the centre limb.

With no airgap in the magnetic circuit the quality of the cores of transformers needs special attention, lamination of course being essential for, unlike rotating machines, the iron loss resistor in the equivalent circuit may have a value below that of the magnetizing reactance X_m, because of the improvement in the magnetic circuit brought about by the absence of an airgap.

So far, topologies have been directed towards single-phase transformers.

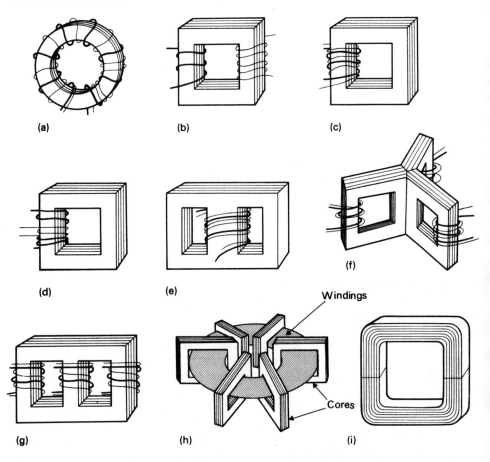

Figure 6.1 Transformer arrangements. (a) Faraday's original transformer. (b) Square ferromagnetic circuit with separate windings. (c) Superimposed primary and secondary. (d) Split primary. (e) 'Shell' type. (f) Three-phase transformer built from three separate single-phase machines (uneconomic and never built commercially). (g) Three-phase, commercial type. (h) Berry type. (i) Modern 'C' core, rolled steel strip construction.

In three-phase designs, one can do much better than to use three separate transformers, even better than employing three cores of the type shown in Fig. 6.1(c) and (d) with a common return limb, as shown in (f), for in a balanced three-phase system the net flux along the common limb is zero, so the core can be eliminated! Where unbalanced conditions exist the core flux will not be the same in all three limbs, but this is no more than that of unequal currents in three-phase transmission lines, or indeed of the windings of the three-phase transformer itself. Unbalance, of course, always involves ineffective use of a part of the materials of apparatus and is therefore to be avoided but not necessarily meticulously so.

The three-phase transformer core therefore emerges as a planar system of

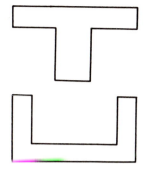

Figure 6.2 Two simple shapes that together form a 'shell' core.

stampings as shown in Fig. 6.1(g), where the cross-sectional areas of all three cores are equal.

First thoughts about how to build a transformer suggest stamping out the complete core shape from steel sheet, with bolt holes at the corners, and making a stack of these to form the magnetic circuit, but at once we see the near impossibility of winding coils in and out of the 'windows' so formed. (The term 'window' is universally accepted for the spaces in the magnetic circuits available for the electric circuits.) If then the core is to be split, the questions are 'where?' and 'how?'. A variation that lasted for over a century is shown in Fig. 6.2. The shapes of individual punchings are known as 'T's' and 'U's' for

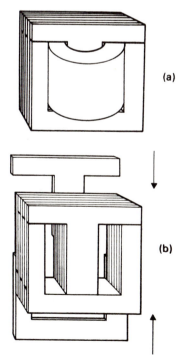

(a)

(b)

Figure 6.3 (a) Two stacks of T's and U's fill and surround the coils. (b) Alternate insertion reduces total reluctance.

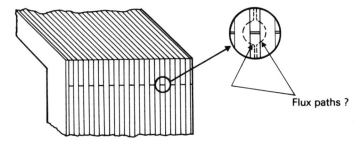

Figure 6.4 The possible 'bridge' action for flux at a corner joint.

obvious reasons. The transformer coils are first wound on a former and the T's are then threaded up the centre and each closed by a U, as shown in Fig. 6.3(a). It was found almost impossible to make good mechanical contact between each T and U pair, so that if all the T's were pushed into the core from one end, the result was a quite large pair of effective airgaps. But if the T's were fed alternately from top and bottom as shown in Fig. 6.3(b) then the resulting equivalent airgap was much reduced. The reason why this is so was the subject of much debate for several decades, for an end view of a joint (enlarged), as in Fig. 6.4, shows that if each continuous part of a U-stamping is to act as 'bridge' across an imperfect joint between the T and U pair on each side of it, the flux is invited to jump from lamination to lamination as shown, and this clearly involves passing through the surfaces of the stampings, a direction known to be capable of inducing substantial eddy currents in the plane of the laminations. In this event one might expect to find the four corners of the steel structure becoming excessively hot. In practice, this is not so! The transformer's action is not so obvious as it might first appear.

An alternative to the T and U stampings is the pairing of an 'E' and an 'I' shape, again alternated, as shown in Fig. 6.5(a). This shape superceded the T and U, largely because the sizes of the various limbs can be designed so that two E-pieces and two I-pieces can be cut from a rectangular sheet entirely without waste, as shown in Fig. 6.5(b), a feat not possible with T and U shapes.

The textbooks of fifty years ago rarely failed to include one other topology for the transformer which represented merely a return to Faraday's anchor ring, and carried the name 'Berry type' transformer (Fig. 6.1(h)). The coils were wound first and the iron strip as it were 'wrapped around the wire'; considered cumbersome to make, it was seldom popular, but modern manufacturing methods have resulted in a return, in part, to this type of construction. The wrapping of steel strip on to a former is a much cheaper process than the stamping out of shapes such as T's and U's or E's and I's. If the core is a rectangle with rounded corners, as shown in Fig. 6.1(i), modern adhesives can hold such a structure rigidly together so that it can then be cut into equal halves as shown, and each half faced off with near optical flatness so that they

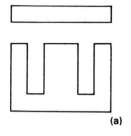

(a)

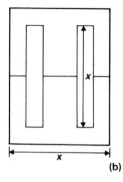

(b)

Figure 6.5 (a) Alternative shapes to the T and U. (b) Preferred dimensions allow matching E- and I-pieces to be cut from a rectangular sheet without waste.

may be clamped around the electric circuits. This topology illustrates a well known but little stated principle of lamination that for a given direction of alternating flux there is always a choice of two axes in which lamination can be made. Only the third orthogonal axis is forbidden. The two alternatives here are exemplified by Fig. 6.1(b) and (c) on the one hand and by (i) on the other.

There is just one other topology in transformer design worthy of mention. Described as an 'open bar' design in early literature, it is shown in Fig. 6.6. The modern engineer is inclined to dismiss such a design as 'ridiculous' in view of 'the enormous airgap that the flux has to cross', 'the disastrously large magnetizing current', and similar phrases. While it is true that the distance from end to end of the core may be ten or more times its thickness and represents the minimum *length* of the magnetic path in air (flux lines that return

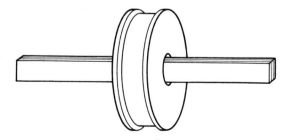

Figure 6.6 An open bar transformer.

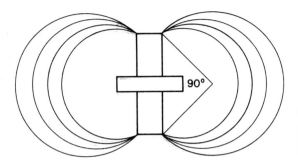

Figure 6.7 Hypothetical flux pattern to form the basis of an approximation to the reluctance in the external space.

a long way out from the bar are longer), the *area* through which the flux can pass stretches to infinity. It is difficult at first sight to reconcile an increased area at the expense of increased length and arrive at any 'common sense' guess as to the equivalent airgap. Let us then merely make one simplification by assuming the bar to be a metre long and to return all its flux within an area defined by Fig. 6.7 in which circular paths are assumed, the longest of which is an arc of some 270°, as shown in Fig. 6.7. It is also assumed that all the flux generated emanates from the ends of the bar. In this way we shall obtain an extremely pessimistic answer for the reluctance of the air path. The maximum path length is easily calculated as $2\pi \times (270 \div 360) \times 0.707\,\text{m} \approx 3.33\,\text{m}$. The path area is $\pi(0.707 + 0.5)^2 \approx 4.6\,\text{m}^2$. The ratio of path length to square root of area is already approaching unity. A larger circle would reduce this ratio below unity, which means that the system has an airgap reluctance less than a ferromagnetic circuit (with $\mu = \infty$), including an airgap–pole dimension of the shape shown in Fig. 6.8(a). The more exact integral for the reluctance has been calculated for a long bar transformer as shown in Fig. 6.6, having a core approximately one metre long and of cross section $6.5\,\text{cm}^2$, carrying coils

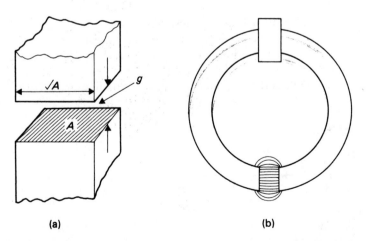

(a)   (b)

Figure 6.8 Equivalent magnetic circuits to those shown in Figs. 6.6 and 6.7.

12.5 cm long, and the magnetic circuit reluctance has been shown to be the equivalent of a ring of steel of the same cross-sectional area with an airgap of the order of 1 mm (Fig. 6.8(b)).[1]

The arguments in favour of the open bar construction were centred around the fact that an airgap in the magnetic circuit meant that fewer and smaller harmonic currents were injected into the system by the nonlinear nature of the *B–H* curve for the steel. The arguments against were that enclosure in a metal tank (not necessarily steel) would result in disastrous losses in the tank. This latter argument, of course, prevailed. But the open bar transformer *did* find application in the new fashion in travel at the turn of the century—the automobile! At the present time a large proportion of all automobiles use an open bar transformer in their coil ignition system.

6.1.2 Principle of Operation

There are many practising power engineers who, if they were honest with themselves, would admit that they had never really appreciated why, when a load current was drawn from the secondary of a transformer, it did not simply shut off the flux. There is no cause for shame in such an admission, for even the Special Theory of Relativity is inadequate to explain the mechanism in purely physical terms. If then we are to proceed from analogy, we are well advised to choose the analogy that makes the explanation most simple.

This is why, in this book, we have used the 'voltage dictates the flux' rule (pages 42, 43), for the action is then obvious. But first let us consider a simple problem using two transformers, intended as a warning against over-confidence in machines that are obviously 'easier' to appreciate than are rotating machines. Two 'perfect' transformers having turns ratios 2:1 and 3:1 respectively have their primary windings connected in series and to a voltage source of 600 V. Their secondary windings are also connected in series, as shown in Fig. 6.9, and the connection sense is such that the open circuit voltage is 240 V. What current will flow when a load resistor of 100 Ω is connected across the secondary pair, i.e., from A to B? What current will flow if the connections to any one of the four windings are reversed? The answers

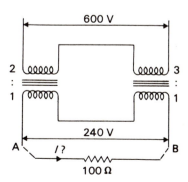

Figure 6.9 A transformer 'puzzle'.

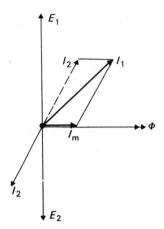

Figure 6.10 Basic phasor diagram of a loaded transformer.

to this problem are preferably given after the theory of operation, for this will be a test of the authors' ability to communicate the theory to the reader!

The primary coil can be seen almost in isolation, having only a resistance and a back e.m.f. due to a changing flux to overcome, whatever is connected to the secondary. Then, looking at the secondary in isolation, it is simply a voltage generator and will supply a current I_2 to an impedance Z according to the law $E_2 = I_2 Z$, provided E_2 is maintained by a constant flux, which we know to exist. Taking now the magnetic circuit's point of view, it will only continue to carry the same flux if the *total* ampere-turns remain constant, which is why the extraction of secondary current necessitates an equal and opposite m.m.f. to exist in the primary. The basic phasor diagram of Fig. 6.10 can be drawn in which I_m is the current needed to maintain a flux Φ, and lags the applied voltage by 90°. The primary current I_1 is then the phasor sum of I_2 reversed and I_m, as shown. This diagram then relates to a transformer that is imperfect only to the extent that it has a magnetic circuit of finite reluctance. At this stage we might draw its equivalent circuit as shown in Fig. 6.11, where the coupled coils are 'perfect' and the load current is delivered to an impedance Z. The rules relating to voltages and currents in the perfect windings are simple to determine, for the magnetic circuit demands that

$$N_1 I_1 = N_2 I_2$$

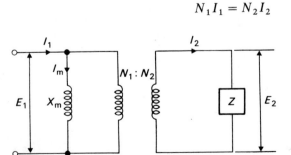

Figure 6.11 Equivalent circuit corresponding to Fig. 6.10.

Further, since the same flux threads both windings, inducing the same volts/turn in each,

$$\frac{E_1}{E_2} = \frac{N_1}{N_2}$$

At this point it is convenient to use the technique of 'lumping of impedances' (Chapter 3, page 82), at the same time noting that the argument can be applied in either direction and primary impedances can be lumped into the secondary by multiplying by $(N_2/N_1)^2$. We recommend that whenever you are in doubt as to whether to multiply by $(N_1/N_2)^2$ or by $(N_2/N_1)^2$, you use *reductio ad absurdum* again and imagine a ridiculous situation where a transformer has a thousand turns on its primary and a single-turn secondary. Since ampere-turns must equate (except for $N_1 I_m$), the secondary winding must be exceedingly thick and its resistance tiny. Its volt drop is still the volts per turn, so when its resistance is lumped into the primary it must appear big enough to absorb at least a few per cent of the total voltage and therefore must be 1000^2 times as resistive. It could not possibly be a tiny resistance *divided* by a million!

The extension of the theory of the transformer to the case of imperfect windings that produce leakage flux and have resistance is very simple. *IR* voltages will be in phase with the *I*, *IX* voltages will be in quadrature. Secondary *IR* and *IX* voltages will *subtract* from the E_2, those of the primary will *add* to the E_1, and the phasor diagram of Fig. 6.10 becomes that of Fig. 6.12 with one further addition of an iron loss current I_L in phase with E_1. I_L and I_m are often shown combined to give I_0, the latter being in effect the no-

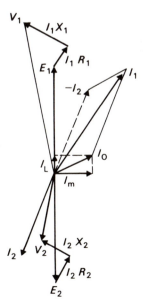

Figure 6.12 Complete phasor diagram.

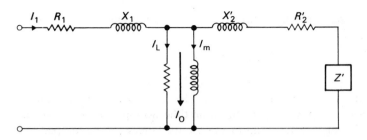

Figure 6.13 Equivalent circuit corresponding to Fig. 6.12.

load current (neglecting $I_0 R_1$ and $I_0 X_1$). The equivalent circuit of Fig. 6.11 merely requires the R and X values to be added as in Fig. 6.13.

Now to the solutions of the problems posed by Fig. 6.9. Whichever way round the connections are made, so long as the primaries and the secondaries are in series, no current can ever be delivered from AB! The equivalent circuit of the device is a voltage source of 600 V in series with an infinite reactance. The reasoning is as follows. Series connection of the primaries demands the same current through each and the secondary voltage observed suggests that we are to assume that the 600 V is divided between the two primaries in the ratio 2:3, but this is only in the absence of current. Series connection of the secondaries demands the same current through each, if any is to flow at all. Perfect transformers must have an ampere-turn balance. Two equal numbers, one of which is multiplied by 2 and the other by 3, cannot yield equal answers. No finite current, therefore, can ever flow and the 'appearance' from the input terminals is that of an open circuit. The dual connection is one in which the two primaries are in parallel and the two secondaries are in parallel. Since voltages are proportional to numbers of turns, the flux is, in effect, being asked to have two different values at one and the same time. The system will react by drawing infinite current and its input impedance will appear to be zero without any load being connected. It *has* to be like that; electromagnetic things have a habit of pairing.

6.1.3 The Design of Transformers

It is clear that the voltage ratio is only determined by the turns ratio of the two windings. In Section 2.7 it was shown that the *number* of turns on each winding was determined by the relative prices of steel and copper. It is often a good idea to work out a numerical example or two, even when studying purely theoretical techniques. In a 2:1 stepdown transformer, having only one turn on the primary and two turns on the secondary and in which the actual voltages involved are 1000 V and 500 V, for example, the 500 V per turn must be balanced by a rate of change of flux. A flux $\phi = \Phi \sin \omega t$ has a rate of change equal to $\omega \Phi \cos \omega t$, which must be equal to 500 (r.m.s.). Hence, for a 50 Hz supply $\Phi/\sqrt{2} = 500/100\pi$ and Φ is equal to the flux density B times the area of

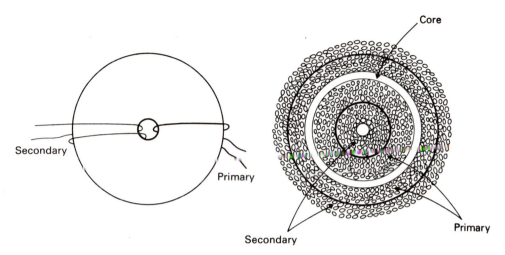

Figure 6.14 Two unacceptable designs for a transformer.

the core in m². Assuming B to have a maximum value of 2.0 T, the area A of core required is given by $\sqrt{2A} = 5/\pi$ or $A = 1.13\,\text{m}^2$. If the transformer is required to deliver 2 amps from the secondary, the wire diameter need be no more than 0.4 mm, and a transformer handling only 1.0 kVA contains over 20 tonnes of steel and just over 10 grams of copper! At the other end of the scale, a transformer of this rating having a million turns of wire on the primary and half a million on the secondary would need at least the same thickness of wire and therefore a pair of coils of minimum cross-sectional area 0.15 m² each with a mass of around 6 tonnes. The steel core would need a cross-sectional area of only 1/60 cm² and weigh about 30 grams. Figure 6.14 shows the two equally unacceptable designs compared with a well designed transformer for 1.0 kV A.

Now there are some authors who declare that the criterion for the optimum design is that of maximum efficiency on full load. Their calculations proceed as follows.

For fixed voltage, and therefore fixed flux, and frequency, the iron losses are fixed. The copper losses are load current dependent as I^2R. Thus the efficiency is given by

$$\eta = \frac{\text{output}}{\text{output} + \text{losses}} = \frac{EI\cos\phi}{EI\cos\phi + I^2R + Fe}$$

where Fe is the fixed iron loss. A straight differentiation of η with respect to I reveals $I^2R = Fe$ or fixed loss = variable loss, a common result in everyday things. But a plot of η against I for a typical large transformer reveals a curve of the form shown in Fig. 6.15, and the efficiency may vary as little as $\frac{1}{4}\%$ between 70% full load and 30% overload. Figure 6.14 contains the true answer as to the proportions of copper and steel and therefore the actual numbers of turns used. The relative costs of iron and copper at the time of

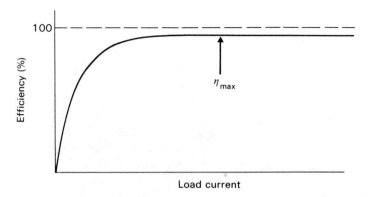

Figure 6.15 The very 'flat' efficiency–load curve of a well designed transformer.

design have a much greater influence than considerations of efficiency. The designer can, by choice of numbers of turns alone, bias a design towards a 'copper' machine (more copper than iron) or an 'iron' machine, depending on market prices.

6.1.4 Transformer Testing

Simple tests on a transformer are based on the fact that with no secondary load current, the input (magnetizing) current is only a few per cent of full load, and the I^2R loss is therefore negligible. An 'open circuit test' with a wattmeter

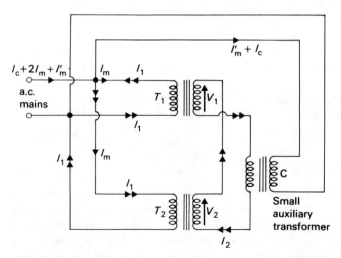

Figure 6.16 The Sumpner 'back-to-back' test for large transformers T_1 and T_2. Full load currents are shown double arrowed. The total power drawn from the mains is very small compared with the *circulating* power.

in the primary will record the iron loss with adequate accuracy. If then the secondary is short circuited (a 'short circuit test') a greatly reduced voltage (again a few per cent of the operating voltage) will pass full load current through both windings and the wattmeter will read the full load copper losses. Efficiency at full voltage and variable load is then easily predictable.

What the open and short circuit tests will not reveal is the ability of the transformer to dissipate its losses without excessive temperature rise. Thermocouples can be incorporated in the structure but the problem of testing is how to dispose of perhaps 100 MV A of output during the test. The problem is solved by making large transformers in pairs (A and B) and connecting them 'back to back' as shown in Fig. 6.16. A relatively very small transformer C is sufficient to drive full load current around both transformers each of which is working at full voltage, and a heat run lasting many hours is achieved for a very small power consumption. The method is accredited to Sumpner. Similar tests for d.c. rotary machines were first performed by Hopkinson in the last century, and much more recently current collection tests at 500 km/h have been performed by a similar 'put in, take off' technique enabling currents corresponding to 17 MW of power at full voltage to be made.[2]

6.1.5 Three-phase Transformers

This section deals specifically with methods of interconnection of three-phase transformers. Either primaries or secondaries can be connected in star or in delta, as shown diagrammatically in Fig. 6.17. But a star–star transformer may not be connected in parallel with a star–delta connected machine, even though primary and secondary line voltages on both primary and secondary sides are identical in magnitude. The reason is shown in Fig. 6.18, which is a phasor diagram for the two transformer secondaries. The red phase of the primary is to be identified as anti-phase in the secondary, wherever that winding appears, and there is therefore a 30° phase shift in all three line voltages between one transformer and the other.

Although engineers attempt to balance the loads on all three phases, there are inevitable periods when imbalance must exist and this has the effect,

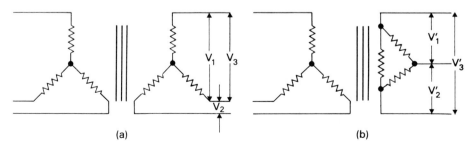

Figure 6.17 Three-phase transformer connections. (a) star–star, (b) star–delta.

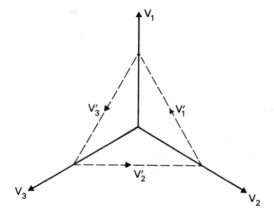

Figure 6.18 Phasor diagram of voltage outputs from a star–star (full lines) and star–delta (dotted) transformer. R_1 and R_2 may be equal in magnitude but will always differ in phase.

through unequal internal impedance voltage drops, of distorting the position of the neutral, thus escalating the effects of internal impedance. Two methods of reducing this effect are used, both of which also assist in eliminating any third harmonic voltages that might have been introduced by saturation or other effects. The first of these is called the 'zig-zag' connection, and is illustrated in Fig. 6.19. Each winding is split into two halves and interconnected as shown. It should be noted at once that this produces an identical phase shift of 30° as if the zig-zag winding had delta connected characteristics. Unlike the delta connection, however, the zig-zag connection does have a neutral point available for earthing or for the extraction of phase voltages, if required. Figure 6.20 shows how a single-phase load (the most extreme case of unbalance) is handled by a star–zig-zag connected

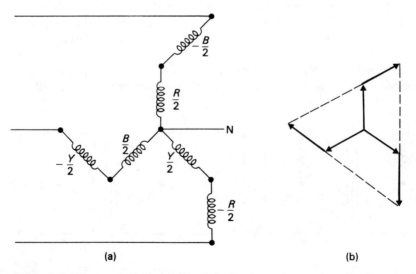

(a) (b)

Figure 6.19 Zig-zag connection; (a) schematic, (b) phasor diagram.

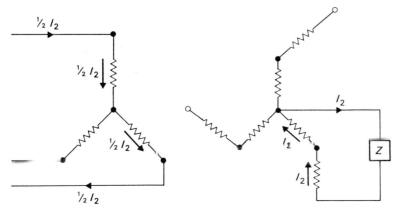

Figure 6.20 Zig-zag connection on single-phase load. The single secondary coil load is shared by two phases in the primary.

transformer. What would otherwise have been a 1, 0, 0 load is reflected into the primary as a 1, 1, 0 load—not ideal, but certainly improved. So far as harmonic suppression is concerned, a series connection of a red phased coil with a negative blue phased coil, and all similar connections, eliminates third harmonics as illustrated in Fig. 5.11.

The second method involves the inclusion of a third set of windings that are connected in delta—the 'tertiary delta', as shown diagrammatically in Fig. 6.21. Here the three sets of third harmonics are put in series with each other and in phase in the tertiary delta winding, which therefore acts as a short circuit to this frequency. So far as unbalanced loads are concerned, the tertiary delta achieves an even better primary load distribution than does the zig-zag connection. Figure 6.21 shows how a 1, 0, 0 load is transformed into a $\frac{1}{2}, \frac{1}{2}, \frac{1}{2}$ distribution, by causing a current $\frac{1}{2}I_2$ to circulate in the tertiary winding. It can be seen that the total currents in each phase of the secondary and tertiary

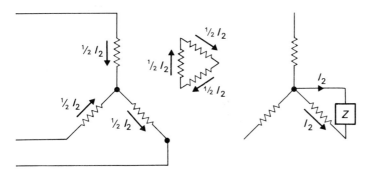

Figure 6.21 Tertiary delta transformer under unbalanced load. Both the primary proper and the tertiary delta are to be regarded as 'primaries'.

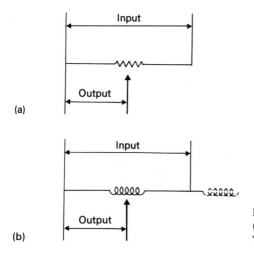

Figure 6.22 Potential dividers; (a) resistive, (b) reactive, generally known as an 'autotransformer'.

combined are equal and opposite to those in the primary. The tertiary delta is usually a low voltage winding whose terminals might be used for the supply of local lighting circuits, etc.

6.2 VARIABLE RATIO TRANSFORMERS

6.2.1 The Autotransformer

A great deal of ingenuity has been used in producing a device that has the characteristics of a transformer with an adjustable turns ratio. In d.c. technology the potential divider (Fig. 6.22(a)) is well known but only useful for small applications in view of the losses in the potentiometer resistance itself and the large voltage drops on load. But where a.c. is involved the resistor can be replaced by a tapped inductor (Fig. 6.22(b)) that incurs very little I^2R loss. What is more, it will achieve what no resistance potentiometer can ever do in that the output voltage can exceed the input voltage, provided extra turns are added beyond the span of the input (as shown dotted), and this is possible because all the turns are made to embrace a common ferromagnetic circuit (not shown in Fig. 6.22(b)).

The only disadvantages in this device are first that it is merely an 'autotransformer' in which primary and secondary circuits cannot be isolated (for example in relation to their potential above earth) and second that the output is obtained via a rubbing contact, which always carries penalties in terms of wear, sparking, mechanical weakness, and so on. Slide contact auto-transformers are common however, in sizes up to 415 volts, 30 amps, 3-phase.

6.2.2 Tap Changing

For large power transformers a compromise is effected by restricting the rubbing contact operation to movement from stud to stud in a discrete

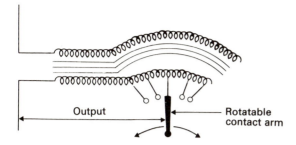

Figure 6.23 Tap changing transformer for adjustable voltage.

number of steps, as shown in Fig. 6.23, and this can be further restricted, if necessary, to periods when the transformer is de-energized (off-load tap changing). The two-winding facility is now retained, so that primary and secondary circuits can be isolated. But it should not be forgotten that the autotransformer, especially when used without the sliding contact facility, carries one advantage over two-winding transformers in that the total I^2R loss is less than that of an equivalent, two-winding device. Consider the two arrangements shown in Fig. 6.24. For simplicity let us assume that the wire section is such as to give the same current density in all parts of each machine. Thus, for (a) the resistance per turn of the primary, R_1, is equal to $(N_1/N_2)^2R_2$, where R_2 is the resistance of the secondary, per turn. Since $N_1I_1 = N_2I_2$, the I^2R losses in primary and secondary are equal, each being $I_1^2N_1R_1$. If the autotransformer is wound with the same number of 'primary' turns, i.e., from A to B (Fig. 6.24(b)), only the part between B and C carries the current I_1. Between A and C, the current is seen to be I_2-I_1, which means that if $I_2 < 2I_1$, the current in AC is less than I_1 and the total I^2R losses in the whole machine are less than those in the primary winding *alone* of the two-winding equivalent and the volume of copper in the whole autotransformer is only one-half that in the two-winding equivalent. What is more usual, however, is to take all the benefit in terms of copper volume so that the winding AC is $(I_2-I_1)/I_1$ times the sectional area of the coils in BC. The ratio of copper volume in the autotransformer to that in the two-winding transformer is therefore

$$\frac{N_2(I_2-I_1)+(N_1-N_2)I_1}{N_1I_1+N_2I_2} = \frac{N_1-N_2}{N_1}$$

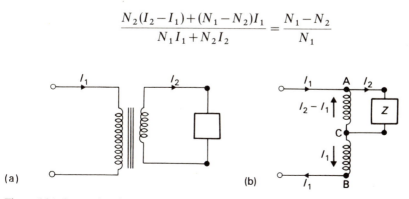

Figure 6.24 Comparison between two-winding and autotransformers under fixed load.

Clearly the greatest benefits accrue as $N_2 \to N_1$, for if $N_2 = N_1$, there is no need for an autotransformer at all!

6.2.3 The Moving Coil Regulator

This machine, frequently omitted from books on a.c. machines, embodies so many of the 'rarer' principles encountered that it might well be considered to be a summary in itself of the physical appreciation of electromagnetic principles. First, it is an example of a machine that employs parallel magnetic circuits and is therefore much more easily treated by the equivalent magnetic circuit technique. Second, it illustrates most forcefully the role of *duals* in electromagnetism, for despite the incorporation of a large *short circuited* winding that embraces the main magnetic circuit, very large machines with efficiencies in the 'high 90 per cent' region are possible. In the series electric world (the dual of the parallel magnetic) the short circuit is a 'friend', the open circuit an 'enemy'. Third, it illustrates the empirical rule: 'Short circuited iron is equivalent to free space.'

The moving coil regulator provides continuous voltage variation right down to zero, without resorting to rubbing contacts.

By way of a simple introduction we will first consider the structures illustrated in Fig. 6.25, emphasizing that such a situation contains only the *elements* of the more sophisticated commercial versions. The short circuiting loop can be moved up and down the left hand limb. When it is over the primary, as in (a), it passes a huge current, but the primary 'underwrites' this in full and still demands (in the absence of primary I^2R drop) the full volts/turn and hence continues to light the lamp connected to the secondary. But when the loop is over the secondary, as in (b), all the flux from the primary finds alternative paths, as shown, in a magnetic circuit designed specially to 'leak' insofar as it has a relatively short length of air, of large area.

Clearly, the enormous short circuit current could not be tolerated in a

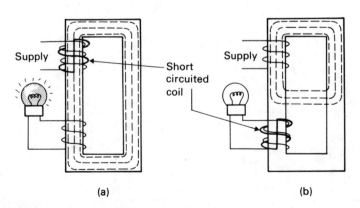

Figure 6.25 Introduction to the moving coil regulator.

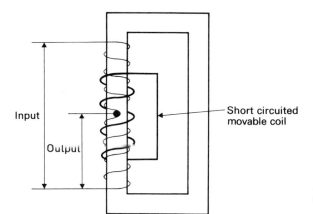

Input

Output

Short circuited
movable coil

Figure 6.26 Schematic diagram
of the windings of a moving coil
regulator.

large commercial machine, but the system becomes viable when the primary winding is made to extend all the way down the limb, to reverse direction at the centre, and to be connected as an autotransformer with the lower half as secondary. The short circuited loop becomes extended into a short circuited coil of half the length of the primary and Fig. 6.26 shows a schematic of the whole arrangement.

It can be seen at once that there will always be some turns of the primary and/or secondary *in series* with the portion opposite the shorted coil, hence the absence of what is normally meant by a 'short circuited' coil. The simplest explanation is now that of equivalent magnetic circuits as shown in Fig. 6.27. In (a) a model of the magnetic circuit reveals a distributed primary–secondary m.m.f. interlaced with parallel reluctances representing the airgap between left and right hand limbs of the core. The short circuited coil becomes a series of transferances per turn of $\mathscr{L}_0 = 1/R_0$ where R_0 is very small, i.e., the system is equivalent to a virtually open magnetic circuit between the ends of the shorted coil. At this stage, the distributed parameters can be reduced to single elements as shown in (b), where $\mathscr{L}_{0T}$ is the sum of all elements $\mathscr{L}_0$ and in theory infinitely large. As the shorted coil is moved, the position of the series of transferances $\mathscr{L}_0$ moves and effectively alters the number of turns N_1 and N_2 on (b). On reconversion to an electric circuit the system becomes simply that shown in (c), with the ratio N_1/N_2 infinitely variable. The short circuited loop does therefore effectively produce a semi-infinite transferance $\mathscr{L}_{0T}$, as would free space, but the electrical connection between turns N_1 and N_2 remains as a tapping point.

An excellent treatment of the moving coil regulator not using magnetic equivalent circuits is to be found in a paper by Rawcliffe and Smith[3] in which they show that the short circuited coil, far from passing normal short circuit current, acts as a second primary, inductively fed, having a current proportional to load current. Their treatment is based entirely on the concept of mutual inductances between the three pairs of windings.

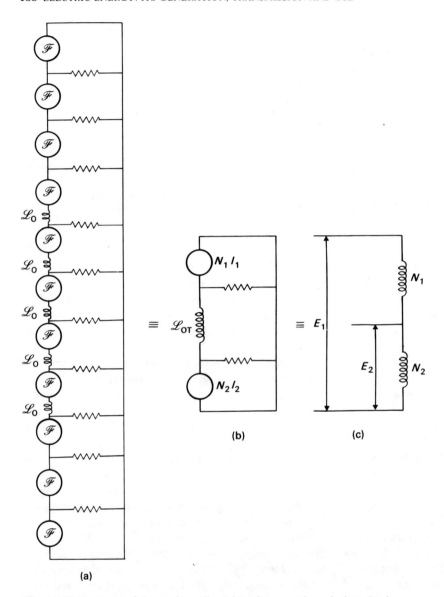

(a)

(b)

(c)

Figure 6.27 Treatment of the moving coil regulator by magnetic equivalent circuit.

Three-phase versions of the moving coil regulator are manufactured, but unlike the diagram of Fig. 6.1(f) the elimination of a common return flux path is not possible as each limb must be allowed to 'leak' on its own and the machine is therefore simply a combination of three single-phase regulators with all three moving coils mechanically coupled. A small pilot motor is usually employed to move the shorted coils.

6.3 THE TRANSMISSION LINE

6.3.1 Introduction

Figure 1.4 shows that electrical energy is transferred from generating stations to consumers through overhead lines and underground cables.

Overhead lines are ideally suited for energy transfer in open country and rural areas, whereas underground cables are ideal for built-up areas. For the same power rating the cost ratio between underground cables and overhead lines is in the region of 10 to 15. Therefore there is a strong incentive to use in a particular system as much overhead line as is practicable. It is interesting to note that the fundamental reason behind this is that overhead lines are immersed in a reasonably good insulation material, i.e., air, while underground cables are imbedded in a good conductor—wet earth. Of course, we capitalize on the latter when we use earth return systems. The high cost of underground cables is not only that of digging trenches, but the cost of very substantial insulating material.

The capital expenditure on the transmission network of a typical power system is about as much as that on the distribution network, the expenditure on both networks being about equal to that of all the generating stations. The capital investment on a planned transmission line may represent millions of pounds or dollars. As shown in Fig. 2.18, transmission line engineers seek an optimum design in which the fixed costs (these include expenditure on conductors, insulators, towers, and substation erection, as well as land costs) plus the variable costs due to energy loss total a minimum. From such studies, a design will be arrived at so that the line will satisfy the required performance without having too high a factor of safety and therefore be too expensive or too low a factor and hence likely to be unreliable. Figure 2.19 illustrates this cumulative experience resulting from such studies.

Overhead line practice encompasses voltages between 120 V and 765 kV, while lines up to 1.5 MV are being considered for the future. For convenience we can label line voltages as follows:

Low voltage (l.v.) distribution	110 V to 415 V
High voltage (h.v.) distribution and subtransmission	6.6 kV to 70 kV
Extra high voltage (e.h.v.) transmission	110 kV to 500 kV
Ultra high voltage (u.h.v.) transmission	735 kV to 1500 kV

The design of lines at the lower end of the voltage scale has become standardized and there are very few basic problems to be resolved. In the u.h.v. range, however, a considerable amount of research and development is being carried out.

6.3.2 Electrical Characteristics

Transmission lines have resistance R due to the resistivity of the conductor, shunt conductance G due to leakage currents in the insulation, inductance L

due to the magnetic field surrounding the conductors, and capacitance C due to the electric field between conductors.

The line parameters determine its performance and equivalent circuits can be set up that enable us to represent the line as lumped components in a power system network. This is of great importance since such power system networks are used to study the flow of active and reactive power, the stability of the system and its performance under fault conditions, and the way the system should be operated to make the cost of generation a minimum.

It is the usual practice for books on power systems to derive from first principles the line parameters. This topic is invariably covered in elementary courses on fields, network theory, or transmission line theory. It seems superfluous to repeat here this material, which is part of general electric theory rather than specifically of power systems. Instead, a short summary of the salient points relating to line parameters is given.

Line resistance and conductance These are the least important of line parameters as they affect the transmission line performance to a small degree. In power lines the effect of shunt conductance is small and is usually neglected. However, for short lines, for which under emergency conditions the loading may be limited by the conductor temperature rise, the series resistance plays an important part in defining the line active power loss and therefore its value should be known. If a calculation involving loss minimization or optimum economic operation is to be undertaken the line resistances should also be known.

The effective a.c. resistance of small diameter conductors at power frequencies is very nearly equal to the d.c. resistance. However, as the conductor cross section increases, the distribution of current becomes non-uniform. This phenomenon is called 'skin effect'. It is caused by the fact that portions of the conductor near the periphery are linked with fewer flux lines than portions near the conductor centre. Since the inductance of a conductor element is proportional to the flux linkages per ampere, the inner areas of the conductor possess higher inductance than the outer areas and the current tends to congregate in the region of the conductor skin. This reduces the effective area and hence increases the effective resistance of the conductor.

The resistance of lines is determined from manufacturers' tables where allowance is made for stranding, composite conductors, and skin effect. Resistance of transmission lines ranges from 0.5 to 0.015 Ω/km, the lower resistance being that of e.h.v. overhead and underground lines.

A typical ratio of a.c. to d.c. resistances at 50 Hz of a 2.5 cm diameter copper conductor is 1.05.

The shunt conductance represents loss due to leakage currents along insulator strings and due to corona, about which more will be said later. There are no reliable data on shunt conductance G of overhead lines as this is heavily dependent on atmospheric conditions and pollution. In the case of underground cables, data are given in manufacturers' tables and represent the loss of the dielectric material.

Line inductance Detailed derivations for the inductance of transmission lines can be found in standard textbooks.[4-6] In such derivations both the partial flux linkages within the conductor cross section and the external flux linkages are taken into account. The inductance of a single-phase transmission line consisting of two conductors of radius r and spacing d is given by

$$L = \frac{\mu_0}{\pi} \ln \frac{d}{R} \text{ H/m} \tag{6.1}$$

where $R = e^{-0.25} \times r = 0.779r$.

Radius R is known as the geometric mean radius (g.m.r.) and represents the radius of a hollow conductor of thickness small enough for no internal flux linkages to be present. Equation 6.1 is valid where the relative permeability of the conductor is unity.

For a three-phase overhead line, the inductance of each phase is different unless the three conductors occupy the vertices of an equilateral triangle, a geometry not usually adopted in practice. To equalize the inductance of the three phases with non-equilateral spacing, the lines are transposed in such a way that each phase occupies successively all three possible locations.

For a transposed three-phase line the inductance per phase is

$$L = \frac{\mu_0}{2\pi} \ln \frac{D}{R} \text{ H/m} \tag{6.2}$$

where R is again the g.m.r., which, if supplied by the manufacturers, takes into account not only the internal inductance but also the composition and stranding effect of the conductor, and D is the geometric mean distance (g.m.d.). This is a function of the distances d between the conductors of the three phases a, b, and c given by

$$D = \sqrt[3]{(d_{ab} \times d_{bc} \times d_{ca})} \tag{6.3}$$

The reactance per phase of overhead lines at 50 Hz ranges in practice between 0.2 and 0.5 Ω/km.

The inductance of cables is complicated by the magnetic interaction between the conductor and sheath.[7] The reactance of e.h.v. cables at 50 Hz ranges between 0.13 and 0.22 Ω/km.

Line capacitance As for the inductance, the derivations can be found in references 4 to 6. On the assumption that the radius of the line conductor is considerably smaller than the distance d between the two conductors of a single-phase line, the capacitance is given by

$$C = \frac{\pi \varepsilon}{\ln D/r} \text{ F/m} \tag{6.4}$$

For a three-phase overhead line, the capacitance of each phase is again different unless the spacing is equilateral or the line is transposed. For a transposed line the capacitance of each phase to neutral is given to a reasonable approximation by

$$C_n = \frac{2\pi\varepsilon}{\ln D/r} \text{ F/m} \tag{6.5}$$

where D is the g.m.d. given by Eq. (6.3).

The capacitive reactance at 50 Hz of e.h.v. lines is of the order of 0.2 MΩ/km.

In the case of cables, the capacitance of the core to the screen is given again by Eq. (6.5) but r and D are now the inner and outer radii of the dielectric and $\varepsilon = \varepsilon_0 \varepsilon_r$ where ε_r is the relative permittivity of the dielectric. The capacitive reactance of e.h.v. cables at 50 Hz is of the order of 4 kΩ/km.

The presence of the earth's surface, which is virtually an equipotential, will influence the electric flux lines between conductors and therefore the capacitance per phase. The problem of calculating the capacitance of a line in the presence of the earth can be solved very neatly using the idea of 'images'. Again, the analysis can be found in standard textbooks on transmission lines or power systems.[5,6]

6.3.3 The Transmission Line Analogue

Whether the transmission line is overhead or underground, its four electrical characteristics R, L, C, and G are distributed evenly along the line length. Figure 6.28 illustrates an approximation of this distributed nature. The larger the number of the lumped parameter sections, the nearer we approach the true distributed nature of the line.

The relationship between the terminal voltages and currents of a perfectly distributed transmission line can be arrived at through differential calculus. Again, this is a topic of general transmission line theory and is usually covered in basic courses on electrical networks and electromagnetism.

With the exception of the study of transients in power networks, a topic not dealt with in this introductory book, the relationships referred to above are not of vital interest in steady state studies, and the exact equations are therefore not included.

From first sight, it seems reasonable to set up for a transmission line an equivalent circuit that has a lumped series resistance and inductance equal to the resistance and inductance per unit length multiplied by the line length. The shunt capacitance and conductance can be similarly calculated. This very 'lumpy' approximation is adequate for short and medium length lines but for long lines the accuracy is poor, and the distributed constant analysis has to be applied. In fact, there is no definite length boundary between medium and short or long lines but, as a general guide, lines up to about 60 km may be considered short and above 250 km long.

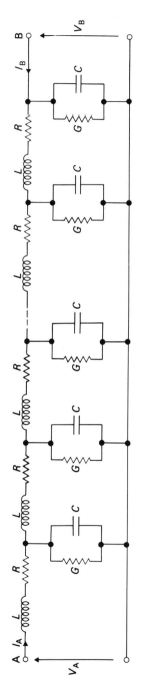

Figure 6.28 Representation of a distributed constant line.

193

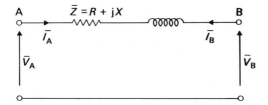

Figure 6.29 Equivalent circuit of a short transmission line.

6.3.4 The Short Line

In short transmission lines the shunt components can be neglected, as the current they absorb is only a fraction of one per cent of the line rated current. The equivalent circuit per phase under balanced three-phase conditions is shown in Fig. 6.29. In Chapter 4 the active and reactive power transfer over such an impedance Z linking voltages V_A and V_B was extensively investigated. For e.h.v. and u.h.v. lines the ratio X/R is in the region 5–15, the higher the line voltage the higher the ratio. In such cases, and where great precision is not required, the resistance can be altogether neglected.

Because of the constant voltage nature of power networks, the per unit drop of voltage across the line, known as 'regulation', is important and will be investigated. With a load of lagging power factor connected across terminals B, i.e., dispatch of reactive power from A to B over the line, the phasor diagram is as shown in Fig. 6.30(a). As the power angle δ is usually small, the projection of $\bar{V}_A$ along $\bar{V}_B$ is very nearly equal to $|\bar{V}_A|$ itself, therefore, numerically,

$$V_A = OC = V_B + ab + bc$$
$$= V_B + I_A R \cos\theta + I_A X \sin\theta$$
$$= V_B + I_A (R \cos\theta + X \sin\theta) \tag{6.6}$$

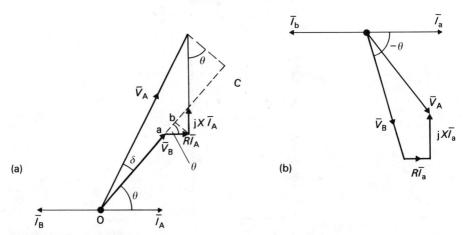

Figure 6.30 Phasor diagrams of a short transmission line. (a) Dispatch of Q from A to B. (b) Dispatch of Q from B to A.

The per unit voltage regulation is defined as the change in voltage from no-load to full load, expressed on the base of the full load voltage. The percentage voltage regulation is given by

$$\text{percentage regulation} = \frac{V_A - V_B}{V_B} \times 100 \qquad (6.7)$$

From Eqs. (6.6) and (6.7) we can write

$$\text{percentage regulation} \simeq \frac{I_A(R\cos\theta + X\sin\theta)}{V_B} \times 100 \qquad (6.8)$$

Usually the maximum voltage regulation of low and medium voltage transmission lines is 10 per cent. For 400 kV and higher voltage lines it is nearer 5 per cent and in many cases lines are operated with zero regulation. The desirability of low voltage regulation is implicit in the analysis of Chapter 4, where it was shown that large voltage differences at the two ends of a line mean large reactive power transfer, high transmission losses, and reduction of active power transfer capability.

With a load of leading power factor connected across terminals B, i.e., dispatch of reactive power from B to A over the line, the phasor diagram is as shown in Fig. 6.30(b). Angle θ is now negative and the regulation, as can be confirmed from Eq. (6.6), may also be negative. A leading power factor load may therefore result in an increase of voltage across the load terminals. This phenomenon was first noticed by Ferranti on overhead transmission lines supplying a lightly loaded and therefore highly capacitive cable network; it is therefore sometimes referred to as the 'Ferranti effect'.

Recalling the two-port generalized relationship

$$\begin{bmatrix} \bar{V}_A \\ \bar{I}_A \end{bmatrix} = \begin{bmatrix} A & B \\ C & D \end{bmatrix} \begin{bmatrix} \bar{V}_B \\ \bar{I}_B \end{bmatrix}$$

from inspection of Fig. 6.29 we can write for a short line

$$A = 1, \quad B = -\bar{Z}, \quad C = 0, \quad D = -1$$

6.3.5 The Medium Line

With a line length between 60 and 250 km the shunt capacitance cannot be neglected. The equivalent circuit of Fig. 6.29 is now augmented with shunt components to form the π-equivalent of Fig. 6.31(a). Admittance Y here represents the admittance per phase to neutral for the total length of the line. Alternatively, the series components could be divided into two equal parts and combined with one lumped shunt admittance to form the T-equivalent of Fig. 6.31(b). Of the two versions, the π-equivalent is of more general use. Also, the analysis of Chapter 4 can be readily applied to the π-equivalent, with the proviso that the reactive powers at ends A and B are augmented by $V_A^2 Y/2$ and $V_B^2 Y/2$, respectively.

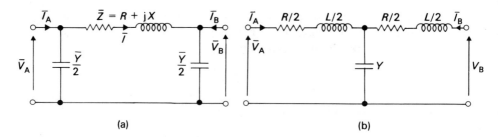

Figure 6.31 Equivalent circuits of a medium length line.

The two-port constants in this case can be found as follows:

$$\bar{V}_A = \bar{I}\bar{Z} + \bar{V}_B \qquad \text{but} \qquad \bar{I} = \bar{V}_B\frac{\bar{Y}}{2} - \bar{I}_B$$

therefore

$$\bar{V}_A = \left(\bar{V}_B\frac{\bar{Y}}{2} - \bar{I}_B\right)\bar{Z} + \bar{V}_B = \left(1 + \frac{\bar{Z}\bar{Y}}{2}\right)\bar{V}_B - \bar{Z}\bar{I}_B$$

Also

$$\bar{I}_A = \bar{I} + \bar{V}_A\frac{\bar{Y}}{2} = \bar{V}_B\frac{\bar{Y}}{2} - \bar{I}_B + \left[\left(1 + \frac{\bar{Z}\bar{Y}}{2}\right)\bar{V}_B - \bar{Z}\bar{I}_B\right]\frac{\bar{Y}}{2}$$

$$= \left(1 + \frac{\bar{Z}\bar{Y}}{4}\right)\bar{Y}\bar{V}_B - \left(1 + \frac{\bar{Z}\bar{Y}}{2}\right)\bar{I}_B$$

therefore

$$A = \left(1 + \frac{\bar{Z}\bar{Y}}{2}\right) = -D, \quad B = -\bar{Z}, \quad C = \left(1 + \frac{\bar{Z}\bar{Y}}{4}\right)\bar{Y}$$

6.3.6 The Long Line

The rigorous analysis of voltage and current in a line with distributed constants leads to differential equations that give the values of voltage and current at any point on the line. For steady state analysis we are interested in the voltage–current relationship at the line terminals and these equations turn out to contain hyperbolic functions.[4-7] From these two-port relationships, the π-equivalent circuit of Fig. 6.32 can be derived that exactly relates the

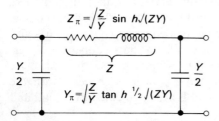

Figure 6.32 Equivalent circuit of a long line.

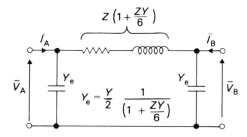

$$Z\left(1 + \frac{ZY}{6}\right)$$

$$Y_e = \frac{Y}{2} \cdot \frac{1}{\left(1 + \frac{ZY}{6}\right)}$$

Figure 6.33 Approximate equivalent circuit of a long line.

input–output quantities. As expected, the elements of the π-network consist of hyperbolic functions of the total series impedance Z and total shunt admittance Y of the line. The equivalent circuit of Fig. 6.32 represents exactly the cumulative effect of an infinite number of cascaded π-sections as in Fig. 6.28.

A convenient way to handle the hyperbolic functions is to use the appropriate series expansion and retain the minimum number of terms necessary to achieve the required accuracy. For most applications and up to line lengths of 400 km, the equivalent circuit of Fig. 6.33, in which only the first two terms have been retained, will provide acceptable results. The accuracy can easily be tested by evaluating the term $\bar{Y}\bar{Z}/6$ and comparing it with unity. In fact, for medium lines this term becomes so small—a fraction of one per cent—that the equivalent circuit reverts to the simple π-equivalent of Fig. 6.31(a).

Example 6.1

Determine the T-circuit equivalent to the equivalent π for a medium line and show that it is not the same as the T of Fig. 6.31(b).

Which of the two equivalents of Fig. 6.31 is likely to indicate the greater value for the line regulation?

Using delta–star transformation to convert the equivalent π-circuit of

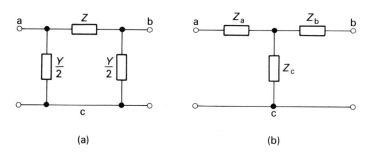

(a)   (b)

Figure 6.34 Example 6.1. (a) Equivalent π-circuit, (b) T-circuit equivalent.

Fig. 6.34 into a T-circuit equivalent,

$$Z_a = \frac{Z_{ab} \times Z_{ca}}{Z_{ab} + Z_{bc} + Z_{ca}} = \frac{Z \times \dfrac{2}{Y}}{Z + \dfrac{4}{Y}} = \frac{Z}{2} \frac{1}{\left(1 + \dfrac{ZY}{4}\right)} = Z_b$$

$$Z_c = \frac{Z_{ca} \times Z_{bc}}{Z_{ab} + Z_{bc} + Z_{ca}} = \frac{4/Y^2}{Z + (4/Y)} = \frac{1}{Y} \frac{1}{\left(1 + \dfrac{ZY}{4}\right)}$$

Therefore the T-circuit equivalent has elements that are $1/(1 + ZY/4)$ times the elements of the T of Fig. 6.31(b).

This discrepancy arises from the fact that both equivalents of Fig. 6.31 are approximations of the distributed nature of the line represented exactly only by Fig. 6.32.

As far as the regulation is concerned, and assuming negligible series resistance, $Z = j\omega L$ and $Y = j\omega C$; therefore $YZ = -\omega^2 LC$, thus

$$\frac{1}{1 + \dfrac{ZY}{4}} = \frac{1}{1 - \dfrac{\omega^2 LC}{4}} > 1$$

Hence both Z_a and Z_b are larger than $Z/2$; therefore the equivalent-π of Fig. 6.31(a) is likely to indicate a greater value for line regulation than the equivalent-T of Fig. 6.31(b).

6.3.7 Construction Aspects of Overhead Transmission Lines

The design and construction of an overhead transmission line involves a variety of technologies, e.g., electrical, mechanical, structural, civil, metallurgical, and chemical. A brief review will be given here of some electrical and mechanical aspects.

Power system planning determines the electrical power transfer, length, voltage, conductor size, and number of circuits on a structure. The object is to design a line that satisfies the planning requirements and the national specifications that govern the minimum factor of safety, as well as to ensure that the number of electrical outages and mechanical failures is extremely low.

Figure 6.35 shows a typical 400 kV tower that forms the backbone of the UK supergrid and, for contrast, the tower of the first North American 735 kV line. A proposed 750 kV d.c. line is also shown and illustrates the economic advantages as far as transmission lines are concerned of using direct rather than alternating current for bulk transfer of electric energy.

Conductor material In the early days of power transmission, copper was used exclusively for conductor material, but since the increase in the cost of copper, aluminium has largely displaced it.

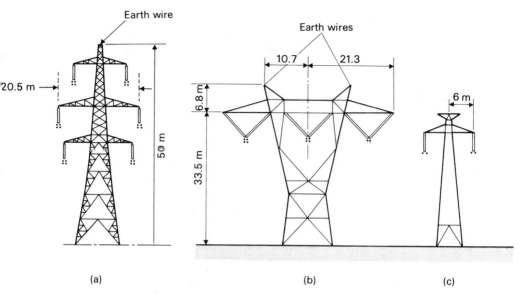

Figure 6.35 Overhead line towers: (a) 400 kV, UK supergrid tower, (b) 735 kV North American tower, (c) Proposed 750 kV d.c.

The most common type of e.h.v. line conductor is made of composite stranding of aluminium conductor, steel reinforced (a.c.s.r.). The reinforcement consists of a central core of galvanized steel wires that are sometimes greased for additional protection against corrosion.

Corona and radio interference The high voltages used in e.h.v. and u.h.v. systems result in high voltage gradients at the conductor surface. If the gradient exceeds 21 kV (r.m.s.)/cm, the breakdown level of air, a discharge takes place, which causes power loss, and emission of electromagnetic waves, hence considerable radio interference (r.i.) and audio noise.

Corona loss, r.i., and audio noise are at a minimum under fine weather conditions and increase by two orders of magnitude during severe weather. For example, the corona loss on a 400 kV line is around 1 kW per mile (0.62 kW per km) in good weather and may reach 150 kW per mile (93 kW per km) during snow and fog.

In general, the yearly average energy loss due to corona is only a small percentage of the conductor I^2R loss.

The voltage gradient on the conductor is therefore of little importance as far as corona loss is concerned but it has to be controlled from the point of view of r.i., which gives rise to interference in both radio and television receivers in the vicinity and to audible noise that may be disturbing to nearby residents.

Bundle conductors If, instead of one, a bundle of two or more conductors is used per phase, a number of advantages is gained. The bundle acts, as far as the electric field lines are concerned, like a conductor of a diameter much larger than that of the component conductors. This reduces the voltage gradient or conversely allows a higher voltage to be utilized for permissible levels of r.i. In fact, all lines above 220 kV employ bundle conductors.

A second advantage is that the g.m.r. of a bundle is high, leading from Eq. (6.1) to a line of low inductive reactance. Equation (4.25) indicates that the maximum power transfer capability of a line with high X/R ratio is inversely proportional to X. Bundling, therefore, has a favourable effect on this capability.

A third advantage of bundling is the easier erection and transportation of the conductor itself.

Earthwires Earthwires perform two important functions.

(1) Prevention of direct lightning strikes to the phase conductors.
(2) Provision of a low resistance path for the fault current in the event of flash-over from the line conductors to the structures.

Galvanized steel wires or line conductors are used for earthwires and the size is determined from the considerations of mechanical strength and fault current carrying capacity.

Insulators Insulators play an important role in all transmission lines but a proportionally greater one at the u.h.v. levels. The installed cost of insulation on typical 132, 400, and 765 kV lines could be 7.5, 12.54, and 24 per cent, respectively, of the total line cost.

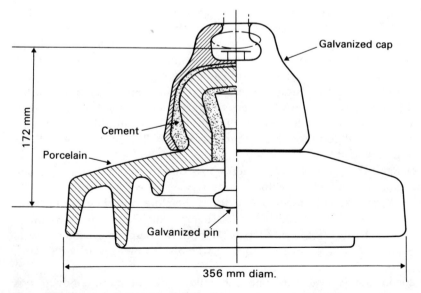

Figure 6.36 Cap and pin type porcelain insulator.

The most common type of insulator used is the cap and pin type made from either glass or porcelain. The cross section of a typical cap and pin insulator is shown in Fig. 6.36. The shape of the sheds under the insulator is determined by pollution conditions. In areas of severe pollution the sheds are designed to provide extra length in the creepage path. The number of units in series in a string is selected to meet the specified insulation level and pollution conditions of the line.

The insulation level of the line depends not on the nominal voltage but rather on the maximum voltage to earth that the line can withstand during transient overvoltages without suffering a flashover.

6.3.8 Rating of Lines

The power transfer capability of lines is a function of several factors. Regardless of voltage, there is a thermal limit on continuous current flow. At this limit, the temperature rise on the conductor is such that expansion has resulted in a line sag approaching the statutory minimum ground clearance. Depending on external factors such as temperature and wind velocity, higher short time ratings may be used during emergencies. A single-circuit 400 kV line with four conductors per bundle has the following thermal ratings.

Air temperature	Current	
°C	A	MVA
18	2000	1400
4–18	2600	1800
4	3200	2200

A second consideration in the rating of lines is the reactive power balance of the line. In Chapter 4 it was stressed that transfer of reactive power over a network is undesirable. One is tempted therefore to ask whether it is possible to operate a line in such a way that the reactive power generated by its capacitance balances the reactive power consumed by its inductance. This condition is satisfied when

$$V_p^2 Y_c = I_p^2 X_L, \text{ therefore } \frac{V_p}{I_p} = \sqrt{(X_L X_C)} = \sqrt{\left(\frac{L}{C}\right)} = Z_0$$

where subscript p stands for phase quantities and Z_0 is known as the characteristic or surge impedance of the line. We can conclude that if the phase load is Z_0 ohms, the line is approximately self sufficient as far as reactive power is concerned. This type of loading is known as 'surge impedance load' (s.i.l.).

Equation (4.25) repeated here, $P_A = V_A V_B / X \sin \delta$, tells us that for a line with large X/R ratio and specified terminal voltages, the power transfer is proportional to the size of the power angle δ. In Chapter 8 we will see that to preserve stability of operation, δ should be kept less than 30°. For long transmission lines the series reactance X is considerable and as δ is con-

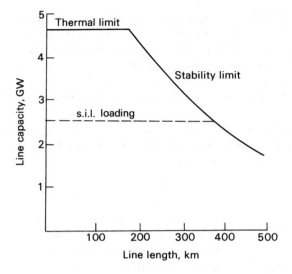

Figure 6.37 Capability of 765 kV transmission line.

strained, a limit on the maximum power transfer is imposed based on certain stability criteria.

Figure 6.37 shows the boundaries that circumscribe the capability of a 765 kV transmission line. The diagram indicates that short lines of low reactance can be loaded appreciably above the s.i.l. but that long lines must operate below the s.i.l.

For very long lines, the limitation on loading due to the large inductive reactance X_L can be relieved at a price, through compensation by series capacitors. Equation (4.25) then becomes:

$$P_A = \frac{V_A V_B}{X_L - X_c} \sin \delta$$

where X_c is the reactance of the series connected capacitors.

Series compensation is often used to improve the power transfer capability of long a.c. transmission lines, the alternative solution being high voltage d.c. transmission. One problem associated with series compensation is the voltage rating of the capacitor. If the rating is based on maximum normal current then the capacitor will break down in the event of overcurrent during faults. Rating the capacitor to withstand the voltage under fault conditions would be hopelessly uneconomical and therefore special protective devices in the form of spark gaps are used to protect the capacitor from overvoltages.

REFERENCES

1. E. R. Laithwaite, 'Some aspects of electrical machines with open magnetic circuits', *Proc. IEE*, **115**, 1275–83, 1968.

2. E. R. Laithwaite (ed.), *Transport Without Wheels*, Elek, London, 1977.
3. G. H. Rawcliffe and I. R. Smith, 'The moving-coil regulator: a treatment from first principles', *Proc. IEE*, **104A**, 68–76, 1957.
4. W. C. Johnson, *Transmission Lines and Networks*, McGraw-Hill, New York, 1950.
5. O. Elgerd, *Electric Energy Systems Theory*, McGraw-Hill, New York, 1971.
6. J. R. Neuenswander, *Modern Power Systems*, Intertex, New York, 1971.
7. B. M. Weedy, *Electric power systems*, 2nd edn, Wiley, London, 1972.

SEVEN

THE UTILIZATION OF ELECTRIC ENERGY

7.1 TYPES OF CONSUMER LOAD

A science fiction film of the nineteen-fifties, *The Day the Earth Stood Still*, imagined a visit from an alien being who, to make his presence known, neutralized all manmade electric devices throughout the world for just one hour. On reflection it is obvious both that the result was a catastrophe and that we take for granted the fact that electricity is always available for our use. We should never fail to convey to present day students of this technology that they should never cease to marvel at the wonder of it all.

The designers of the British grid system are to be admired for their forward thinking. A *three*-phase supply of a.c. rather than a d.c. supply would be needed, they argued, for more electricity would be used to produce mechanical power than would merely be turned into heat *per se*. It is one of the modern wonders of the world, surely, that under the pavements beneath our feet is the energy of motion, motion that began in the power stations and is effectively transmitted as such, temporarily locked in ducts we call 'cables', to be released at will by every householder as and when they wish. It should be noted that of all the electrical energy that enters a workshop full of machine tools through the main cable, over ninety-nine per cent finally appears as heat *within* that workshop, but what a store of ingenious and delightful objects has it made on the way to warming the room for those who use it! It is easy to become so preoccupied with this thought that one is ready to declare it sacrilege simply to plug in a domestic heater, cooker, or similar device! Nevertheless, the fact remains that heating and lighting must take second place to electromechanical energy conversion in a book of this kind and must be dismissed almost as 'obvious', even though the daily habits of humans using electricity mainly as a source of heat can be assessed to an amazing degree by observing the demand for electric power from a national network. (For example, a sharp increase in demand at 9.15 on a winter's evening often implies that an extremely popular television programme has broken off for commercial advertisements and ninety per cent of viewers have demanded the switching on of a heating appliance for the making of a hot beverage, which event takes place in a different room, thus requiring an extra light source.)

The only other topic we propose to mention in connection with non-mechanical power conversion is to suggest that the question of the destination of the one per cent of energy that was fed into the workshop that failed to be converted into warmth within the walls could form a useful educational discussion topic for a study group.

7.2 SYNCHRONOUS MOTORS

The description of the parts and construction of a synchronous motor has already been covered (Chapter 5), for it is simply an alternator with the active power flow reversed. If an appreciation of its properties when run as a motor is to be readily achieved, however, we suggest that a simpler approach than that of the two-axis theory and the synchronous impedance method can be more helpful. One could even begin with a simple model using only permanent magnets, as shown in Fig. 7.1. If one set of magnets is accelerated rapidly, the other magnets' inertia will prevent them from 'locking on' to their opposite members. All that will happen is that each time unlike poles approach each other, as in Fig. 7.2(a), the rotor magnet will experience a short attractive impulse to the left. A fraction of a second later the outer magnet will have passed and will be receding, as in (b), and the rotor magnet experiences a short impulse to the right. Continuous rotation of the outer magnets at high speed

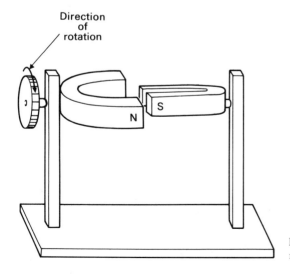

Figure 7.1 Model of a synchronous motor using permanent magnets.

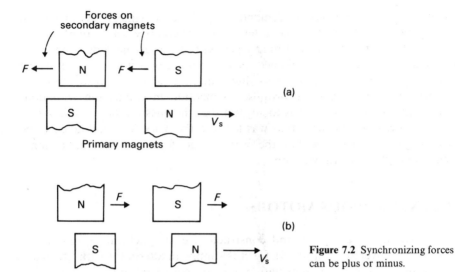

Figure 7.2 Synchronizing forces can be plus or minus.

therefore results only in a rapid vibration of the rotor with no net rotation. But if the relative speed of the outer magnets is slow enough for the rotor magnets to be dragged into synchronism then the two sets will thereafter rotate as one unit.

This simple model should be committed to memory by every student of the synchronous machine, for it contains every facet of the phenomena exhibited by such devices. It gives an immediate impression of the experiences of an 'observer' who could see magnetic flux, fix himself to the rotor, and revolve with it. The only modification that need be made to the simple model is that the magnets should carry pole shoes as do the excitation magnets of water wheel alternators so as to distribute the flux sinusoidally in space.

A few examples will illustrate these assertions. First, the lock-in phenomenon as the outer magnets approach their opposite numbers corresponds to the switching on of the stator of a real machine when the rotor has been driven almost up to synchronous speed by external means. Look at the model and think what will happen in practice. The rotor magnets will not simply be pulled into exact alignment, and rotate in synchronism from that instant. They will overshoot and thereafter oscillate about the position of alignment. The forces that can damp such an oscillation are those of bearing friction, and the hysteresis and eddy current losses in the iron of the magnets themselves.

The transfer of thought from the model to the real machine always involves merely adding to the quasi-static phenomena of the model an additional rotation of the whole system in the direction of the slow rotation, so as to bring the outer members up to synchronous frequency. At once we see that position oscillations in the model imply speed oscillations in the real machine, and as these are obviously undesirable it is important that the

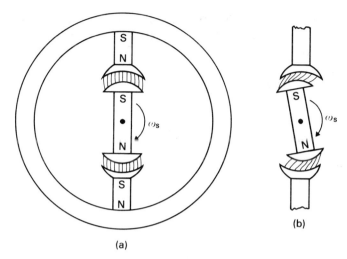

Figure 7.3 Synchronizing torque seen as a Maxwell stress.

damping forces should be considerable. Friction and hysteresis losses are insufficient. So also are eddy currents unless we make provision for their enhancement. The usual method is to embed a grid of copper bars and associated end rings very similar to the 'cage' of an induction motor rotor (page 219). Since an outer set of magnets that, in the model, actually rotate, is to be replaced by a set of static coils carrying polyphase a.c. in the real machine, it would be a disaster to incorporate such a highly conducting grid into the stator, for it would constitute a permanent short circuit to such windings. But the pole faces of the rotor of a real machine of either turbo or water power type do actually rotate, like the inner member of the model, and accordingly the damper grid is incorporated into the rotor pole faces.

When we come to consider the operation of the system when the outer magnets of the model are turned so as to drag the inner magnets around against a load torque, the model is equally useful, for it illustrates at once the 'load angle'. If pole centre is exactly opposite pole centre as in Fig. 7.3(a) then there can clearly be no development of torque. But if the rotor rotates, still at synchronous speed, but with a *lag* as shown in (b), then the Maxwell stress (strands of elastic) approach shows at once that torque is produced and that the bigger the load torque the greater will be the angle of lag. It is precisely this angle that is given the name 'load angle', for obvious reasons.

7.2.1 The Generation of Rotating Magnetic Fields

This topic has already been discussed in Chapter 2 (pages 38–41). It is relevant to alternators, synchronous motors, induction motors, and to all types of a.c. commutator motor. It embodies one of the great mysteries of electromagnetism, whereby a mechanical model in which actual solid objects take the place of a flux, which is an object only of the mind, follows the same pattern of behaviour, and a new situation can be predicted *by* that mechanical model.

Starting with the travelling wave equation (Eq. (2.3)), we can find the velocity of travel as follows.

At any fixed horizontal position x, the magnetizing current h replaces y and

$$\frac{\partial h}{\partial t} = A\omega \cos\left(\omega t - \frac{\pi x}{p}\right)$$

At any instant of time,

$$\frac{\partial h}{\partial x} = -\frac{\pi}{p} A \cos\left(\omega t - \frac{\pi x}{p}\right)$$

Now, since

$$\frac{dx}{dt} = \frac{\partial h}{\partial t} \bigg/ \frac{\partial h}{\partial x} = \text{the velocity } v$$

then

$$v = -\frac{p\omega}{\pi}$$

or in terms of the frequency of rise and fall $f\ (= \omega/2\pi)$

$$v = -2pf \tag{7.1}$$

which means that the wave progresses horizontally by one wavelength per cycle of f, a well known result. The only significance of the minus sign in Eq. (7.1) is the notation adopted for measuring positive x and positive t in Eq. (2.3), in relation to the direction of travel.

In terms of rotary machines it is more usual to convert v into a rotary velocity, e.g., revolutions per second, and to express it in terms of the number of poles around the machine, or preferably the number of pole pairs, P. The circumference being $2\pi r$, where r is the radius of the airgap, $P \times 2p = 2\pi r$. Writing $v = r\Omega$, where Ω is the angular velocity of the rotor, Eq. (7.1) transforms into

$$\Omega = \frac{v}{r} = -\frac{2pf}{r} = -\frac{2pf \cdot 2\pi}{2pP} = \frac{2\pi f}{P} = \frac{\omega}{P}$$

The most profound point to remember in respect of travelling fields is that when we place a row of electromagnets, as in Fig. 2.12, and feed each with alternating current of corresponding phase to those of the rod model, we can argue correctly that if flux density could be 'seen' then it will indeed travel from end to end of the row, but we have no assurance that a slab of conductor placed on the surface will be so moved, as was the ball, unless we return to fundamental experiments such as those of Michael Faraday in 1831, or to fundamental particle physics involving both Special and General Relativity.

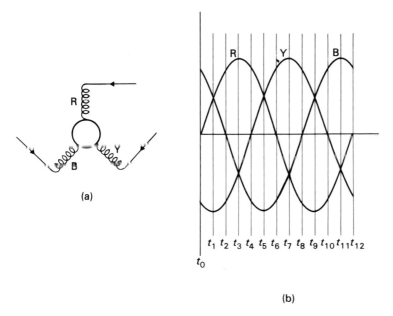

Figure 7.4 A simple, three-coil system (a), fed with three-phase a.c. as shown in (b).

The properties of travelling fields will now be developed again by the inductive method. First, let us consider the three-coil system of Fig. 7.4(a) fed by a three-phase system of currents defined in (b). We will assume that a positive current in any coil produces a magnetic field directed *towards* the centre of the system. This choice was quite arbitrary. Figure 7.5 shows the fields produced by each individual coil as phasors, and hence the combined result, double-arrowed, for the various time instants marked in Fig. 7.4(b). The production of a rotating field vector is more than a mere suggestion, even by

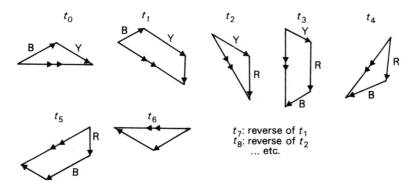

Figure 7.5 Direction of resultant field (double-arrowed) at the centre of the coil system in Fig. 7.4(a) at instants of time defined in Fig. 7.4(b).

this method. What it lacks is any hint that the field is sinusoidally distributed in space.

Formal proof of the travelling wave equation, however, is not difficult. Taking the origin of time as the instant when the flux density due to the red phase is zero and the origin of position to be that at which it is zero at all times, then the flux density b_R at distance x from this position at time t is given by

$$b_R = B \sin \omega t \sin \frac{\pi x}{p}$$

It follows that, due to the yellow phase,

$$b_Y = B \sin \left(\omega t - \frac{2\pi}{3} \right) \sin \left(\frac{\pi x}{p} - \frac{2\pi}{3} \right)$$

the negative signs merely denoting the phase sequence. Likewise

$$b_B = B \sin \left(\omega t - \frac{4\pi}{3} \right) \sin \left(\frac{\pi x}{p} - \frac{4\pi}{3} \right)$$

Each product of two sine functions can be transformed into the difference of two cosines, thus:

$$b_R = \tfrac{1}{2}B \left[\cos \left(\omega t - \frac{\pi x}{p} \right) - \cos \left(\omega t + \frac{\pi x}{p} \right) \right]$$

$$b_Y = \tfrac{1}{2}B \left[\cos \left(\omega t - \frac{\pi x}{p} \right) - \cos \left(\omega t + \frac{\pi x}{p} - \frac{4\pi}{3} \right) \right]$$

$$b_B = \tfrac{1}{2}B \left[\cos \left(\omega t - \frac{\pi x}{p} \right) - \cos \left(\omega t + \frac{\pi x}{p} - \frac{2\pi}{3} \right) \right]$$

The three second terms in each bracket are mutually displaced by $\tfrac{2}{3}\pi$ and therefore sum to zero, leaving

$$B_{xt} = \tfrac{3}{2}B \cos \left(\omega t - \frac{\pi x}{p} \right)$$

(See also page 38.)

7.2.2 A Simplified Approach to Synchronous Motors

The d.c. machine is not covered in this work, since its operation is usually well covered in standard textbooks of physics and in more elementary works, but the concept of a d.c. motor having an applied e.m.f. which, when the armature moves, is opposed by a back e.m.f. is a useful one with which to begin a study of synchronous machines used as motors. It is permissible to consider all phasor diagrams as representing quantities *per phase* in a polyphase machine. If then a machine runs on zero load, the phasor diagram for each phase is simply that shown in Fig. 7.6(a), the back e.m.f. due to rotation being exactly equal and opposite to the applied e.m.f. The instant a load is applied, the rotor

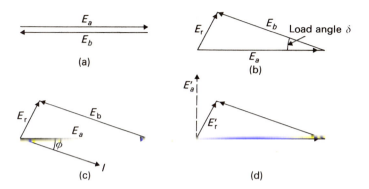

Figure 7.6 Simple phasor diagrams to illustrate synchronous motor action.

will fall back in phase, as is most easily seen from the primitive magnet model of Fig. 7.1. If the load is sustained and the damping has reduced any rotor oscillations to zero, the phasor diagram is now as shown in Fig. 7.6(b) and a resultant phasor E_r is free to drive current through the stator winding. It is at this point that we have departed from d.c. machine theory, for the subtraction of E_b from E_a is not an arithmetic but a phasor subtraction. Likewise, the current that flows as the result of E_r is not in phase with it; indeed, so great is the combined effect of armature reaction and leakage reactance that the angle of lag can be taken, in this simplified approach, to be 90°. The current phasor can then be added, as shown in Fig. 7.6(c).

In taking a 90° lag we have assumed, not an infinite equivalent synchronous reactance, but a zero winding resistance, i.e., there is no power loss in the stator. Hence any input power must all be delivered as mechanical output. Herein lies the strength of the simplified approach, for many of the properties of synchronous motors follow directly, if only qualitatively. For example, Fig. 7.6(c) can be used at once to show that the power input is $E_a I \cos \phi$, which must be equal to $T\omega_s$ where T is the torque delivered at synchronous speed ω_s. The effect of varying the excitation can at once be assessed simply by drawing a variety of phasors for E_b and observing how the load angle δ must change in order to maintain $E_a I \cos \phi$ constant. This process may be simplified, however, by assuming, rather than that $E_a - E_b$ is the cause of I, that the dotted line E'_a in Fig. 7.6(d) is the applied voltage, and that E'_r is drawn to the new scale such that $E'_r = E_r/X_s$ numerically, where X_s is the synchronous reactance. Power output is thus indicated merely as the vertical ordinate of E'_r (numerically multiplied by E_a). Changes in load and changes in excitation are now easily plotted as loci, as shown in Fig. 7.7(a) and (b).

The important deductions that follow at once are:

(1) Increase in load produces increase in load angle, not proportionately, but as dictated by the circular arc OY.

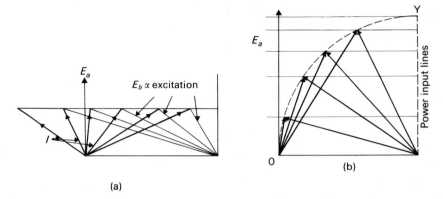

Figure 7.7 Phasor diagrams illustrating (a) the effect of variation in excitation, (b) the variation in applied load.

(2) There is a maximum load, for any fixed value of excitation (which fixes the size of E_b), beyond which the load angle $\delta = 90°$ can no longer increase to supply that load. Beyond this, therefore, the machine stops. In terms of Fig. 7.1, the rotor magnets have finally 'lost contact' with the primary system. The speed–torque characteristic of a synchronous motor on fixed excitation is therefore as shown in Fig. 7.8, the height of the line at ω_s being the 'pull-out torque' or 'ultimate load'.

(3) It follows at once that the pull-out torque is proportional to the excitation and that the machine is not self starting.

(4) On fixed load, variations in excitation, and therefore in E_b, cause the motor to draw the same active power from the supply, but at different values of power factor. In particular, when the excitation is increased beyond that required to synchronize, the motor draws active power at leading power factor and supplies reactive power to the mains.

This last result accounts for a considerable proportion of the power invested in synchronous machines run as motors, for a single machine of

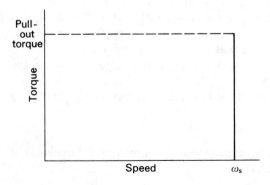

Figure 7.8 The speed–torque characteristic of a synchronous motor.

modest proportions can be made to behave like an enormous capacitor, of the order of farads of capacitance, that otherwise would have required a bulk of static capacitors occupying the volume of an aircraft hangar. At the same time, the machine can supply a useful mechanical torque. Had this leading power factor facility not been available, few large synchronous motors would have been used as mechanical drives, since their inability to operate unless run up to speed by an auxiliary drive and synchronized before they could be used would have been regarded as a prohibitive disadvantage. As it is, a single synchronous motor can be used to correct the power factor of a number of induction motors run from the same supply.

7.3 INDUCTION MOTORS

As an industrial drive the induction motor is the 'king' of electric motors. It dominates the scene to the extent probably of over ninety per cent of the total power. Its advantages of a robust rotor requiring no electrical contact has encouraged engineers designing systems to use it in tandem with a mechanical speed adjuster in situations where wide speed range is essential, rather than to seek the more sophisticated commutator motors or to pay for power frequency conversion equipment, although modern developments in solid state devices have done much to bring the controllable frequency inverter into competition with mechanical speed adjusters.

The disadvantages of the induction motor are easily distinguished. Basically it is a fixed speed motor, capable of high efficiency only when run within a few per cent of one of the speeds listed in the table on page 25. Ingenious switched windings developed by Rawcliffe and others[1-3] in the last two decades have extended the usefulness by allowing a choice of two or three fixed speeds for virtually no loss of power/weight ratio or efficiency and therefore at the cost, only, of a switch. The second disadvantage is the motor's incapability of being run at unity power factor, but the overexcited synchronous motor (often known as a 'synchronous capacitor') has removed this disadvantage for many applications.

7.3.1 Principle of Operation

The teaching of the principle of the induction motor has been virtually omitted from school physics textbooks; the d.c. machine, despite its complications of brushes and rubbing contacts, has somehow always appealed to the physicist as 'simpler', yet the principle of the induction machine, if introduced through a good analogy, is not only simple to appreciate but represents an example of an extremely fundamental and far-reaching concept in the whole of the physical world—the action of a body subject to the pressure of fluid flow. Perhaps the necessity of regarding flux as rather more 'real' than is required in, say, the study of permanent magnets, acts as a deterrent, but we believe the proof of the basic efficiency of the device, developed in Chapter 3 (pages 90–92) in purely mechanical terms, to be the most elegant we have seen.

Equation (3.5) is the most fundamental statement of induction motor action, implying that for each increment of force F there is an inescapable increment of loss. The force F is readily obtainable from Eq. (3.5). Therefore

$$\text{input} = Fv_s = \frac{\text{loss}}{s}$$

and

$$F = \frac{\text{loss}}{sv_s} \tag{7.2}$$

Thus

$$s = \frac{Fv_s - Fv}{Fv_s} = \frac{\text{loss}}{Fv_s} = \frac{\text{loss}}{\text{input}}$$

It is only at this point that we need to specify an electrical system and begin to introduce electrical units. The above calculations relate, of course, to a *linear* propulsion system, whereas the majority of induction machines are rotary, but the only modification required is that angular velocities then replace v_s and v and torque T replaces F, so that Eq. (7.2) becomes:

$$T = \frac{\text{loss}}{s\omega_s} \tag{7.3}$$

In the following adaptation it should be noted that the equation remains an *equation* and does not degenerate to a proportionality. In many texts, the tangential force on an induction motor rotor that leads to the torque is evaluated from the concept

$$T \propto \Phi I_2 \cos \phi \tag{7.4}$$

where Φ is the flux in the airgap, I_2 the secondary current, and ϕ the phase angle between them. Apart from the difficulty of deciding whether ϕ is a space angle or a time angle, the result can never be more than a proportionality, requiring a constant to convert it to an equation, a constant that eventually is seen not to be nondimensional.

In Eq. (7.3) the loss is only that developed in the rotor and therefore readily calculable if we assume that, in the first instance, the rotor is perfectly laminated and produces no hysteresis loss, and that the rotor carries a three-phase winding whose leakage impedance per phase at mains frequency $2\pi f_s$ is given by $R_2 + j2\pi fL_2$, where L_2 is the leakage inductance per phase. Let this impedance be denoted $R_2 + jX_2$.

Now when the rotor moves at speed ω, the frequency of e.m.f.s induced by the primary (stator) winding is reduced from f_s at standstill to sf_s at slip s. If there are N_1 turns per phase in the stator winding and N_2 turns per phase in the rotor, and the stator is fed from a supply voltage E_1 per phase, the induced voltage in the rotor at standstill is $(N_2/N_1)E_1$ and at slip s is $(sN_2/N_1)E_1$. The leakage impedance at slip s is clearly $R_2 + sX_2$.

Hence the rotor loss per phase is given by

$$I_2^2 R_2 = \frac{\left(\dfrac{sN_2 E_1}{N_1}\right)^2 R_2}{(R_2^2 + s^2 X_2^2)}$$

and Eq. (7.3) becomes

$$T = \frac{s\left(\dfrac{N_2}{N_1}\right)^2 R_1 F_1^2}{\omega_s (R_2^2 + s^2 X_2^2)} \tag{7.5}$$

(The torque equation derived from the proportionality (7.4) leads to the same expression with an unknown constant of proportionality in the numerator replacing $1/\omega_s$.)

For simplicity in appreciation of the form of Eq. (7.5), it is convenient to divide numerator and denominator by R_2/X_2^2 and express the result as:

$$T = \left[\left(\frac{N_2}{N_1}\right)^2 \frac{E_1^2}{\omega_s X_2}\right]\left[\frac{s(R_2/X_2)}{s^2 + (R_2/X_2)^2}\right]$$

which, so far as the ratio R_2/X_2 $(=a)$ and the speed as represented by s $(=(\omega_s - \omega)/\omega_s)$ are concerned, becomes

$$T = K\left(\frac{sa}{s^2 + a^2}\right) \tag{7.6}$$

A set of speed–torque curves for a fixed value of X_2 (and therefore of K) but variable R_2 (and hence a) is as shown in Fig. 7.9, for positive torque and speeds between standstill and ω_s. Taking a typical curve A, and continuing the

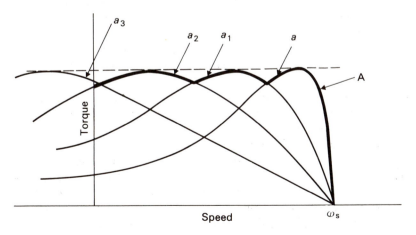

Figure 7.9 Speed–torque curves for induction motors having different values of $a(= R_2/X_2)$. $a < a_1 < a_2 < a_3$.

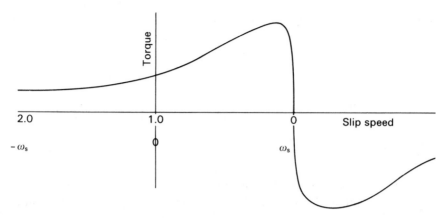

Figure 7.10 Speed–torque curve of an induction motor including values of slip that are negative or greater than unity.

evaluation of T for negative values of s (speeds in excess of ω_s) and for values of $s > 1$ (negative speeds), gives a complete four-quadrant plot as shown in Fig. 7.10. If the speed of the rotor is greater than ω_s, the significance of negative T is that the machine must be driven by an auxiliary device, in which case its action becomes that of a generator of active power, which is fed back into the mains supply. If ω is reversed, again the machine must be being driven backwards against the direction of the stator field travel. In either mode, the driving torque can be the inertia of the motor and its load. This situation can arise as the result of supplying a running motor with a frequency less than that required to generate a field speed ω_s, or by interchanging any pair of stator supply leads, so as to reverse ω_s. Both techniques are used in 'dynamic braking'. The first is known as 'regenerative braking', for the loss of kinetic energy from the rotor is transformed into electrical energy returned to mains. The second action is known as 'plugging' and is uneconomical in that more power must be fed to the stator in order to slow the machine, all of which appears as heat in the rotor. The principal reasons why the energy-wasting plugging technique is often preferred is that the supply of reducing frequency a.c. to the stator requires an expensive power conditioner, and this can only operate down to a low speed and not to standstill, for the system 'runs out of Goodness Factor', as it were, long before $\omega = 0$. A plugging system can produce considerable braking torque right down to standstill.

There is a popular misconception that the shape of the speed–torque curves of Figs. 7.9 and 7.10 is a 'natural' result inherent in the construction of an induction machine. This is not so. If the magnetic circuit were perfect so that X_2 were zero, the speed–torque relationship would be simply defined by Eq. (7.2) and the graph would be a straight line, as shown in Fig. 7.11. As with many d.c. motors, the user often insists on a very small speed drop on load and this demands a very steep speed–torque line, as shown broken in Fig. 7.11. The starting torque (at $s = 0$) for such a machine would be monstrous, and would

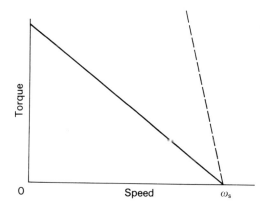

Figure 7.11 Hypothetical speed–torque curves for a motor with a perfect magnetic circuit.

be associated with an intolerably high starting current. Accordingly, the designer manages to limit the starting current by *exploiting* leakage reactance despite the fact that leakage is an imperfection. The curves in Fig. 7.12 show how the torque–speed curve can be modified by the introduction of X to an otherwise leakage-free machine.

7.3.2 Equivalent Circuit

By the technique of lumping, secondary components can be lumped into the primary, as if the machine were simply a transformer with a curious kind of load resistor, for as we have seen, Eq. (7.5) tells us that the input power $T\omega_s$ is given by the $I_2^2 R$ loss divided by s. It is therefore permissible to subtract from $I_2^2 R_2/s$ the *actual* rotor secondary loss. What remains must be the mechanical output and is seen to be $I_2^2 R_2[(1-s)/s]$. Thus the lumping of $I_2^2 R_2/s$ into the primary leaves the equivalent circuit (as viewed from the airgap) as the leakage reactance $(N_1/N_2)^2 X_2$, together with a total (apparent) loss resistor

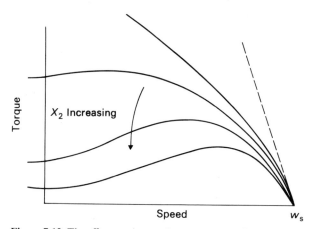

Figure 7.12 The effect on the speed–torque curve of changing X_2.

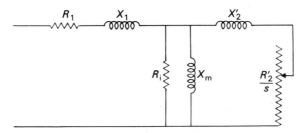

Figure 7.13 Complete equivalent circuit for one phase of a polyphase machine.

$(N_1/N_2)^2 R_2/s$, which component must be used in full when calculating torque, but only a fraction $(1-s)/s$ of this when calculating output.

The rest of the equivalent circuit is added by exactly the same processes as were used in the development of the transformer equivalent circuit, i.e., a magnetizing reactance component X_m and a stator iron loss resistor R_i are shown in parallel with the lumped secondary, and a primary leakage impedance $R_1 + jX_1$ is added in series, to give the complete equivalent circuit as shown in Fig. 7.13. It should be remembered that all the components used in such a diagram refer to 'per phase' values in a polyphase machine.

What now follows is interesting, for most modern induction machines do not have three-phase windings on the rotor. Rather, the rotor slots are filled with copper or aluminium, usually the latter because of its better casting properties. The slots are filled with solid bar conductors, all joined around each end of the rotor by equally solid end rings, the whole conductor system resembling that of a bird or animal's cage, the name 'cage rotor' being uniformly accepted for this type of construction. In modern machines the end rings and slot conductors are cast as a whole, and fan blades attached to the end rings are often incorporated in a single casting operation.

The justification for using an equivalent circuit of the form shown in Fig. 7.13 and for using the concept of a rotor leakage impedance 'per phase' is interesting, because it is merely an extension of the two-axis technique already described in relation to synchronous machines, except that resolution takes place along three axes, mutually 120° apart, rather than two axes at right angles. It matters not, so far as input impedance viewpoint is concerned, whether the rotor consists of a polyphase, insulated winding, a cast cage construction, or merely a hollow cylindrical tube of conductor with a moving or stationary iron core. The actual *values* of the equivalent circuit components will, of course, vary with the type of rotor adopted, for example the hollow cylinder type (often known as a 'drag cup' rotor, for fairly obvious reasons) has almost negligible X_2 in relation to R_2.

7.3.3 Types and Performance of Induction Motors

Around the turn of the century most induction machines had three-phase distributed windings on both rotor and stator. The rotor windings were

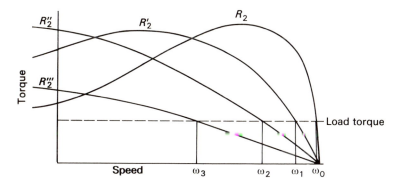

Figure 7.14 Speed control by adjustment of rotor resistance in a slip ring machine. The curves correspond to different values of R_2 where $R_2''' > R_2'' > R_2' > R_2$.

usually star connected and their free ends were brought out and connected to three slip rings. One of the principal reasons for doing this, at that time, was to enable a bank of variable value resistors to be put in series with the rotor, so that the windings did not burn out during the run-up period, especially if the motor was required to run up from rest against the load torque. A simple theory of this process that neglects primary leakage impedance shows that there is a whole family of speed–torque curves for constant voltage input, each curve being applicable to a different value of secondary resistance (Fig. 7.9). It is easy to see how a motor can be started on load by running along the thickened lines, transfer from line to line being made by progressing from stud to stud on a stepped variable resistor bank.

This insertion of resistance in the rotor circuit still persists today, although not with starting current reduction as a prime objective, for, as will be seen in the next paragraph, there are now better methods of starting. The fact is that despite all modern developments, especially that of solid state electronics, the wound rotor with added resistance is still the *cheapest overall* adjustable speed motor for many applications, notably those in which the speed range required is less than 1.5:1. Figure 7.14 shows how additional resistance increases the slip, rather than changes the synchronous speed. In terms of an equivalent circuit it means that the rotor input $T\omega_s$ remains fixed at all times and that speed reduction is obtained simply by burning up most of the difference between $T\omega_s$ and $T\omega$ in the external resistors. The efficiency is always $(1-s)$, so 50% speed reduction reduces the basic, potential efficiency from 100 to 50%. The additional resistor bank often consists of vats of copper sulphate solution containing plate type electrodes that can be moved further apart when more resistance is needed.

Historically, it took twenty years before designers of starting mechanisms realized that the control of *reactance* was far preferable to methods that involved rubbing contacts and brushes. On the way to the modern machine, a switching arrangement became popular that allowed a three-phase machine

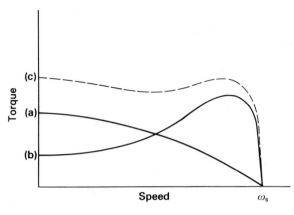

Figure 7.15 Speed–torque curves for rotors with (a) thin, shallow slots, (b) deep slots and thick conductors, and (c) a combination of the two.

with a simple cage of solid conductor to be started in star connection and switched to delta connection as full running speed was approached. But between 1900 and 1910 the great French engineer P. Boucherot developed a series of new designs that led to the modern machine—the idea behind which was the 'double-cage rotor'. Whether the rotor contains two separate, insulated, but short circuited windings, two separate cage rotors, or two integrated cage rotors is of little consequence in appreciating the *basic* theory, which is as follows.

A secondary winding that is made of thick conductor sunk into deep slots will have a low value of R_2, but quite a high value of X_2, in its equivalent circuit. On the other hand, a thin set of conductors in shallow slots will have high R_2, low X_2. The speed–torque curve appropriate to each is shown in Fig. 7.15. Used *together*, the combined thrust curve is shown as a broken line and approaches the rectangular shape that is often regarded as ideal for many purposes. The high reactance–resistance combination at standstill reduces input current on starting to three or four times full load current, which is quite acceptable in most cases. The low R_2 near full speed increases the slope of the curve in that region.

Boucherot was an engineer of great imagination and versatility. He deserves more, perhaps, than merely being remembered for the double-cage rotor. As designs progressed, the two sets of slots were combined as shown in Fig. 7.16(a), so that the whole could be cast at a single operation. Later still, it was realized that simpler slot shapes as shown in (b) and then (c) could be adopted, the latter often being called the 'deep bar' rotor. It should always be remembered that the starting mechanism of the direct on-line induction motor

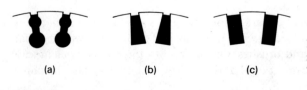

Figure 7.16 Cross sections of rotor slots designed to exploit the 'double-cage rotor' principle.

is a classic example of the exploitation of an imperfection, in this case, leakage of a magnetic circuit. Too often in the nineteen-seventies imperfections have been fought as 'enemies'. The good engineer, like the expert in judo, knows how to use the power of his opponent in order to succeed. Do we not exploit the imperfection of frictional contact each time we walk?

7.3.4 Single-phase Induction Motors

There are connoisseurs of food and drink who will pronounce upon the quality of a restaurant on the basis of its 'sweet trolley' alone. We have known industrialists who have employed secretaries on the basis of a handshake alone. For our part, we have often judged the soundness of a textbook on machines by its treatment of the single-phase induction motor. All too often, the approach is oversimplified and emerges with qualitative results that appear most reasonable but will not hold good quantitatively for any but the tiniest of machines whose input impedance is virtually constant for all speeds from zero to synchronism. The fallacious approach forms a useful starting point, for it uses a valid technique, albeit operating on the wrong quantity. It is a fact that a pulsating magnetic field, such as that obtained from a single, air-cored coil, as shown in Fig. 7.17, is equivalent to a pair of counter rotating flux vectors as shown, insofar as one can resolve the latter into x-axis components $(B/2)\cos \omega t - (B/2)\cos \omega t = 0$, and y-axis components $(B/2)\sin \omega t + (B/2)\sin \omega t = B\sin \omega t$, which is the flux produced by the single coil. But the worm is already in the apple! Such a technique makes the bold assumption that the flux in a single-phase motor's airgap is simply $B\sin \omega t$, which is only valid at standstill. The further point that the technique takes no account of the spatial distribution of the flux is, by comparison, a mere detail, sweeping though it is!

The fallacy was first pointed out to us in Cyril Veinott's excellent book *Theory and Design of Small Induction Motors*[4] where he makes the point that, historically, Ferraris is credited (or discredited, according to your upbringing!) with the first concept of the counter rotating field vectors, but goes on to say effectively that if 'field' is interpreted as magnetomotive force rather than flux, i.e., as H rather than B, the analytical method becomes rigorous. According to Veinott, (a point which we heartily endorse) Ferraris was genuinely trying to help the students of his time to wrestle with this most difficult phenomenon, electromagnetism, applied in such sophisticated pieces of hardware as is the case in slotted cylindrical magnetic structures, and it was the second

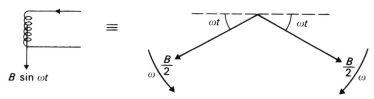

Figure 7.17 The counter-rotating field concept.

generation of teachers (some of whom taught us!) that gave the split flux a reality to which it was never entitled. See how easy it is to prove $1 = -1$ by solid argument based on split flux of constant magnitude B.

Constant flux implies, of course, constant voltage applied across the magnetizing reactance of the equivalent circuit, i.e., it ignores R_1 and X_1. This is not a serious omission in itself. The assumption that a field may be divided into components, each of which can be treated as separately producing torque, can and has been justified by Piggott.[5] (Piggott, during the preparation of the paper cited, pointed out that in the usual four-terminal element handling a complex waveform such as a modulated carrier radio signal, it was only possible to split the input into components, operate on each separately and add the result to obtain the output, provided that the relationship between output and input was linear. In calculating the torques of electrical machinery, the relationship between torque T and flux density B is always non-linear, i.e., $T \propto B^2$. Yet one deals with harmonics by the component technique without question. In proving, as he does in his paper, that 'the modes do not couple' he justifies rigorously the technique for all machines, perhaps for the first time.) So we can apparently proceed to draw speed–torque curves for the forward and backward going fields as shown in Fig. 7.18 and subtract them to give the

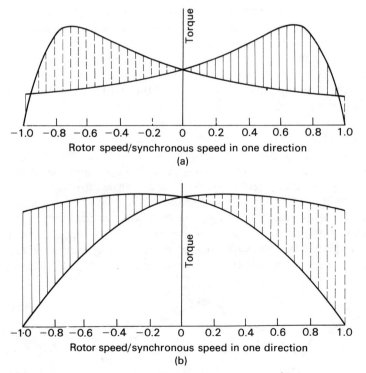

Figure 7.18 Torque prediction by addition of torques due to each flux component: (a) $R/X_L < 1$, (b) $R/X_L > 1$.

shaded areas, whose ordinates must be a plot of the total speed–torque characteristics of the motor. After all, see how many of the known properties of single-phase machines are at once predictable:

(1) There is no starting torque.
(2) The machine will run in either direction once given a start.
(3) The machine never quite attains the full synchronous speed, even when on ideal, zero load.

Now let us examine why all these correct answers have emerged from wrong arguments. Let us first be sure that the machine will only develop positive going torque provided that the forward field develops more torque than does the backward and that this situation only occurs near standstill when the speed–torque curve due to the forward going field has an *upward* slope at $s = 1$, i.e., that the curve has a peak between $s = 1$ and $s = 0$. Let us then ask what quantities fix the position of the peak and we shall at once receive the answer: 'where $s = R_2/X_2$'. If then a motor fails to run at all, it must be safe to assume that its speed–torque curve peaks at $s > 1$, i.e., that its secondary resistance is bigger than its secondary leakage reactance. It would appear, therefore, that all one has to do is to increase X_2 and all will be well. There may be those who, in the light of what has been said about the successful exploitation of X_2, may still argue that such a technique would succeed. But the theory makes no demands on *how* the value of X_2 could be raised. One method is to increase the airgap. Does the machine in Fig. 7.19(b) seem more likely to run than that in (a)? The Goodness Factor of (b) must be less than 0.1. In matters of *fundamental* importance, does it seem likely that the question of 'run–no run' is resolved by the mere ratio of the imperfections of electric and magnetic circuits?

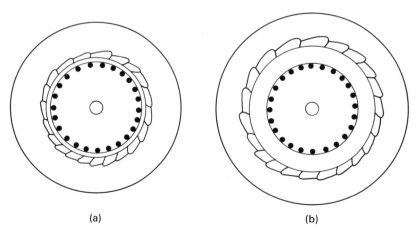

(a)   (b)

Figure 7.19 Ridiculous result obtained by deductions made from Fig. 7.18. It predicts that machine (b) will run whereas machine (a) will not.

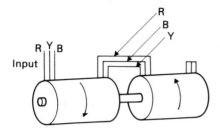

Figure 7.20 Correct analogue of the single-phase motor. The two three-phase machines are connected in *series*.

The alternative approach to the mechanism developed in pages 225–230 will show at once that the forward and backward going fluxes are far from equal except at standstill and that a running, single-phase motor can have an almost perfectly 'circular' rotating field. All that has been proved is that if two identical polyphase motors are connected *in parallel* with opposite phase sequence and coupled to the same shaft, the pair will only run up when given a start, if $R_2/X_2 < 1$. To split the *m.m.f.* into components is an entirely different matter, since the resulting flux can adjust to the resultant of both primary *and* secondary m.m.f. The only way to ensure that a pair of identical machines can be used to simulate the action of a single-phase machine is to connect them in *series*, as shown in Fig. 7.20. It is the operation of each at constant *current* rather than at constant voltage that is relevant. Let us examine the speed–torque curve of a polyphase motor at constant current. A convenient way of doing this is to use the equivalent circuit, for the primary leakage reactance is then of no consequence. Iron loss can be ignored for the purpose of this exercise, which is largely based on establishing a dual with the simplified constant voltage operation where, having ignored R_1 and X_1, the parallel components R_i and X_m are irrelevant and the system is reduced to an X_2 and an R_2/s in series, yielding the equation

$$T_v = \frac{kas}{a^2 + s^2}$$

where a has the value R_2/X_2.

Similarly the torque T_c at constant current that divides only as between a magnetizing reactance X_m and a secondary load resistor R_2/s (X_2 being ignored) leads to the identical form of equation with a different constant k, and a now having the value R_2/X_m. It is perhaps not surprising therefore that confusion arose over the counter rotating field theory, for when two polyphase motors are connected for opposite rotation and connected in series, the only certain fact about their operation is that their stators carry the same *current*. Constant current theory, rarely used in evaluation of mains-fed machines, *is* needed for assessment of the performance of single-phase induction motors.

There is, however, an alternative method that in the main is to be preferred. It is the method of two-axis resolution that led the way to Generalized machine theory. It is a pointer to the misinterpretation of the intermediate generations of teachers that a classic paper of the nineteen-twenties by Karapetoff[6] showed clearly the complete agreement between the two-axis ('cross-field') theory and the counter rotating approach properly applied. The cross-field theory is the one adopted by Langsdorf in his standard work on a.c. machine theory.[7] The whole problem of analysis of electromagnetic devices lies rooted in the fact that having created a concept of a 'field' (to avoid the cumbersome and virtually unmanageable relativistic approach, as we now know it—relativity was unknown to the originators of field theory) it virtually defies representation, for it has the following associated properties:

(1) a magnitude (in the case of sinusoidal variation an 'amplitude');
(2) a direction in space;
(3) a time variation (for sinusoids a 'phase').

Phasor diagrams will take care of (1) and (3) simultaneously. Vector concepts will lead to illustration of (1) and (2) simultaneously (as in 'lines of force' or flux plots). But to tackle all three simultaneously one has almost to abandon any hope of a 'physical' picture and return to Maxwell's vector equations and a computer that can never reassure the user that he has fed it with the appropriate boundary conditions.

We believe in the approach used by Langsdorf in which a phasor diagram is drawn for quantities such as induced voltages, currents, and fluxes, but each resolved along the direct axis (now appropriately called the *transformer axis*) and the quadrature axis (in induction motor terms, the *speed axis*). Each phasor carries a capital letter (*E* for voltages, *I* for currents, Φ for fluxes) with two subscripts. The first subscript indicates to which axis the quantity refers—'t' for transformer, 's' for speed. The second, used only for induced voltages, indicates whether the voltage was produced by rotation through a

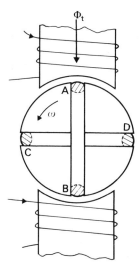

Figure 7.21 Primitive machine in which the rotor carries only two short circuited loops of which AB and CD are cross sections.

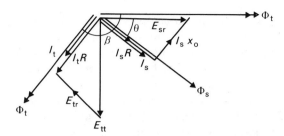

Figure 7.22 Phasor diagram for the machine shown in Fig. 7.21.

certain value of flux (which we know was given the name 'flux cutting rule' by the engineers of the last century and is now identified with Special Relativity) and is denoted 'r'. The alternative second suffix is 't', meaning 'by transformer action' (now known to be predictable by General Relativity).

Figure 7.21 shows a primitive machine in which the primary consists of a single winding producing a sinusoidal variation of flux Φ_t. The rotor is considered to consist of only two single coils whose sides are AB and CD; the two coils are located at right angles to each other in space, and at the instant considered have their axes parallel to the speed axis and transformer axis respective to AB and CD. The 'mechanism' of torque production when the rotor revolves at speed ω in the direction shown is as follows.

A and B are moving through flux Φ_t. At any instant the value ϕ of the flux at A is given by $\phi = \Phi \sin \omega t$. Thus Φ_t is chosen as reference phasor in the analysis that follows. Rotation through ϕ will produce a 'flux cutting' e.m.f. always proportional to ϕ. Hence the e.m.f. E_{sr} as a phasor will always be in phase with Φ_t. E_{sr} will cause a current I_s in AB that in turn will set up a flux Φ_s, in phase with I_s. Rotation of CD through Φ_s will now induce a voltage E_{tr} in phase with Φ_s as previously. This is the equivalent of the 'back e.m.f.' of a d.c. motor and will largely (for high values of G) oppose the transformer e.m.f. E_{tt} set up in CD by transformer action. Current I_t is driven by the resultant of E_{tt} and E_{tr} and is assumed to be restricted only by the resistance of the coil CD (leakage neglected). The complete phasor diagram is as shown in Fig. 7.22.

The forward torque will emerge from the ensuing calculations as the phasor product of Φ_s and I_t. The backward torque, strangely enough, is produced by the (apparently) 'main' flux Φ_t acting on I_s. Tesla did not succeed in making his induction motor run until he strengthened the magnetic circuit in the speed axis to increase Φ_s. The phasor diagram shows that the ideally perfect rotating field with $\Phi_s = \Phi_t$ and at right angles to it is seen not to be vital to the production of net torque.

7.3.5 An Analysis of the Continuous Conductor Machine

We return now to the single-phase induction motor, this time with cage rotor or continuous conducting cylinder (the ultimate generality). Each portion of rotor conductor shown in Fig. 7.23 is resolved for an instant of time t, into an

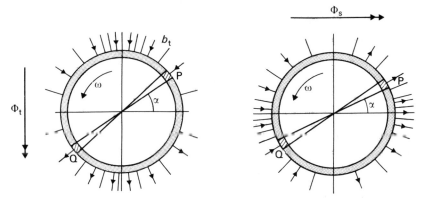

Figure 7.23 Method of treating a motor whose rotor carries a uniform conducting cylinder.

element of the kind represented by coil AB of Fig. 7.21, reduced by the sine of α, together with an element of the coil CD kind reduced in proportion to the cosine of α. The choice of the positive direction for flux lines of Φ_s and Φ_t as indicated by the arrows is quite arbitrary, as is the choice of the direction of the rotor speed ω, but great care must be exercised when relating these to the flux threading the elementary loop PQ and to the directions of the forces produced by the fluxes at positions such as P and Q. No loss of generality results from the consideration of a two-pole system so long as it is remembered that the rotor synchronous speed ω_s does not equal the angular frequency of the supply, as here, but is a submultiple of it in a multi-polar machine.

It is also assumed that ϕ_t is sinusoidally distributed in space around the airgap. Thus e_{sr} will be sinusoidally space distributed as will i_s and therefore ϕ_s, since $b_s \propto \int i_s \, d\alpha$. It will be convenient to assume the machine to be of unit length perpendicular to the diagrams.

$$b_t = B_t \sin \omega_s t \sin \alpha$$

$$b_s = B_s \sin(\omega_s t - \theta) \cos \alpha$$

Hence

$$\Phi_t = r \int_0^\pi b_t \, d\alpha = 2rB_t \sin \omega_s t$$

and

$$\Phi_s = r \int_{-\pi/2}^{\pi/2} b_s \, d\alpha = 2rB_s \sin(\omega_s t - \theta)$$

Thus

$$B_t = \frac{\Phi_t}{2r}, \qquad B_s = \frac{\Phi_s}{2r}$$

It is interesting to note that the values of B are the same as would be obtained if the flux distributed itself uniformly across a diameter.

Total flux threading the elementary loop PQ at angle α is given by

$$\phi = r \int_{\alpha}^{\pi + \alpha} b_t \, d\alpha + \int_{\pi + \alpha}^{\alpha} b_s \, d\alpha$$

$$= 2rB_t \sin \omega_s t \cos \alpha + 2rB_s \sin(\omega_s t - \theta) \sin \alpha$$

$$= \Phi_t \sin \omega_s t \cos \alpha + \Phi_s \sin(\omega_s t - \theta) \sin \alpha$$

Note that the sign is positive because the convention adopted in the diagrams is such as to make both Φ_t and Φ_s thread the loop PQ in the same direction.

Now the induced e.m.f. is given by $e = d\phi/dt$ or

$$e = \omega_s \Phi_t \cos \omega_s t \cos \alpha - \omega_r \Phi_t \sin \omega_s t \sin \alpha$$
$$+ \omega_s \Phi_s \cos(\omega_s t - \theta) \sin \alpha + \omega_r \Phi_s \sin(\omega_s t - \theta) \cos \alpha$$

Current density is given by $j = e/2\rho$ therefore current in elementary loop $= rj \, d\alpha = re \, d\alpha/2\rho$ and the force on one side of the loop $= rbj \, d\alpha = r/2\rho$ $(be \, d\alpha)$. Thus

$$\text{torque} = \frac{r^2}{\rho} \int_0^{\pi} be \, d\alpha$$

i.e.,

$$\text{torque} = \frac{r}{2\rho} \int_0^{\pi} [\Phi_t \sin \omega_s t \sin \alpha - \Phi_s \sin(\omega_s t - \theta) \cos \alpha]$$

$$\times [\omega_s \Phi_t \cos \omega_s t \cos \alpha - \omega_r \Phi_t \sin \omega_s t \sin \alpha$$
$$+ \omega_s \Phi_s \cos(\omega_s t - \theta) \sin \alpha + \omega_r \Phi_s \sin(\omega_s t - \theta) \cos \alpha] \quad (7.7)$$

Note again that because of the convention adopted, the fluxes b_t and b_s are in opposite directions at P and are therefore subtracted.

Only contributions from Eq. (7.7) are from products giving $\sin^2 \alpha$ or $\cos^2 \alpha$.

For all terms in $\sin \alpha \cos \alpha$,

$$\int_0^{\pi} = 0$$

Also

$$\int_0^{\pi} \sin^2 \alpha \, d\alpha = \int_0^{\pi} \cos^2 \alpha \, d\alpha = \frac{\pi}{2}$$

Thus the torque is

$$\frac{\pi r}{4\rho} [-\omega_r \Phi_t^2 \sin^2 \omega_s t + \omega_s \Phi_s \Phi_t \sin \omega_s t \cos(\omega_s t - \theta)$$

$$- \omega_s \Phi_s \Phi_t \cos \omega_s t \sin(\omega_s t - \theta) - \omega_r \Phi_s^2 \sin^2(\omega_s t - \theta)]$$

Each term such as $\sin^2 \omega_s t$ gives a steady torque of one-half amplitude plus a pulsating torque.

The steady torque only is therefore given by

$$\frac{\pi r}{8\rho}[-\omega_r \Phi_t^2 - \omega_r \Phi_s^2 + 2\omega_s \Phi_s \Phi_t \sin \theta]$$

$$= -\frac{\pi r}{8\rho}[\omega_r(\Phi_t^2 + \Phi_s^2) - 2\omega_s \Phi_s \Phi_t \sin \theta]$$

$$= -\frac{\pi r \omega_r}{8\mu}\left[\Phi_t^2 + \Phi_s^2 - \frac{2\omega_s}{\omega_r}\Phi_s \Phi_t \sin \theta\right]$$

The relationship between Φ_s and Φ_t may be deduced as follows:

$$E_{sr} = 2 \times \text{e.m.f./conductor} = 2B_r r\omega_r \sin \omega_s t$$

therefore

$$|E_{sr}| = 2B_t r\omega_r = \Phi_t \omega_r$$

Now

$$I_s x_0 = E_{sr} \sin \theta \text{ (from Fig. 7.22)} = \Phi_t \omega_r \sin \theta$$

which must amount to $d\Phi_s/dt$. But

$$\Phi_s = 2rB_s \sin(\omega_s t - \theta)$$

so that

$$\frac{d\Phi_s}{dt} = 2rB_s \omega_s \cos(\omega_s t - \theta)$$

and

$$\frac{d\Phi_s}{dt} = 2rB_s \omega_s = \Phi_s \omega_s$$

therefore

$$\frac{\Phi_s}{\Phi_t} = \frac{\omega_r}{\omega_s}\sin \theta$$

and steady torque is

$$-\frac{\pi r \omega_r}{8\rho}\left[\Phi_t^2 + \left(\frac{\omega_r}{\omega_s}\right)^2 \Phi_t^2 \sin^2 \theta - 2\frac{\omega_s}{\omega_r}\frac{\omega_r}{\omega_s}\Phi_t^2 \sin^2 \theta\right]$$

$$= \frac{\pi r \omega_r \Phi_t^2}{8}\left[\sin^2 \theta\left\{1 - \left(\frac{\omega_r}{\omega_s}\right)^2\right\} - \cos^2 \theta\right]$$

so that for zero torque $\omega_r = 0$ or

$$\cot^2 \theta = 1 - \left(\frac{\omega_r}{\omega_s}\right)^2$$

or

$$\omega_r = \omega_s\sqrt{(1 - \cot^2 \theta)}$$

where $\cot \theta = R_2/x_0$.

Now x_0 is the effective reactance at supply frequency of all the rotor conductors operating into the reactance of the cross axis which is not linked to the stator winding. In a symmetrical iron structure this reactance is the same on all axes and is therefore to be interpreted as the magnetizing reactance X_m in an equivalent circuit and

$$\omega_r = \omega_s \sqrt{\left[1 - \left(\frac{R_2}{X_m}\right)^2\right]}$$

so that the criterion that a single-phase induction motor shall be capable of running at all is $X_m/R_2 > 1$ or, in terms of the Goodness Factor, $G > 1$.

7.3.6 Space and Time Harmonics in Polyphase Induction Motors

Having established the validity of handling each component of a travelling field separately, the treatment of harmonics is relatively simple. *Time* harmonics occur as the result of the application of non-sinusoidal waveforms to the stator. Each harmonic involves a component of higher frequency than the fundamental and therefore a travelling field a multiple *faster* than the speed at which the motor will ever run. So far as any harmonic field is concerned, therefore, the rotor will always appear to be running at very high slip ($s = \frac{4}{5}$ for the fifth harmonic, $\frac{6}{7}$ for the seventh, and so on). So while time harmonics produce useful torque they do it at low efficiency and there is little more that need be added to this conclusion.

Space harmonics, however, are different. They arise because it is impossible to distribute the stator windings 'perfectly', i.e., the slots form distinct 'lumps' of m.m.f. that make the instantaneous flux distribution different from the idealized $b = B \sin \pi x/p$. The effect is a *reluctance* effect due to the uneven permeance of the airgap caused by the slotting. In severe cases where the number of rotor slots is related to the number of stator slots by fairly simple number ratios such as $2:1$, $3:4$, etc., the machine may indeed 'lock on' to the tooth pattern and run as a reluctance motor, which so far as its action as an induction device is concerned would be a disaster, for the reluctance speed is almost by definition less than $\frac{1}{6}\omega_s$. The speed–torque curve would be weird indeed (Fig. 7.24). Thus every induction machine with a

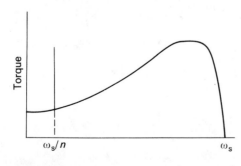

Figure 7.24 Speed–torque curve of an induction motor with an unfortunate choice of rotor/stator slot numbers. (A synchronous torque occurs at a sub-multiple of ω_s.)

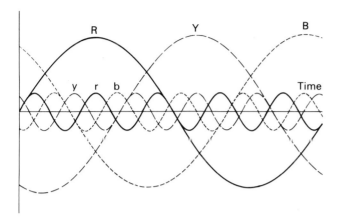

Figure 7.25 Waveforms of a three-phase system in which each phase carries a fifth harmonic, 'in phase' as it were with its fundamental. (Note that the order R, Y, B is reversed in the harmonic waves y, r, b.)

ferrous magnetic circuit carries a small 'parasite' of reluctance motor, just as each reluctance motor without infinitely thin lamination carries a parasitic induction motor, but the 'irritation' of the latter is negligible compared with that due to the former. But induction motor action due to the *slower* fields produced by space harmonics can also take its toll on the efficacy of a machine. Let us consider the fifth and seventh space harmonics. Figure 7.25 shows the waveforms of the fundamental and fifth harmonic whose zeros are such that one in five corresponds with the zero of the fundamental. Notice that the fifth harmonics are also space displaced mutually by 120° in relation to their own pole pitch $p/5$, and that their phase sequence is *reversed* in relation to that of the fundamental. This is because

$$5 \times \underline{120°} = 600° = 360° + \underline{240°}$$

and

$$5 \times \underline{240°} = 1200° = 3 \times 360° + \underline{120°}$$

The field due to the fifth space harmonic therefore rotates *backwards* at $\omega_s/5$. Consideration of the seventh harmonic shows no change in phase sequence and hence a *forward* going field, thus:

$$7 \times \underline{120°} = 840° = 2 \times 360° + \underline{120°}$$

and

$$7 \times \underline{240°} = 1680° = 4 \times 360° + \underline{240°}$$

and in general the $(3n-1)$th harmonic will produce a backward going field, the $(3n+1)$th a forward going.

Backward fields are rarely troublesome for motors, unless the plugging mode is important, except for the fact that their torques *subtract* from the

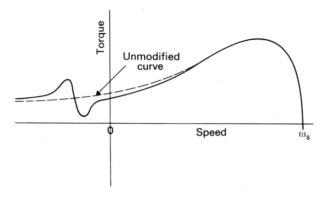

Figure 7.26 Effect of certain harmonics on the speed–torque curve.

useful output in the plugging region (Fig. 7.26) while the associated losses are additive. A study of the seventh harmonic torque (Fig. 7.27), however, shows how it modifies the motoring zone to the extent that if a motor with such a characteristic is required to start under an increasing load torque such as is provided by a fan (shown by a broken line), the motor may fail to run up beyond the stable slope of the harmonic interference and will run until the protection device disconnects it, because of rapid overheating, at roughly $\omega_s/7$. This running mode is often accompanied by a harsh *noise*. The phenomenon is known as 'crawling'.

The subject of noise in general is much more complicated and, in the main, is a problem that refuses to yield to analysis. All that is certain is that it arises as the result of an unfortunate choice of stator/rotor slot numbers. Most of the knowledge on this topic takes the form of case history and each manufacturer has his own confidential list of slot combinations opposite two tick columns headed 'machines known to be noisy' and 'machines known to be quiet'.

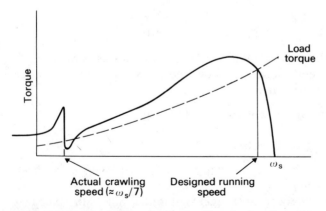

Figure 7.27 The cause of 'crawling' is the effect of a space harmonic on the speed–torque curve.

Usually fewer than ten per cent of the combinations have a tick in one or the other column!

7.3.7 Half-speed Running

If one phase of a three-phase wound rotor becomes open circuit, if some of the bars of a cage rotor become disconnected from the end rings, or if the rotor electric circuit otherwise becomes electrically unbalanced, the machine may fail to run above half speed for the following reason. Such imbalance may be represented as a balanced rotor circuit, together with a single-phase component. The latter, regarded as m.m.f., splits into counter-rotating m.m.f.s. The forward going half will always lock with the stator m.m.f. to produce useful torque, for its speed at slip s will be $\omega_r + s\omega_s = \omega_s$. But the backward going half will have a speed in space given by $\omega_r - s\omega_s$, which is nothing in particular unless $s = 0.5$, in which case $\omega_r - s\omega_s = 0$ and the field is stationary in space, i.e., relative to the stator frame. If now there be any anisotropy in the magnetic circuit (and it may be no more than grain orientation in the steel or a keyway in the shaft) the backward going field component (of zero *absolute* speed) may lock on to the anisotropy as a *reluctance* device. The effect was first observed by Geörges and often carries his name.

7.3.8 Transient Overspeeding

When an induction motor is suddenly switched on to full voltage, as is common in modern practice, it would be strange indeed if it displayed no transient behaviour comparable with that of passive networks when subjected to step functions of voltage. But in rotating machines the situation is complicated by the inertia of the moving parts. In particular, if the motor is run up initially on no-load and its rotor inertia is low, it may overshoot its normal running light speed, as shown in Fig. 7.28. One might deduce that its unloaded speed–torque curve is as shown in Fig. 7.29. This curve can be

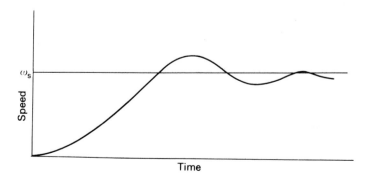

Figure 7.28 Overshoot of synchronous speed when started on light load.

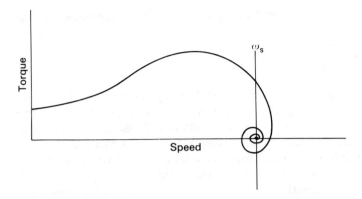

Figure 7.29 Apparent speed–torque curve operative during high acceleration.

derived geometrically by assuming that at each instantaneous speed during the run-up, the motor 'remembers' where it has been a short time previously (owing to inductance) and has failed to adjust to the new condition. Successive subtraction of abscissae as shown in Fig. 7.30 gives a physical picture of the effect.

What is probably more profitable for most readers, however, is to use the Generalized machine approach in which the m.m.f. of the rotor, always rotating at speed ω_s $(=\omega_r + s\omega_s)$, can be regarded as a synchronous source of m.m.f., as from a permanent magnet, for example. If then the stator is represented also as a rotating permanent magnet, the effect of sudden acceleration of either member is to produce oscillation of one magnet axis in relation to the other. In synchronous machines proper this oscillation is the change of lead–lag angle. In an induction machine it is a speed oscillation—

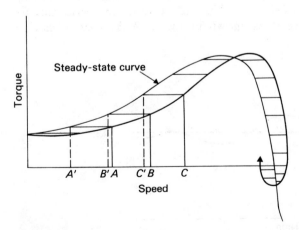

Figure 7.30 Figure 7.29 can be obtained by assuming a simple time lag. The rotor has accelerated to A while its flux pattern suggests that it is only at speed A', etc.

the transient overspeed phenomenon. It is interesting to note that with specially low inertia rotors (drag cup rotors) a first overshoot in which the speed exceeded $2\omega_s$ has been recorded.

7.3.9. Unbalanced Magnetic Pull (U.M.P.)

The forces of induction can be likened to a mechanical shearing stress in which the force is applied at right angles to both flux and current. But both rotor and stator of an induction machine usually contain windings in slots—they are electromagnets fed with a.c., but no matter *how* fed, they are still electromagnets with iron cores that face each other with N-pole opposite S-pole. This has nothing to do with induction machine action, but results in very large radial forces that exist quite separately (as tensile stresses) from the induction forces. That both designer and manufacturer try their best to make rotary machines have perfect cylindrical symmetry, is due to the fact that any asymmetry in the magnetic circuit can give rise to very large radial forces, simply because the magnetic attractive force ($B^2/2\mu_0$/unit pole area) is not the same at opposite ends of a diameter. This problem is amplified in induction machines by the requirement to maintain an average airgap of less than 0.1 in (2.5 mm), even in large machines. A rotor eccentric by only 0.01 in makes the airgaps of a 'one-millimetre-gap-machine' at opposite ends of a diameter become 0.75 mm and 1.25 mm. Since most primaries are series connected, the flux densities at standstill are inversely proportional to gap and magnetic pulls are proportional to $1/(\text{gap})^2$. In the example quoted, the unbalanced pull is $(1.25/0.75)^2$ at opposite ends of a diameter, i.e., 2.78 times.

It has been the lament of engineers since Boucherot in 1905 that these radial, magnetic forces cannot be harnessed, for the typical mean value of B in the gap of a good induction machine can be as high as 1.0 T, making $B^2/2\mu_0$ of the order of 8 kgf/cm^2. All the designer can do is to use the shearing stress $B \times J$ per unit area and a typical value of J is 30 000 A/m, making the induction stress of the order of 0.03 kgf/cm^2, some 25 times smaller than the radial force.

Of course, standstill is the worst possible condition of u.m.p. Once the rotor spins, its short circuited conductors object strongly to 67 per cent changes in flux every half revolution. Rotor current flows to balance the flux at low values of slip, but it is interesting to note that this implies rotor current and hence rotor loss where $s = 0$, i.e., a magnetic imperfection manifests itself as an electric circuit inefficiency. It has been our experience that not all manufacturers use the same formula for the calculation of u.m.p. and that many ignore the effect of rotor spin, assuming the force to be that obtaining at standstill. Their fears of the enhancement of u.m.p. by a shaft whirling phenomenon invariably results in their designing a much larger diameter shaft than is required. In linear motors, the u.m.p. is a quite different manifestation, and fear of enormous values of u.m.p. probably did more than anything else to set back the progress in linear motors for over a century (see Chapter 10).

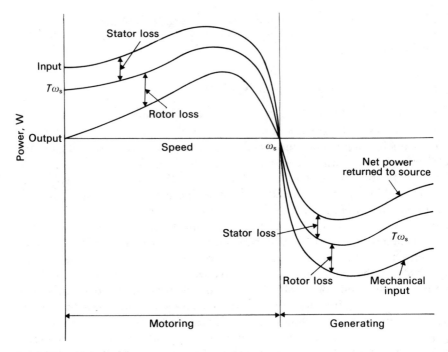

Figure 7.31 Power allocation in the generating zone. Only the $T\omega_s$ curve is skew-symmetric about the axes.

7.3.10 Operation as a Generator

The simplest approach to the reversal of power flow is to continue to plot Eq. (7.6) for $v_s - v < 0$, i.e., for negative value of slip. Figure 7.31 shows the resulting curve that illustrates the following properties of an induction machine when used in this region.

(1) The torque is negative. This implies that the machine is being mechanically driven.
(2) If T is negative, $T\omega_s$ is negative and the machine is attempting to return this power to the supply.
(3) The $T\omega_s$ curve is skew-symmetric in the generating region compared with its shape in the motoring region, but
(4) whereas, as a motor, the rotor I^2R loss must be subtracted to obtain the net *mechanical* power output, as a generator the losses must also be subtracted from the $-T\omega_s$ curve to obtain the net *electrical* output. The curve, indicating the output in each mode, is therefore not symmetrical.

The above approach, however, does not face up to the real difficulties that can confront the student of this subject if questions such as this are posed: 'If the stator terminals of an induction machine are disconnected from the supply and the rotor is driven above its synchronous speed, where does the electrical output flow to?' The obvious answer to this question is that there cannot *be* any electrical output in this situation. Further thought will suggest that the reason for this is connected with the idea that an electrically disconnected induction machine can have no indication of an operating frequency and hence no 'knowledge' of a synchronous speed ($2pf$). While this is correct, it has introduced still further complications, as we are about to indicate.

But first let us return to the T–s curve, which gave such simple answers and itself was derived from such simple mechanical concepts as a piece of wood drifting in a river. Was there an underlying assumption that was taken for granted in the mechanical analogy? The answer is that there *was*, but it was extremely fundamental. We assumed that there *was* a river! In electrical terms this means that there was not only a travelling magnetic field, but that something determined its *speed*. To set up an alternating flux of any kind in an imperfect magnetic circuit requires an m.m.f., and hence a current. That current will *lag* the applied e.m.f. by 90°. There is *no mechanism* in an induction machine for the generation of reactive power. There is no equivalent of residual magnetism in a d.c. machine. If the stator of a cage rotor machine carries any residual flux, rotation of the rotor will simply demolish it.

Yet it is not necessary for an induction machine to be connected to a major busbar system for it to be capable of generating. All that is necessary is for its stator terminals to be connected to a polyphase source of reactive power that will also monitor frequency and thus define the speed above which it will generate.

A synchronous motor will do this. What is more, it need not be as large a machine as the induction generator, for it is only required to supply magnetizing current and leakage flux. Figure 7.32 shows a system that will generate power to a bank of resistors when the slip is negative. But it *must* be

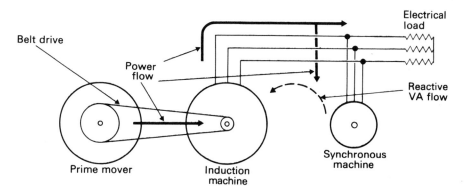

Figure 7.32 Induction generator connected to a mechanical power source and a 'pacemaker' synchronous machine.

noted that as the value of negative slip is increased, the output *power* of the induction machine will demand a load capable of absorbing it. At first sight this appears to be satisfied by an increase in the working voltage, yet the latter is set by the excitation of the synchronous machine alone, apparently. If the latter is not raised in sympathy with the rise in speed of the mechanical drive (and this situation can only continue until either machine *saturates* its magnetic circuit) then something else must happen.

Examination of the problem soon shows that there is now only *one* other thing that can change to compensate—the induction device can feed *power* to the synchronous machine and accelerate it to a higher speed. At once the synchronous machine sets a higher frequency and hence a higher value of ω_s in the synchronous machine. The negative slip is at once reduced, the available power output falls, and a stable system is obtained.

In starting up a system such as that shown in Fig. 7.32 the synchronous machine must first be run up, as an alternator, by means of a separate drive, in order to establish a 'river'. It is instructive to disconnect the electrical load and to attach a large flywheel to the induction machine. Once a reasonably large speed has been established for the set, disconnect the mechanical drive to the synchronous machine and, by means of instruments, observe the electrical and mechanical changes that thereafter occur. Not being flywheel assisted, the synchronous machine tries to slow down more rapidly (due to windage and friction) than does the induction device. But the instant it succeeds, it feeds a magnetizing current of lower frequency to the induction machine which at once becomes a generator and feeds *power* to the synchronous machine to supply its mechanical losses, and to *maintain* its speed. The synchronous machine, being still excited, continues to supply the reactive power that the induction machine needs. The pair *must* slow down *together* and all the flywheel energy must appear as I^2R loss in the windings of the two machines. This process can take a long time, but will be greatly accelerated of course by the switching in of an electrical load to the stator terminals. Even so, the excitation of both machines will remain until the speed has fallen to perhaps only a few per cent of its initial value. The synchronous–induction combination can be no better described than by analogy with the famous nursery rhyme:

> *Jack Sprat could eat no fat.*
> *His wife could eat no lean.*
> *And so you see, between them both,*
> *They licked the platter clean.*

This subject is of great importance in relation to the emergency braking systems of high speed vehicles driven by linear motors, particularly in the presence of external power failure (see Chapter 10, page 349).

Yet there remains one more 'brain teaser' in relation to an induction machine in the generator mode. Imagine a three-phase induction machine, connected to mains as shown in Fig. 7.33 and driven at exactly synchronous

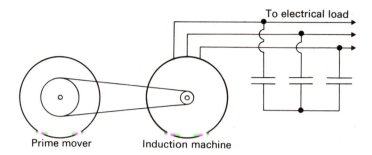

Figure 7.33 Induction generator with capacitor bank only.

speed by a separate drive. A capacitor bank that tunes out exactly the reactive power demand of the induction device is now connected. Then the main power supply is switched off. What happens if the drive to the induction machine is now accelerated? The machine is excited, its reactive power supplied, and its frequency fixed by the equation $X_m = 1/C\omega$, so it is now possible to generate active power.

Again, the answer must be that the active power can only go towards accelerating the induction motor. This being so, the only way the equation X_m $(= L_m\omega) = 1/C\omega$ can be upheld is that ω increases. At first sight this seems impossible, for either L_m or C must change. What in fact *can* occur (and since this is the only possibility *must* occur), is that the voltage rises until the iron saturates. Saturation lowers the value of L_m, increases $1/L_mC$, and hence ω, and all is accounted for!

This apparently highly complex affair turns out to be identical to the self excitation of a d.c. shunt generator that schoolchildren of seventeen take in their stride. A small amount of residual magnetism in a d.c. machine is *amplified* (as in the amplidyne, page 165) and produces more field current and hence m.m.f. to add to the excitation and so on, and this positive feed-back situation would excite the machine to infinity, were it not for the shape of the *B–H* curve of the magnetic circuit. What might happen in an air cored machine, initially triggered by a battery, can be guessed! A similar phenomenon in reverse was provided by the Zeta project in which the 'pinch effect' of a current, in the case of a conducting plasma, shrank down to atomic level and shattered the nucleus!

We feel that we cannot conclude this most intriguing use of an induction machine without recalling an experiment done, 'just for fun', by the late Sir Frederic Williams in Manchester in the nineteen-fifties. Having tuned a driven induction motor, he noted that the loose laminations of the stator vibrated at the tuned frequency to emit sound. He then connected up a bank of capacitors of varying sizes, arranged a 'keyboard' of switches allowing different values to be switched in or out, and succeeded in playing the national anthem on a 56 hp rotary machine!

7.4 OTHER TYPES OF ROTATING MACHINE

Space does not permit a full treatment of the principles of d.c. machines, a.c. commutator motors, both single phase and polyphase, and reluctance and hysteresis (the 'magnetic') machines. We therefore propose to treat the whole subject of commutator machines by concentrating mainly on the purpose of a commutator itself and by a qualitative approach only, with some underlying philosophy and economics. The action of the magnetic machines will be reduced to a physical explanation of their behaviour only.

7.4.1 The Mechanism of a Commutator

The simple physical theory of d.c. machines suggests that the purpose of a commutator is to *rectify* what would otherwise be a harmonic ridden a.c. wave that was nearly rectangular. The very nature of magnetism is such that a south pole must follow a north and any generated or supplied e.m.f. must be alternating in nature. But a commutator is very much more than a rectifier. Let us consider the two basically different windings shown in Figs. 7.34 and 7.35. In both cases the windings are shown Gramme ring fashion, merely to simplify the diagrams. In real machines external field would emanate radially from the cores into the stators. In type A the winding is tapped at three points that are connected via slip rings to stationary brushes. In type B the winding is tapped at a plurality of points that are connected to a corresponding set of commutator segments. Three brushes spaced 120° apart make contact with a succession of the conducting segments. The winding of both rotors is to be regarded as a three-phase, two-pole, delta connected system. This in no way restricts the theory to three phases, two poles, or to this form of connection.

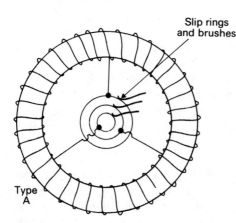

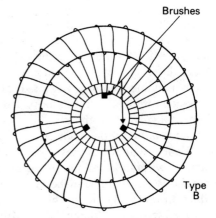

Figure 7.34 A rotor winding tapped at three points and connected to slip rings (subsequently referred to as 'type A').

Figure 7.35 A fundamentally different type of winding, tapped at many points and connected to commutator segments (subsequently referred to as 'type B').

When each rotor is at rest and a three-phase, balanced supply is fed to the brushes, the windings produce effects that are identical. Each field rotates at ω_s relative to the stationary stator. Each winding presents the same reactance per phase to the a.c. supply and hence the same impedance per phase. If now the rotors are rotated in the same direction as the field rotates at velocity ω, the speed of the field of A is increased to $(\omega_s + \omega)$, while that of B remains at ω_s, since the coil system at any instant 'sees' itself as stationary and fed from the same three points in space. The reactance of A does not change with changes in ω, since its own field accelerates in step with the windings. But the rate at which winding B makes and breaks linkages with its own field reduces as ω increases, from ω_s at standstill to $(\omega_s - \omega)$. Its reactance therefore falls by a factor $(\omega_s - \omega)/\omega_s$ $(= s\omega_s)$. The frequency of the currents in rotor A remains at f_s $(= \omega_s/2\pi)$, those of B reduce to sf_s.

Let us now reverse the power flow to each machine by assuming that an externally impressed two-pole rotating field of velocity ω_s threads each system, and that electrical power is collected from the brushes. The frequency collected from machine A will be sf_s; that of B will be f_s at all times. The only way that a frequency other than f_s can be collected is by rotation of the brush system itself in relation to the stator.

The conclusion should now be clear. A commutator is a polyphase *frequency changer* in which the frequency of the e.m.f. at the brushes (whether energy is fed in or extracted) is a measure of the relative velocity between the angular speed of the field and that of the brushes, and of nothing else. We can now check this finding for the relatively simple case of the d.c. machine. The field coils and hence the field itself are stationary; so are the brushes. The relative velocity, field to brushes, is zero. Therefore the frequency at the brushes is zero, i.e., it is d.c.!

Armed with this information we can now proceed to a consideration of a.c. commutator machines along two entirely contrasting paths, one of which needs the above result while the other does not. The first facilitates the understanding of polyphase machines; the latter is preferable for single-phase commutator motors.

7.4.2 Polyphase Commutator Motors

We begin with the basic Eq. (7.3), developed on page 214, rearranged slightly:

$$s = \frac{\text{rotor loss}}{\text{rotor input}} \tag{7.8}$$

The speed control of induction motors using added secondary resistance that can be located outside the machine entirely suggests that the energy lost therein might be returned to the supply, were it to be recast into the proper frequency and phase, for clearly the heat produced in external resistors could be used to make steam, which in turn could drive a turboalternator. The fact that such a system would be enormously costly and the efficiency of the steam producer very low does not detract from the thought: 'It *can* be done.' In engineering there is usually more than one way to achieve a result. It is the engineer's task to find the best. It is certain that Eq. (7.8) can now be written in a more optimistic form:

$$\text{slip} = \frac{\text{rotor power extracted}}{\text{rotor input}}$$

and since an extraction mechanism other than a resistor might be able to operate as a *negative* article as well as a positive, the final form of the basic equation is:

$$\text{slip} = \frac{\text{rotor power extracted or injected}}{\text{rotor input} \ (= T\omega_s)}$$

Negative values of slip simply indicate speeds in excess of ω_s, and why not, since energy is being injected into the system? The only problem with the slip ring arrangement is that the extracted energy is at the wrong frequency (sf_s instead of f_s). But if the rotor winding is of type B (Fig. 7.35) rather than type A, the frequency at the brushes will be a measure of the field speed of the stator, i.e., f_s at all times. A polyphase commutator motor uses a rotor of this kind together with a variable ratio transformer or transformer-cum-phase-shifter (an induction machine with lockable (but movable) rotor) to extract rotor power and feed it back to supply, or to add *conductively* to the rotor energy already being supplied by the stator *inductively*. If the coupling transformer between brushes and line is connected in series with the stator of the motor then the latter will exhibit the series characteristics of a d.c. series motor, as shown in Fig. 7.36. If parallel connection is made then the characteristics change to the nearly flat speed–torque curve of the shunt motor.

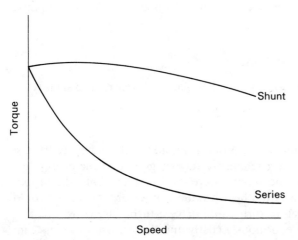

Figure 7.36 Characteristics of shunt and series commutator motors (d.c. or a.c.).

Polyphase commutator machines at the start of the twentieth century were basically adjustable speed motors where the magnitude only of the conductively fed power was under the control of the operator. But it was also realized that a type B rotor, with its magnetic circuit closed by means of a windingless stator, and driven slightly above the 'electrical speed' (f/P) fed to the brushes, would appear to have a negative reactance, i.e., capacitive reactance per phase. As such it could be run in parallel with an induction motor perhaps twenty or thirty times its weight, yet bring the power factor of the system up to unity. One name for such a device was a 'phase advancer' and it should have been obvious that more than mere reactive power might have been obtained from a machine whose stator was almost 'redundant' in electromagnetic terms. It was some time before a combined speed and power factor control emerged.

7.4.3 The Modern Commutator Motors

The Schrage motor filled this role for several decades. Its rotor carried *both* a type A *and* a type B winding. The former was connected to the three-phase supply and if the stator winding was short circuited the machine could be described as a simple induction motor 'inside out'. But the type B winding carried not three brushes but three *pairs*, each pair being capable of being separated angularly, and able to pass by each other so that they could be 'negatively separated' or, of course, rest side by side on the same commutator segment. Rotation of all six brushes through an angle controlled the power factor; separation positively extracted energy from the rotor, negative separation added to it. In practice it was generally found necessary only to preset the phase angle of all six, then move only one brush from each pair to control speed and maintain a high power factor simultaneously.

But a.c. commutator motors suffered commutation problems of a magnitude such as d.c. machines never had. In the first instance, for a given r.m.s. current, the brushes were called upon to switch $\sqrt{2}$ times as much current in the worst condition. What was worse, transformer e.m.f.s were induced in the coils undergoing commutation, a fact more easily demonstrated in respect of the single-phase machines about to be described. It was generally reckoned that the size of a Schrage motor was limited by commutation to a maximum output of 34 hp per pole. Teago[8] has described the A and B winding combination as equivalent to a very special kind of rotating transformer, having a variable voltage ratio, a variable frequency ratio, and a variable primary–secondary phase relationship.

In the nineteen-thirties came perhaps the ultimate commutator machine, at least the only one to compete still with solid state frequency processing systems. Invented by Schwarz, it was named simply the 'N-S' motor and embodied a refinement in commutation at least equal to the effect of interpoles in a d.c. machine. (Interpoles cannot be used with a.c. for the phase of the flux from the interpoles is out of phase with the flux it is supposed to neutralize.

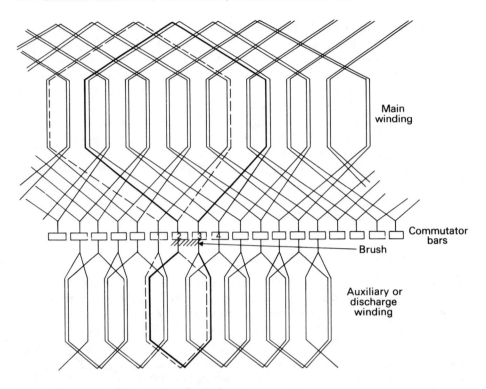

Figure 7.37 Section of the winding of an N-S motor.

Attempts were made to incorporate phase splitting circuits but these were found to give cancellation only at one value of speed and load.) In the N-S motor the rotor carries a type B winding, but in the same slots is housed a winding of one-third the pitch, with the number of turns adjusted to cause no short circuit current between the two, even though the two windings are tightly coupled magnetically and are coil-for-coil connected to identical pairs of adjacent commutator segments. The interconnection, however, is made with a subtle 'half overlap' best describable in a developed diagram as in Fig. 7.37. The small-pitched winding is known as a 'discharge' winding, for being magnetically coupled to the primary it is able to hand on any spurious e.m.f. induced during commutation by a succession of inductive and conducting couplings in each direction, until the reactive effect that the spurious e.m.f. would have otherwise produced is shared among *all* the coils of the rotor as if in parallel and the effective reactance is thus divided by the *total* number of coils, i.e., it is *very* small. The rotor is effectively a type B with an additional built-in set of transformers that rotate on the same shaft. Figure 7.38 attempts to show a simplified arrangement to illustrate the forward and backward energy transfers. N-S motors have been built for drive power of the order of 10 000 hp in a single unit.

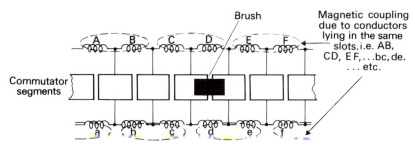

Figure 7.38 Conductive and inductive couplings in an N-S motor enable stored energy in the coil undergoing commutation to be shared with coils both in front and behind it.

7.4.4 Single-phase A.C. Commutator Motors

Now follows the second approach to the mechanism of a.c. commutator machines that is formulated to simplify single-phase devices. It is based on the fact that if the current flow in both armature and field windings of a d.c. motor are reversed simultaneously, the machine continues to develop torque in the same direction. It could therefore be expected to run when fed from a.c. However, a shunt motor carries a field winding necessarily having a very large number of turns (to 'absorb' the full line voltage without an enormous magnetic circuit cross section). Its inductance is such that the application of even the full a.c. supply voltage produces a trickle of current only (of the order of a few milliamps). Shunt motors for single-phase a.c. are never attempted. But the series motor with its field winding of a few turns of thick wire carrying the full current *is* possible, with modifications. First the iron parts of the whole machine and not merely the armature must be laminated. Even the armature of a motor designed for d.c. would have too high a reactance. Compensation mechanisms to neutralize the effect have included a quadrature winding as shown in Fig. 7.39(a) or effectively a short circuited winding on the stator

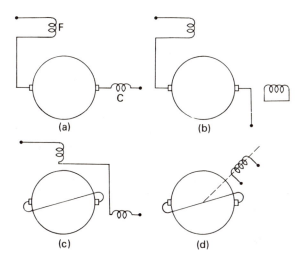

Figure 7.39 (a), (b) Quadrature windings in single-phase, a.c. commutator motors to neutralize the armature ampere-turns. Diagrams (b)–(d) illustrate the development of the repulsion motor.

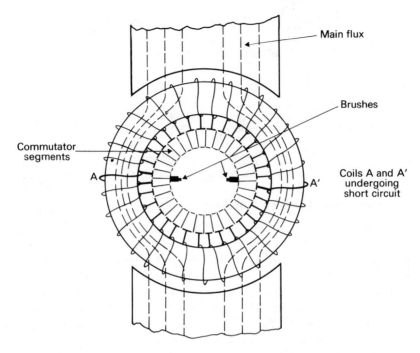

Figure 7.40 Schematic diagram illustrating the most serious cause of commutation problems in a.c. machines.

cross axis, as shown in (b). But the latter concept was immediately developed most ingeniously by two topological steps illustrated in (c) and (d). First the armature winding, in series with the field in diagram (c), is interchanged with the short circuit winding. Then the two stator windings are combined to give the result in (d), a machine with a conventional stator winding and a short circuited single-phase rotor. Because of an early explanation of its action involving the determination of the instantaneous polarities of field poles and armature steel, the motor was called a 'repulsion motor'.

The basic troubles of single-phase motors are of course associated with the process of commutation. Figure 7.40 illustrates, with a simple Gramme ring rotor, how the coils A and A', which are short circuited by the brushes for a few milliseconds each half-revolution, have their axes coincident with the transformer axis and are liable therefore to send a heavy current through the brushes. While such might be tolerable since the winding only suffers the current for a small fraction of a revolution, the brushes must carry it at all times and will certainly burn out within minutes unless steps are taken to minimize it. The transformer induced e.m.f. is proportional to the flux per pole, the frequency, and the number of turns per coil.

Accordingly, in single-phase a.c. machines the following differences are to be found compared with a d.c. motor of similar design.

(1) The a.c. machine has many more poles (>12) to maintain the same total flux (which after all, produces the output) and yet reduce the flux per pole.
(2) The number of turns per armature coil is reduced to *one* (the ultimate minimum), but this involves:
(3) The use of a great deal more rotor slots and commutator segments. Yet each segment must handle the same current. Consequently:
(4) The commutator segments are much longer, axially.
(5) In large machines, the supply frequency must be reduced. Before the days of solid state devices, this was usually done (as in European railway systems) by means of back-to-back mercury arc converters that divided the 50 Hz supply frequency by a factor of three.

A famous remark attributed to Steinmetz says: 'For an a.c. commutator motor, the ideal frequency is zero!'—which we interpret as meaning that if a designer is prepared to go to such lengths in the design of an a.c. machine and the user then decides to run it on d.c., the performance will be superb! The reason why the study of single-phase a.c. commutator motors is important is that many drives, especially those in household equipment, need speeds in excess of 3000 (or 3600) rev/min, which cannot be obtained by straight induction, nor by a d.c. motor, for the supply is a.c. The one thing in common in household devices is that the power requirement is low. In small machines the value of G is low, and by working on this factor by adding a few extra imperfections such as high resistance brushes, the necessity for reduced frequency can be removed and the constraints (2) to (4) of the above list can be relaxed a little. The fact that these motors will run equally well on d.c. gave rise to their being named 'universal' motors.

7.4.5 The 'Magnetic' Machines

Neglecting simple electromagnets such as are used in telegraphic relays, there are only two types of magnetic machine, the 'reluctance' motor and the 'hysteresis' motor. The first of these is in general use also as a generator, particularly in aircraft systems where the standard frequency is 400 Hz and the power/weight ratio, in consequence, is far higher than anything that a 50 or 60 Hz machine can achieve. Two to three kilowatts per kg is not uncommon in these high speed alternators that are force cooled to a degree where 13 000 A/in^2 ($= 2 \times 10^7$ A/m^2) is a tolerable current density in the copper windings.

Figure 7.41 shows a typical layout of an electric clock motor. This, as a reluctance device, is a very unsophisticated design, very cheap to manufacture, and its action we propose to deal with in an unsophisticated way also. The laminated stator and rotor consists of no more than a few stampings (<10) of fairly thick steel (perhaps a millimetre or more). The electric circuit is a single, simple-bobbin coil. Tooth faces tooth between rotor and stator, a position that will obtain if any flux at all is set up in the magnetic circuit. If the flux is alternating and the rotor runs at such a speed that the time interval between a

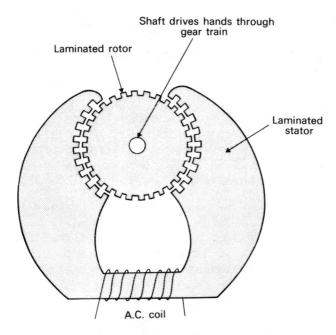

Figure 7.41 Basic mechanism of a mains-fed electric clock.

first alignment of teeth and the next alignment is half a period of the supply, a condition of minimum energy is established and this running condition continues. If for any reason the rotor fails to come into alignment owing to friction or other small load, the peak flux will occur when the rotor teeth centres *lag* slightly, as in any loaded synchronous machine, and the rotor receives accelerating torque. Conversely, if the rotor tries to go ahead, retarding forces will be developed. Because of the complex nature of the B–H relationship in steel, there is not a lot of established theory of clock motors and the designer uses experience to know that, for example, the tooth tips should be rounded (not shown), to avoid sudden 'locks' when the rotor stops dead. The large number of teeth makes the synchronous speed, and therefore the rotor momentum, low, so that the chances of a rapid deceleration due to a speck of dust in the bearings would otherwise be high.

Single-phase reluctance motors are started by accelerating them beyond synchronous speed and then releasing the rotors. In the case of electric clocks this can be done with the fingers on a suitably terminated shaft. An automatic start can be provided by giving the mechanism an impulse delivered from a pre-set spring.

In the more sophisticated aircraft reluctance generator, the magnetic circuit is given an additional m.m.f. (of fixed value) as excitation. Unlike the standard alternator, however, both a.c. and d.c. windings are housed in the stator, as shown in Fig. 7.42. The fact of having both an exciting winding and

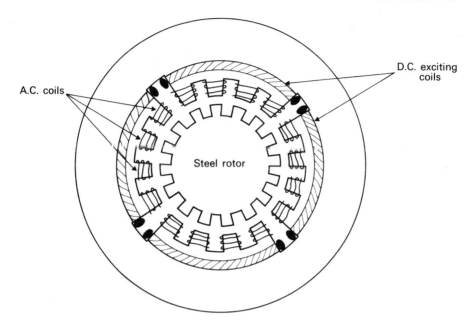

Figure 7.42 Aircraft-type alternator with both excitation and output windings on the stator. Flux density is modulated by reluctance only, giving the stator the electromagnetic 'appearance' of a transformer.

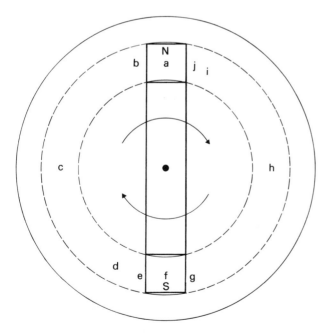

Figure 7.43 The action of a hysteresis motor.

an output does not allow the machine to qualify as an 'electromagnetic' machine, for the variation of flux through the output windings is achieved only by reluctance change, which, as discussed in Chapter 5 (page 133), becomes proportionately smaller the larger the machine. The use of 100 kW reluctance generators does not refute the argument 'the smaller, the better', for the 400 Hz machine is really a number of small pole pairs distributed around a not very large diameter rotor (< 20 cm). The impressive output is due to the high speed, the intricate design of the cooling system, and the use of the very best insulating and magnetic materials. The 400 Hz machine may weigh only a tenth as much as its 50 or 60 Hz counterpart of the same power, but the high frequency machine may still have the higher initial cost!

Hysteresis motors obviously operate by exploiting the nonlinear relationship between B and H in ferromagnetic material. The following description is purely qualitative but is, we believe, quite satisfying, in that it explains with relative ease an otherwise impossible looking speed–torque curve. Let the effect of the stator be seen to be a rotating magnetic field represented in Fig. 7.43 by a pair of permanent magnets and pole shoes, physically rotating around a steel cylinder of high hysteretic loss. Let us assume that there is a relative velocity in the direction indicated.

Figure 7.44 shows a typical B–H loop for the rotor steel. Points marked in capital letters on this figure relate to points on the rotor of Fig. 7.43 (in small letters), indicating corresponding states of magnetization. Maximum m.m.f. occurs opposite pole centres a and f which therefore correspond to A and F

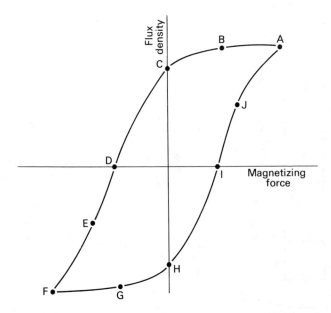

Figure 7.44 Points in the magnetization cycle corresponding to points on the rotor.

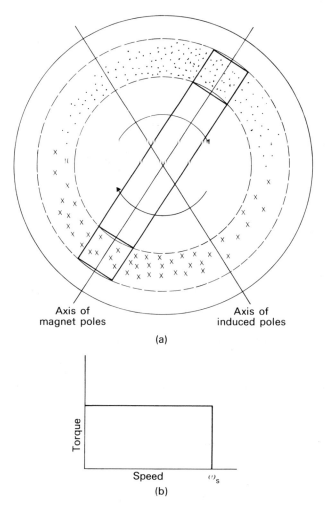

Axis of
magnet poles

Axis of
induced poles

(a)

Torque

Speed ω_s

(b)

Figure 7.45 Instantaneous flux pattern in a hysteresis motor, (a), and speed/torque curve, (b).

in Fig. 7.44. Positions such as b and g on the rotor have just been under the influence of maximum m.m.f. and are therefore still highly fluxed (points B and G in Fig. 7.44). The zero m.m.f. positions c and h still allow a large remanent flux (C and H) to exist. Only at D and I does the flux fall to zero as the result of reversed m.m.f. Beyond D and I, the flux is rapidly reversed to maximum values at F and A. Let us now draw in a flux pattern for the airgap that will fulfil these demands on flux values (Fig. 7.45). The Maxwell stress pattern clearly indicates torque production in a direction trying to reduce the relative velocity.

Now none of the foregoing argument had need to refer to the *value* of the relative velocity, for the flux distortion is purely the result of a magnetic

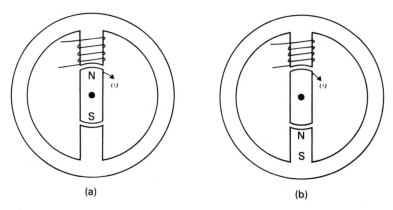

Figure 7.46 The difference between an electromagnetic machine, (a), and a magnetic machine, (b), is that the secondary of the latter carries no excitation.

'history'—a hysteretic lag that occurs equally at all speeds, *including zero*! Accordingly, the speed–torque curve of the machine is as shown in Fig. 7.45(b), and what could be better for driving a hi-fi record player or tape deck than a synchronous motor with full torque during run-up? Were this machine to lie on the electromagnetic side of the 'Great Divide'[9], induction motors would hardly ever be used!

Owing to skin effect, the rotors of hysteresis motors are usually made of thin walled cylinders, since the starting flux can only penetrate a highly permeable material to the extent of a few millimetres.

7.4.6 A Comparison Between a Synchronous Machine and a Reluctance Machine

Figure 7.46 shows primitive structures of two types of machine that physically are very similar, yet whose characteristics vary with scale in quite opposite directions. Structurally, the magnetic circuits are identical, the stator coils are identical, and the rotor of each is driven at the same speed. In fact, the only physical difference between the two is that the excitation magnet (marked N-S), which could equally well be replaced by an iron cored electromagnet fed with d.c., is the *rotor* in (a) but a part of the stator in (b). Within the definition here adopted, (b) is clearly a *magnetic* machine, while (a) is electromagnetic.

Let us first measure the flux that threads the stator coil. In machine (a) it alternates between saturation level in one direction and an equal value in the opposite direction at a frequency ω (the rotor speed). In machine (b) the flux never changes direction and in theory (where magnetic circuits could be 'insulated') it varies from zero to maximum at double the frequency of the flux in machine (a). The latter is shown by the unbroken line in Fig. 7.47(a). The current rating of each machine is identical, so a comparison of power output from each amounts to a comparison of induced voltage in the stator coils.

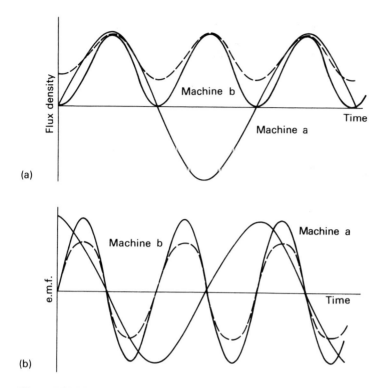

Figure 7.47 Fluxes and induced e.m.f.s in the two machines shown in Fig. 7.46.

Induced e.m.f. is proportional to the rate of change of flux and thus the waveforms of e.m.f. for the two machines are as seen in the unbroken lines in Fig. 7.47(b), having the same amplitudes. The loss of the factor of two in flux variation is balanced by a gain of two due to increased frequency. The two machines are apparently of equal rating.

But in practice, magnetic circuits cannot be insulated and when the rotor of machine (b) is in the quadrature position, as shown in Fig. 7.48, the flux

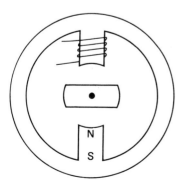

Figure 7.48 When the rotor is in the quadrature position shown, the flux linking the coil is not zero.

through the stator coil is far from zero, which is not the case with machine (a), whose flux not only falls to zero, but *reverses*. The true flux through the coil of machine (b) is shown by the broken line in Fig. 4.47(a) and the e.m.f., therefore, is as shown by the broken line in (b). The output of (b) is fundamentally less than that of (a) by an amount depending on the ratio of the reluctances in the direct and quadrature axes. More than this, the peak flux in the direct axis position cannot exceed the saturation value, but the minimum flux is set only by the reluctance in the quadrature position. The reluctances of magnetic circuits with similar geometries vary as length/area (i.e., proportionally to $1/L$). Thus, as the scale of machines (a) and (b) is increased, the broken curves in Fig. 7.47 reduce in amplitude in relation to the maxima of flux density and e.m.f., and the reluctance machine (b) demands tangential force less than proportional to pole area and hence input torque (force × radius) less than proportional to volume. This result expresses the law 'the smaller the better' in terms of specific output. The above argument, of course, is as valid for motor action as it is for generation.

7.4.7 Fractional Horsepower Motors

Although some of the material under this heading has already been covered, a number of interesting mechanisms remain to be discussed. How, for example, can single-phase induction motors and electric clocks be made to start, other than by spinning with the fingers? In the case of induction motors there are several methods:

(1) An auxiliary cross field winding is put in series with a capacitor and connected in parallel with the main winding. This is the 'capacitor start' mechanism. It is only necessary to produce a component of flux in time and space displacement from that of the main flux to produce an 'elliptic' field, as shown in Fig. 7.49, which is seen to be the equivalent of a pulsating field and a small rotating field superposed.

(2) The auxiliary winding itself can be designed to have a different R/X

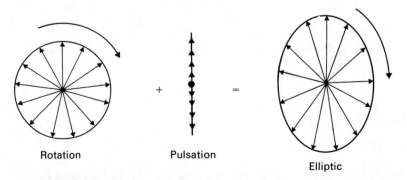

Rotation   Pulsation

Elliptic

Figure 7.49 The definition of an elliptic field.

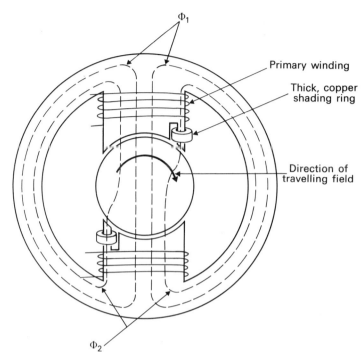

Figure 7.50 A shaded pole mechanism.

ratio from that of the main winding, thus achieving the same elliptic field effect.

(3) The motor may incorporate a 'shaded pole' device, which will now be described with reference to Fig. 7.50. The pole pieces are slotted, and a thick copper loop surrounds the tooth tip so isolated. The flux due to the primary winding now has two possible *parallel* paths, one avoiding the loop, the other passing through it. To keep the initial argument simple, let us assume that there are, in the first instance, no rotor conductors whatever. As is often the case, there is need for more than one simple explanation of the action, for in electromagnetism all explanations are in the nature of 'parables'.

First, then, the long established phasor diagram method. The flux path avoiding the loop is an open circuit transformer situation. That *through* the loop is a short circuit counterpart whose diagram is more complex. Let us therefore begin with the more difficult instance and draw a typical phasor diagram for a loaded transformer as shown in Fig. 7.51(a). It matters little whether we assume that a short circuited loop produces in-phase or lagging current; let us therefore keep the situation as general as possible and assume a lag. The flux Φ_2 is the flux through the loop.

But the primary winding embraces *both* magnetic circuits, so the whole of the current I_1 in Fig. 7.51(a) is available as magnetizing current for the open

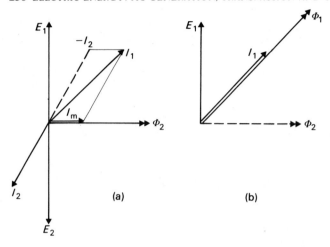

Figure 7.51 Phasor diagrams for the fluxes Φ_1 and Φ_2.

magnetic circuit and produces, as in Fig. 7.51(b), a flux Φ_1 that is at once seen to be bigger than Φ_2 and to lead it by a large angle. Interpreting this on the physical diagram (Fig. 7.50), the flux Φ_1 comes to its maximum *before* that of Φ_2, and therefore there is a component of travelling field from the unshaded part of the pole *towards the shaded part*. Such field component is sufficient to start a small, single-phase motor.

The name 'shaded pole' is better appreciated perhaps if the physical structure is as shown in Fig. 7.52, where the shading ring is actually a sheet of conductor on the surface. It should also be noted forcibly that the action of a shading conductor so placed will also produce force *on itself*, ejecting it if not secured to the pole. This phenomenon, together with the ability of a single-phase motor to increase its own speed *due* entirely *to* that speed, makes it indeed an object of wonder, comparable to the impossible concept of pulling oneself into the air by one's own bootlaces!

For readers who have 'digested' magnetic equivalent circuits, the phasor diagram approach will appear cumbersome, for the magnetic model of the

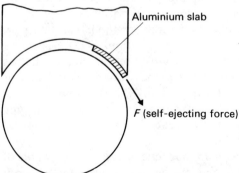

Aluminium slab

F (self-ejecting force)

Figure 7.52 Alternative form of pole shading.

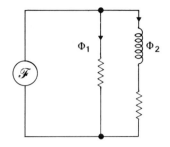

Figure 7.53 Magnetic equivalent circuit of the shaded pole mechanism.

system is as shown in Fig. 7.53 and flux Φ_2 obviously lags Φ_1 by an angle $\tan^{-1}(\mathscr{L}\omega/\mathscr{R}) = \tan^{-1}(L\omega/R)$, where $\mathscr{L} = 1/R$, $\mathscr{R}$ is the airgap reluctance, L is the self inductance of the loop, and R is its resistance.

These results are usually as far as the theory of the shaded pole device is taken in most standard works. But it will not withstand the test of experiment when the rotor itself contains a cage of conductors or is faced with a conducting cylinder. Without a shading device, the rotor itself now shades each edge of the poles and produces travelling fields as shown in Fig. 7.54. The fact that these all cancel owing to symmetry obscures the action entirely. But if a step is cut in each pole, as shown in Fig. 7.55, then Φ_2 will be seen to lead Φ_1

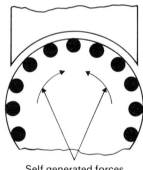

Self generated forces

Figure 7.54 Self shading effect of rotor conductors due to a pole edge.

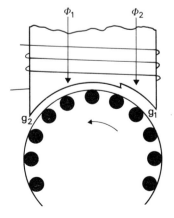

Figure 7.55 A reluctance start mechanism.

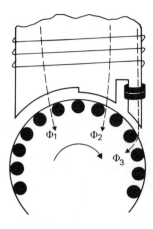

Figure 7.56 The structure of a tri-flux motor—a combination of shaded pole and reluctance start.

across the step, not because there is a change of airgap from g_1 to infinity, but rather because the gap has changed from g_1 to g_2 and hence G has changed from G_1 to G_2. The more general rule for shaded pole action is that the resultant field will move from the less tightly coupled region (small G) to the greater (large G). The stepped pole mechanism has been used commercially and is described by Veinott,[10] as is a combination of shaded pole and step as shown in Fig. 7.56 where Φ_1 leads Φ_2 and Φ_2 leads Φ_3. The step alone method is known as a 'reluctance start' and the combination of Fig. 7.56 is called a 'tri-flux' motor.

The stepped pole device has been extended recently by Eastham and Williamson[11] to a series of steps and hence ultimately to a continuous gradation as shown in Fig. 7.57. It is interesting to note that the pole shape suggests that the sharp pole tips emit a stream of particles that impinge on the rotor to propel it, or that it resembles electric discharge from sharp points. Eastham went on to show that the proper explanation of conventional shaded pole motors has little to do with phasor diagrams as described above, but that the action is simply that of Fig. 7.54 with an imbalance produced by shading

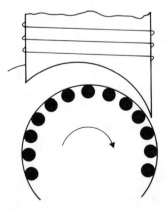

Figure 7.57 Continuous change of airgap in a reluctance start mechanism.

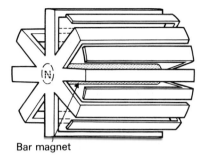

Bar magnet

Figure 7.58 Structure of a simple dynamo rotor, as used on pedal cycles, and in more sophisticated form as an aircraft alternator.

rings. It is simply the result of reducing the *magnitude* of the rotor shading at the edges with additional shading, that the *phase* produced by the shading rings is irrelevant and that the locations of the starting forces are not on the shaded pole tips but on the opposite pair of edges! These findings can easily be checked by search coil experiments. The pole regions within the shading rings are, as the late H. P. Young once remarked so delightfully in relation to the trailing pole tips of a d.c. motor without interpoles, 'dee-nuded of flux'!

Another interesting piece of pure topology in small machines relates to a permanent magnet alternator often used on pedal cycles for lighting. A bar magnet is rotated axially and carries a slotted disk at each end, the teeth of which are folded over, as shown in Fig. 7.58, to form an interlaced system of induced alternate poles operating inside a conventional stator coil system. This device is known as a claw pole construction and the principle has been extended to aircraft reluctance type alternators.

An alternative geometry for a hysteresis motor that offers improved torque/inertia and torque/$\sqrt{}$(inertia) (the useful criterion in feedback control systems) over the thin-walled cylinder rotor is shown in Fig. 7.59(a). The rotor steel is divided into a series of disks that allow the primary flux to spread between the disks and enter the disk faces, as shown in (b). The surface area is greater than that of the equivalent thin cylinder; the inertia is less.[12]

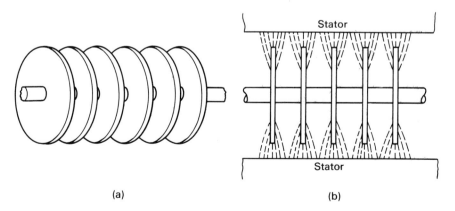

Stator

Stator

(a)   (b)

Figure 7.59 Divided disk rotor for an improved hysteresis motor.

REFERENCES

1. G. H. Rawcliffe, R. F. Burbidge and W. Fong, 'Induction-motor speed-changing by pole-amplitude modulation', *Proc. IEE*, **105A**, 411–19, 1958.
2. G. H. Rawcliffe and W. Fong, 'Speed-changing induction motors: further developments in pole-amplitude modulation', *Proc. IEE*, **107A**, 513–28, 1960.
3. G. H. Rawcliffe and W. Fong, 'Speed-changing induction motors: reduction of pole number by sinusoidal pole-amplitude modulation', *Proc. IEE*, **108A**, 357–68, 1961.
4. C. G. Veinott, *Theory and Design of Small Induction Motors*, p. 17, McGraw-Hill, New York, 1959.
5. L. S. Piggott, 'A theory of the operation of cylindrical induction motors with squirrel-cage rotors', *Proc. IEE*, **109C**, 270–82, 1962.
6. V. Karapetoff, 'The equivalence of the two theories of the single-phase induction motor', *Journal AIEE*, **40**, 640–1, 1921.
7. A. S. Langsdorf, *Theory of Alternating-current Machinery*, McGraw-Hill, New York, 1937.
8. F. J. Teago, *The Commutator Motor*, Methuen, London, 1930.
9. E. R. Laithwaite, 'Magnetic or electromagnetic? The great divide', *Electronics & Power*, **19** (14), 310–12, 1973.
10. C. G. Veinott, *Theory and Design of Small Induction Motors*, p. 108, McGraw-Hill, New York, 1959.
11. J. F. Eastham and S. Williamson, 'Generalised theory of induction motors with asymmetrical airgaps and primary windings', *Proc. IEE*, **120**, 767–75, 1973.
12. E. R. Laithwaite and M. T. Hardy, 'Rack-and-pinion motors: hybrid of linear and rotary machines', *Proc. IEE*, **117**, 1105–12, 1970.

EIGHT

THE SYSTEM AS AN ENTITY

8.1 INTRODUCTION

Power systems were designed to provide consumers with electrical energy of a certain standard or quality.

Four factors determine the quality of supply:

> constancy of frequency
> constancy of voltage
> level of reliability
> purity of sinusoidal waveform

Constancy of frequency ensures constancy of speed of induction and synchronous motor drives, reliability of time keeping of electric clocks, and of use of the mains frequency for other timing purposes. Constancy of speed of motor drives is particularly crucial in power stations where the performance of the turboalternators themselves is highly dependent on the performance of all the auxiliary drives associated with the fuel, the boiler, and the cooling systems.

The frequency of a system is dependent on the active power balance. With the power infeed being equal to the power demand plus system losses, the frequency is constant. If this balance is upset, a positive or negative variation in frequency takes place. A power system is, of course, never in equilibrium because the demand varies continuously as consumers switch on or off their loads. A considerable reduction in frequency could precipitate a disastrous situation where the extra demand required from the alternators could not be supplied because of the reduced performance of all the power station auxiliary drives.

Furthermore, in a network containing transformers and induction motors, a considerable drop in frequency unaccompanied by a drop in voltage could result in high magnetizing currents. For all these reasons, the frequency is controlled by statute in most countries; in the UK the permissible tolerance is 1 per cent or ± 0.5 Hz, except of course in emergency conditions.

The desirability for constant voltage was stressed in section 2.5 and later in Chapter 4, where it was shown that in power networks the voltage is primarily dependent on the reactive power flow.

There is an important distinction between the coupling of the frequency-active power and voltage-reactive power pairs. Frequency is a common factor throughout the network. Therefore an increase in active power demand at a load point is reflected throughout the network by a reduction of frequency. In contrast, an increase in reactive power demand at a load node is felt only locally in terms of a reduction of voltage at that node and perhaps in terms of attenuated voltage reduction at adjacent nodes.

The level of reliability depends on the ability of the power system to survive sudden faults, overloads, and loss of generating sets, transformers, and transmission lines without interruption of supply to consumers. Clearly, if the contingency is severe enough, interruption of supply, at least to some consumers, will take place. As an exceedingly secure supply would require duplication or triplication of equipment, the cost of which would be reflected in prohibitively high electric energy cost, a compromise is reached. Power systems are normally designed to withstand certain contingencies that through experience are known to be most likely to occur. In special cases where even very short term power interruption could prove disastrous, e.g., a hospital operating theatre, standby supplies are installed that take over literally instantaneously if the mains supply is lost.

The final item in the 'quality' list, i.e., purity of sinusoidal waveform, is perhaps the least important at present but is likely to increase in prominence. Any load possessing a non-linear characteristic absorbs a non-sinusoidal current, even from a perfectly sinusoidal voltage source. The non-sinusoidal current can, through Fourier analysis, be decomposed into a purely fundamental sinusoidal component plus a number of sinusoidal harmonics. These harmonics flowing through the network impedance produce harmonic voltage drops. The flow of such harmonic currents in a complex power system network may produce voltage distortions at consumer terminals in the neighbourhood of and sometimes at a distance from the non-linear load. Due to resonance of inductive–capacitive power system elements, magnification of harmonics and large distortions may result.

Rectifiers and non-linear loads, such as fluorescent lights, have been the traditional causes of voltage distortion. The recent expansion of power electronics in the mass production domestic appliance field has exacerbated the problem. Power transistors and thyristors are used in millions for rectification in television sets, for dimming lights, for controlling the operation of washing machines and mixers. Regulations exist defining the maximum harmonic current absorption of such equipment, but as their number multiplies it is likely that the rules will be increasingly tightened.

The following list gives a summary of the undesirable effects caused by harmonic currents and voltages in a power network:

(1) Capacitors used for power factor correction offer a low reactance to harmonic voltages and can be overloaded through excessive harmonic currents.
(2) Harmonic currents in a power network may, through electromagnetic coupling, interfere with telephone, railway signalling, and other networks carrying signals in the audio range.
(3) Increased losses in electric motors.
(4) Errors in energy meters.

The power system of an industrialized country is a very complex network consisting of hundreds of nodes at which generators inject and loads extract active and reactive power, these nodes being interconnected by hundreds of transmission lines and transformers. We demand that this network should transfer in some predetermined manner, usually defined by economic considerations, active and reactive power from generator to loads so that active power balance ensures constancy of frequency and reactive power balance ensures maintenance of node voltages within specified limits.

We also require that if a set of specified contingencies were to occur, the power system should be so structured that it would survive the shock, both immediately after its occurrence and later, when the first transients have subsided. Such performance will satisfy the specified criteria of reliability.

It should be clear that this kind of network analysis is considerably more complex and demanding than the usual application of Kirchhoff's laws to the solution of ordinary networks. Here the computational power provided by modern digital computers comes to our aid.

In the following sections the interplay between active power and frequency and next between reactive power and voltage will be examined and the analytical tools required to study power system flows and reliability will be introduced.

8.2 ACTIVE POWER AND FREQUENCY CONTROL

A power flow diagram for a thermal power system is shown in Fig. 8.1. The energy is converted from chemical to thermal form in the boiler, from thermal to mechanical in the turbine, from mechanical to electrical in the generator, and finally from electrical to thermal, mechanical, light, or chemical form at the load.

For the frequency to remain fixed, the fuel energy input to the boiler must be controlled so that it balances the variable consumer demand. This is achieved through two main feedback control loops, the boiler control, and the turbine speed governor control. The boiler, because of its physical size, has typically five full-load minutes of energy storage that acts as a 'buffer' stage

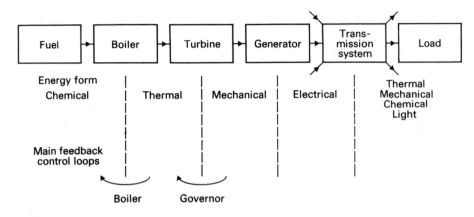

Figure 8.1 Active-power flow diagram for thermal power generation.

making manual control practicable. However, the stored energy in the rotating mass of the generator is only of the order of five full-load seconds and automatic control is necessary. In most power networks this automatic control of turbogenerator output to meet demand fluctuations is carried out by local governors. These draw upon the boiler stored energy and are assisted by manual or automatic readjustment of their set points.

A typical governor mechanism is shown in Fig. 8.2. It consists of two weights on a spindle that rotates in synchronism with the turbine shaft. The weights move radially outwards as the shaft speed increases, thus moving a sleeve on the spindle. The sleeve movement is transmitted by a lever mechanism and a hydraulic circuit to a pilot valve piston that activates a hydraulic servomotor, this in turn operating the main steam inlet valve to the

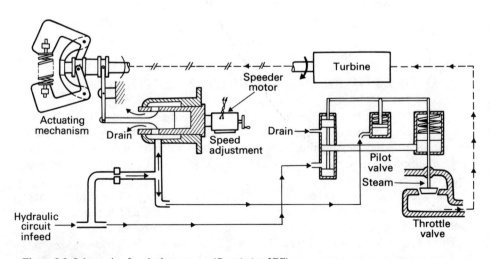

Figure 8.2 Schematic of typical governor. (*Permission IEE*)

turbine. Modern large plant is now normally fitted with electric governing systems that eliminate the non-linearities inherent in mechanical systems. In such governors, the speed sensing is done electrically and the desired droop is introduced electronically.

The mechanical characteristics of the 'ball' governor determine the droop of the speed–power relationship of the set; in the UK this is of the order of a 4 per cent speed change for 100 per cent load change (or 50 per cent load change per Hz on a 50 Hz system). The governor sleeve and hence the main

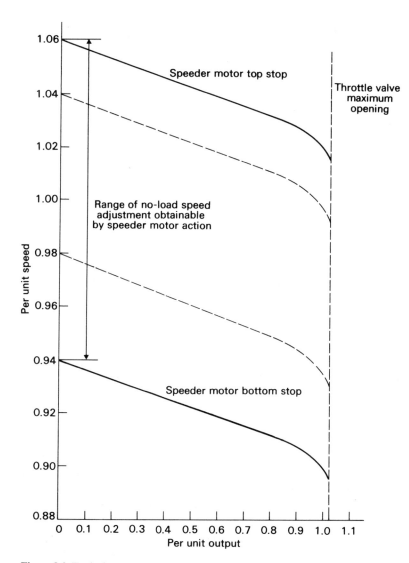

Figure 8.3 Typical speed governor characteristic.

valve position can also be changed by a motor known as the 'speeder motor', this adjustment enabling manual or automatic control of the set.

The effect of this control action is depicted in Fig. 8.3, where a family of curves having the same droop are shown for different speeder motor settings. The governor characteristic decides the output of the machine when a sudden load change occurs. The steady state sharing of load among several generators operating in parallel is decided by the control engineers or, in a fully automated system, by a computer, through variations in speeder motor setting. This sharing is based on economic grounds that are discussed in Chapter 9.

The frequency of an interconnected power system depends on the combined effect of the speeder motor settings and droops of all the generator governors. It also depends on the combined active-power–frequency characteristics of all the loads. Heating and lighting loads are insensitive to frequency variations but motor drives are frequency sensitive. A drop in frequency reduces motor speed which, in turn, reduces the mechanical and therefore the electrical load. Such drives may exhibit a 2–3 per cent active power demand drop for a 1 per cent fall in frequency.

Power systems contain a considerable amount of stored energy of kinetic form in the rotating mass of generators and motors and in mass flow in boilers. A sudden change in generation or demand will not produce an immediate shift to a new state but some time will elapse before an equilibrium is achieved.

Figure 8.4 shows a typical system frequency and power input transient following a loss of generation on an isolated power system without automatic generation control. Although the loss is immediate, the frequency follows a gradual decline during the subsequent few seconds while energy is extracted from the decelerating rotors connected to the system. After about one second, the governors of the part loaded generators respond to the decline in speed and act with a resulting surge of input power from boiler stored energy. This causes a power input overshoot, the frequency recovering to a value determined by the combined mean droop of the governors. In the example, the loss of generation is severe, the frequency decreasing gradually owing to boiler falloff in stored energy. Control action is eventually taken to dispatch further power through steam generation, gas turbines, or a pumped storage scheme. With power input now above demand, the downward trend in frequency is reversed.

If the change is not as severe as depicted in Fig. 8.4 then the system will have settled to a new lower frequency unless an 'integral control' is implemented manually or automatically to eliminate the frequency error through adjustment of the set points of selected governors.

The first few cycles immediately after a severe change are crucial to the stability of the system. In section 8.5.4 it will be shown that if the change is large enough then one or more generators may lose synchronism with the rest of the system, in which case they will be tripped out by protective action. This would further enhance the generation loss and cascade tripping of other

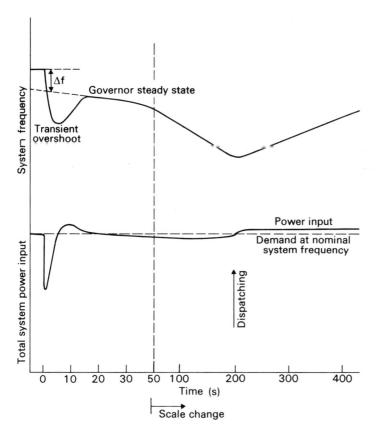

Figure 8.4 Typical grid frequency transient and system power input transient following a generation loss.

generators could take place with complete loss of power supply to many consumers. It is therefore important to study not only the steady state condition before and after a contingency but also the transient system response between these two states.

We have seen that as the frequency drops, governor action increases the active power output of generators whereas the active power demand of loads declines. The net change of power in the system ΔP must be equal to the difference between the increase in generated power ΔP_g and the increase in load power ΔP_l, i.e.,

$$\Delta P = \Delta P_g - \Delta P_l \tag{8.1}$$

If for a small variation ΔP it is assumed that this net power change is linearly related to frequency, then the active-power–frequency relationship is given by

$$\frac{\Delta P}{\Delta f} = -K \tag{8.2}$$

where K is a constant dependent upon the load and governing characteristics of the system; K is normally expressed in MW/Hz and is known as the power–frequency characteristic, frequency response characteristic, or system gain. The negative sign of Eq. (8.2) indicates that a negative change in frequency results in a positive change in active power.

K is most accurately estimated by providing a step power change ΔP on the system, usually by tripping out a generator, and measuring the resulting frequency changes. This may involve special tests, but values of K at random times can be obtained from the study of the system response to the instantaneous loss of a generator due to a fault. To ensure stable operation of the power system after a credible incident, the value of K should be such that the system frequency does not fall to a value which leads to mal-operation of power station auxiliaries. Experience in the UK shows that a value of K of about 20–25 per cent of synchronized generation capacity per Hz is adequate for this purpose.

Example 8.1

The two alternators of Fig. 8.5(a) supply a load of 100 MW. Both alternators are fitted with governors having a droop of 4 per cent. Determine the division of load between the alternators.

From Fig. 8.5(b)

$$\frac{P_A}{\Delta f} = \frac{50}{0.04} \quad \text{and} \quad \frac{P_B}{\Delta f} = \frac{100}{0.04}$$

therefore

$$\frac{P_A}{P_B} = \frac{1}{2}$$

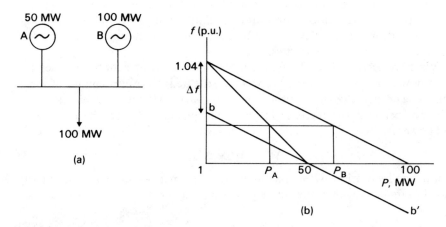

Figure 8.5 Diagram for Example 8.1.

and, as

$$P_A + P_B = 100\,\text{MW},$$

$$P_A = \frac{100}{3} = 33.3\,\text{MW} \quad \text{and} \quad P_B = \frac{200}{3} = 66.66\,\text{MW}$$

The generators share the load in proportion to their ratings.

Through change in governor settings, the share can be adjusted to satisfy other requirements, e.g., economic operation.

For example, let us assume that the cost of generation of unit A is lower than that of unit B; we would then wish to load A up to its full 50 MW rating. This could be achieved through a change in the governor set point of generator B so that its characteristic is shifted to bb′ in Fig. 8.5(b).

Example 8.2

Three power systems A, B, and C are interconnected by tie-lines AB, BC, and CA, as shown in Fig. 8.6(a). From tests on the three systems it is found that the active-power–frequency constants K_A, K_B and K_C are 650, 500, and 450 MW/Hz, respectively.

Lines AB and BC are protected so that after a time delay they trip out of service when the power transfer exceeds 300 and 120 MW respectively.

At a time when the system frequency is 50.00 Hz, A is exporting 250 MW to B and 100 MW to C and C is exporting 75 MW to B, a fault takes place and line AC is tripped out of service.

Calculate the consequent frequencies attained by the separate systems and the power flows over any remaining lines.

From Eq. (8.2) $\Delta P + K\Delta f = 0$.

For two coupled systems 1 and 2

$$\Delta P_{\text{total}} = \Delta P_1 + \Delta P_2 = -K_1\Delta f - K_2\Delta f = -(K_1 + K_2)\Delta f$$

After the tripping of line AC, system frequency is unaltered but 100 MW is now transferred to C through AB and BC. Therefore line AB carries 350 MW and trips out of service.

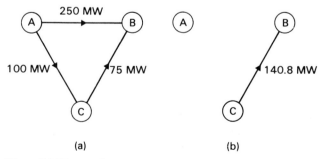

(a)   (b)

Figure 8.6 Diagram for Example 8.2.

The system is now split up into A and B+C as shown in Fig. 8.6(b).
For system A

$$-350 = -K_A(f_A - f) = -650(f_A - 50)$$

and

$$f_A = 50 + \frac{350}{650} = 50.54 \text{ Hz}$$

For system B+C

$$\Delta P_{BC} = +350 = -(K_B + K_C)(f_{BC} - 50) = -950(f_{BC} - 50)$$

and

$$f_{BC} = 50 - \frac{350}{950} = 50 - 0.368 = 49.63 \text{ Hz}$$

The 350 MW increase in demand is supplied as follows by systems B and C:

$$\Delta P_B = -500(-0.368) = 184.2 \text{ MW}$$
$$\Delta P_C = -450(-0.368) = 165.6 \text{ MW}$$

As a consequence, the power transfer from C to B increases by $165.8 - 100 = 65.8$ MW and line BC carries $75 + 65.8 = 140.8$ MW and trips.
With all the tie-lines lost, the frequencies of systems B and C are

$$\Delta P_B = 140.8 = -K_B(f_B - f_{BC}) = -500(f_B - 49.63)$$

whence

$$f_B = 49.63 - \frac{140.8}{500} = 49.35 \text{ Hz}$$

and

$$\Delta P_C = -140.8 = 450(f_C - 49.63)$$

thus

$$f_C = \frac{141}{450} + 49.63 = 49.94 \text{ Hz}$$

8.3 REACTIVE POWER AND VOLTAGE CONTROL

A discussion on the interdependence of reactive power and voltage was given in Chapter 4 where it was stressed that, as with active power, a balance exists between the generated and consumed reactive power.
  Let us look again at the issue of reactive power balance. Consider a power system that momentarily is in a stable condition and in which, therefore, the reactive power generated by all the synchronous machines and capacitors exactly balances the load demand plus the inductive transmission losses. If the

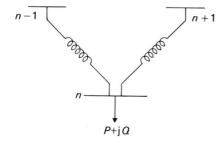

Figure 8.7 Effect of increase in reactive power demand.

system is well run, the per unit voltage drop across the lines is small; therefore the node voltage profile throughout the system is 'flat' and near to 1 p.u., with the consequences that (1) the transmission system is used efficiently, i.e., mainly for active power transfer, and (2) the voltage at consumer terminals is within the permissible limits.

Let us next postulate a sudden increase in reactive power demand by a consumer connected to node n in Fig. 8.7. After the initial transient associated with the switching of components in networks has died out, the steady state voltage V_n at node n would have dropped due to the extra transfer of reactive power from nodes $n-1$ and $n+1$. The last two nodes will also experience a reduction of voltage. This will not be as severe as that of node n and will depend on the following considerations:

(1) If a synchronous machine with adequate reactive power reserve is connected to either node then its automatic voltage regulator (a.v.r.) will sense the voltage drop and will increase the excitation, thus generating more reactive power at the node and restoring the voltage.

(2) If loads are connected at either node then the voltage reduction will have the effect of reducing the reactive power demand of these loads, which, in turn, will relieve the severity of the voltage drop.

(3) If nodes $n-1$ and $n+1$ have no synchronous machines connected to them but are themselves supplied through transmission lines from the rest of the system then these nodes will experience a voltage drop as the incremental reactive power routed through them will flow from the system through transmission lines. If the synchronous plant on the system has no adequate reserve then the same will apply but to a lesser degree.

In general, the extent of penetration of the voltage reduction to adjacent nodes depends on a variety of factors, i.e., proximity of a reactive power source, reactance of transmission lines in the locality, and reactive power–voltage characteristics of loads connected to local nodes. In any case, a steady state will be reached in which the slope of the voltage profile from node to node will be such that a reactive power balance is obtained. Restoration of the voltages to the original level can be achieved by injection of reactive power at the point of demand, i.e., through power factor 'improvement' or 'correction'.

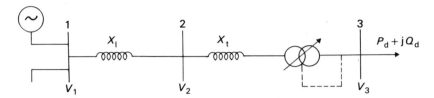

Figure 8.8 Operation of a tap-change transformer.

8.3.1 Tap Change Transformers

The major method of controlling voltage in power systems is through tap changing of transformers. Such transformers usually have a tapped high voltage winding and mechanical tap selectors that permit change of taps on load. The tap selector is usually activated by a controller that endeavours to maintain the voltage on the transformer low voltage side to a prescribed level. The object of the exercise is, of course, to provide the consumer with constant voltage. Many low voltage systems do not, therefore, operate strictly at constant voltage but at a voltage profile that partly offsets the varying series loss between the tap change point and the consumer.

As shown in Fig. 8.8, a complex power demand on node 3 is supplied from an alternator through a transmission line of reactance X_1 and a tap change transformer of reactance X_t. We can take for granted that the voltage of node 1 is maintained constant through the action of the alternator a.v.r. or, in other words, through ample availability of reactive power, and that the transformer reactance X_t is the same on all taps.

If Q_d were to increase, V_3 and V_2 would drop by ΔV_3 and ΔV_2, respectively. The automatic tap change mechanism, however, would increase V_3 to the original value, the effect of which would be to enhance the load reactive power demand and the voltage drop at node 2, which would now be $\Delta V_2'$, where $\Delta V_2' > \Delta V_2$. The tap change operation then maintains the consumer voltage constant at the expense of increased voltage drop at the transformer primary. This is permissible within certain limits. Excessive reduction of V_2 could lead to 'voltage instability', as illustrated by Fig. 4.20 in Chapter 4. For a line of a given reactance, there is a maximum power transfer to a load of a given power

Table 8.1 Transformer parameters

Voltage ratio kV	Rating MVA	Type	Impedance p.u.	Tap range per cent	No. of taps
400/132	240	Auto	0.20	+15 to −5	15
275/66	120	Double wound	0.20	+15 to −15	19
132/11	30	Double wound	0.225	+10 to −20	19

factor. With large values of X_l and X_t in Fig. 8.8 and for a poor load power factor, a situation may occur where transformer tapping-up action produces a decrease rather than an increase in secondary voltage. In a well designed power system, measures will be taken to support V_2 by injection of reactive power at node 2 or 3 from a capacitor or a synchronous compensator long before such an eventuality is reached. Alternatively, the active power flow over the line would be reduced by improving the active power balance at node 3.

Typical characteristics of transmission transformers used for voltage control in the UK network are shown in Table 8.1.

8.3.2 Control of Voltage

The most important factors in the control of voltage are:

(1) the availability of reactive power generation spread as widely as possible throughout the network with adequate reserves to meet contingencies;
(2) the controlled tap change of transformers to ensure desirable voltage levels.

Customers are encouraged to help keep the reactive power–voltage problem manageable through tariffs that penalize low lagging power factor loads. In these tariffs a charge is made for reactive as well as for active power. It is, however, not only the reactive power of loads that has to be supplied but also that of the transmission plant. Table 8.2 gives the reactive power requirement of transmission plant as affected by loading.

Unloaded transmission lines supply reactive power owing to their shunt capacitance but when fully loaded operate beyond their 'natural load' and absorb reactive power. In contrast, underground cables supply reactive power under all conditions of loading. Transformers absorb low levels of reactive power for excitation under no-load but their demand increases considerably on full load owing to the reactive power loss in their series reactance.

Table 8.2 Reactive power requirement of transmission plant

Equipment	Reactive power requirement (M VAR)	
	No load	Full load
Overhead lines		
400 kV, 150 km	− 105	+ 1250
132 kV, 30 km	− 1.6	+ 10
Underground cables		
400 kV, 15 km	− 540	− 470
132 kV, 8 km	− 14	− 13
Transformers		
400/275 kV, 750 MVA	+ 0.5	+ 90.0
132/11 kV, 90 MVA	+ 0.2	+ 20.5

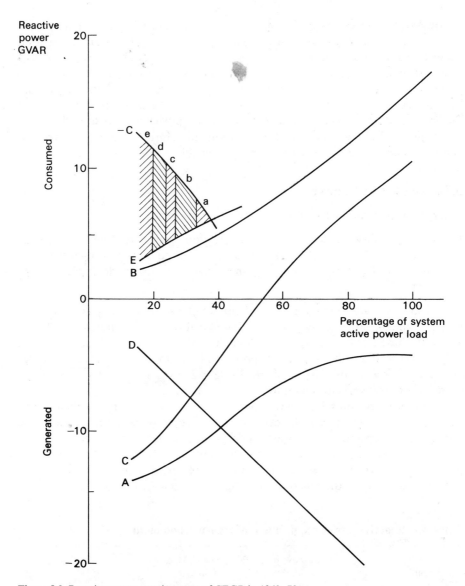

Figure 8.9 Reactive power requirements of CEGB in 1969–70.

Figure 8.9 shows the reactive power requirements of the UK system in 1969–70 as a function of percentage of active power demand. The graphs bring to focus the complexity of the reactive power balance control problem. Earlier it was mentioned that, as far as practicable, reactive power is balanced locally; still, it is instructive to look at the system globally, as in Fig. 8.9.

Curve A represents the reactive power generated by the whole network. As expected, this is particularly high at light loads. Curve B shows that the reactive power absorbed by the load is approximately proportional to the active power demand. Curve C is the sum of curves A and B and shows a considerable swing (23 000 M VAR) from generation at light load to absorption at full load that must be coped with by variable reactive power equipment.

In Chapter 5 we found that alternators have a capability of generating and absorbing reactive power, and that a reduction or 'part-loading' on active power enhances the reactive power generation or absorption capability. Curves D and E show the generation and absorption capability of alternators. It is clear that there is more than sufficient generation capability to cover the demand at high system load. But the crisis comes at light load when the absorption capability is far less than that generated by the combined load and network. Provision for additional absorption capability should therefore be made if transmission system voltages at light load are not to become dangerously high.

A final point should be made about the ample generation capacity at high active load demand level. Although this capacity is available, it may be located at points of the network where it is not required, therefore equipment capable of supplying reactive power at selected points is still necessary.

8.3.3 Reactive Power Compensation Equipment

(1) *Synchronous compensators*. Synchronous machines running light, i.e., without a prime mover or mechanical load, and referred to as 'synchronous compensators', are used for voltage control. These are connected on the tertiary winding of a transformer linking the transmission to the sub-transmission system as in Fig. 8.10. Automatic voltage control on the h.v.

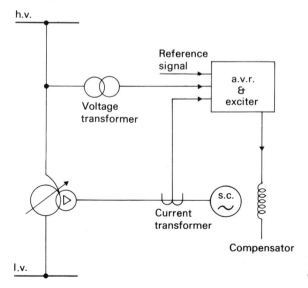

Figure 8.10 Synchronous compensator and controls.

side is effected through a feedback loop that adjusts the synchronous compensator excitation. This method of compensation, though costly, is particularly useful if for the maintenance of a node voltage within the prescribed limits it is required under light load to absorb, and under heavy load to inject, reactive power.

(2) *Static compensation.* Cheaper schemes for the generation or absorption of reactive power consist of static capacitors or reactors connected to the tertiary transformer winding of Fig. 8.10 or directly to the network. Taps on reactors and switchable capacitor banks can provide a measure of flexibility, though not, of course, as fine as that provided by the synchronous compensator.

Infinitely variable capability can however be provided from static equipment if a transductor is connected in parallel with a capacitor. A transductor is a saturable reactor whose reactance can be adjusted through changes in a d.c. exciting current controlling the degree of core saturation. More recently, variable reactive power equipment has been installed with thyristors to provide the regulating function.

Finally, a scheme for reactive power absorption that requires only existing hardware is extensively used in the UK. The problem of voltage control is particularly acute during periods of light load from late night to early morning. Long transmission lines connecting large city conurbations to power stations near coalfields or to remote hydroelectric schemes may experience an excessively high voltage at the receiving end. During such periods, the reactive power load seen by the transmission line is negative as it consists of the light resistive–inductive load of consumers plus the considerably larger capacitive load of the extensive primary and secondary distribution cable network of the city. If now at bulk power substations the taps of parallel-connected tap change transformers are not moved in unison, as is the normal practice, but are staggered, a current will circulate within the transformers. The transformer windings' X/R ratio is of the order of 40 and the power loss associated with this circulating current will be mainly inductive.

Returning to Fig. 8.9, we see that for this particular power system, when the active load falls below 33 per cent there is a discrepancy between curves $-C$ and E, i.e., there is a problem of reactive power absorption. A possible policy to deal with this situation is outlined below and illustrated in the figure by bands a to e.

(a) All unnecessary underground cables and overhead lines are switched out. The cost of this operation is small.
(b) Shunt reactors are brought in; these have X/R ratios of 200 and therefore low loss.
(c) Synchronous compensation and unloaded gas turbine alternators in underexcited mode are brought in. Rotational losses here are not negligible.
(d) Tap stagger on transformers is implemented.

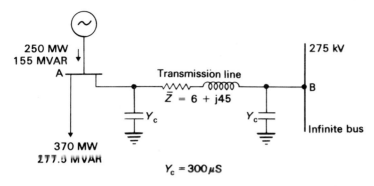

Figure 8.11 Network for Example 8.3.

(e) Finally, generating plant is part loaded, a situation that incurs a penalty as more plant is on the bars than is strictly necessary to supply the active power requirement. The extra cost incurred is mainly due to the 'no-load' cost of the additional plant.

Example 8.3

A power station generating 250 MW and 155 M VAR is linked to a 275 kV infinite bus through a transmission line, as shown in Fig. 8.11.

With the generator bus supplying a load of 370 MW and 277.5 M VAR, determine the generator bus voltage magnitude and its angle with respect to the infinite bus voltage.

Two solutions will be given for this problem. In the first, an answer will be sought through explicit solution of the system equations; in the second, one of a large number of possible iterative techniques will be used.

The latter will serve as an introduction to iterative solutions for power system problems, a topic to be covered in detail in the next section.

(1) The generator and load on bus A can be replaced by an impedance $\bar{Z}_2$ that absorbs a complex power $\bar{S}_2 = P_2 + jQ_2$ where $P_2 = 370 - 250 = 120$ MW and $Q_2 = 277.5 - 155 = 122.5$ M VAR. The circuit then can be redrawn as shown in Fig. 8.12 where $\bar{Z}_1 = 1/\bar{Y}_c = jB$, $\bar{V}_B = V_B e^{j0}$ is the infinite bus reference voltage and $\bar{V}_A = V_A e^{j\delta}$, the voltage of bus A leading $\bar{V}_B$ by an angle δ.

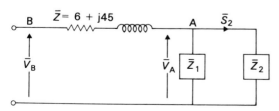

Figure 8.12 Network for Example 8.3.

The ratio of the two bus voltages is given by

$$\frac{\bar{V}_B}{\bar{V}_A} = 1 + \bar{Z}\left(\frac{1}{\bar{Z}_1} + \frac{1}{\bar{Z}_2}\right)$$

bearing in mind that

$$\bar{S}_2^* = \frac{V_A^2}{\bar{Z}_2} \qquad \text{and} \qquad \frac{1}{\bar{Z}_2} = \frac{P_2 - jQ_2}{V_A^2}$$

the ratio can be written

$$\frac{V_B}{V_A e^{j\delta}} = 1 + (R + jX)\left[\frac{P_2 - jQ_2}{V_A^2} + jB\right]$$

which when rearranged gives

$$V_A V_B e^{-j\delta} = V_A^2 + (R + jX)[P_2 + j(BV_A^2 - Q_2)]$$
$$= [V_A^2 + RP_2 - X(BV_A^2 - Q_2)] + j[XP_2 + R(BV_A^2 - Q_2)]$$

Separating real and imaginary parts:

$$V_A V_B \cos\delta = V_A^2 + RP_2 - X(BV_A^2 - Q_2) = V_A^2[1 - XB] + [RP_2 + Q_2]$$
$$V_A V_B \sin\delta = -[XP_2 + R(BV_A^2 - Q_2)] = -RBV_A^2 - [XP_2 - RQ_2]$$

and rewriting these equations in terms of $K = V_A/V_B$

$$K\cos\delta = K^2(1 - XB) + \left[\frac{RP_2 + XQ_2}{V_B^2}\right] \tag{8.3}$$

$$K\sin\delta = -K^2(RB) - \left[\frac{XP_2 - RQ_2}{V_B^2}\right] \tag{8.4}$$

Squaring these two equations and adding we get an equation of the form $K^4 + MK^2 + N = 0$, hence we can solve for K^2 and take the square root. Let us first evaluate the coefficients of Eqs. (8.3) and (8.4).

$$(1 - XB) = (1 - 45 \times 300 \times 10^{-6}) = 0.9865$$
$$RB = 6 \times 300 \times 10^{-6} = 0.0018$$

$$\frac{RP_2 + XQ_2}{V_B^2} = \frac{6 \times 120 + 45 \times 122.5}{275^2} = 0.082$$

$$\frac{XP_2 - RQ_2}{V_B^2} = \frac{45 \times 120 - 6 \times 122.5}{275^2} = 0.061$$

Substituting into Eqs. (8.3) and (8.4):

$$K\cos\delta = 0.985K^2 + 0.082$$
$$K\sin\delta = -0.0018K^2 - 0.061$$

which when squared and added give

$$K^4 - 0.86K^2 + 0.01075 = 0$$

therefore

$$K^2 = 0.43 \pm \sqrt{(0.1849 - 0.0108)} = 0.847$$

and

$$K = \sqrt{0.847} = 0.92 \quad \text{and} \quad V_2 = 275 \times 0.92 = 253 \, \text{kV}$$

From above, $K \sin \delta = -0.0018 \times 0.847 - 0.061 = 0.0625$, therefore $\sin \delta = -0.068$ and $\delta = -3.9°$.

An approximate but perfectly adequate solution can be arrived at if some engineering judgement is used. In practice, the power angle δ is small, therefore $\cos \delta \simeq 1.0$ and as BR is small it can be neglected; Eqs. (8.3) and (8.4) then simplify to

$$K \simeq K^2(1 - XB) + \frac{RP_2 + XQ_2}{V_B^2}$$

and

$$K \sin \delta \simeq -\left(\frac{XP_2 - RQ_2}{V_B^2}\right)$$

From these, K and δ can be calculated directly as follows.

$K \simeq 0.9865K^2 + 0.082$, the solution of which gives $K = 0.923$ and $0.923 \sin \delta \simeq -0.061$, which yields $\delta = 3.8°$.

(2) As P and Q have to be imported from B to A, $V_A < 275 \, \text{kV}$ and $\bar{V}_A$ will lag $\bar{V}_B$.

To start the iterative solution and using our engineering experience let us assume that $V_A = 260 \, \text{kV}$; then the reactive power injected by the capacitor at A is

$$Q_c = 3(260/\sqrt{3})^2 \times 300 \times 10^{-6} = 20.28 \, \text{M VAR}$$

The P and Q delivered at A by the line are

$$P_A = 120 \, \text{MW and } P_B = 122.5 - 20.28 = 102.22 \, \text{M VAR}$$

Equations (4.21) and (4.22) for end A of the line are not convenient for our purposes as they are not easily solvable. In contrast, Eqs. (4.23) and (4.24) are suitable; however, an assessment of P_B and Q_B will have to be made.

To calculate the line active and reactive power loss, first calculate the approximate line current from

$$P_A = 120 = \sqrt{3} \times 260 \times I_1 \cos\left(\tan^{-1} \frac{102.32}{120}\right) \times 10^{-3}$$

therefore

$$I_1 = 350.2 \, \text{A}$$

and

$$Q \text{ loss} = 3 \times 350.2^2 \times 45 = 16.56 \, \text{M VAR}$$

$$P \text{ loss} = 3 \times 350.2^2 \times 6 = 2.2 \, \text{MW}$$

therefore

$$P_B = 120 + 2.2 = 122\,\text{MW} \quad \text{and} \quad Q_B = 102.29 + 16.56 = 118.85\,\text{M VAR}$$

Also

$$Z = \sqrt{(45^2 + 6^2)} = 45.4, \qquad \alpha = \tan^{-1}\frac{45}{6} = 82.4°$$

$$\cos_{\bullet}\alpha = 0.132, \qquad\qquad \sin\alpha = 0.99 \simeq 1.00$$

Using now Eqs. (4.23) and (4.24),

$$122.2 = \frac{275^2}{45.4} \times 0.132 - \frac{275 V_A}{45.4}\sin(82.4 - \delta)$$

$$118.85 = \frac{275^2}{45.4} - \frac{275 V_A}{45.4}\sin(82.4 - \delta)$$

from which

$$\tan(82.4 - \delta) = \frac{1546.92}{97.68} \quad \text{and} \quad \delta = -3.986°$$

Substituting δ into the first equation of the above pair,

$$V_A = \frac{1546.92 \times 45.4}{275\sin 86.38} = 256\,\text{kV}$$

These values can be used to recalculate Q_c, P_{loss}, Q_{loss}, P_B, and Q_B and hence to arrive at improved values of V_A and δ. The process is halted when little difference results in V_A and δ between two successive iterations.

8.4 POWER FLOW ANALYSIS

8.4.1 The Load Flow Equations

Figure 8.13 shows a small power system network consisting of two generating stations, one load, three transmission lines, and a static capacitor connected to the load bus. For simplicity, let us assume that the line shunt admittances are negligible, that the network is symmetrical and is operating under balanced conditions, that the frequency is constant, and that we are interested in the steady state solution. The classical method of solution of such a problem is achieved through the application of Kirchhoff's laws and can take the form of the mesh current or nodal voltage method. The latter method is particularly suited to power system problems where all node voltages are expressed with respect to a common 'neutral' node and where generators and consumers inject or absorb currents at the system nodes.

The application of the nodal voltage method to a general three-node network gives the classical equations

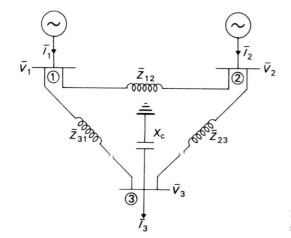

Figure 8.13 Network for load flow solution.

$$\bar{I}_1 = \bar{Y}_{11}\bar{V}_1 + \bar{Y}_{12}\bar{V}_2 + \bar{Y}_{13}\bar{V}_3$$
$$\bar{I}_2 = \bar{Y}_{21}\bar{V}_1 + \bar{Y}_{22}\bar{V}_2 + \bar{Y}_{23}\bar{V}_3 \qquad (8.5)$$
$$\bar{I}_3 = \bar{Y}_{31}\bar{V}_1 + \bar{Y}_{32}\bar{V}_2 + \bar{Y}_{33}\bar{V}_3$$

which can be written in shorthand or matrix form as

$$[\bar{I}] = [\bar{Y}][\bar{V}] \qquad (8.6)$$

For our specific network, Eq. (8.5) takes the following form

$$\bar{I}_1 = \left(\frac{1}{\bar{Z}_{12}} + \frac{1}{\bar{Z}_{31}}\right)\bar{V}_1 - \frac{1}{\bar{Z}_{12}}\bar{V}_2 - \frac{1}{\bar{Z}_{31}}\bar{V}_3$$

$$\bar{I}_2 = -\frac{1}{\bar{Z}_{12}}\bar{V}_1 + \left(\frac{1}{\bar{Z}_{12}} + \frac{1}{\bar{Z}_{23}}\right)\bar{V}_2 + \frac{1}{\bar{Z}_{23}}\bar{V}_3 \qquad (8.7)$$

$$-\bar{I}_3 = -\frac{1}{\bar{Z}_{31}}\bar{V}_1 - \frac{1}{\bar{Z}_{23}}\bar{V}_2 + \left(\frac{1}{\bar{Z}_{13}} + \frac{1}{\bar{Z}_{23}} + \frac{1}{X_c}\right)\bar{V}_3$$

Note that all mutual admittance terms have a negative sign and all injected currents are positive but extracted currents are negative.

In Chapter 4 it was stressed that in a power network the working quantities are active and reactive powers rather than currents because basically we require to transfer P and Q from generators to consumers, at the same time keeping the network voltages within specified limits.

Here, a further justification for the adoption of these working quantities will be given.

In a power station, through the adjustment of governor settings, i.e., prime mover torques, a specified active power is injected into the power network. For reasons explained in section 8.3, through the action of voltage regulators the voltage at the generator terminals is maintained within specified limits. Therefore a node to which a generating station is connected is associated with a constant active power injection and constant voltage magnitude. Such a node is known as a P, V or voltage control bus.

In section 8.3.1 it was pointed out that the requirement of constant voltage at consumer terminals is enforced through tap change transformers. Thus a substation node on the primary side of such a transformer experiences a constant P and Q load demand, irrespective of the voltage level at the node. Such a node is known as a P, Q or load bus.

The complexity of the problem is now apparent. Generators are not specified as e.m.f.s behind impedances or as current sources, and loads are not specified as fixed impedances.

Equations (8.5) are written below in terms of node complex powers rather than currents:

$$\left(\frac{P_1 + jQ_1}{\bar{V}_1}\right)^* = \bar{Y}_{11}\bar{V}_1 + \bar{Y}_{12}\bar{V}_2 + \bar{Y}_{13}\bar{V}_3$$

$$\left(\frac{P_2 + jQ_2}{\bar{V}_2}\right)^* = \bar{Y}_{21}\bar{V}_1 + \bar{Y}_{22}\bar{V}_2 + \bar{Y}_{23}\bar{V}_3 \qquad (8.8)$$

$$\left(\frac{P_3 + jQ_3}{\bar{V}_3}\right)^* = \bar{Y}_{31}\bar{V}_1 + \bar{Y}_{32}\bar{V}_2 + \bar{Y}_{33}\bar{V}_3$$

On each node or bus we have four variables, namely active and reactive power and voltage magnitude and angle. For the three-bus system there are twelve variables but the complex Eqs. (8.8) would only provide six equations on separation of real and imaginary parts. We must, by necessity, reduce the number of unknowns from twelve to six to match the number of equations. This can be done in accordance with the type of node as mentioned earlier. At a generator node, the P and V are specified and therefore Q and δ are unknowns. At a load node there is a good estimate of the customer demand and P and Q are therefore specified, V and δ being the unknowns. There is, however, a snag in this procedure. We cannot, *a priori*, specify all the active powers at generation nodes because this would imply that we know the system losses before solving the problems, an impossible mathematical feat! Consequently, we should refrain from specifying the active generation into *one* node. We *must* specify, however, for the problem to be solvable, two variables at each node; we therefore take the opportunity to specify the voltage angle at this one node, usually by assigning it zero degrees. A node at which the voltage is specified in magnitude and angle is known as the slack, swing, or reference bus as it is at this bus that numerically we take up the 'slack' in the system due to the unknown losses.

The effect of this formulation is to reduce by one the number of simultaneous equations we have to solve. Let node 1 in Fig. 8.13 be the reference bus at which V_1 and δ_1 are specified. Only the second and third equations of (8.8) have to be solved simultaneously to determine the four unknowns Q_2, δ_2, V_3, and δ_3. After the solution, the first equation is evaluated to give P_1 and Q_1, the slack bus complex power. If a bus n has a generating station, subscript g, and a load, subscript l, connected to it, then the net bus power is $P_g - P_l$. The solution of the load flow problem will yield a reactive power Q_n for this node; the generator reactive power is then given by $Q_g = Q_n + Q_l$.

8.4.2 The Solution of the Load Flow Equations

The observant reader should have noticed that Eqs. (8.8) are non-linear, i.e., they contain products of the unknown quantities. Analytical solutions for such equations are either very difficult or usually impossible to obtain. This should not perturb us, since with the aid of a digital computer numerical solutions can be used.

Such solutions are of iterative nature, i.e., initially an informed guess is made of the value of the unknowns, the equations are solved, and improved values of the unknowns are determined. The procedure is stopped when little improvement in the unknowns is produced in successive iterations. Several hundred papers have appeared in the technical journals proposing an amazing variety of methods for the solution of the load flow problem.

Here two methods will be described. The first is based on the Gauss–Seidel algorithm and was described in a paper by Glimn and Stagg.[1] It is of great simplicity and therefore easy to understand and program. Most of the early power flow programs were based on this algorithm.

The second is based on the Newton–Raphson method, a powerful technique that 'homes in' very rapidly and therefore requires few iterations. Unfortunately, this method is more difficult to understand and program; however, it is now used extensively because of its desirable characteristics.

We will consider a power network with N buses for which the following data is available:

(1) The impedances between nodes and admittances to ground.
(2) The active power generated and/or consumed at all buses but one.
(3) The reactive power consumed at all load buses.
(4) The voltage magnitude at all voltage control buses.
(5) The magnitude and angle of the voltage at one node of the network, the reference bus.

The Gauss–Seidel (GS) method From Eqs. (8.8) we can write the equation for the kth busbar of an n-bus system:

$$\left(\frac{P_k + jQ_k}{\bar{V}_k}\right)^* = \sum_{i=1}^{n} \bar{Y}_{ki} \bar{V}_i \tag{8.9}$$

which can be rewritten

$$\frac{P_k - jQ_k}{\bar{V}_k^*} = \bar{Y}_{kk} \bar{V}_k + \sum_{\substack{i=1 \\ i \neq k}}^{n} \bar{Y}_{ki} \bar{V}_i$$

from where

$$\bar{V}_k = \frac{P_k - jQ_k}{\bar{Y}_{kk}\bar{V}_k^*} - \frac{1}{\bar{Y}_{kk}}\sum_{\substack{i=1 \\ i \neq k}}^{n} \bar{Y}_{ki}\bar{V}_i \qquad (8.10)$$

Equation (8.10) is the heart of the iterative algorithm.[1] First, we have to make an informed guess of the magnitude and angle of the voltage at all load buses and of the voltage angle at all generator buses. If we have not previously solved the same network for similar operating conditions, in which case that solution could very well be a good starting point, then we postulate a 'flat' voltage start. By 'flat', we mean that all load voltages have a one per unit magnitude and zero angle and that all generator voltages have the specified magnitude and zero angle. This guess is not far from the truth, as a well designed power system operates with voltages having magnitudes close to the nominal level and load angles of a few degrees.

Assuming that busbars are numbered 1 to n, computation starts at bus 1 followed by 2, etc. When the slack bus is reached no computation is performed. This procedure is followed until all buses have been dealt with, i.e., one iteration has been completed.

If the kth bus happens to be a load bus then Eq. (8.10) is used. On the right hand side, P_k and Q_k are known and the best available values of voltage are utilized. If this is the pth iteration, the best values are $\bar{V}_1^p, \bar{V}_2^p, \ldots, \bar{V}_{k-1}^p$, $\bar{V}_k^{p-1}, \bar{V}_{k+1}^{p-1}, \ldots, \bar{V}_n^{p-1}$. The evaluation of Eq. (8.10) gives $\bar{V}_k^p$, which is an improved value in comparison with $\bar{V}_k^{p-1}$.

If the kth bus is a generator bus, the following procedure takes place. Rearranging Eq. (8.9), we get

$$Q_k = -\text{Im}\left[\bar{V}_k^* \sum_{i=1}^{n} \bar{Y}_{ki}\bar{V}_i\right] \qquad (8.11)$$

where Im stands for 'imaginary'.

Introducing in the right hand side the best available values of voltage, Q_k is calculated and then introduced into Eq. (8.10) to provide an updated value for $\bar{V}_k$. Denoting the specified voltage magnitude by V_{ks} and the updated value by $\bar{V}_k' = e_k + jf_k$, we aim to scale the magnitude of V_k' to conform to V_{ks}. This scaling is implemented through

$$\bar{V}_k'' = \frac{V_{ks}}{\sqrt{(e_k^2 + f_k^2)}}(e_k + jf_k) \qquad (8.12)$$

On completion of each iteration, a test is performed to determine whether convergence has been reached. The test compares for each bus the voltage from the last iteration with that of the last but one. If the difference is within a certain tolerance for all buses, the load flow problem is considered solved.

The convergence test for bus k takes the following form

$$\begin{aligned} |e_k^p - e_k^{p-1}| &< \varepsilon \\ |f_k^p - f_k^{p-1}| &< \varepsilon \end{aligned} \qquad (8.13)$$

where ε is a precision index and determines the precision of the solution. In more sophisticated Gauss–Seidel algorithms, meaningful convergence is achieved if the mismatch between the specified and the calculated values of active and/or reactive power at all buses, excepting the slack, is less than a given tolerance. This is because the difference between the voltages of all the system buses is perhaps within the band ± 10 per cent, while the differences between P and Q transfers over all the lines could be 100 per cent. In other words, some lines may be fully loaded and others running at practically no-load. In addition, if the total transmission loss, usually a few per cent of the base power, is to be calculated, the P and Q transfers must be precise to a fraction of one per cent.

In the Gauss–Seidel method it is usual to specify a voltage tolerance of 0.0001 p.u. When the voltage convergence test is satisfied, the P and Q mismatches are calculated and if these are higher than, say, 0.005 p.u., the voltage tolerance is decreased and further iterations are performed.

The Gauss–Seidel algorithm is simple to program but requires a large number of iterations to reach convergence. The rate of convergence can be increased considerably through the use of an acceleration factor. This is a multiplier that enhances the correction between the values of voltage in two successive iterations, i.e.,

$$\bar{V}_k^{(p+1)'} = \bar{V}_k^p + [\bar{V}_k^{p+1} - \bar{V}_k^p]\alpha$$

where $\bar{V}_k^{(p+1)'}$ is the accelerated value of voltage and α is the acceleration factor, usually in the range 1.4 to 1.6.

When the convergence test has been satisfied, the P and Q of the slack bus is obtained through Eq. (8.9). If required, the P and Q flows over all the lines and the line losses are then calculated and the results printed out.

A flow diagram describing a simple Gauss–Seidel algorithm is shown in Fig. 8.14.

Newton–Raphson (NR) method This is an iterative technique for solving a set of simultaneous non-linear equations in an equal number of unknowns.

Let the n equations in n unknowns be

$$\left. \begin{aligned} f_1(x_1, x_2, \ldots, x_n) &= k_1 \\ f_2(x_1, x_2, \ldots, x_n) &= k_2 \\ \ldots \\ f_n(x_1, x_2, \ldots, x_n) &= k_n \end{aligned} \right\} \tag{8.14}$$

and assume that we start the iterations with an initial estimate of the solution $\bar{X}^0 = x_1^0, x_2^0, \ldots, x_n^0$. Let $\Delta\bar{X}^0 = \Delta x_1, \Delta x_2, \ldots, \Delta x_n$ be the corrections necessary so that the equations are exactly satisfied, i.e.,

$$\left. \begin{aligned} f_1(x_1^0 + \Delta x_1, x_2^0 + \Delta x_2, \ldots, x_n^0 + \Delta x_n) &= k_1 \\ f_2(x_1^0 + \Delta x_1, x_2^0 + \Delta x_2, \ldots, x_n^0 + \Delta x_n) &= k_2 \\ \ldots \\ f_n(x_1^0 + \Delta x_1, x_2^0 + \Delta x_2, \ldots, x_n^0 + \Delta x_n) &= k_n \end{aligned} \right\} \tag{8.15}$$

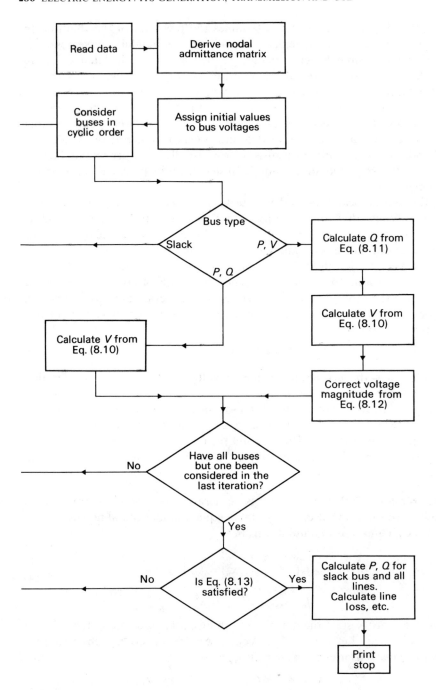

Figure 8.14 Flow diagram for Gauss–Seidel load flow algorithm.

Each equation in (8.15) can be expanded using Taylor's theorem as follows:

$$f_i(x_1^0 + \Delta x_1, x_2^0 + \Delta x_2, \ldots, x_n^0 + \Delta x_n)$$

$$= f_i(x_1^0, x_2^0, \ldots, x_n^0) + \left(\frac{\partial f_i}{\partial x_1}\right)_0 \Delta x_1 + \left(\frac{\partial f_i}{\partial x_2}\right)_0 \Delta x_2, \ldots, + \left(\frac{\partial f_i}{\partial x_n}\right)_0 \Delta x_n$$

$$+ \text{higher order terms} \qquad (8.16)$$

the partial derivatives being evaluated at the solution estimate X^0.

The higher order terms could be neglected if our initial solution estimate is close to the true solution.

Expanding as in Eq. (8.16) all the equations of the set (8.15) and re-arranging, we arrive at

$$
\begin{bmatrix}
k_1 - f_1(x_1^0, x_2^0, \ldots, x_n^0) \\
k_2 - f_2(x_1^0, x_2^0, \ldots, x_n^0) \\
\ldots \\
k_n - f_n(x_1^0, x_2^0, \ldots, x_n^0)
\end{bmatrix}
=
\begin{bmatrix}
\Delta f_1^0 \\
\Delta f_2^0 \\
\ldots \\
\Delta f_n^0
\end{bmatrix}
=
\begin{bmatrix}
\dfrac{\partial f_1}{\partial x_1} \dfrac{\partial f_1}{\partial x_2}, \ldots, \dfrac{\partial f_1}{\partial x_n} \\
\dfrac{\partial f_2}{\partial x_1} \dfrac{\partial f_2}{\partial x_2}, \ldots, \dfrac{\partial f_2}{\partial x_n} \\
\ldots \\
\dfrac{\partial f_n}{\partial x_1} \dfrac{\partial f_n}{\partial x_2}, \ldots, \dfrac{\partial f_n}{\partial x_n}
\end{bmatrix}
\begin{bmatrix}
\Delta x_1 \\
\Delta x_2 \\
\\
\Delta x_n
\end{bmatrix}
\qquad (8.17)
$$

If the solution estimate $\bar{X}^0$ were exact then the left hand side of Eq. (8.17) and therefore the correction $\Delta \bar{X}^0$ would be zero. However, as $\bar{X}^0$ is only an estimate, the errors $\Delta f_1^0, \Delta f_2^0, \ldots, \Delta f_n^0$ are finite.

Equation (8.17) provides a linearized relationship between the errors Δf and the correction Δx through a matrix of partial derivatives known as the Jacobian of the simultaneous equations. A solution for $\Delta \bar{X}$ can be obtained by applying any suitable method for the solution of a system of linear equations.

Updated values of x can be obtained from

$$x_i^1 = x_i^0 + \Delta x_i$$

and the process repeated until the errors $\Delta f_1, \Delta f_2, \ldots, \Delta f_n$ are lower than a specified tolerance.

This procedure of linearization of a non-linear problem and the use of successive displacements to arrive at a solution is a technique employed extensively in science and engineering. It is also interesting to note that the elements of the Jacobian indicate the 'sensitivity' of the function to changes in the variables.

We will now apply the NR method to the solution of a power flow problem.[2]

Let the voltage and complex power at bus k of an n-bus system be

$$\bar{V}_k = e_k + \mathrm{j}f_k \qquad (8.18)$$

and

$$\bar{S}_k = P_k + jQ_k \tag{8.19}$$

respectively.

To begin we may assume that the kth node is a load bus for which $\bar{S}_k$ is specified to be $\bar{S}_{ks}$.

At the pth iteration the complex power at the kth bus in terms of the system voltages is given by

$$\bar{S}_k^p = P_k^p + jQ_k^p = \bar{V}_k^p(\bar{I}_k^p)^* = \bar{V}_k^p \left[\sum_{i=1}^n \bar{Y}_{ki} \bar{V}_i^p \right]^* \tag{8.20}$$

Assuming that we have not yet reached convergence, i.e., that $\bar{V}_1, \bar{V}_2, \ldots, \bar{V}_n$ deviate from the right values by the corrections $\Delta\bar{V}_1, \Delta\bar{V}_2, \ldots, \Delta\bar{V}_n$, respectively, there will be a difference $\Delta\bar{S}_k^p$ between $\bar{S}_{ks}$ and $\bar{S}_k^p$.

The linear relationship between the deviations $\Delta\bar{S}_k$ and the corrections $\bar{V}_k$ is given by Eq. (8.17), i.e.,

$$\begin{bmatrix} \Delta\bar{S}_1^p \\ \Delta\bar{S}_2^p \\ \cdots \\ \Delta\bar{S}_n^p \end{bmatrix} = \begin{bmatrix} \dfrac{\partial\bar{S}_1}{\partial\bar{V}_1} \dfrac{\partial\bar{S}_1}{\partial\bar{V}_2}, \ldots, \dfrac{\partial\bar{S}_1}{\partial\bar{V}_n} \\ \dfrac{\partial\bar{S}_2}{\partial\bar{V}_1} \dfrac{\partial\bar{S}_2}{\partial\bar{V}_2}, \ldots, \dfrac{\partial\bar{S}_2}{\partial\bar{V}_n} \\ \cdots \\ \dfrac{\partial\bar{S}_n}{\partial\bar{V}_1} \dfrac{\partial\bar{S}_n}{\partial\bar{V}_2}, \ldots, \dfrac{\partial\bar{S}_n}{\partial\bar{V}_n} \end{bmatrix}_p \begin{bmatrix} \Delta\bar{V}_1 \\ \Delta\bar{V}_2 \\ \Delta\bar{V}_n \end{bmatrix} \tag{8.21}$$

For the kth bus and the pth iteration, Eq. (8.21) takes the form

$$\Delta S_k^p = \Delta P_k^p + j\Delta Q_k^p = \sum_{i=1}^n \left(\frac{\partial\bar{S}_k}{\partial\bar{V}_i}\right) \Delta\bar{V}_i$$

$$= \sum_{i=1}^n \left\{ \left(\frac{\partial P_k}{\partial e_i} + j\frac{\partial Q_k}{\partial e_i}\right)^p \Delta e_i^p + \left(\frac{\partial P_k}{\partial f_i} + j\frac{\partial Q_k}{\partial f_i}\right)^p \Delta f_i^p \right\} \tag{8.22}$$

Separation of the real and imaginary parts of Eq. (8.22) leads us to an alternative, compact form of writing Eq. (8.21) as follows

$$\begin{array}{|c|c c|c|} \hline \Delta P & \dfrac{\partial P}{\partial e} & \dfrac{\partial P}{\partial f} & \Delta e \\ \hline \Delta Q & \dfrac{\partial Q}{\partial e} & \dfrac{\partial Q}{\partial f} & \Delta f \\ \hline \end{array} \tag{8.23}$$

An iterative algorithm can now be devised. With the knowledge of all bus voltages at the pth iteration, $\Delta\bar{S}_k^p$, the deviation of $\bar{S}_k^p$ from $\bar{S}_{ks}$ is calculated from Eq. (8.20). Next, the corresponding changes in $\bar{V}_k^p$ are obtained from Eq. (8.22) and an improved value $\bar{V}_k^{p+1} = \bar{V}_k^p + \Delta\bar{V}_k^p$ is calculated. This sequence is repeated until the calculated $\Delta\bar{S}_k$ satisfies a precision index ε, i.e.,

$$\Delta P_k \leqslant \varepsilon$$
$$\Delta Q_k \leqslant \varepsilon \qquad (8.24)$$

It is now necessary to spell out the way in which the elements of the Jacobian of Eq. (8.23) are derived. Let

$$\bar{Y}_{ki} = G_{ki} - jB_{ki} \qquad (8.25)$$

and let the injected current at node k be

$$\bar{I}_k = a_k + jb_k = \sum_{i=1}^{n} \bar{Y}_{ki} \bar{V}_i \qquad (8.26)$$

Introducing Eqs. (8.18) and (8.25) into (8.26)

$$a_k = \sum_{i=1}^{n} (e_i G_{ki} + f_i B_{ki}) \qquad (8.27)$$

and

$$b_k = \sum_{i=1}^{n} (f_i G_{ki} - e_i B_{ki}) \qquad (8.28)$$

Finally the real and reactive power can be written in terms of voltages and admittances

and
$$\bar{S}_k = P_k + jQ_k = \bar{V}_k \bar{I}_k^* = (e_k + jf_k)(a_k - jb_k)$$
$$P_k = a_k e_k + b_k f_k, \qquad Q_k = a_k f_k - b_k e_k \qquad (8.29)$$

Equations (8.29) together with (8.27) and (8.28) enable us to calculate the differential coefficients of Eq. (8.22).

For load buses, Eqs. (8.29) are used; for voltage control buses where the voltage magnitude is specified as V_{ks}, the Q_k equation is replaced by the following voltage equation

$$|\bar{V}_k|^2 = e_k^2 + f_k^2 \qquad (8.30)$$

Using matrix notation and denoting the Jacobian by J, the equations involved in the NR power flow analysis method are given by

$$
\begin{array}{|c|}
\hline
\Delta P \\
\hline
\Delta Q \text{ or } \Delta|\bar{V}|^2 \\
\hline
\end{array}
=
\begin{array}{|c|c|}
\hline
J_1 & J_2 \\
\hline
J_3 & J_4 \\
\hline
\end{array}
\begin{array}{|c|}
\hline
\Delta e \\
\hline
\Delta f \\
\hline
\end{array}
\qquad (8.31)
$$

where for the kth row and pth iteration

$$\Delta P_k = P_{ks} - P_k^p$$
$$\Delta Q_k = Q_{ks} - Q_k^p$$
or
$$\Delta|\bar{V}_k^p|^2 = V_{ks}^2 - |\bar{V}_k^p|^2 \qquad (8.32)$$

The solution or, in matrix jargon, the 'inversion' of Eq. (8.31) will result in values for Δe and Δf wherefrom improved voltage values can be obtained for the kth bus

$$e_k^{p+1} = e_k^p + \Delta e_k^p$$
$$f_k^{p+1} = f_k^p + \Delta f_k^p \qquad (8.33)$$

Table 8.3

Part	Off-diagonal terms, $i \neq k$ Element	Value	Diagonal terms, $i = k$ Element	Value
J_1	$\partial P_k/\partial e_i$	$e_k G_{ki} - f_k B_{ki}$	$\partial P_k/\partial e_k$	$a_k + e_k G_{kk} - f_k B_{kk}$
J_2	$\partial P_k/\partial f_i$	$e_k B_{ki} + f_k G_{ki}$	$\partial P_k/\partial f_k$	$b_k + e_k B_{kk} + f_k G_{kk}$
		For load buses		
J_3	$\partial Q_k/\partial e_i$	$e_k B_{ki} + f_k G_{ki}$	$\partial Q_k/\partial e_k$	$-b_k + e_k B_{kk} + f_k G_{kk}$
J_4	$\partial Q_k/\partial f_i$	$-e_k G_{ki} + f_k B_{ki}$	$\partial Q_k/\partial f_k$	$a_k - e_k G_{kk} + f_k B_{kk}$
		For generation buses		
J_3	$\partial V_k^2/\partial e_i$	0	$\partial V_k^2/\partial e_k$	$2e_k$
J_4	$\partial V_k^2/\partial f_i$	0	$\partial V_k^2/\partial f_k$	$2f_k$

Let us now derive a few sample elements of the Jacobians J_1 to J_4. The off-diagonal element of J_1 for the kth row and ith column will be $\partial P_k/\partial e_i$; this can be expressed in terms of the network constants and node voltages with the help of Eqs. (8.29), (8.27), and (8.28).

$$\frac{\partial P_k}{\partial e_i} = e_k \frac{\partial a_k}{\partial e_i} + f_k \frac{\partial b_k}{\partial e_i} = e_k G_{ki} - f_k B_{ki}$$

We next derive the diagonal element $\partial Q_k/\partial f_k$ of J_4:

$$\frac{\partial Q_k}{\partial f_k} = \frac{\partial}{\partial f_k}(a_k f_k) - e_k \frac{\partial b_k}{\partial f_k} = a_k + f_k B_{kk} - e_k G_{kk}$$

Finally we require the diagonal element $\partial |\bar{V}_k|^2/\partial f_k$ of J_4. From Eq. (8.30) we get

$$\frac{\partial |\bar{V}_k|^2}{\partial f_k} = 2f_k$$

All the elements of the Jacobian have been derived in this way and are given in Table 8.3.

It is interesting to note that $\partial P_k/\partial e_i = -\partial Q_k/\partial f_i$ and $\partial P_k/\partial f_i = \partial Q_k/\partial e_i$. This offers considerable advantage in evaluating the Jacobian matrix as it is only necessary to compute the diagonal elements of J_1, J_2, J_3, and J_4 and the off-diagonal elements of only two of the four matrices. For an $n \times n$ Jacobian of P, Q buses, the elements to be evaluated will be $(n^2/4) + (3n/2)$ rather than n^2.

In power networks each node is connected to one, two, perhaps three, or rarely to more than four other nodes. As a consequence the admittance matrix is not a 'full' but a 'sparse' matrix, i.e., an element Y_{ki} exists only if a transmission line links nodes k and i. Table 8.3 indicates that the same applies in the case of the Jacobian for which only a few terms have to be calculated.

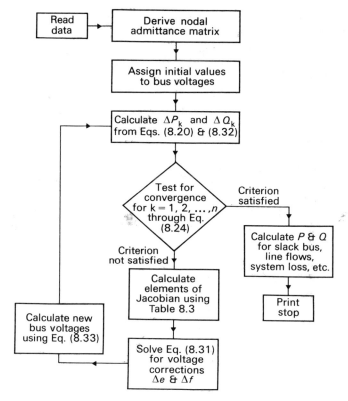

Figure 8.15 Flow diagram for Newton–Raphson load flow algorithm.

Advantage can be taken of the sparsity of such matrices in order to reduce the number of arithmetic operations per iteration.

A simplified flow diagram giving the steps in the NR power flow analysis is shown in Fig. 8.15.

Comments on power flow analysis methods The NR method is considerably more complicated than the GS method; however, it has advantages that far outweigh its shortcomings of complexity. Since the late nineteen-sixties, considerable ingenuity has been invested in making the NR method computationally efficient through skilful programming. The details of these advances can be found in the literature but are out of place in an elementary book. The following list, however, should give an appreciation first of the inherent problems in load flow analysis and second of the way in which the NR method has proved superior over other techniques.

(1) The NR method's convergence is faster than that of any other method devised, solution to a high accuracy being achieved nearly always in two to five iterations from a flat start. In contrast, the Gauss–Seidel method

would take hundreds of iterations to converge if a system with several hundred buses were to be analysed.

(2) The NR method convergence is not sensitive to the choice of reference bus. This is not the case with other methods.

(3) Occasionally load flow problems are met, known as ill-conditioned, that are difficult to solve iteratively. The NR method is the most reliable and powerful technique for the solution of such problems.

Example 8.4 A Load Flow Study

(1) *The load flow problem.* The GS and NR methods will be applied to the solution of the network of Fig. 8.13. Because of the simplicity of the problem all the steps in the solution will be shown and this should go a long way towards illuminating the obscurity inherent in formal presentation of algorithms. The solution, using a pocket calculator, is worked out below. As an exercise, the reader may wish to embark on further iterations. For a system with more than four nodes, the pocket calculator method is very time consuming and a program should be written on the lines indicated by Figs. (8.14) and (8.15).

We start by defining the network constants in p.u.:

$$\text{Let} \qquad \begin{aligned} \bar{Z}_{12} &= 0.09 + j0.33 = 0.3420 \angle 74.7449 \\ \bar{Z}_{13} &= 0.05 + j0.25 = 0.2549 \angle 78.6901 \\ \bar{Z}_{23} &= 0.02 + j0.15 = 0.1513 \angle 82.4053 \\ X_c &= -j10 \end{aligned}$$

Knowledge of the magnitude and angle of the three bus voltages defines uniquely the load flows and through Eqs. (8.7) we can then calculate the injected currents and complex powers at the buses. The complex power flows over the three lines can be calculated using Eqs. (4.14) or (4.15). Our aim is to formulate the load flow problem by arbitrarily selecting node 1 as the reference bus, thus defining V_1 and δ_1, node 2 as a generator bus, thus defining V_2 and P_2, and node 3 as the load bus, thus defining P_3 and Q_3. However, we also wish to know the exact solution to the problem so that we can assess the performance of the GS and NR algorithms. All this can be satisfied by starting with specified bus voltages on the basis of which P_2, P_3, and Q_3 can be derived. Then we will attempt to arrive at the specified voltages through the iterative algorithms.

Let us start by defining the three bus voltages

$$\bar{V}_1 = 1.1 \angle 0°, \quad \bar{V}_2 = 1.08 \angle -3°, \quad \bar{V}_3 = 0.97 \angle -9°$$

Rather than solve the simultaneous equations (8.7) we can apply repeatedly Eqs. (4.23) and (4.24) to determine P_3, Q_3, and P_2.

The active power delivered by line 13 to bus 3 is given by

$$P_{3(13)} = \frac{0.97^2}{0.2549} \cos 78.6901 - \frac{1.1 \times 0.97}{0.2549} \cos(78.6901 - 9) = -0.7290$$

Similarly, from Eq. (4.24) the reactive power is

$$Q_{3(13)} = \frac{0.97^2}{0.2549} \sin 78.6901 - \frac{1.1 \times 0.97}{0.2549} \sin (78.6901 - 9) = -0.3061$$

and

$$P_{3(23)} = \frac{0.97^2}{0.1513} \cos 82.4053 - \frac{1.08 \times 0.97}{0.1513} \cos (82.4053 - 6) = -0.8053$$

$$Q_{3(23)} = \frac{0.97^2}{0.1513} \sin 82.4053 - \frac{1.08 \times 0.97}{0.1513} \sin (82.4053 - 6) = -0.5657$$

The complex power associated with bus 3 is therefore

$$P_3 = P_{3(13)} + P_{3(23)} = -1.5343$$

$$Q_3 = Q_{3(13)} + Q_{3(23)} - \frac{0.97^2}{10} = -0.9659$$

Note that the negative sign means that P_3 and Q_3 are 'generated' at bus 3 and that the third term in the equation for Q_3 represents the local injection of reactive power by the capacitor.

To determine P_2 injected by generator 2, we employ Eq. (4.21):

$$P_{2(12)} = \frac{1.08^2}{0.3420} \cos (74.7449) - \frac{1.08 \times 1.1}{0.3420} \cos (74.7449 - 3) = -0.1907$$

$$P_{2(23)} = \frac{1.08^2}{0.1513} \cos (82.4053) - \frac{1.08 \times 0.97}{0.1513} \cos (82.4054 + 6) = 0.8261$$

therefore

$$P_2 = 0.8261 - 0.1907 = 0.6355$$

The problem now can be stated:

Node 1 is the reference bus, $\bar{V}_1 = 1 \angle 0°$
Node 2 is a voltage control bus, $|\bar{V}_2|_s = 1.08$, $P_{2s} = 0.6355$
Node 3 is a load bus, $P_{3s} = -1.5343$, $Q_{3s} = -0.9659$

Determine P_1, Q_1, δ_2, Q_2, V_3, and δ_3.
We first calculate the elements of the admittance matrix:

$$\bar{Y}_{12} = -\frac{1}{\bar{Z}_{12}} = -0.7692 + j2.8205$$

$$\bar{Y}_{23} = -\frac{1}{\bar{Z}_{23}} = -0.8734 + j6.65502$$

$$\bar{Y}_{13} = -\frac{1}{\bar{Z}_{13}} = -0.7692 + j3.8461$$

$$\bar{Y}_{11} = -\bar{Y}_{12} - \bar{Y}_{13} = 1.5385 - j6.6513$$

$$\bar{Y}_{22} = -\bar{Y}_{21} - \bar{Y}_{23} = 1.6426 - j9.3707$$

$$\bar{Y}_{33} = -\bar{Y}_{31} - \bar{Y}_{32} + j0.1 = 1.6426 - j10.3964$$

(2) *The Gauss–Seidel method.* We start with a flat voltage profile, i.e.,

$$\bar{V}_2 = 1.08 + j0, \qquad \bar{V}_3 = 1 + j0$$

Equation (8.11) gives a better value for $\bar{V}_3$

$$\bar{V}_3^1 = \frac{1}{\bar{Y}_{33}} \left[\frac{P_3 - jQ_3}{\bar{V}_3^*} - \sum_{i=1}^{n} \bar{Y}_{3i} \bar{V}_i \right]$$

$$= \frac{(-1.5343 + j0.9659) - 1.1(-0.7692 + 3.8461) - 1.08(-0.8733 + j6.5502)}{(1.6425 - j10.2963)}$$

$$= 0.9828 - j0.132 = 0.9916 \angle -7.6496°$$

For bus 2, Eq. (8.10) gives Q_2

$$Q_2 = -\operatorname{Im} \left[\bar{V}_2^* \sum_{i=1}^{3} \bar{Y}_{3i} \bar{V}_i \right]$$

$$= -\operatorname{Im} \{ 1.08 [1.08(1.6425 - j9.3701) + 1.1(-0.7692 + j2.8205)$$

$$+ (0.9828 - j0.132)(-0.8733 + j6.5502)] \} = 0.5022$$

A better value for $\bar{V}_2$ is given by Eq. (8.10)

$$\bar{V}_2^1 = \frac{1}{\bar{Y}_{22}} \left[\frac{P_2 - jQ_2}{\bar{V}_2^*} - \sum_{\substack{i=1 \\ i \neq 2}}^{3} \bar{Y}_{2i} \bar{V}_i \right]$$

$$= \{ [(0.6355 - j0.5022)/1.08] - 1.1(-0.7692 + j2.8205)$$

$$- (0.9828 - j0.132)(-0.8733 + j6.5502) \} / (1.6425 - j9.3707)$$

$$= 1.0737 - j0.0358 = 1.0743 \angle -1.9096°$$

Equation (8.12) scales the magnitude of $\bar{V}_2^1$

$$\bar{V}_2^1 = \frac{1.08}{1.0743} (1.0737 - j0.0358) = 1.08 \angle -1.9096°$$

This first iteration brought $\bar{V}_2$ and $\bar{V}_3$ closer to the correct values. Further iterations should successively improve the solution.

(3) *The Newton–Raphson method.* Equation (8.27) is written below in detail for the three-bus network.

ΔP_2		$\partial P_2/\partial e_2$	$\partial P_2/\partial e_3$	$\partial P_2/\partial f_2$	$\partial P_2/\partial f_3$		Δe_2	
ΔP_3		$\partial P_3/\partial e_2$	$\partial P_3/\partial e_3$	$\partial P_3/\partial f_2$	$\partial P_3/\partial f_3$		Δe_3	
ΔQ_3	=	$\partial Q_3/\partial e_2$	$\partial Q_3/\partial e_3$	$\partial Q_3/\partial f_2$	$\partial Q_3/\partial f_3$		Δf_2	(8.34)
ΔV_2^2		$\partial V_2^2/\partial e_2$	$\partial V_2^2/\partial e_3$	$\partial V_2^2/\partial f_2$	$\partial V_2^2/\partial f_3$		Δf_3	

Starting again with a flat voltage profile, i.e., $e_1 = 1.1$, $f_1 = 0$, $e_2 = 1.08$, $f_2 = 0$, $e_3 = 1$, $f_3 = 0$, the elements of the Jacobian are evaluated through Table 8.3.

$$\frac{\partial P_2}{\partial e_2} = 1.08 \times 1.6426 - 1.1 \times 0.7692 + 1.08 \times 1.6426 - 1 \times 0.8734 = 1.8285$$

$$\frac{\partial P_2}{\partial e_3} = -1.08 \times 0.8734 = -0.9432$$

$$\frac{\partial P_3}{\partial e_2} = -1 \times 0.8734 = -0.8734$$

$$\frac{\partial P_3}{\partial e_3} = 1 \times 1.6426 - 1.1 \times 0.7692 - 1.08 \times 0.8734 + 1 \times 1.6426 = 1.4958$$

$$\frac{\partial P_2}{\partial f_2} = 1.08 \times 9.3707 + 1.1 \times 2.8205 - 1.08 \times 9.3707 + 1 \times 6.5502 = 9.6527$$

$$\frac{\partial P_2}{\partial f_3} = -1.08 \times 6.5502 = -7.0742$$

$$\frac{\partial P_3}{\partial f_2} = -1 \times 6.5502 = -6.5502$$

$$\frac{\partial P_3}{\partial f_3} = 1 \times 10.3964 + 1.1 \times 3.8461 + 1.08 \times 6.5502 - 1 \times 10.2963 = 11.4049$$

$$\frac{\partial Q_3}{\partial e_2} = -1 \times 6.5502 = -6.5502$$

$$\frac{\partial Q_3}{\partial e_3} = 1 \times 10.3964 - 1.1 \times 3.8461 - 1.08 \times 6.5502 + 1 \times 10.3964 = 9.4877$$

$$\frac{\partial Q_3}{\partial f_2} = 0.8733$$

$$\frac{\partial Q_3}{\partial f_3} = -1 \times 1.6425 - 1.1 \times 0.7692 - 1.08 \times 0.8734 + 1 \times 1.6426 = -1.7894$$

$$\frac{\partial |\bar{V}_2|^2}{\partial e_2} = 2.16, \qquad \frac{\partial |\bar{V}_2|^2}{\partial f_2} = 0$$

Next ΔP_2, ΔP_3, ΔQ_3, and $\Delta |\bar{V}_2|^2$ are calculated assuming a flat voltage profile.

At bus 3,

$$P_3^0 - jQ_3^0 = \bar{V}_3^* \sum_{i=1}^{3} \bar{Y}_{3i} \bar{V}_i = -0.1468 + j1.0086$$

therefore

$$\Delta P_3 = P_{3S} - P_3^0 = -1.5343 + 0.1468 = -1.3875$$
$$\Delta Q_3 = Q_{3S} - Q_3^0 = -0.9659 + 1.0086 = 0.0427$$

at bus 2

$$P_2^0 = \mathrm{Re}\left\{ \bar{V}_2^* \sum_{i=1}^{n} \bar{Y}_{2i} \bar{V}_i \right\} = 0.05843$$

Table 8.4

Row No.	Δe_3	Δf_2	Δf_3	$\Delta P, \Delta Q$	Operation
1	−0.9432	9.6527	−7.0742	0.5767	
2	1.4958	−6.5502	11.4049	−1.3875	
3	9.4877	0.8734	−1.7894	0.0427	
4	1	−10.2339	7.5002	−0.6114	row 1 ÷ −0.9432
5	1.4958	−15.3079	11.2188	−0.9145	row 4 × 1.4958
6	9.4877	−97.0962	71.1596	−5.8008	row 4 × 9.4877
7	0	8.7577	0.1861	−0.4730	row 2 − row 5
8	0	97.9696	−72.9490	5.8435	row 3 − row 6
9		1	0.0212	−0.0540	row 7 ÷ 8.7577
10		97.9696	2.0770	−5.2904	row 9 × 97.9696
11		0	−75.0260	11.1339	row 8 − row 10

therefore

$$\Delta P_2 = P_{2s} - P_2^0 = 0.6355 - 0.0588 = 0.5767$$

for the first iteration $\Delta|\bar{V}_2|^2 = 0$. Introducing the numerical values into Eq. (8.34) we arrive at the following set of linear simultaneous equations:

$$
\begin{vmatrix} 0.5767 \\ -1.3875 \\ 0.0427 \\ 0 \end{vmatrix}
=
\begin{vmatrix} 1.8285 & -0.9432 & 9.6527 & -7.0742 \\ -0.8734 & 1.4958 & -6.5502 & 11.4049 \\ -6.5502 & 9.4877 & 0.8734 & -1.7894 \\ 2.16 & 0 & 0 & 0 \end{vmatrix}
\begin{vmatrix} \Delta e_2 \\ \Delta e_3 \\ \Delta f_2 \\ \Delta f_3 \end{vmatrix}
\quad (8.35)
$$

For the first iteration the last row of Eq. (8.35) gives $\Delta e_2 = 0$, therefore we can delete the first column and the last row of the Jacobian.

The task facing us now is to solve the three remaining simultaneous equations in (8.35) in the three unknowns Δe_3, Δf_2, and Δf_3. This is achieved below using an ordered procedure known as Gaussian elimination. In spite of the daunting name, this is only a tidy method of organizing the elimination of unknowns until an equation with only one unknown is reached. The remaining unknowns are then calculated through back substitution. The method should be self-explanatory, the operation performed on the left hand and right hand sides of the equations being described in the last column of Table 8.4.

From row 11 $\quad \Delta f_3 = -\dfrac{11.1339}{75.0260} = -0.1484$

From row 7 $\quad 8.7577\Delta f_2 - 0.1861 \times 0.1484 = -0.4730$

therefore

$$\Delta f_2 = \frac{-0.4730 + 0.0276}{8.7577} = -0.0508$$

From row 2 $1.4958\Delta e_3 + 6.5502 \times 0.0508 - 11.4049 \times 0.1484 = -1.3875$

therefore

$$\Delta e_3 = \frac{-1.3875 - 0.3327 + 1.6925}{1.4958} = -0.0185$$

The updated values of voltage are given by

$$\bar{V}_2^1 = 1.08 - j0.0508 = 1.0812 \angle 2.69°$$

$$\bar{V}_3^1 = (1.000 - 0.0185) - j0.1181 = 0.9815 - j0.1484 = 0.9926 \angle -8.598°$$

The results show that one iteration of the NR algorithm brought us closer to the solution than did one iteration of the SG method.

8.5 SECURITY ANALYSIS

8.5.1 Introduction

Continuity of supply of electric energy is of vital importance to modern society. One need only recollect the chaos that followed in New York and in France after the power system failures to appreciate the priority that security of supply demands.

Provisions for system security have always been an integral part of power system planning and design. However, owing to mainly economic considerations, only a certain degree of security can be built into a system. In the past, any abnormality of operation requiring action beyond that provided by protection devices was taken care of by a human operator. With ever increasing expansion and interconnection of power networks, the task of the human operator to provide judicial action has become increasingly difficult. Digital computers have recently been used to aid the operator in the complex process of making decisions on security. More recently, such computers have taken over the direct implementation of actions necessary to enhance security. In general, however, the human operator is an integral part of the design of the control system.

The operating conditions of a power system are characterized in terms of three operating states—normal, emergency, and restorative.[3]

The normal state is defined as the operating state that satisfies the active and reactive power demand on the system without violation of the operating limits of its component parts. In other words generators, lines, and transformers are not overloaded with regard to either voltage or current. In response to the small instant-to-instant changes in load, the power system may be viewed as going from one normal state to another. If, however, a severe disturbance occurs such as a large load change, a loss of generator or transmission line, or a short circuit, the system may settle down to a new normal state or may be driven into an emergency or restorative state.

In the emergency state all or practically all of the load demand is satisifed but with simultaneous violation of operating limits in one or more system components, e.g., line or transformer overloading. Corrective action is now required to prevent or limit the damage to the overloaded equipment. If the overload is caused by a severe fault or short circuit, fast corrective action is taken by the protection system which through circuitbreakers isolates the faulted part of the network. Fault analysis is the mathematical procedure that determines the level of abnormal currents in a network resulting from faults. The rating of circuitbreakers and the setting of relays is based on the outcome of such fault studies.

The tripping of a piece of equipment may result in overloading of other equipment. In a well designed system such overloading is not excessive and may be tolerated for a reasonable period until corrective action is taken to reschedule the pattern of power flow and return the system from the emergency to the normal state. Contingency analysis is the mathematical procedure through which a selected number of power system components are removed in turn and the effect of such contingencies on the rest of the network is determined.

On rare occasions, a disturbance may occur that causes the tripping of a component, this causing further severe component rating violations and leading to a cascade tripping effect with a partial or total system breakdown. In such situations, neither the load demand nor the component operating limits are being met and the power system is driven into the restorative state. A major contributory factor to such a catastrophe is the loss of stability among interconnected synchronous machines. System stability analysis is the mathematical procedure that studies the stability of integrated systems and the corrective actions necessary to retain stability during severe disturbances.

The overall objective of security control is to keep the power system operating in the normal state.

8.5.2 Contingency Analysis

The normal operating state can be classified as either secure or insecure.[3] The system is secure if it can ride a disturbance or 'contingency' without going into the emergency state. The system is insecure if such a disturbance could bring about an emergency condition. Owing to economic and technical limitations, no power system is secure from all possible disturbances. In practice, system security is determined with reference to a selected list of contingencies. Experience dictates the contingencies contained in the list. Typical contingencies included are loss of any line and loss of any generating set. The more disturbances are added in the list, the more tight the security requirements become.

Contingency analysis consists of the simulation of the occurrence of each of the contingencies in the given list to determine whether the operating constraints of the power system component parts are violated. It should be appreciated that the time required for the analysis is proportional to the length of the contingency list and therefore it is desirable to analyse only such contingencies as are known from previous studies, or from experience, to be most severe and to have a high probability of occurrence. Contingency analysis therefore is nothing more than a repetitive solution of a load flow problem executed as many times as the number of contingencies in the list.

The results of contingency analysis will indicate whether the system is generating in the secure or the insecure state. If in the latter, it is possible to calculate the necessary preventive control actions to lead the system into the secure region. As will be shown in the next chapter the selection of the control actions is made in accordance with an appropriate criterion for optimum performance.

From the computational point of view, line outages are the most demanding contingencies because they alter the structure of the network. Contingency analysis algorithms can be used off line, in which case unlimited computation time could be devoted to derive results of excellent accuracy, or on line, in which case speed is of primary importance. Considerable research has been pursued recently in the development of fast and accurate algorithms for on-line use. These are based broadly on two principles: (1) Matrix algebra theorems can be used that introduce the changes in the network due to the outage without the need to modify the admittance matrix in the NR load flow. (2) A line outage can be simulated by injecting, at the nodes connected by the line whose outage is considered, appropriate amounts of complex power. Again this technique does not interfere with the 'topology' of the network.

Detailed consideration of such methods is beyond the compass of this book; however, the topic was touched upon since the student should be aware of the importance of contingency analysis.

8.5.3 Fault Analysis

Section 2.12 dealt with the whys and hows of protection and circuitbreaking. Here, we are concerned only with the calculation of fault currents and the rating of circuitbreakers.

Let us look again at the simple power network of Fig. 8.13 and assume that a solid symmetrical three-phase short circuit has occurred on the transmission line that feeds the load from bus 3. To rate the circuitbreaker interposed between bus 3 and the line, the fault current must be calculated. Before embarking on this calculation we can introduce certain approximations that will simplify the problem considerably without affecting unduly the accuracy of the solution.

(1) The transmission line impedances are predominantly reactive, therefore the resistive part may be neglected. It follows that in the case of a solid short circuit on a previously unloaded system there is only reactive power flow in the network.

(2) If on the basis of the demanded complex power at load buses we were to calculate the load impedances, we would find that these are about an order

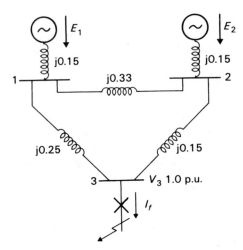

Figure 8.16 Network for fault analysis (Example 8.5).

of magnitude larger than the transmission line reactances. There is then good justification in neglecting the pre-fault current distribution in the network when calculating post-fault currents. This is also underpinned by the fact that the load demand and therefore the pre-fault distribution of power in the network are mostly active. This would contribute only very marginally to the preponderantly reactive power flows under fault conditions.

(3) The synchronous machines can be represented by an e.m.f. behind a reactance. The reactance should be either the subtransient, if we wish to determine the current immediately after the fault, or the transient, if we are interested in the current after about 3 cycles. The latter figure is generally of interest as modern air blast circuit breakers operate in the region of 2.5 cycles of 50 Hz from the detection of the fault by the protection equipment.

(4) In normal operation, the bus voltages of a power network are kept close to one per unit. It can be taken therefore that the pre-fault voltage at any part of the network is one p.u.

Example 8.5

On the basis of the above assumptions the network of Fig. 8.13 has been simplified to that of Fig. 8.16. Here the transient reactance of the alternators is taken as 0.15 p.u. The fault current can be easily calculated using Thévenin's theorem. The pre-fault voltage at bus 3 is clearly the Thévenin voltage E_t and the Thévenin impedance Z_t is the source impedance looking into bus with E_1 and E_2 shorted. Figure 8.17(a) is reduced to 8.17(b) through a delta–star transformation and this again is easily reduced to Fig. 8.17(c). The fault current is

$$\bar{I}_f = \frac{1.0}{j0.17} = -j5.88 \text{ p.u.}$$

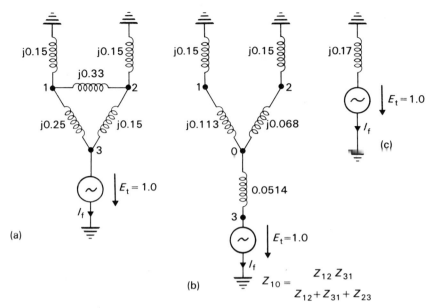

Figure 8.17 Network reduction for fault analysis.

A circuitbreaker in this location should be rated so that it can safely interrupt the severest fault current and so that when open it should withstand the network voltage of 1 p.u. without insulation breakdown. The product of these two quantities in MVA is known as the short circuit level (s.c.l.) of the bus.

To calculate the s.c.l. at bus 3 we require the base voltage and base MVA of the system. Let us choose $V_b = 132\,\text{kV}$ and $\text{MVA}_b = 50$; then the base current is given by

$$I_b = \frac{50 \times 10^3}{\sqrt{3 \times 132}} = 218.6\,\text{A}$$

and the fault current is $I_f = 5.88 \times 218.6 = 1285\,\text{A}$.

The s.c.l. at the bus and consequently the rating of the circuitbreaker is

$$\text{s.c.l.}_3 = \sqrt{3} \times 132 \times 1285 \times 10^{-3} = 292\,\text{MVA}$$

A quicker way of calculating the s.c.l. is shown below. The fault current is

$$I_f = \frac{V_b}{\sqrt{3}Z_{t\Omega}}$$

where $Z_{t\Omega}$ is the Thévenin impedance in ohms, but from Eq. (2.7)

$$Z_{tpu} = Z_{t\Omega}\frac{S_b}{V_b^2}$$

therefore

$$Z_{t\Omega} = \frac{Z_{tpu} V_b^2}{S_b}$$

also

$$\text{s.c.l.} = \sqrt{3} V_b I_f = \sqrt{3} V_b \frac{V_b}{\sqrt{3} Z_{t\Omega}}$$

$$= \frac{V_b^2 S_b}{Z_{tpu} V_b^2} = \frac{S_b}{Z_{tpu}} \tag{8.36}$$

For our numerical example

$$\text{s.c.l.}_3 = \frac{50}{0.170} = 294\,\text{MVA}$$

Equation (8.36) indicates the obvious fact that the lower the Thévenin impedance at a bus, the higher the s.c.l. A bus at the secondary distribution level, i.e., at the extremities of the network, will possess a high Z_t and a low s.c.l. A bus at the transmission level is 'electrically close' to the generators, therefore it possesses a low Z_t and a high s.c.l. The s.c.l. at the highest voltage level of an interconnected system is in tens of thousands of MVA.

In this section only the most severe faults, i.e., symmetrical three-phase short circuits, were discussed. The majority of faults on power systems are, however, line to ground, or line to line. The analysis of such faults requires treatment by a special technique known as 'symmetrical components' not covered in this elementary book.

8.5.4 Stability Analysis

A comprehensive assessment of security includes an analysis of stability. The stability of a synchronous generator may be defined as its ability to remain in synchronism with the power system to which it is connected. Figure 8.18 shows a synchronous generator connected to a 'load' through an impedance Z. The 'load' could be a simple impedance, an induction motor, a synchronous motor, or any combination of these, or it could be an infinite bus. Power transfer to an impedance load was examined in section 4.8, where it was shown that there is an upper limit to the amount of active power supplied by the generator to the load. The system cannot however become unstable or lose synchronism.

With an induction motor load, the system has a power limit; it can become unstable, in the sense that the motor may stall, but it cannot lose synchronism. However, if the 'load' is a single or several interconnected synchronous machines, the system has an upper active power limit given by Eq. (4.25) which, if exceeded, may lead to loss of synchronism.

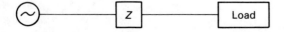

Figure 8.18 Alternator connected to load.

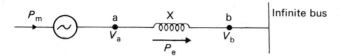

Figure 8.19 Alternator connected to infinite bus.

When a synchronous machine loses synchronism or 'falls out of step' with the rest of the system, it rotates at a higher or lower speed than that required to generate voltages at system frequency. The 'slip' between the generated and the system set of voltages results in heavy overcurrents that through the protection system trip the offending machine out of the network.

We will examine more closely this mechanism of instability.

In Fig. 8.19 a synchronous generator is connected through a reactive impedance to an infinite bus b; P_m is the mechanical input power to the machine, V_a is the voltage behind the synchronous impedance, and X represents the machine and transmission line impedances both taken as reactive.

For a lossless system and under steady state operation, Eq. (4.25) tells us that

$$P_m = P_e = V_a V_b \sin \delta / X \tag{8.37}$$

The operating point is shown in Fig. 8.20 and the system transfers active power with a load angle δ_0.

If the prime mover power is very gradually increased with the machine excitation and therefore V_a kept constant, a maximum value of P_e is reached at $\delta = \pi/2$. If P_m is made larger than $V_a V_b / X$ there is more power input than output, with the consequence that the machine rotor accelerates, pole-slips, and loses synchronism. We would then say that the 'steady state stability limit' has been exceeded. Loss of steady state stability is a rare occurrence, since normal operating ranges of prime mover power and excitation levels leave adequate steady state stability margins. (See also Section 7.2.2 and Figs. 7.6 and 7.7.)

Let us now assume that the system of Fig. 8.19 which is operating under steady state stable conditions experiences a severe disturbance. This could be a sudden change either in P_m caused by a transient in the mechanical system or in P_e caused by a sudden change in the ability of the electrical transmission

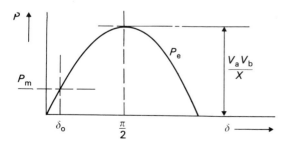

Figure 8.20 Power angle characteristic.

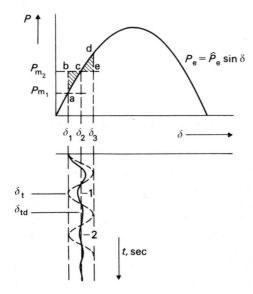

Figure 8.21 Oscillatory response of alternator.

system to maintain the predisturbance power due, for example, to a fault or a loss of a transmission line.

To study the behaviour of the system we will consider the case of Fig. 8.21 where the mechanical input power P_m is suddenly increased from the original steady state value P_m at a to P_{m2} at b. The excess of input power over the output at a is $\Delta P = P_{m2} - P_e \sin \delta_1$ and causes the rotor to accelerate towards the new equilibrium operating point c. Owing to its inertia, the rotor cannot move instantaneously from δ_1 to δ_2 but follows the curve P_e from a to c, the difference between P_{m2} and P_e at any instant representing accelerating power. On reaching point c the rotor cannot stop instantaneously but overshoots δ_2. The difference ΔP between P_e and P_{m2} is now negative, i.e., the output power exceeds the input and the rotor decelerates. The overswing of δ reaches some maximum value δ_3. In the absence of losses the oscillations continue unabated, as shown by the time plot of δ_t in Fig. 8.21. In practice, owing to the losses in the damper bars of the machine, the oscillations will decay as illustrated by δ_{td}.

The swing equation To determine whether stability and synchronism will be retained after a disturbance it is necessary to derive the 'swing equation'. A disparity ΔP between input and output power causes the machine rotor to accelerate or decelerate. The equation of rotary motion is

$$T = I\alpha \tag{8.38}$$

where T is the accelerating torque, I is the moment of inertia of rotating mass, and α is the angular acceleration.

Multiplying both sides of Eq. (8.38) by ω, the instantaneous angular velocity,

$$T\omega = I\omega\alpha \tag{8.39}$$

During a disturbance, the oscillation of δ is superimposed on the steady rotational synchronous speed ω_s, but $d\delta/dt$ is so much smaller than ω_s that for all intents and purposes it can be assumed that the machine speed does not differ much from synchronous unless stability is lost and pole slipping takes place. With this simplifying assumption Eq. (8.39) becomes

$$T\omega_s = I\omega_s \alpha$$

which can be written as

$$\Delta P = M\alpha - P_{\text{m}} \quad P_{\text{e}} \tag{8.40}$$

where $M = I\omega_s$ is the machine angular momentum and can be treated as a constant. Expressing Eq. (8.40) as a function of δ gives the swing equation

$$M \frac{d^2\delta}{dt^2} = P_{\text{m}} - \hat{P}_{\text{e}} \sin \delta \tag{8.41}$$

The formal solution for δ is difficult; however, numerical techniques can be used on a digital computer to determine the plot of δ against t as depicted in Fig. 8.21. If such a study shows that, following a transient disturbance, δ increases to a maximum and then proceeds to decrease, it is likely that stability will not be lost. Subsequently, δ oscillates about the new equilibrium point. The inclusion of damping in Eq. (8.41) gives

$$M \frac{d^2\delta}{dt^2} + K_{\text{d}} \frac{d\delta}{dt} = P_{\text{m}} - \hat{P}_{\text{e}} \sin \delta \tag{8.42}$$

and the oscillations become successively smaller—as shown by the plot of δ_{td}. Here, K_{d} is the damping coefficient.

The following sweeping statements have been made on the assumption that Eq. (8.41) or (8.42) will provide a true trajectory of δ with respect to time.

(1) P_{m} remains constant during the transient, i.e., there is no governor action.
(2) P_{e} remains constant during the transient, i.e., there is no a.v.r. action.
(3) The machine can be represented by a voltage behind a fixed source reactance.

The equal area criterion For the case of one machine connected to an infinite bus or a two-machine system, information about the maximum excursion of δ can be obtained from a diagram such as that of Fig. 8.21. Earlier, we established that $\Delta P = T\omega_s$; therefore the acceleration torque is

$$T = \frac{P_{\text{m}} - P_{\text{e}}}{\omega_s} \tag{8.43}$$

and the energy gained by the rotor during the angular displacement δ_1 to δ_2 is

$$\text{energy gained} = \int_{\delta_1}^{\delta_2} T \, d\delta = \frac{1}{\omega_s} \int_{\delta_1}^{\delta_2} (P_{\text{m}} - P_{\text{e}}) \, d\delta \approx \text{area abc}$$

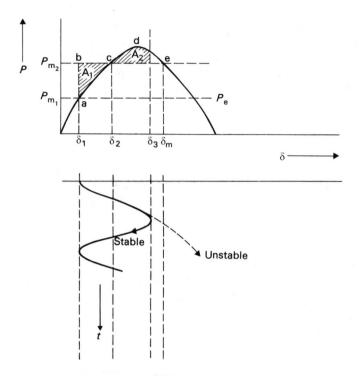

Figure 8.22 The equal area criterion.

During deceleration

$$\text{energy lost} = \int_{\delta_2}^{\delta_3} T\,\mathrm{d}\delta = \frac{1}{\omega_s}\int_{\delta_2}^{\delta_3} (P_e - P_m)\,\mathrm{d}\delta \approx \text{area cde}$$

Ignoring damping during the oscillations, the energy gained is equal to the energy lost, therefore area abc = area cde. This 'equal area criterion' enables us to determine the maximum excursion of δ and therefore the stability of the system without recourse to Eq. (8.41).

For example, in the situation illustrated by Fig. 8.21, we can determine the maximum excursion of δ. Using the equal area criterion we write

$$(\delta_2 - \delta_1)P_{m2} - \int_{\delta_1}^{\delta_2} \hat{P}_e \sin\delta\,\mathrm{d}\delta = \int_{\delta_2}^{\delta_3} \hat{P}_e \sin\delta\,\mathrm{d}\delta - P_{m2}(\delta_3 - \delta_2) \quad (8.44)$$

The steady state values δ_1 and δ_2 can be calculated from $P_{m1} = \hat{P}_e \sin\delta_1$ and $P_{m2} = \hat{P}_e \sin\delta_2$, therefore the only unknown δ_3 can be determined.

The criterion will now be used to determine the maximum permissible increase in P_m if stability is to be preserved. In Fig. 8.22 a larger step in P_m has been applied. The system will be stable only if an area A_2 at least equal to A_1 can be located *above* P_{m2}. If $A_1 >$ area cde then $\delta_3 > \delta_m$ and stability will be lost. This is because for values of δ larger than δ_m, P_m is larger than P_e and the torque is accelerating rather than decelerating.

The limiting value of P_{m2} for which A_1 = area cde can be found either graphically or analytically from the equal area criterion and represents the 'transient stability limit' for the given conditions of operation.

Example 8.6

An alternator is supplying 1 p.u. active power to an infinite bus of 1 p.u. voltage through a transmission line of 0.2 p.u. reactance and negligible resistance. The alternator reactance is 0.3 p.u. and the e.m.f. behind the reactance is 1.3 p.u.

A three-phase short circuit fault takes place electrically close to the alternator terminals. Determine the load angle before which the fault must be cleared by a circuitbreaker if stability is to be preserved.

The active power transfer is given by Eq. (4.25):

$$P = \frac{V_a V_b}{X} \sin \delta = \frac{1.3 \times 1}{0.3 + 0.2} \sin \delta_1 = 2.6 \sin \delta_1 = 1$$

therefore

$$\sin \delta_1 = \frac{1}{2.6} = 0.385, \qquad \delta_1 = 0.395 \, \text{rad}$$

During a short circuit close to the alternator terminals the electrical output from the alternator is zero as the short circuit current is purely reactive. The situation is illustrated by Fig. 8.23 in which, after the fault, P_e has collapsed to zero and all the input power P_m is expended in accelerating the rotor. The fault should be cleared before δ reaches δ_2 for which $A_1 = A_2$.

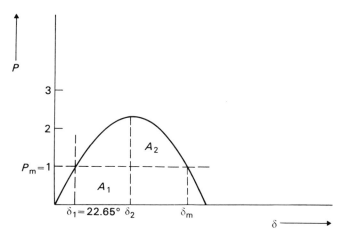

Figure 8.23 Power angle characteristic for Example 8.6.

$$\delta_m = \pi - 0.395 = 2.747 \, \text{rad}$$

$$A_1 = 1 \times (\delta_2 - \delta_1) = \delta_2 - 0.395$$

$$A_2 = \int_{\delta_2}^{\delta_m} 2.6 \sin \delta \, d\delta - 1 \times (2.747 - \delta_2) = 2.6(-\cos \delta_m + \cos \delta_2) - 2.747 + \delta_2$$

Making $A_1 = A_2$,

$$\delta_2 - 0.395 = 2.4 + 2.6 \cos \delta_2 - 2.747 + \delta_2$$

therefore

$$\cos \delta_2 = \frac{0.048}{2.6} \quad \text{and} \quad \delta_2 \simeq 89°$$

The value of δ_2 at which A_2 is just equal to A_1 is known as the 'critical clearing angle'. As the name implies, the fault should be cleared just before this angle is attained if stability is to be preserved.

Example 8.7

The alternator of Fig. 8.24(a) is delivering 1 p.u. power to an infinite bus through a double-circuit transmission line.

One of the transmission lines experiences a solid three-phase fault to ground, during which occurrence the system reactances are as shown in Fig. 8.24(b).

Determine the critical clearing angle before which the circuitbreakers of the faulted line should operate if stability is to be preserved.

The prefault power angle characteristic is given by

$$P_e = \frac{1.4 \times 1}{X} \sin \delta$$

where X is the effective reactance between a and c. Therefore

$$1 = \frac{1.4 \times 1}{0.25 + 0.3} \sin \delta_1 = 2.545 \sin \delta_1$$

$$\sin \delta_1 = 0.3928 \quad \text{and} \quad \delta_1 = 23.13°.$$

The power angle characteristic during the fault can be determined from Fig. 8.24(b) through a successive delta–star, star–delta transformation.

These two transformations are shown in Fig. 8.24(c). In the final star–delta transformation only the reactance between nodes a and c need be calculated as the other two shunt reactances do not contribute to active power transfer from a to c.

The power angle characteristic during the fault is therefore

$$P_f = \frac{1.4 \times 1}{1.8} \sin \delta = 0.778 \sin \delta \tag{8.45}$$

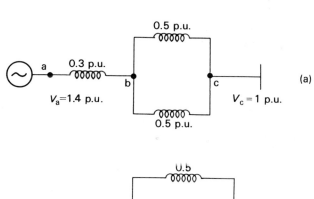

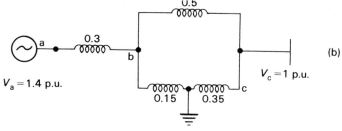

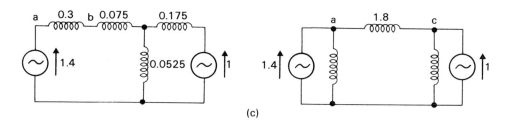

(c)

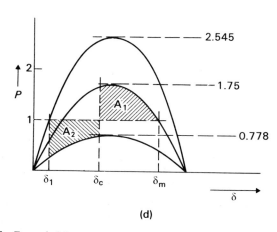

(d)

Figure 8.24 Diagrams for Example 8.7.

Finally, the post-fault power angle characteristic is easily derived from Fig. 8.24(a) with one line out of circuit.

$$P_{\text{pf}} = \frac{1.4 \times 1}{0.8} \sin \delta = 1.75 \sin \delta \qquad (8.46)$$

The power angle diagram for this three-stage problem is shown in Fig. 8.24(d).

While the fault persists, accelerating torque is available owing to the difference between P_{m} and Eq. (8.45). With the faulted line cleared, decelerating torque is present owing to the difference between Eq. (8.46) and P_{m}. The maximum angle of swing can be found from

$$1 = 1.75 \sin \delta_{\text{m}}, \quad \text{therefore} \quad \delta_{\text{m}} = 145.15°$$

For stability $A_1 = A_2$, therefore

$$1 \times (\delta_{\text{c}} - 23.13) \frac{\pi}{180} - \int_{\delta_1}^{\delta_{\text{c}}} 0.778 \sin \delta \, d\delta$$

$$= \int_{\delta_{\text{c}}}^{\delta_{\text{m}}} 1.75 \sin \delta \, d\delta - 1 \times (145.15° - \delta_{\text{c}}) \frac{\pi}{180}$$

$$-0.4037 + 0.778 \cos \delta_{\text{c}} - 0.7155 = 1.436 + 1.75 \cos \delta_{\text{c}} - 2.533$$

$$0.977 \cos \delta_{\text{c}} = 0.0222, \quad \text{therefore} \quad \delta_{\text{c}} = 88.69°$$

Dynamic stability The equal area criterion determines the critical fault clearing angle. It does not provide information on the time period permitted for clearing the fault—a necessary factor in the specification of circuitbreaker performance. This critical clearing time can be calculated from approximate step-by-step methods or through numerical integration methods of the swing equation. Such techniques are beyond the terms of reference of this book.

Before closing the subject of transient stability we will look at the effect of removing the simplifying assumptions on which the derivation of Eq. (8.42) was based. A more precise relationship between δ and t is given by the following equation

$$M \frac{d^2\delta}{dt^2} + K_{\text{d}} \frac{d\delta}{dt} = P_{\text{m}}(t) - P_{\text{e}}(\delta, t)$$

where $P_{\text{m}}(t)$ is the mechanical power, as varied by governor action, and $P_{\text{e}}(\delta, t)$ is the electrical power, now also a function of time due to a.v.r. action.

During the first 1 to 1.5 second period following the disturbance, the governor controls do not respond due to their long time constant. However, a.v.r. controls respond and endeavour to maintain the generator terminal voltage at its nominal value. In reality, the power angle characteristic is not a sine wave but a curve whose shape depends on the characteristics of the a.v.r. and excitation system. Transient stability refers to the ability of the power system to maintain first-swing synchronization.

The transient period is followed by the dynamic period during which the effect of the governor comes into play and overlaps that of the a.v.r. A system can be first-swing stable and go dynamically unstable on the second or subsequent swings. The difficulty of determining the dynamic stability of an integrated power system should now be apparent. A large disturbance in a multimachine system will set in action all the a.v.r.s and governors and the nominal system frequency may drift. The equal area criterion will be of no help in such a situation!

A dynamic stability study on a multimachine system is perhaps the most onerous task a power system engineer may have to face. Extensive modelling of the generators, a.v.r.s, governors, and system hardware must be undertaken and the differential swing equations of all machines should be solved simultaneously. Powerful numerical techniques exist for solving such problems on a digital computer but because of the enormous variety of possible contingencies only a limited number of cases can be studied. The following list of factors that affect system stability should bring home the difficulties involved in stability studies.

System topology
Transmission line impedances
Prefault load flow level on system
Type of fault and fault impedance
Location of a fault
Protection system philosophy
Speed of clearing fault
Inertia of all rotating machines
Excitation system and a.v.r. characteristics
Governor characteristics
Machine reactances and damping constants

REFERENCES

1. A. F. Glimn and G. W. Stagg, 'Automatic calculation of load flows', *Trans. AIEE*, **76**(III), 817, 1957.
2. W. F. Tinney and C. E. Hart, 'Power flow solution by Newton's method', *IEEE Trans. on Power Apparatus and Systems*, **86**, 1449, 1967.
3. T. E. Dy Liacco, 'Real-time computer control of power systems', *Proc. IEEE*, **62**(7), 884, 1974.

NINE

POWER SYSTEM CONTROL

9.1 INTRODUCTION—THE AUTOMATED POWER SYSTEM

The objectives of power system control are to provide a secure supply at a minimum cost.[1]

Figure 9.1 illustrates the operation of and the data flow in a modern power system. The flow diagram has been drawn on the assumption of a fully automated power system based on real-time digital computer control. Although such an extreme degree of automation has not yet been implemented, the activities in the boxes are performed by most utilities. In some cases computation is performed off line, in others on line, the degree of human supervision or intervention varying considerably from utility to utility.

There are three basic stages in system control, namely generator scheduling or unit commitment, security analysis, and economic dispatch. Generator scheduling involves the hour-by-hour ordering of generator units on or off the system to match the anticipated consumer load and to allow a safety margin. Information on the anticipated load is provided by load forecasting. With a given power system topology and a number of generators on the bars, security analysis, a topic already covered in section 8.5.2, assesses the system response to a set of contingencies and provides a set of constraints that should not be violated if the system is to remain in the secure state.

Finally, economic dispatch orders the minute-to-minute loading of the connected generating plant so that the cost of generation is a minimum with due respect to the satisfaction of the security and other engineering constraints.

These three control functions require a reliable knowledge of the system configuration, i.e., circuitbreaker and isolator position and of the system actual P and Q flows. This data is collected from thousands of metering devices and transmitted to control centres, usually over hired telephone lines. It is statistically inevitable that owing to the numbers of devices involved,

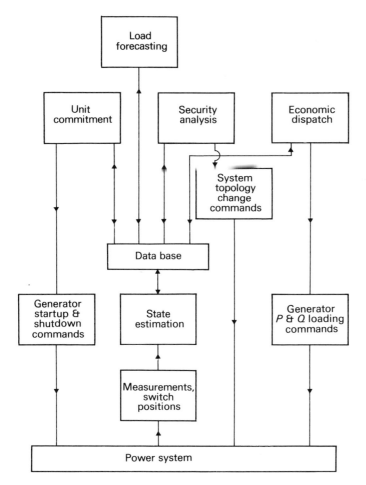

Figure 9.1 Power system control activities.

unreliable data will be present. Interference over communication lines may further corrupt the reliability of data arriving at the control centre. State estimation is a mathematical algorithm that provides a reliable data base out of an unreliable set of information.

For this to be possible, the total number of measurements must be greater than that required for a load flow solution. The more the redundant data, the greater the reliability of the data base provided by the state estimator. In traditional power system control centres where all activities are channelled through a human operator, the experienced control engineer looking at a wall mimic diagram of the power system takes in a multiplicity of data. He mentally assesses their compatibility and with good degree of confidence he can pinpoint a grossly corrupted piece of information. Human beings are very good state estimators!

To summarize, the timescale involved in the various management activities on a power network is as follows:

> Unit commitment—hours to days
> Economic dispatch—minutes to hours
> Security analysis—every few minutes and on demand
> System equipment automatic voltage control,
>   i.e., tap changers and excitation control, and
>   generator set governor control—milliseconds to seconds

9.2 LOAD FORECASTING

The following list contains some characteristics of power systems:

(1) Electrical energy cannot be stored economically. It can be stored as potential energy in hydro systems and pumped storage schemes; however, these represent a small fraction of the installed capacity of most industrialized nations.
(2) The larger portion of generating plant is thermal, therefore the demand must be met as and when it occurs.
(3) For thermal plant, a cold turboalternator set requires 6 to 8 hours of preparation in readiness for synchronization. A hot unit can be synchronized within 15 minutes and fully loaded in 30–60 minutes.

Because of the absence of storage capability and the long time lags involved in loading thermal plant, it is essential that the consumer demand is forecasted well in advance in order to prepare and load generating plant.

Electricity supply authorities invest considerable effort in short term forecasting. Through years of experience they have evolved sophisticated mathematical techniques to correlate weather and electricity demand. All methods are essentially based on the fact that system demand exhibits regular patterns. There are similarities between the demand during a given hour from day to day, during a given day from week to week, during a given week from year to year. Forecasting techniques adjust past demands to present weather conditions. Meteorological data is required on temperature, wind speed, humidity, cloud cover, and visibility. These factors have an important bearing on heating and lighting demand.

The art of load forecasting has been refined to such an extent that estimates are rarely in error by more than ± 3 per cent and on average they are accurate within ± 1 per cent.

9.3 UNIT COMMITMENT

Load forecasting gives a fairly accurate picture of the expected demand over the following few hours. In anticipation of the variations in demand and for reasons of operating economy, some of the less efficient generating units are connected on the bars to satisfy the imminent increases in load and stopped when the demand declines.

Start-up and shut-down costs are incurred when a unit is committed or decommitted. Therefore it may, in the long run, be more economical to maintain a lightly loaded unit on the bars during a trough in demand, even though the instantaneous operating costs would be less if the unit were stopped.

The total generating capacity required to be available on the bars is always larger than the anticipated load. The difference between these two quantities is called 'system spare' or 'spinning reserve', a notion mentioned in section 2.9 when the benefits of system interconnection were discussed.

The purpose of the 'unit commitment' activity in Fig. 9.1 is to schedule the start-up and shut-down of units in such a manner that the spinning reserve requirement is satisfied and the fuel cost is minimized.

The unit commitment activity involves such long time lags that little benefit would accrue from the use of on-line automatic control. The problem is ideally suited to off-line computation involving sophisticated optimization methods such as dynamic programming.

9.4 SPINNING RESERVE

Within limits, the larger the available spinning reserve the greater the reliability of the system; however, this additional capacity on the bars significantly increases the system fuel cost.

The spinning reserve (s.r.) for a given generating unit can be defined as the extra amount of active power that can be obtained from that unit within a specified interval of time (a few minutes) by loading it at its maximum rate through governor action. The total s.r. of a power system will be available to make up the outage of any generating unit should this contingency arise. The s.r. should be at least equal to the rating of the largest unit on the bars. The system characteristics will determine the post-outage interval after which the s.r. must be available if excessive drop in frequency is to be averted.

The specified post-outage time and the maximum loading rate of a generating unit will fix its ceiling of s.r. The maximum loading rate of turboalternator units is determined empirically and is dictated by thermal considerations. Only a limited fraction of the apparent available capacity of thermal plant will be truly available at the end of the specified post-outage interval. Typical maximum loading rates of turboalternators are in the region of 2–5 MW/min; in contrast, gas turbines may be loaded at a rate of 30 MW/min.

Figure 9.2 shows a typical s.r. characteristic for the ith thermal generator of a power system. Superscripts M and m indicate maximum and minimum, respectively. For the generator operating at power $P_{g,i}$ the s.r. available is

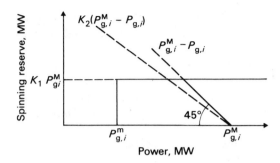

Figure 9.2 Spinning reserve of a generator.

given by $K_1 P_{g,i}$ where K_1 is a constant numerically less than unity and depending on the set maximum loading rate and the specified post-outage interval. When P_g approaches $P_{g,i}^M$ the apparent spare capacity $P_{g,i}^M - P_{g,i}$ is multiplied by a safety factor $K_2 \simeq \frac{2}{3}$.

Reserve capacity is required not only to cover the instantaneous loss of the largest unit on the bars but also to meet unexpected (i.e., not forecasted) increases in system demand.

Fast response reserve capacity can be provided by hydro or pumped storage schemes and by gas turbines. Such fast response plant is invaluable in instances such as the end of popular television programmes when within a few minutes large load increases are experienced by the system. Such plant can be started up automatically when the frequency falls below a critical value.

The decision of how much reserve capacity the system should carry depends on diverse factors such as type of generating plant, unit sizes, and degree of desirable reliability and security. It usually amounts to less than 10 per cent of the load. At the time of writing the daytime spinning reserve on the CEGB system is around 1000 MW, dropping to 680 MW at night. Of the 1000 MW, 640 MW is provided by partly loaded sets on the bars capable of supplying the demand within 5 minutes and sustaining this output. The remaining 360 MW is available from the Ffestiniog pumped storage scheme. There is also a 'standing reserve' of 500 MW provided by gas turbines not in synchronization with the system but able to supply the demand within 5 minutes. Finally there is a 'standby reserve' of 800 MW of gas turbine plant not included in the standing reserve capacity capable of achieving the demand within 3 hours.

9.5 ECONOMIC DISPATCH

9.5.1 Introduction

Having solved the unit commitment problem and having ensured through security analysis that the present system is in a secure state, the economic dispatch box in Fig. 9.1 endeavours to adjust the loading on individual generators to achieve minimum production cost on a minute-to-minute basis.

In this section we will consider the static case in which a load demand P_d and Q_d on the system is specified, a number of generators n is specified as being on the bars, and we wish to determine $P_{g,i}, Q_{g,i}: i = 1, 2, \ldots, n$ so that the total cost of generation is a minimum.

First let us distinguish the basic difference between a load flow analysis problem and a minimization problem such as the optimum economic dispatch (o.e.d.). In a load flow analysis, the number of unknowns (or degrees of freedom) is matched by the available number of equations or 'equality constraints'. In a minimization problem, the number of variables exceeds the number of equality constraints. Under such circumstances a solution can be found by setting up a 'cost function' expressed in terms of the variables. The cost function is then minimized through adjustment of the variables with the proviso that the equality constraints are also satisfied. The solution of such optimization problems is the province of a branch of mathematics called 'mathematical programming'. The label is somewhat confusing as the word 'programming' has nothing to do with computer programming although, of course, computers are invariably used for the solution of such problems.

In the following sections, a few elementary ideas on mathematical programming will be introduced which will enable us to formulate and solve some simple power system o.e.d. problems.

9.5.2 Formulation of the O.E.D. Problem

Of the four variables (P, Q, V, and δ) associated with each bus of a power network, two are specified and the other two can be determined from load flow analysis. In the o.e.d. problem, further degrees of freedom are necessary, in other words some elbow room is available within which the variables can be adjusted for the purpose of minimizing the operating cost. It seems therefore that some quantities that are specified when performing load flow analysis should be allowed to vary when performing o.e.d. The quantities that come immediately to mind are the active power injections at generation buses. The cost of energy production is directly related to these injections and it can therefore be conveniently minimized by their adjustment.

For the purpose of the o.e.d. analysis we can now classify the variables in a power system into three categories.[2] This classification is a general one developed for the study of all systems, therefore it should strike a familiar note to the reader conversant with control systems theory.

At the outset we have to specify the system structure or topology and the values assigned to the branches linking the nodes, i.e., the node admittance matrix. We then have to specify any other constants such as the P and Q demand at load buses. These are outside our control and are defined by load forecasting. We are now ready to specify the system variables.

(1) Control or decision variables U: these are variables over which we have complete control, within specified limits. Typical control variables are the active power injection and voltage magnitude at the generator buses.

(2) State or dependent variables X: we have no direct control over these as their value is not known until the completion of a load flow study. Typical dependent variables are the voltage magnitude and angle at the load buses.

(3) Output variables Z: these are functions of other variables at least one of which is a state variable. The output variables are determined after the completion of a load flow study. Typical Z's are the P and Q injected at the slack bus, the complex power flows over the transmission lines, the cost of power generation, the network losses etc.

Armed with all this background we are now ready to formulate the o.e.d. problem.

The total cost of generation in a power system with n generators is given by

$$C = C_1 + C_2 + \ldots C_n = \sum_{i=1}^{n} C_i(P_{g,i}) \tag{9.1}$$

as it is reasonable to assume that the generation cost is a function only of the generated active power. As the slack bus active power injection is a Z variable, we can write Eq. (9.1) in a shorthand form

$$C = \sum_{i=1}^{n} C_i(P_{g,i}) = f(X, U) \tag{9.2}$$

Our purpose is to minimize Eq. (9.2) and to simultaneously satisfy the following sets of constraints.

Network constraints Under steady state conditions there is a balance of active and reactive power, therefore

$$\sum_{i=1}^{n} P_{g,i} - (P_d + P_l) = 0$$

and

$$\sum_{i=1}^{n} Q_{g,i} - (Q_d + Q_l) = 0$$

where P_l and Q_l are the network losses. The above two sets of equations are no more than Kirchhoff's network laws embodied in the load flow relationships described by Eqs. (8.8). These are expressed in terms of both control and state variables, therefore mathematically can be written in the shorthand form

$$g(X, U) = 0 \tag{9.3}$$

Engineering constraints Cost minimization is performed through adjustment in the value of the control variables. This adjustment, however, is restricted within specified limits imposed by engineering considerations, e.g., the active power injected by a thermal generator set has an upper limit imposed by the rating of the set and a lower limit imposed by boiler or other thermodynamic considerations. The engineering or operational constraints that follow are conveniently expressed as inequalities.

(1) *Active power generation limits.* Owing to the reasons mentioned above the active power generation of each unit is restricted between upper and lower limits:

$$P_{g,i}^{m} \leqslant P_{g,i} \leqslant P_{g,i}^{M}: \quad i = 1, 2, \ldots, n \tag{9.4}$$

(2) *Reactive power generation limits.* In section 5.2.6 it was shown that there is an upper limit to the reactive power generated by a synchronous generator imposed by rotor heating and a lower limit imposed by considerations of stability:

$$Q_{g,i}^{m} \leqslant Q_{g,i} \leqslant Q_{g,i}^{M}: \quad i = 1, 2, \ldots, n \tag{9.5}$$

(3) *Voltage limits.* As mentioned repeatedly in earlier chapters, for optimum power system operation the bus voltages should not deviate appreciably from one p.u., therefore

$$V_i^{m} \leqslant V_i \leqslant V_i^{M}: \quad i = 1, 2, \ldots, m \tag{9.6}$$

where m is the number of buses.

(4) *Transformer tap limits.* There is an obvious limitation imposed by the highest and lowest available taps.

$$t_i^{m} \leqslant t_i \leqslant t_i^{M}: \quad i = 1, 2, \ldots, p \tag{9.7}$$

where p is the number of tap change transformers.

(5) *Transmission line loading.* For each line there is an upper limit to its current carrying capacity determined by the thermal rating of the line or imposed by requirements from security analysis:

$$I_{ij} \leqslant I_{ij}^{M}: \quad i = 1, 2, \ldots, m, j = 1, 2, \ldots, m \tag{9.8}$$

where I_{ij} is the current in the line linking the ith and jth buses.

(6) *Spinning reserve limit.* If the available spinning reserve of the ith unit is S_i and the minimum specified s.r. for the whole system is S^m then

$$\sum_{i=1}^{n} S_i \geqslant S^{m}: \quad i = 1, 2, \ldots, n \tag{9.9}$$

The active power inequality (9.4) can be written as

$$P_{g,i}^{m} - P_{g,i} \leqslant 0 \quad \text{and} \quad P_{g,i} - P_{g,i}^{M} \leqslant 0$$

It follows that all the remaining inequalities can take the same form. A mathematical shorthand expression can now be written to encompass all the engineering constraints

$$h(U, X) \leqslant 0 \tag{9.10}$$

The problem we are faced with, and it is no mean task, is to minimize Eq. (9.2) subject to the satisfaction of Eq. (9.3) and the inequality (9.10).

The reader may rightly suspect that the solution of the o.e.d. problem, unless drastic simplifications are made, has to be solved through an iterative algorithm. In other words, successive adjustments are made to the control variables within their limits so that the cost function is minimized. However, the load flow solution following the minimization may result in some state and output variables that have overridden their limits. To prevent this and to ensure quick convergence, tremendous ingenuity has been expended by power engineers in devising powerful algorithms. Hundreds of papers on the topic of o.e.d. have appeared in journals and conferences.

In this elementary book we cannot possibly solve the fully fledged o.e.d. problem but we can, with little effort and simple mathematical tools, solve useful o.e.d. problems in which sensible simplifying assumptions have reduced the complexity.

9.5.3 Mathematical Background

The authors know from experience that it is difficult to extract from books written by mathematicians the few simple facts necessary for the understanding of optimization theory as applied to the o.e.d. problem. In this section a distillation of these facts is provided with minimum mathematical rigour and, it is hoped, with maximum clarity.

Unconstrained optimization The search for the minimum or maximum of a function of one variable is an easy matter. Differential calculus teaches us that if $y = f(x)$ the value x^0 at which y is stationary can be found from the solution of

$$\frac{\mathrm{d}}{\mathrm{d}x} f(x^0) = f'(x^0) = 0$$

The test on whether the stationary point is a maximum or a minimum is based on the sign of the second derivative evaluated at x^0.

If $f''(x^0) < 0$ we have a maximum, if $f''(x^0) > 0$ we have a minimum.

In optimization problems we are basically interested in functions not of one but of several variables or, in other words, in functions of a *vector* variable

$$f(x_1, x_2, \ldots, x_n) = f(X)$$

It is not surprising that by analogy to the function of a single variable the procedure to determine the stationary points of $f(X)$ is

$$\frac{\partial f}{\partial x_i} = 0: \quad i = 1, 2, \ldots, n \tag{9.11}$$

Solving simultaneously the resulting n equations we get the solution vector

$$X^0 = x_1^0, x_2^0, \ldots, x_n^0$$

Unfortunately, the test on whether X^0 corresponds to a minimum or a maximum cannot be found by stretching further the analogy and checking whether

$$\frac{\partial^2}{\partial x_i^2} f(x_1^0, x_2^0, \ldots, x_n): \quad i = 1, 2, \ldots, n$$

are all greater or less than zero.

A formal method does exist, but as o.e.d. problems invariably converge to a minimum cost, we will not need to perform such a test.

It is progressively harder to visualize a function of one, two, and finally three variables. In the first two cases we can show the plots on two dimensions, but three dimensions are required for the last case. When more than three variables are involved it is impossible to form a mental picture of the 'multidimensional' or 'hyper-' space we are working in and we have to rely solely on the maths to guide us.

Example 9.1

Plot the function $f(X) = 2x_1^2 + 5x_2^2$ on an x_1, x_2 plane and explore the meaning of $\partial f/\partial x_1$ and $\partial f/\partial x_2$, when evaluated at one point on the function.

A simple way of plotting the function $f(X)$ on an x_1, x_2 plane is to plot contours of equal value of $f(X)$ or, as they are generally known, equicost contours. This is achieved very easily by choosing any value for $f(X)$, selecting a series of values for x_1, and obtaining corresponding values of x_2 from the functional relationship.

Such a set of equicost contours is shown in Fig. 9.3 for $f(X) = 7$, 18, and 28. The minimum value attainable by this function is zero when $x_1 = x_2 = 0$.

Next, let us evaluate the partial derivatives of $f(X)$ with respect to the two variables:

$$\frac{\partial f}{\partial x_1} = 4x_1 \quad \text{and} \quad \frac{\partial f}{\partial x_2} = 10x_2$$

Consider the point $x_1 = x_2 = 2$ on the $f = 28$ contour. At this point $\partial f/\partial x_1 = 8$ and $\partial f/\partial x_2 = 20$. These partial derivatives give us the rate at which $f(X)$ changes with respect to changes in x_1 and x_2, however the maximum

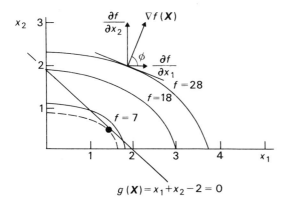

Figure 9.3 Equicost contours for Example 9.1.

local increase in $f(X)$ is given by a vector pointing in the direction of higher equicost contours and being at right angles to the tangent at $(2, 2)$. This vector is known as the gradient of $f(X)$, written $\nabla f(X)$, and has $\partial f / \partial x_1$ and $\partial f / \partial x_2$ as components.

In the case of the example and using matrix notation

$$\nabla f(X) = \begin{bmatrix} \dfrac{\partial f}{\partial x_1} \\[2mm] \dfrac{\partial f}{\partial x_2} \end{bmatrix} = \begin{bmatrix} 4x_1 \\ 10x_2 \end{bmatrix} = \begin{bmatrix} 8 \\ 20 \end{bmatrix}_{x_1 = x_2 = 2} = \sqrt{(8^2 + 20^2)} \ \angle \ (\phi = \tan^{-1} \tfrac{20}{8})$$

In multidimensional space it is not possible to visualize the gradient, however, by analogy,

$$\nabla f(X) = \left[\frac{\partial f}{\partial x_1}, \frac{\partial f}{\partial x_2}, \dots, \frac{\partial f}{\partial x_n} \right]^T$$

Equality constraints Our next problem is to optimize a function $f(x_1, x_2, \dots, x_n)$ subject to the satisfaction of m equality constraints $g_i(x_1, x_2, \dots, x_n) = 0: i = 1, 2, \dots, m$. It is also necessary to postulate that $m < n$, otherwise there would be no 'elbow room' to optimize $f(X)$.

Because of the m equality constraints we have $n - m$ independent variables and in principle we can solve $g(X) = 0$ for $x_{n-m+1}, \dots, x_n$ in terms of $x_1, x_2, \dots, x_{n-m}$, then substituting into $f(X)$ to get $f(x_1, x_2, \dots, x_{n-m})$, which can then be treated as an unconstrained function.

Example 9.2

Minimize the function of Example 9.1 subject to the equality constraint $x_1 + x_2 = 2$.

Here the equality constraint $g(X) = x_1 + x_2 - 2 = 0$ is plotted on Fig. 9.3. The solution point, indicated by a black point, lies on the equality constraint and on the equicost contour with the minimum possible cost. From the diagram it is clear that the said equicost contour is tangential to the equality constraint at the solution point.

Converting now the problem from a constrained to an unconstrained optimization

$$x_2 = 2 - x_1, \quad \text{therefore} \quad f(x_1) = 2x_1^2 + 5(2 - x_1)^2$$

$$f(x_1) = 7x_1^2 - 20x_1 + 20, \quad \frac{\partial f}{\partial x_1} = 14x_1 - 20 = 0, \quad \text{from where}$$

$$x_1 = 1.43, \quad x_2 = 0.57, \quad \text{and} \quad f(X)_{\min} = 5.71$$

The method of Lagrange multipliers In most practical problems $g(X)$ is a set of non-linear equations and as a consequence it is not possible to express explicitly the $x_{n-m+1}, \dots, x_n$ variables in terms of $x_1, \dots, x_{n-m}$.

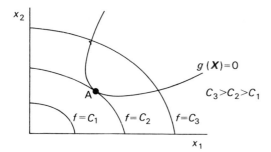

Figure 9.4 Constrained minimization

The method of Lagrange multipliers offers a way out of this impasse.

Consider the cost function $f(x_1, x_2)$ that has to be minimized subject to $g(x_1, x_2) = 0$. Figure 9.4 indicates that the solution is at point A where the equality constraint meets tangentially the particular equicost contour $f(x_1, x_2) = C_2$.

At the solution point A in Fig. 9.5 the tangency requirement implies that the gradient vectors $\nabla f(X)$ and $\nabla g(X)$ are colinear. In the diagram it has been arbitrarily assumed that curves $g(X) > 0$ are shifted away from $g(X) = 0$ and towards the origin. As the gradient vector represents the maximum local rate of increase of a function, $\nabla g(X)$ has been drawn pointing downwards.

It follows that a constant of proportionality links the two gradients at A.

$$\nabla f(X) = -\lambda \nabla g(X) \tag{9.12}$$

therefore

$$\begin{bmatrix} \dfrac{\partial f}{\partial x_1} \\ \dfrac{\partial f}{\partial x_2} \end{bmatrix} = -\lambda \begin{bmatrix} \dfrac{\partial g}{\partial x_1} \\ \dfrac{\partial g}{\partial x_2} \end{bmatrix} \tag{9.13}$$

and

$$\frac{\partial f/\partial x_1}{\partial g/\partial x_1} = \frac{\partial f/\partial x_2}{\partial g/\partial x_2} = -\lambda \tag{9.14}$$

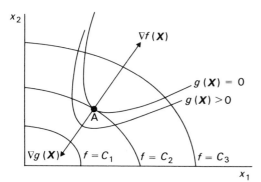

Figure 9.5 Constrained minimization using a Lagrange multiplier.

The constant of proportionality linking the gradients of f and g is known as the Lagrange multiplier.

Rearranging Eq. (9.14) we arrive at

$$\left.\begin{aligned}
\frac{\partial f}{\partial x_1} + \lambda \frac{\partial g}{\partial x_1} &= 0 \\[2mm]
\frac{\partial f}{\partial x_2} + \lambda \frac{\partial g}{\partial x_2} &= 0
\end{aligned}\right\} \tag{9.15}$$

which contains three unknowns.

To solve for these unknowns, we must add a third equation to the set, the obvious candidate being the equality constraint, therefore

$$\left.\begin{aligned}
\frac{\partial f}{\partial x_1} + \lambda \frac{\partial g}{\partial x_1} &= 0 \\[2mm]
\frac{\partial f}{\partial x_2} + \lambda \frac{\partial g}{\partial x_2} &= 0 \\[2mm]
g(x_1, x_2) &= 0
\end{aligned}\right\} \tag{9.16}$$

The minimization problem has now been transformed into a set of three equations for three unknowns, x_1, x_2, *and* λ.

The introduction of the extra variable has helped us to set up Eqs. (9.16) whose simultaneous solution yields the optimum point. In addition, a bonus has accrued. The value of λ gives the 'sensitivity' of the cost to changes in the equality constraint. In optimization problems equality constraints are associated with system parameters. At the end of a study, the parameters related to the largest values of λ can be pinpointed and if changed marginally a solution with a much improved cost can be obtained.

Equation (9.16) can be derived through a formal technique that apparently converts a constrained optimization problem to an unconstrained one. The original cost function $f(x_1, x_2)$ is 'augmented' as follows:

$$F(x_1, x_2, \lambda) = f(x_1, x_2) + \lambda g(x_1, x_2) \tag{9.17}$$

This augmented function is minimized as if it were an unconstrained function, i.e., partial derivatives of F with respect to all variables are taken and equated to zero:

$$\frac{\partial F}{\partial x_1} = \frac{\partial f}{\partial x_1} + \lambda \frac{\partial g}{\partial x_1} = 0$$

$$\frac{\partial F}{\partial x_2} = \frac{\partial f}{\partial x_2} + \lambda \frac{\partial g}{\partial x_2} = 0$$

$$\frac{\partial F}{\partial \lambda} = g(x_1, x_2) = 0$$

The above set is identical to Eqs. (9.16).

The general method of Lagrange multiplier for n variables and m equality constraints can now be formulated:

Problem: Optimize $f(x_i)$ subject to $g_j(x_i) = 0$: $i = 1, 2, \ldots, n$; $j = 1, 2, \ldots, m$

Solution: Form augmented function

$$F(x_i, \lambda_j) = f(x_i) + \sum_{j=1}^{m} \lambda_j g_j(x_i): \quad i = 1, 2, \ldots, n \tag{9.18}$$

Differentiate the augmented function with respect to all x_i and λ_j to get the following $n + m$ equations:

$$\frac{\partial f}{\partial x_i} + \sum_{j=1}^{m} \lambda_j \frac{\partial g_j}{\partial x_i} = 0: \quad i = 1, 2, \ldots, n \tag{9.19}$$

$$g_j(x_i) = 0: \quad j = 1, 2, \ldots, m \tag{9.20}$$

Solve the simultaneous equations to determine the n variables and the m Lagrange multipliers.

Example 9.3

Solve the minimization problem of Example 9.2 using the method of Lagrange multipliers.

The augmented function is

$$F(X) = 2x_1^2 + 5x_2^2 + \lambda(x_1 + x_2 - 2)$$

Differentiating with respect to all variables

$$\partial F / \partial x_1 = 4x_1 + \lambda = 0$$
$$\partial F / \partial x_2 = 10x_2 + \lambda = 0$$
$$\partial F / \partial \lambda = x_1 + x_2 - 2 = 0$$

wherefrom $x_1 = 1.43$, $x_2 = 0.57$, and $\lambda = -5.72$.

A negative value of λ implies that both gradients at the solution point A of Fig. 9.3 are pointing in the same direction.

Inequality constraints We are now ready to deal with the fully fledged non-linear optimization problem that can be described mathematically by

Optimize $\qquad f(x_i)$: $\quad i = 1, 2, \ldots, n$

subject to

$$g_j(x_i) = 0: \quad j = 1, 2, \ldots, m \tag{9.21}$$

and

$$h_k(x_i) \leqslant 0: \quad k = 1, 2, \ldots, l$$

where $h(X)$ are the l inequality constraints.

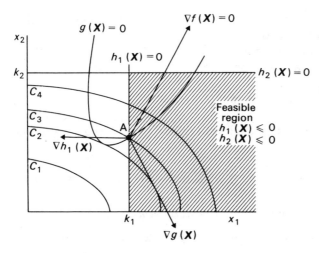

Figure 9.6 Minimization with equality and inequality constraints.

Let us look closely at the simple example of Fig. 9.6 where only two variables are involved and which is described by

Minimize $\qquad\qquad f(x_1, x_2)$

subject to

$$g(x_1, x_2) = 0$$

and

$$h_1(x_1, x_2) \leqslant 0 \quad [\text{In Fig. 9.6 } k_1 - x_1 \leqslant 0]$$
$$h_2(x_1, x_2) \leqslant 0 \quad [\text{In Fig. 9.6 } x_2 - k_2 \leqslant 0]$$

Because of the inequality constraints, x_1 and x_2 can take values only within the shaded area known as the admissible or feasible region. As the solution point must lie on $g(X) = 0$ it is clear that the minimum cost point which satisfies this and does not violate the inequality constraints is A. We can also observe that inequality $h_2(X)$ is 'inactive', i.e., can be disregarded in arriving at a solution, but that inequality $h_1(X)$ is 'active', i.e., the solution point is *on* its boundary and therefore to all intents and purposes can be treated as an equality constraint.

The general conclusion can then be drawn that a minimum cost solution either lies within the feasible region, in which case all the inequalities are 'inactive' and can be disregarded, or it lies on the boundary of the region, in which case one or more inequalities are 'active' and therefore can be treated as equality constraints.

We have now resolved the problem of incorporating the inequality constraints in our optimization method using Lagrange multipliers. For the two-variable problem we can set up an augmented function including the inequality constraints:

$$F(x_1, x_2, \lambda_1, \mu_1, \mu_2) = f(x_1, x_2) + \lambda_1 g(x_1, x_2) + \mu_1 h_1(x_1, x_2) + \mu_2 h_2(x_1, x_2)$$

Differentiating with respect to all the variables

$$
\left.
\begin{aligned}
\frac{\partial F}{\partial x_1} &= \frac{\partial f}{\partial x_1} + \lambda_1 \frac{\partial g}{\partial x_1} + \mu_1 \frac{\partial h_1}{\partial x_1} + \mu_2 \frac{\partial h_2}{\partial x_1} = 0 \\[6pt]
\frac{\partial F}{\partial x_2} &= \frac{\partial f}{\partial x_2} + \lambda_1 \frac{\partial g}{\partial x_2} + \mu_1 \frac{\partial h_1}{\partial x_2} + \mu_2 \frac{\partial h_2}{\partial x_2} = 0 \\[6pt]
\frac{\partial F}{\partial \lambda_1} &= g(x_1, x_2) = 0 \\[6pt]
\frac{\partial F}{\partial \mu_1} &= h(x_1, x_2) = 0 \ \text{ for } \ \mu_1 > 0 \ \text{ or } \ \mu_1 = 0 \\[6pt]
\frac{\partial F}{\partial \mu_2} &= h_2(x_1, x_2) = 0 \ \text{ for } \ \mu_2 > 0 \ \text{ or } \ \mu_2 = 0
\end{aligned}
\right\}
\qquad (9.??)
$$

where the μ's are known as the Kuhn–Tucker multipliers. The basic difference between λ's and μ's is that the former are always active, i.e., they are non-zero (either positive or negative) while the latter may be active, in which case they are positive, or inactive, in which case they are zero.

To see why the μ's are only positive when active, refer back to Fig. 9.5 and replace $g(X)$ by $h(X)$, in which case the feasible region extends from the boundary $h(X) = 0$ to all points where $h(X) < 0$. The minimum cost solution may lie either within the feasible region, in which case the inequality is inactive and $\mu = 0$, or on the boundary, in which case μ is finite. In the latter case, there *must* be a lower cost outside the feasible region, i.e., $\nabla f(X)$ points into the feasible region. By definition, $\nabla h(X)$ points away from the feasible region. We can conclude that $\nabla f(X)$ and $\nabla h(X)$ are colinear and always in opposition, therefore the μ multipliers in Eq. (9.22), if finite, are positive.

We are now ready to set up a formal solution to the problem posed by Eq. (9.21).

Form the following augmented function:

$$F(x_i, \lambda_j, \mu_k) = f(x_i) + \sum_{j=1}^{m} \lambda_j g_j(x_i) + \sum_{k=1}^{l} \mu_k h_k(x_i):$$

$$i = 1, 2, \ldots, n; \ j = 1, 2, \ldots, m; \ k = 1, 2, \ldots, l$$

Differentiate this function with respect to all x_i, λ_j, and μ_k to get $n + m$ plus *two* sets of l equations. Solve these to determine the n variables, the m Lagrange multipliers, and the l Kuhn–Tucker multipliers.

The Kuhn–Tucker multipliers express the sensitivity of the cost to changes in the inequality constraints. Considerable insight can be obtained from them into the way in which design and engineering constraints affect the cost of operating a power system. Relatively small relaxation of constraints associated with large Kuhn–Tucker multipliers could result in considerable cost benefits.

The merit of the Lagrange, Kuhn–Tucker optimization method is that it

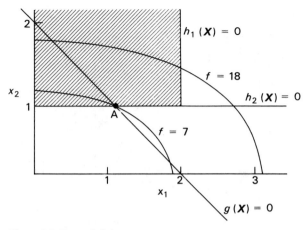

Figure 9.7 Example 9.4.

makes unnecessary the explicit solution of some variables in terms of others and that insight into the system is offered by the multipliers. It should be appreciated that in most cases the equations that have to be solved simultaneously are non-linear, therefore iterative numerical techniques will have to be applied.

Example 9.4

Solve the minimization problem of Example 9.3 subject to the following inequality constraints

$$h_1(x_1, x_2) = x_1 - 2 \leqslant 0$$
$$h_2(x_1, x_2) = 1 - x_2 \leqslant 0$$

The problem and its solution (point A) is illustrated in Fig. 9.7. This is of course a trivial example but it will serve to illustrate the short cuts necessary to arrive at a solution.

Equations (9.22) for this problem give

$$
\left.
\begin{aligned}
\frac{\partial F}{\partial x_1} &= 4x_1 + \lambda_1 + \mu_1 = 0 \\[4pt]
\frac{\partial F}{\partial x_2} &= 10x_2 + \lambda_1 - \mu_2 = 0 \\[4pt]
\frac{\partial F}{\partial \lambda} &= x_1 + x_2 - 2 = 0 \\[4pt]
\frac{\partial F}{\partial \mu_1} &= x_1 - 2 = 0 \text{ if } \mu_1 > 0 \text{ or } \mu_1 = 0 \\[4pt]
\frac{\partial F}{\partial \mu_2} &= 1 - x_2 = 0 \text{ if } \mu_2 > 0 \text{ or } \mu_2 = 0
\end{aligned}
\right\} \qquad (9.23)
$$

A formal way of solving the problem is to solve the first three equations successively with the four possible sets obtained from the last two equations, calculate the four costs, and pick as the solution the lowest cost that satisfies the inequality constraints. This is a laborious procedure and instead the following reasoning can be used.

If X_p^* is the optimal point with p inequality constraints active and $C(X_p^*)$ is the corresponding cost, then it is reasonable to assume that the cost $C(X_{p+1}^*)$ with $p+1$ constraints active will be higher than $C(X_p^*)$. In other words, we are seeking the cost with the minimum number of active constraints. A reasonable strategy is to start with all inequality constraints inactive, i.e., all values of $\mu = 0$ and solve the problem. If this solution violates a number of inequalities, these are brought in one at a time and in combinations until a minimum cost solution is found.

Applying this strategy to the solution of our problem, we know from Example 9.3 that the solution without inequality constraints is $x_1 = 1.43$, $x_2 = 0.57$. This solution violates $h_2(X)$, therefore we have to solve Eqs. (9.23) with $\mu_1 = 0$, $\mu_2 > 0$.

$$4x_1 + \lambda_1 = 0$$
$$10x_2 + \lambda_1 - \mu_2 = 0$$
$$x_1 + x_2 - 2 = 0$$
$$1 - x_2 = 0$$

which give

$$x_2 = 1, x_1 = 1, \lambda_1 = -4, \mu_2 = 6, f_{\min} = 7$$

The relative values of λ_1 and μ_2 indicate that the cost is more sensitive to changes in the inequality rather than the equality constraint.

9.5.4 The Solution of the O.E.D. Problem

We have now acquired the tools to tackle simple o.e.d. problems, but first let us look at the difficulties involved in solving the problem in its full complexity.

The relationship between cost and injected power in Eq. (9.1) could be of quadratic order. Owing to the slack bus active power injection being a Z variable, the total cost of generation of Eq. (9.2) turns out to be a complicated non-linear function of U. If the system loss is not negligible, the generation cost is not only a function of the active power injections at generation nodes but also of the way the reactive power is routed through the system from suppliers to consumers. We therefore should ideally minimize the cost with respect to injected active and reactive powers. The complications are compounded by the engineering constraints that impose limits not only on U variables but also on X and Z variables whose values are not under our direct control.

Such complications render the solution of the o.e.d. problem by the straightforward Lagrange, Kuhn–Tucker multiplier method extremely uneconomical in computing time. Other more powerful techniques and short cuts were therefore developed.

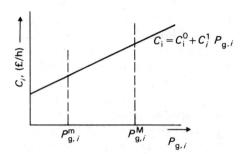

Figure 9.8 Linear cost function.

In what follows it is assumed that the power system under consideration has short transmission distances and that the losses are therefore negligible. This has the tremendous benefit of simplifying the equality constraint and making the solution independent of the reactive power flows or in other words the voltage profile. The two cases will be examined where the generation cost is first a linear and then a quadratic function of the injected active power.

(1) Linear cost function Some turbo-alternator sets have a linear cost function as shown in Fig. 9.8 where the cost in pounds per hour is plotted against the generated active power which is limited between a maximum and a minimum value.

The o.e.d. problem is described by the following:

Minimize
$$C = \sum_{i=1}^{n} C_i(P_{g,i})$$

subject to
$$g(P_{g,i}) = 0 = P_d - \sum_{i=1}^{n} P_{g,i}$$

and
$$h_i(P_{g,i}) \leqslant 0: \quad i = 1, 2, \ldots, n$$

which can be written
$$\begin{matrix} P_{g,i}^m - P_{g,i} \leqslant 0 \\ P_{g,i} - P_{g,i}^M \leqslant 0 \end{matrix} \quad i = 1, 2, \ldots, n$$

To solve the problem, form an augmented cost function C^*

$$C^* = \sum_{i=1}^{n} (C_i^0 + C_i' P_{g,i}) + \lambda \left(P_d - \sum_{i}^{n} P_{g,i} \right)$$
$$+ \sum_{i=1}^{n} \mu_i^m (P_{g,i}^m - P_{g,i}) + \sum_{i=1}^{n} \mu_i^M (P_{g,i} - P_{g,i}^M)$$

Taking partial derivatives of C^* with respect to all variables

$$\frac{\partial C^*}{\partial P_{g,i}} = C_i' - \lambda - \mu_i^m + \mu_i^M = 0 \tag{9.24}$$

$$\frac{\partial C^*}{\partial \lambda} = P_d - \sum_{i=1}^{n} P_{g,i} = 0 \tag{9.25}$$

$$\frac{\partial C^*}{\partial \mu_i^m} = P_{g,i}^m - P_{g,i} = 0 \text{ for } \mu_i^m > 0 \text{ or } \mu_i^m = 0 \tag{9.26}$$

$$\frac{\partial C^*}{\partial \mu_i^M} = P_{g,i} - P_{g,i}^M = 0 \text{ for } \mu_i^M > 0 \text{ or } \mu_i^M = 0 \tag{9.27}$$

For Eqs. (9.24), (9.26), and (9.27), $i = 1, 2, \ldots, n$.

Rather than considering all the possible permutations among Eqs. (9.24) to (9.27) let us take the following short cuts:

(1) We can rule out the possibility that for some i, $\mu_i^m > 0$ and $\mu_i^M > 0$ as $P_{g,i}$ cannot be at the same time on its upper *and* lower limit.

(2) If for some i the inequality constraints are inactive, i.e.,

$$\mu_i^m = \mu_i^M = 0 \text{ then } P_{g,i}^m < P_{g,i} < P_{g,i}^M$$

and from Eq. (9.24) $C_i' = \lambda$.

Furthermore, if $C_j' < C_i' = \lambda$ then from Eq. (9.24) we can conclude that $\mu_j^M > 0$ and from (1) above that $\mu_i^m = 0$ therefore from Eq. (9.27) $P_{g,j} = P_{g,j}^M$.

(3) If $C_j' > C_i' = \lambda$ then the converse is true, i.e.,

$$\mu_i^M = 0, \qquad \mu_i^m > 0$$

and from Eq. (9.26)

$$P_{g,j} = P_{g,j}^m$$

The short cuts have led us to the conclusion that if the ith generator is between its limits, the remaining generators are either at their lower or upper limit, depending on whether their C' is larger or smaller than C_i'.

The analysis leads to the following strategy for o.e.d. A table is made up of the available generating units with their corresponding values of the incremental cost coefficient C' in ascending magnitude, e.g.,

Unit	C' (£/MW h)	
2	C_2'	
5	C_5'	
7	C_7'	Ascending
13	C_{13}'	magnitude
10	C_{10}'	↓
1	C_1'	
etc.	etc.	

For a given load if unit 13 is operating between its limits, units 2, 5, and 7 are at their upper limit and units 10, 1, etc. at their lower limit. In practice it is

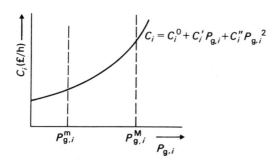

Figure 9.9 Quadratic cost function.

arranged that not all the units below 13 are at their lower limit but perhaps only 10 and 1, so that spinning reserve is ensured.

The above table is known as the merit order list of the units and this method of ordering generation is known as the 'order of merit' method. This policy of o.e.d. is of course so obvious that the solution of the above problem using λ and μ multipliers resembles the proverbial sledgehammer to crack a nut! Nevertheless, the solution illustrates the application of the method and the tricks required to arrive at an answer with relatively little labour.

(2) Quadratic cost function The majority of generating units have a non-linear generation cost function that can be adequately described by the quadratic cost of Fig. 9.9.

For simplicity, assume at the outset that there are no inequality constraints; this reduces the problem to minimizing

$$C = \sum_{i=1}^{n} C_i = \sum_{i=1}^{n} C_i^0 + C_i' P_{g,i} + C_i'' P_{g,i}^2$$

subject to

$$g(P_{g,i}) = P_d - \sum_{i=1}^{n} P_{g,i}$$

The augmented function is

$$C^* = \sum_{i=1}^{n} C_i + \lambda \left[P_d - \sum_{i=1}^{n} P_{g,i} \right]$$

and the partial derivatives give

$$\frac{\partial C^*}{\partial P_{g,i}} = \frac{\partial C_i}{\partial P_{g,i}} - \lambda = 0: \quad i = 1, 2, \ldots, n \tag{9.28}$$

$$\frac{\partial C^*}{\partial \lambda} = P_d - \sum_{i=1}^{n} P_{g,i} = 0 \tag{9.29}$$

From Eq. (9.28)

$$\frac{\partial C_i}{\partial P_{g,i}} = \lambda: \quad i = 1, 2, \ldots, n$$

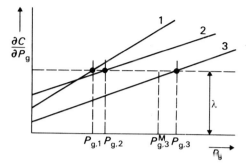

Figure 9.10 Equal incremental cost solution.

where $\partial C_i/\partial P_{g,i}$ is known as the 'incremental cost' of the ith generator. For a quadratic cost function

$$\frac{\partial C_i}{\partial P_{g,i}} = C_i' + 2C_i'' P_{g,i} = \lambda: \quad i = 1, 2, \ldots, n \tag{9.30}$$

i.e., for optimum economic dispatch the incremental cost of all generators should be identical and equal to λ subject to the satisfaction of Eq. (9.29).

Figure 9.10 shows the equal incremental cost solution for a three-generator system. The value of λ should be such that

$$P_{g,1} + P_{g,2} + P_{g,3} = P_d$$

Generation upper and lower limits can be taken into account without the explicit use of μ multipliers. Let us, for example, assume that in the three-generator system the unconstrained solution for $P_{g,3}$ in Fig. 9.10 exceeds $P_{g,3}^M$. In that case we set $P_{g,3} = P_{g,3}^M$ and we solve the equal incremental cost problem for $P_{g,1}$ and $P_{g,2}$ only, with a modified demand given by $P_d - P_{g,3}^M$.

(3) The lossy system Finally a few words will be said about the lossy system. If the transmission loss P_l is not negligible, the augmented cost function is

$$C^* = \sum_{i=1}^{n} C_i + \lambda \left(P_d + P_l - \sum_{i=1}^{n} P_{g,i} \right)$$

the partial derivatives of which give

$$\frac{\partial C^*}{\partial P_{g,i}} = \frac{\partial C_i}{\partial P_{g,i}} - \lambda \left(1 - \frac{\partial P_l}{\partial P_{g,i}} \right) = 0: \quad i = 1, 2, \ldots, n \tag{9.31}$$

$$\frac{\partial C^*}{\partial \lambda} = P_d + P_l - \sum_{i=1}^{n} P_{g,i} = 0 \tag{9.32}$$

From Eq. (9.31) the incremental cost of the ith generator is

$$\frac{\partial C_i}{\partial P_{g,i}} = \lambda \left(1 - \frac{\partial P_l}{\partial P_{g,i}} \right)$$

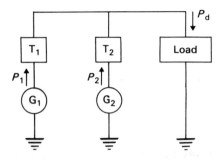

$C_1 = 0.1 - P_1 + P_1{}^2$ $\qquad$ $C_2 = 0.75 + 0.5 P_2 + 0.5 P_2{}^2$

$\qquad\qquad$ $P_d = 3.5$ p.u. $\qquad\qquad\qquad$ **Figure 9.11** Example 9.5.

which can be written as

$$\frac{\partial C_i}{\partial P_{g,i}} w_i = \lambda \tag{9.33}$$

where

$$w_i = \cfrac{1}{\left(1 - \cfrac{\partial P_1}{\partial P_{g,i}}\right)}$$

The system loss is a Z variable and therefore a complicated function of X and U variables, therefore the evaluation of $P_1/P_{g,i}$ is not easy. Such difficulties do not concern us here; however, we are interested in the insight provided by Eq. (9.33). The fraction $\partial P_1/\partial P_{g,i}$ is known as the 'incremental transmission loss' and describes the extra system loss incurred by an increment of active power injection by the ith generator. The larger the incremental transmission loss, the larger is the 'penalty factor' w_i, the harder the generator is penalized. In other words, an economic generating unit located at the end of a long transmission line may be less attractive than a less economic unit located near a load centre.

Example 9.5

In the power system of Fig. 9.11 two generators with fuel costs C_1 and C_2 are supplying load L through transmission lines T_1 and T_2.

The transmission losses associated with the powers P_1 and P_2 injected by the generators are given approximately by $P_{11} = 0.06P_1^2$ and $P_{21} = 0.03P_2^2$.

Using the Lagrange multiplier method calculate P_1 and P_2 for optimum economic dispatch.

The augmented cost function is

$$C^* = C_1 + C_2 + \lambda(P_1 + P_2 - 0.06P_1^2 - 0.03P_2^2 - P_d)$$

The partials are

$$\partial C^*/\partial P_1 = -1 + 2P_1 + \lambda(1 - 0.12P_1) = 0 \tag{9.34}$$

$$\partial C^*/\partial P_2 = 0.5 + P_2 + \lambda(1 - 0.06P_2) = 0 \tag{9.35}$$

$$\partial C^*/\partial \lambda = P_1 + P_2 - 0.06P_1^2 - 0.03P_2^2 - 3.5 = 0 \tag{9.36}$$

Eliminating λ from Eqs. (9.34) and (9.35)

$$\frac{1 - 0.12P_1}{1 - 0.06P_2} = \frac{-1 + 2P_1}{0.5 + P_2}$$

from where

$$P_1 = 0.728 + 0.456P_2 \tag{9.37}$$

Substituting Eq. (9.37) into Eq. (9.36)

$$0.728 + 0.456P_2 + P_2 - 0.06(0.728 + 0.456P_2)^2 - 0.03P_2^2 - 3.5 = 0$$

which after rearrangement becomes

$$0.0425P_2^2 - 1.416P_2 + 2.804 = 0$$

the solution of which is

$$P_2 = 2.117 \, \text{p.u.}$$

and from Eq. (9.37)

$$P_1 = 1.679 \, \text{p.u.}$$

Finally

$$\lambda = \frac{1 - 2P_1}{1 - 0.12P_1} = -2.95$$

9.6 SECURE ECONOMIC DISPATCH

In this final section of the chapter the ideas developed on automated power system control are implemented on a power system model controlled in real time by a digital computer.[3]

There is really no need to involve the reader in a detailed description of the model and the computer, as we are interested only in the outcome of the simulation. Very briefly, the model used consists of generators, loads, transmission lines, transformers, circuit breakers, instrumentation for monitoring bus voltages, active and reactive powers, and breaker status. The generating plant is simulated by electronic analogue models of the turbine, governor, synchronous generator, and a.v.r. The loads are also simulated by electronic models that allow an infinitely variable choice of active and reactive load settings. These settings can be adjusted in real time by the digital computer to match typical load demand patterns.

The digital computer communicates with the model through an interface consisting of analogue-to-digital (a–d) and digital-to-analogue (d–a) converters. A block diagram of the on-line control strategy is shown in Fig. 9.12. The data from the model instrumentation are collected by the computer and processed by a state estimator to obtain a reliable data base. An optimum

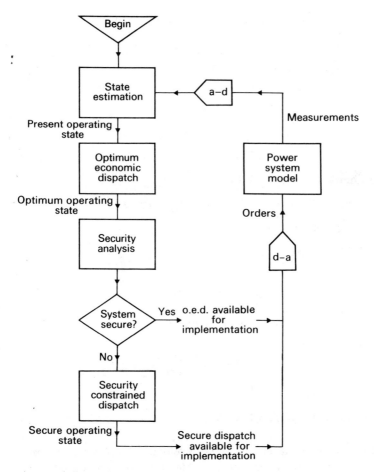

Figure 9.12 Block diagram of on-line control strategy.

economic dispatch is then performed with the information supplied by the state estimator. The sophistication of the o.e.d. program can be tailored to the character of the network under control. A security analysis is then carried out on the optimum operating state. If this state is found to be secure, the difference between the present and the o.e.d. schedule of generation is the control required to satisfy at minimum cost the present demand of the system. If the security analysis (which simulates the occurrence of line outages) reports line overloadings, a set of constraints is derived which if satisfied ensure secure operation. These constraints are incorporated in a simple o.e.d. algorithm that determines the necessary rescheduling of power which departs minimally from the most economic schedule and simultaneously satisfies the security criteria.

There are certain situations when the security-constrained o.e.d. fails to

Table 9.1 Security list

Outage of line	Effect on line	Pre-outage current	Post-outage current	Capacity	Comment
1–2	1–3	0.256 63	0.883 86	0.400	OVERLOADED
1–3	1–2	0.544 67	0.814 69	0.600	OVERLOADED
2–3	1–3	0.256 63	0.329 81	0.400	
2–3	2–4	0.679 01	0.830 42	1.000	
2–4	1–3	0.256 63	0.477 16	0.400	OVERLOADED
2–4	2–3	0.228 97	0.739 00	0.650	OVERLOADED
2–4	3–5	0.334 43	0.892 83	1.000	
3–6	1–2	0.544 67	0.575 70	0.600	
3–6	5–6	0.170 34	0.539 37	0.650	
3–5	1–2	0.544 67	0.387 10	0.600	
3–5	2–4	0.679 01	0.849 30	1.000	

find a feasible solution. In that case the program endeavours to arrive at a schedule of generation resulting in an operating state that is less vulnerable, and reports to the control engineer those outages whose occurrence would result in other lines becoming overloaded.

The network of Fig. 9.13 was set up on the model to test the behaviour of the control system. A gross error was introduced in the P and Q measurement of line 1–2. The data shown in parentheses correspond to the system state as assessed by the state estimator. For comparison, the measured line flows are also given. These measurements are, of course, also subject to error, nevertheless the reasonable agreement with the estimated values indicates the effectiveness of the state estimator in producing reliable data from corrupted measurements.

Table 9.1 shows a line outage security analysis performed on the network of Fig. 9.13 on one particular operating point. Four lines are seen to be overloaded. Table 9.2 gives the costs of generation in arbitrary units before economic dispatch, after an o.e.d., and finally after a security-constrained o.e.d. It is to be expected that there will be a cost increase when the extra constraints due to security have to be satisfied in the o.e.d. A security analysis using the

Table 9.2 Cost of different generation schedules

Unit	Present operation Generated power	Cost	Economic dispatch Generated power	Cost	Secure dispatch Generated power	Cost
1	0.851 3	89.21	0.500 2	46.27	0.380 0	33.56
2	0.350 6	35.58	0.244 8	23.62	0.351 6	35.70
3	0.116 5	8.41	0.552 9	48.61	0.564 0	49.81
	Cost units	133.20		118.50		119.07

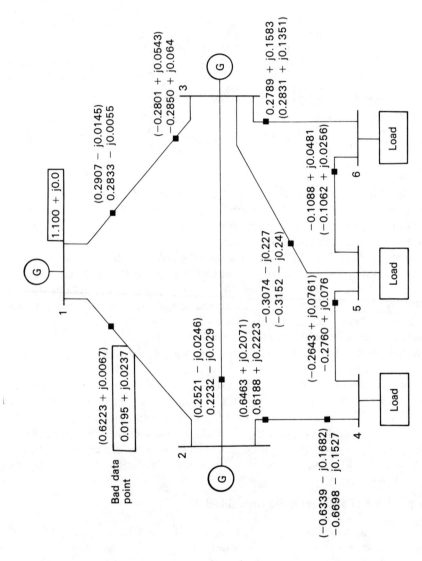

Figure 9.13 State estimation results on test system.

338

Table 9.3 Security analysis after optimum generation rescheduling

Outage of line	Effect on line	Pre-outage current	Post-outage current	Capacity	Comment
1–2	1–3	0.107 3	0.372 8	0.400	
2–4	3–5	0.410 9	0.892 7	1.00	
3–6	5–6	0.140 6	0.539 5	0.65	
3–5	6–3	0.370 2	0.598 5	0.70	

generation schedule under the secure dispatch of Table 9.2 confirms in Table 9.3 that all line overloads have been successfully eliminated. Table 9.3 contains only lines whose post-outage current is above 80 per cent of their capacity.

REFERENCES

1. W. F. Tinney and M. K. Enns, 'Controlling and optimising power systems', *IEEE Spectrum*, June 1974, p. 56.
2. N. Nabona and L. L. Freris, 'Optimisation of economic dispatch through quadratic and linear programming', *Proc. IEE*, **120**(5), 574, 1973.
3. E. Arriola-Valdes, L. L. Freris, C. B. Giles and M. J. Short, 'Real-time hybrid power system simulation for on-line control studies', *IEE Conf. on On-line Operation and Optimisation of Transmission and Distribution Systems*, London, 1976, p. 43.

TEN

FUTURE PROSPECTS

10.1 DEVELOPMENTS IN POWER SYSTEMS

The impact of digital computers, the intense global awareness of environmental and future energy shortage problems, and the realization of the vulnerability of power systems to breakdown, have opened up in the nineteen-seventies innumerable avenues for exciting research.

In this last chapter only some of these research avenues are explored very briefly, the intention being to convince students that some very exciting things are happening in the power field.

10.1.1 Power System Analysis and Planning

Traditional optimum economic dispatch programs can be augmented to incorporate functions that minimize the production of pollutants discharged in the atmosphere and the ageing effects of turboalternators. The efficiency of most generator units decreases and the maintenance costs increase when they are subjected to rapid power output fluctuations. Such aspects could be incorporated in o.e.d. programs. Furthermore, strategies could be devised to control the system optimally during energy shortages.

There is an urgent need for improvement in transient stability computation. For a large system, several tens of minutes of computing time are required on a powerful computer to simulate one second of real time. Such programs are hopelessly slow for on-line system stability assessment. However, hybrid computers (a combination of analogue and digital computers) can be used for simulation of power system dynamics and can be made to operate at speeds 100 times faster than real time. If cheap hybrid computers are developed in the future through breakthroughs in solid state technology, they could well be an indispensable tool for on-line assessment of system stability.

Power system planning, i.e., studies related to the future expansion of generation and transmission capability to meet expected demand growth, is increasingly performed on digital computers. It should be possible from such studies to determine the optimum kind, size, and location of generator units subject to reliability, size limit, fuel, environmental, or political constraints. Transmission planning studies determine when, where, and what kind of transmission lines should be built to provide reliable service between generators and consumers.

10.1.2 Power System Control

Security constrained optimization action could be expanded to include starting up of new generating units, load shedding, transformer tap changing, and reactive power adjustments. Such programs could be expanded to take action not only when the system is in its normal-insecure state but also when it is in the emergency or restorative state.

Communication between computer and control engineer, i.e., the computer–man interface, can be enhanced through the use of graphic c.r.t. terminals enabling the control engineer to absorb data readily or to introduce information in the computer.

The recent explosion in microcomputers is permeating the power scene and microprocessors are now used for substation protection and in the near future are likely to be used in complex control operations such as start-up and shut-down of generating sets. This multiplicity of computers in future power systems poses the problem of the relationship between central and satellite computers.

10.1.3 Power System Transmission

If we were to assume a future growth in demand, the power system engineer would be faced with a dilemma. Is it preferable to increase the number of large power stations that are invariably located remotely from load centres or to build a large number of smaller power stations near the load centres with the possibility of using total energy schemes? The first solution requires expansion of the transmission system with the related problems of rights-of-way and visual pollution. Alternatively, existing rights-of-way could be exploited more intensively through u.h.v. transmission or use of superconducting cables.

The second solution is attractive if the capital cost of the total energy scheme and the more stringent emission control from chimneys are not prohibitively expensive.

Microwave transmission provides an attractive alternative if microwave generators could be designed to operate at very high powers.

10.2 ALTERNATIVE ENERGY SOURCES AND CONCEPTS

At this point we may ask some pertinent questions. How sensible is it to pursue blindly an ever-increasing expansion and complexity of power systems? Is it not likely that such future power systems may offer more problems than solutions to our energy needs? Complexity could reach such an extent that no one person could adequately grasp the system and all its internal interactions. Local and central computers would then be taking decisions on the basis of programs written by power system engineers with only superficial knowledge of the workings of the system. Under severe contingency conditions it may happen that no computer or control engineer knows what is the best action to take to avert system breakdown.

Excessive centralization is vulnerable and, some would say, socially undesirable. It is vulnerable in the sense that considerable disruption could be caused by damage to overhead lines by a weapon as simple as a rifle. It is socially undesirable in the sense that technical specialization of personnel in power stations means that political power resides in fewer and fewer workers. If the miners can bring the UK to its knees in eight weeks the power engineers could do it in eight minutes.

Centralization has other disadvantages. At least half of an average consumer's electricity bill is fixed distribution costs to pay the overheads of the energy system. This includes not only transmission lines, transformers, and meters and people to read them, but also planners, accountants, billing computers, and advertisers. At present, power systems are supplied mainly from non-renewable fuels. Some economists claim that the cost of such fuels should not be determined by impersonal market forces but that they should be defined by a replacement philosophy. If that was seriously accepted then fossil fuels would become very expensive and energy from renewable sources would become economic overnight.

The power engineer should therefore think very hard on the pros and cons of centralized electric systems and of the effective exploitation of renewable energy sources.

By their nature some renewable energy sources are more suitable to decentralized applications, e.g., solar and wind energy, while others are more suitable to large scale exploitation, e.g., tidal and wave energy. In any case, these sources distribute the technical risk among many diverse technologies and the engineering involved is of an altogether different and more forgiving order than that required in development of, e.g., fast breeder reactors. The cost of failure is also lower in both loss of hardware and damage to people. Critics of alternative energy technologies argue that such technologies are speculative and would absorb a great deal of time and money for their development, as if the technology of large fast breeder reactors and controlled nuclear fission consumes little money and effort and is assured of success!

The power system engineer's job is energy management. Whether he likes it or not energy is now, and will increasingly be, an issue involving not only

Figure 10.1 The 2 MW aerogenerator at Tvind. (*Courtesy of Vestjysk Energikontor.*)

technical but also political, social, and even ethical decisions. The engineer should face this fact and be prepared to declare his policy rather than retire to his laboratory and let politicians and accountants decide for him.

The two examples which follow illustrate the sort of research pursued at present in the exploitation of renewable energy sources.

Figure 10.1 shows the 2 MW windmill built by a college community at Tvind in Denmark. The three-blade rotor has a diameter of 54 m and is

Figure 10.2 Wave energy extraction system. (*Courtesy of the University of Edinburgh.*)

mounted on a 53 m tall slipformed concrete tower. The rotor drives an alternator through a gearbox. The intention is to use the energy output for the heating of the college and to feed into the local electricity grid any spare energy.

Figure 10.2 shows an artist's impression of a string of 'nodding ducks' for the extraction of energy from waves. The ducks, which are being developed in the UK, would rock to and fro and are designed to extract a very high percentage of the energy in the waves.

10.3 POWER ELECTRONICS

Developments in solid state technology have influenced power engineering not only through the extensive use of digital computers but also through solid state devices whose rating classifies them as 'power' rather than 'electronic' components.

Thyristors have been developed with voltage ratings of several kilovolts and current ratings of several hundred amps. Transistors are following close behind with voltage and current ratings one order of magnitude lower but nevertheless increasingly used in small and medium sized motor drives.

Present electric locomotives and electric cars under development are based on solid state switching devices for the control of speed.

Thyristors have now completely displaced gas and plasma valves in the field of rectification and have played a major role in the spread of d.c. transmission round the world. Transmission of electric energy using a.c. is beset by a number of problems, some of which are enumerated below:

(1) With long transmission lines the series reactance of the line becomes so large that it imposes a severe limit to the maximum power that can be transmitted.
(2) Underground or undersea high voltage a.c. cables are limited in length to a few tens of kilometres because of the considerable reactive current associated even with short runs of such cables.
(3) If it is desirable to interconnect neighbouring power systems (of the same nominal frequency) within a country or over national frontiers the systems have to be synchronized; this presents considerable problems. If the systems are of different frequencies, a.c. interconnection cannot be used.
(4) With ever increasing expansion and interconnection of power systems, short circuit levels are on the increase. This requires uprating of circuit breakers.

Direct-current transmission, in which a.c. is converted into d.c. at a rectifier station, then electric energy is transmitted over a d.c. line to an inverter station where d.c. is converted back into a.c., can solve all the problems that bedevil a.c. transmission. In fact eighteen d.c. links are in operation at the time of writing and another six are under construction.

A considerable boost was given to d.c. transmission when mercury arc valves were recently replaced by thyristors in the rectifier and inverter stations. Such a thyristor valve rated at 133 kV and 2 kA in bridge connection is shown in Fig. 10.3. There is no mistaking that solid state devices will find increasing applications in the power systems of the future.

It is worth mentioning also that considerable research is being conducted in the development of cheap solid state photoelectric devices. A breakthrough here will have an enormous impact on the energy scene.

The problem of developing an 'ideal' adjustable speed drive has yet to be solved. D.C. machines have their commutation problems. Induction motors need power conditioning equipment which 'dislikes' lagging power factor and is expensive. For very large machines, especially in the transport business, the size and weight of a solid state inverter is still excessive and the search for the variable speed induction motor not preceded by a power-conditioning unit goes on.

A 'near miss' in this direction occurred in the nineteen-fifties when an exotic form of induction motor with a spherical rotor having a two-dimensional copper grid embedded in it produced continuously variable speed with constant efficiency, but only at a cost and weight penalty that fell short of the demands of the economy.[1] A 150 hp motor weighed approximately five

Figure 10.3 Thyristor valve for d.c. transmission under test. (*Courtesy of GEC Power Engineering Ltd.*)

times as much as a fixed speed drive for the same power. Ordinarily, there is always a power/weight penalty when variable speed is demanded, but it is of the order of three times the constant speed value, rather than five. With induction motors the *basic* efficiency η depends on the amount by which the rotor speed v falls below the speed of the travelling magnetic field v_s (see Chapter 7), thus $\eta = v/v_s$. Efficient speed control is therefore obtained only by a change in v_s rather than in v, and v_s is determined from Eq. (7.1) i.e.

$$v_s = 2(\text{pole pitch}) \times (\text{supply frequency})$$

v_s can therefore be varied only by variation of pole pitch or frequency.

Before the days of solid state devices, a few installations had limped along (relatively) on frequency changing using steel tank versions of the mercury arc converter. A quite large proportion of the railways of Europe used a.c. commutator motors supplied at 50/3 Hz, the 'divide by 3' being effected in mercury arc converters, and studies were made of the use of these devices to act as spongy links that would allow interconnection between two large distribution systems whose frequencies could not be guaranteed to coincide.[2]

Even in a self contained distribution network a.c. is not without its disadvantages. Peak voltage on an a.c. system is $\sqrt{2}$ times the equivalent d.c. value and since the modern level of transmission voltage is sufficient to rip electrons off the atoms of air near to cables, corona loss would be reduced by transmitting d.c. or, what is more useful, the transmission voltage could be raised for the *same* corona loss. D.C. cables would not radiate and interfere with telephone lines and other systems. Conversion to and from a.c. could be effected at efficiencies matching those of the transformer, whose services would still be required, for the alternator must remain, for as far ahead as we can yet see, the principal generating device of nations. Yet even here we can never afford to be complacent. Contrary to popular opinion, research into 'heavy' electrical engineering has not 'all been done'.

10.4 NEW TYPES OF ELECTRICAL MACHINE

Progress in a science or a technology can rarely be expressed in graphical form as a steadily rising graph against a base of time. Rather, it is a series of steep slopes, each of which reaches a new 'plateau'. Each plateau may occupy months, years, decades, or even centuries. The electrical engineers of the late nineteenth and early twentieth centuries were so ingenious that the plateau on electrical machine innovation lasted for close on half a century before new materials, new demands, and a revolution in economic accounting produced new gradients in the progress chart. It will suffice here to illustrate each of these three facets with a single example, for to do more is to risk the ever present tendency to put the most recent decade under a lens, as it were, that magnifies its importance out of all proportion in relation to what has gone before.

Under 'new materials' is included the use of superconductor. To be granted a metallic substance with *zero* resistance should surely be, for the engineer, the equivalent of satisfying the greed of a latter-day King Midas, yet as in the legend of that foolish king, the blessing carries a sting in the tail. All electric currents that flow in conductors, whether superconducting or otherwise, are known to produce magnetic field. When the magnitude of the

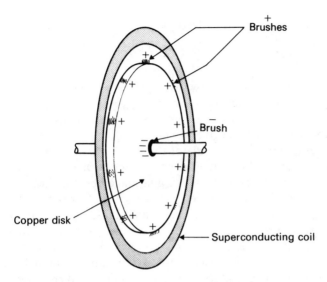

Figure 10.4 Basic topology of a superconducting d.c. generator.

current changes, so does that of the field and such change produces the property we call inductance. A circuit of superconductor therefore has a time constant (L/R) of infinity, a Goodness Factor of infinity, surely as desirable as Midas's gold? The only snag is that it takes an infinite time to set up finite current within such a circuit! Yet our gods are more merciful than were those of Midas, and there *are* ways of getting a current to flow in superconducting circuits.

Nevertheless, industry has been slow to take up large scale application of this technology. A homopolar, d.c. generator built in Newcastle upon Tyne, England, at a cost of about a million pounds serves to point out the necessity for essentially simple shapes of superconductor, in this case a single circular coil; and although the complete design was more sophisticated than that shown in Fig. 10.4, the disk being multiplexed and some iron included near to the disks in an otherwise open-air magnetic circuit, one has to admit that the basic topology was certainly that of Fig. 10.4, which is, of course, that of Faraday's disk dynamo. Nor can it be said that, as in the case of the latter machine, natural developments will follow the same course as did those of the nineteenth century, for the later shapes need no inventing. They are both known and seen to be unsuitable.

10.4.1 Linear Motors and Magnetic Levitation

The only place where any other large scale use of superconductor has been attempted is where the second of our conditions obtains, i.e., in a situation of new demand. In this case the demand is for higher speeds in ground transport

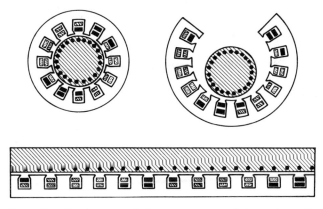

Figure 10.5 Development of a linear motor by 'splitting and unrolling' a rotary machine.

to replace inland air flights, as noise, pollution and fuel shortage all begin to militate against aircraft. High speed transport developments in the nineteen-sixties and seventies have been aimed at replacing the wheel either as driving member, or as both driving member and weight supporter.[3] The high speed propulsion unit of the future will undoubtedly be some form of 'linear' motor,[4] that is, a motor whose form can be imagined by considering a conventional cylindrical motor to have been cut along a radial plane and 'unrolled', as shown in Fig. 10.5. Any kind of rotary motor can be so treated, but the magnetic machines (reluctance and hysteresis) are ruled out for transport on scale considerations. The 'big three'—induction, synchronous, and d.c. machines—are all undergoing development for transport in linear form.

So far as electromagnetic suspension is concerned, there are three distinct systems under investigation. Two of these have both been confusingly listed under the same name—'Maglev'—yet one is a magnetic system, the other an electromagnetic. The design constraints in regard to the size limitations in the two systems are diametrically opposed. In the first, electromagnets, mounted on the vehicle and fed from an amplifier, lie beneath a pair of steel rails and support the vehicle by magnetic attraction. Stabilization is achieved by a sensing mechanism that monitors the current fed from the amplifier so as to maintain a clearance of the order of a centimetre between magnets and rail. This clearance cannot be greatly exceeded and this is the limitation imposed by the 'smaller the better' rule. Track rails require very accurate alignment for such a system and it is very doubtful whether it can be made commercial for transport beyond the urban and suburban range of speeds (up to perhaps 80 mile/h (130 km/h)).

The second 'Maglev' system uses superconducting coils on the vehicle with open magnetic circuits. When such d.c.-carrying coils move rapidly over aluminium or copper sheets laid in the track, induced currents in the latter largely oppose the primary currents and repulsion occurs between the two. It is generally reckoned that sufficiently large lifting forces for full scale vehicles occur only at speeds above 50 mile/h (80 km/h). Stabilization laterally requires vertical track plates and the whole may be combined in a U-shaped guideway. The disadvantage of the superconducting system merely for levitation is that large inductive drag forces are produced, but the latter can be overcome if the levitation flux is also used to propel the vehicle. This can be done by fitting what amounts to a linear 'armature' winding in the track that may reproduce either that of a d.c. machine, or the a.c. stator winding of a synchronous machine. In both cases, solid state power-conditioning equipment is required in trackside stations, for the track must be energized over short sections only, that move with the vehicle, for two reasons:

(1) The cost of energization.
(2) The ability to run more than one vehicle at a time on the same track.

The present state of the art is that the Japanese National Railways[3] are developing the d.c. linear motor with cryogenic 'Maglev', while a German industrial combine on the one hand, and Canadian industry/university[3] resources on the other, are developing the synchronous machine with cryogenic 'Maglev'. The magnetic 'Maglev' system is being developed by Japan Air Lines, British Rail,[5] and a German consortium.

In the UK, a third alternative has been described as a 'magnetic river'.[6] In this system no superconductor is used, but a single-sided linear induction motor has been so shaped that it provides lift and guidance simultaneously from the same set of coils that provides the forward thrust. This invention arose as a byproduct of more fundamental research into linear motor applications. The speed of the field of an a.c. rotary machine is given by the supply frequency f divided by the number of pole pairs. In linear machines the speed is independent of the *number* of poles; the more fundamental concept, that any travelling wave moves along one complete wavelength λ in one cycle of events, serves to set the rule for linear speed v_s thus:

$$v_s = f\lambda$$

or, writing pole pitch $p(= \lambda/2)$,

$$v_s = 2pf$$

This equation applies equally well, of course, to rotary machines, provided v_s and p are measured around the airgap periphery. From consideration of Goodness Factor it emerges that good induction motors that convert large quantities of power should only very rarely have values of v_s smaller than 10 m/s. Experience of industrial machines bears out this truth absolutely.

At first sight, this one rule appears to throw out almost all possibilities for linear motors, except in high speed transport. The fact that this is not so is due to two causes, the first of which is the last of the three new developments with which we began this chapter, i.e., an awareness of the importance of overall economics. The second is that there are fundamentally different design concepts in linear motors from those well proven in rotary machine design. We shall deal with each of these in turn.

In the early days of a new technology the leading question is invariably: 'Can it be done at all?' When the fact that it can is established, the next question is always: 'Is it economically viable?' In the case of electrical machines in the era 1900–40 this question was immediately converted to, 'What is its efficiency? What is its power factor?'—and nothing else. Even in the mid nineteen-seventies, the product of efficiency and power factor was still being used as sole argument against the use of linear motors for high speed transport. In other fields of application, however, the questions asked in respect of rotary machines in the earlier part of the century were also asked—'What will it cost?' 'What will it weigh?'

The success of linear motors commercially was not due to consideration of any of these questions alone. (Incidentally, all of them are G-dependent.) Other economic factors, none of which depends on G, outweighed the usual 'big four' (efficiency, power factor, power/weight, power/cost). They were:

reliability;
absence of maintenance costs;
ease of transportation from location to location;
absence of noise;
absence of pollution;
convenience;
cleanliness;
absence of physical contact, and others.

A linear motor scores virtually 100 per cent on each of these items.

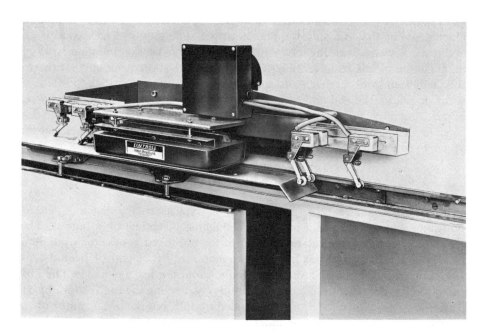

Figure 10.6 A linear motor fitted to operate a sliding door. (*Courtesy of Linear Motors Limited.*)

Figure 10.7 Back tension being applied by linear motors, without contact, to aluminium sheet during its manufacture. (*Courtesy of Alcan Aluminium Ltd. and Redman B. & K. Ltd.*)

Figures 10.6 and 10.7 show two typical applications of linear induction machines. The first is a single application to a sliding door. The second is an application where nothing else will do so well. Sheet aluminium, during manufacture, needs back tension applied while the sheet is moving. Hitherto this had been done by felt pads rubbing on the surface. A single particle of swarf or grit on the pad and surface scratches are produced. Contactless force, in this case, improved the end product beyond what any other device could do.

The second facet that put linear motors into the economic market was an attack on the G-dependent quantities by application of the equation

$$\frac{B_g}{J_s} = k \frac{p}{g} \qquad \text{(see ref. (3))}$$

Figure 10.8 compares the geometry of a typical rotary machine stator punching and a linear punching for a machine of comparable output. The larger slot, carrying with it opportunities for improved conductor/insulation ratio, enables the current loading J_s to be increased by a factor of around 4, as compared with the rotary motor having the same slot leakage factor. The flux density B_g is reduced by a factor of 5 (simply by dividing the tooth width by 5). Thus the specific force ($\propto B_g \times J_s$) is divided by 1.25, but the linear motor often involves the addition of stator units only, as in travelling crane applications

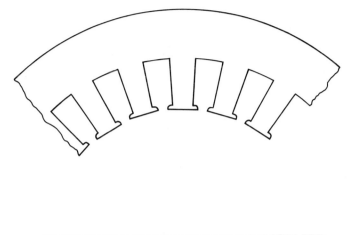

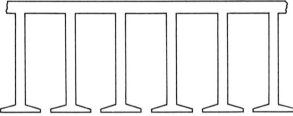

Figure 10.8 Comparison between the slot geometries of rotary and linear induction motor stators.

where the stator operates directly into the already existing steel girder.[7] Thus the linear motor shows advantage in first cost (especially where rotary drives involve gearing) and in thrust/weight—two G-dependent factors.

The most recent developments in linear induction machines have been concerned with overcoming the problem of long pole pitches in machines required for high speeds, where mains frequencies have been almost mandatory. In such cases the primary and secondary cores have produced a 'bottleneck' in the magnetic circuit and demanded prohibitively large amounts of steel, especially in the track member of a transport system. A new family of machines (from which the 'magnetic river' emerged also) was developed in which the main flux was returned transversely, as illustrated in Fig. 10.9, which is schematic only. The construction of a transverse flux machine is shown in Fig. 10.10 where both longitudinal and transverse primary lamination has been used for ease of manufacture. In such cases the magnetic circuit is three-dimensional, as shown in Fig. 10.11, rather than the more usual essentially planar circuits of rotating machines and transformers.[8]

One variation in linear motor topology involves the 're-rolling' of a flat linear motor, as shown in Fig. 10.12. The resulting tubular structure carries the advantage of producing linear motion from stator coils completely devoid of end windings. The disadvantages stem first from the need to support the

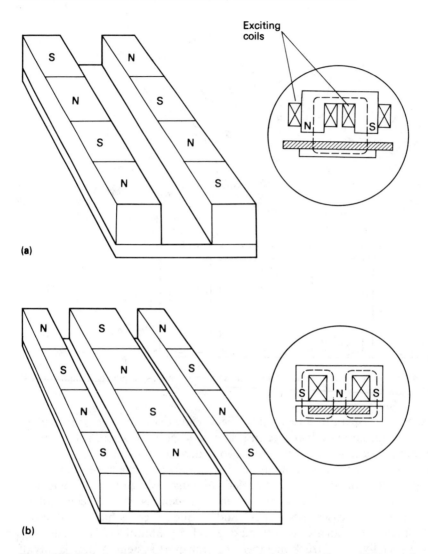

Figure 10.9 Basic topology of a transverse flux motor (t.f.m.): (a) C-core, (b) E-core. Insets show cross sections, indicating how the magnetic circuits would be closed by the track members in transport applications.

central secondary core and conductor and this can only be done conveniently at the ends of the primary. Second, the whole of the flux per pole must traverse the secondary axially and this can restrict the power output severely. However, this second disadvantage was removed entirely by the invention, in 1971, of the transverse flux tubular motor[9] whose helical stator windings (Fig. 10.13) project flux diametrically through the central core, enabling laminated steel disks to suffice as a secondary core. In many cases the available space into

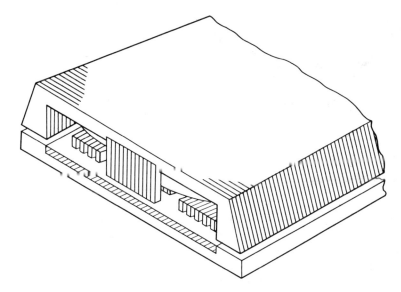

Figure 10.10 One method of constructing a t.f.m. using crossed laminations (lying in two planes).

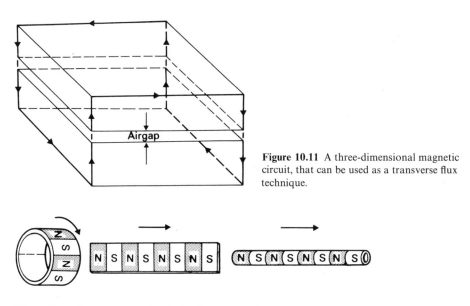

Figure 10.11 A three-dimensional magnetic circuit, that can be used as a transverse flux technique.

Airgap

Figure 10.12 Development of a tubular linear motor by a 're-rolling' of a flat motor.

which the primary flux can spread, outside of the windings, is sufficient to remove the need for primary steel entirely.

There are over three thousand published papers on linear machines. A useful summary is shown as reference 10.

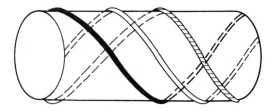

Figure 10.13 Transverse flux tubular motor windings are helical.

10.4.2 Slotless Machines

An interesting speculation, to be treated merely as an exercise in appreciating just how near are the properties of copper, steel, and free space to those that would be economically prohibitive to the whole of power engineering success as we know it, is to imagine that it was announced last week that a new material had been discovered having twenty times the conductivity of copper at normal temperatures and costing no more than copper per metre of wire. The question is, how would it change the design of machines radically?

The answer, we believe, is that it would eliminate the use of slots in both primary and secondary members, certainly of induction machines. The earliest d.c. machines carried their conductors on the surface, mainly because it was believed that the flux cutting rule demanded that the working flux be detectable *at the actual conductor position*. The usual flux density in a conductor at the bottom of a slot is less than ten per cent of the airgap flux. That the 'linkage' rule applies in the flux cutting situation so far as absolute position is concerned was more or less forced upon the Victorian engineers by their inability to hold surface conductors in place against the centrifugal and electromagnetic forces.

Modern developments in bonding would have eliminated this hazard and indeed a number of organizations are now asking the question: 'Will ordinary copper be good enough to make a surface wound machine?' The answer to this final question will rest, as did those to all previously solved questions, with those who are prepared to try.

REFERENCES

1. F. C. Williams, E. R. Laithwaite and J. F. Eastham, 'Development and design of spherical induction motors', *Proc. IEE*, **106A** (30), 471–84, 1959.
2. H. Caillez, W. Casson, P. Laurent and H. R. Schofield, 'Design and construction of the cross-Channel d.c. interconnector', *Proc. IEE*, **110**, 603–18, 1963.
3. E. R. Laithwaite (ed.), *Transport Without Wheels*, Elek, London, 1977.
4. E. R. Laithwaite, *Induction Machines for Special Purposes*, Newnes, London, and Chemical Publishing Company, New York, 1966.
5. D. Linder, 'Design and testing of a low speed magnetically suspended vehicle', *Proc. IEE 2nd Conf. on Advances in Magnetic Materials and their Applications*, London, 1976.

6. J. F. Eastham and E. R. Laithwaite, 'Linear induction motors as "electromagnetic rivers"', *Proc. IEE*, **121**, 1099–1108, 1974.
7. G. V. Sadler and A. W. Davey, 'Applications of linear induction motors in industry', *Proc. IEE*, **118**, 765–76, 1971.
8. E. R. Laithwaite, J. F. Eastham, H. R. Bolton and T. G. Fellows, 'Linear motors with transverse flux', *Proc. IEE*, **118**, 1761–67, 1971.
9. J. F. Eastham and J. H. Alwash, 'Transverse-flux tubular motors', *Proc. IEE*, **119**, 1709–18, 1972.
10. E. R. Laithwaite, 'Linear electric machines—a personal view', *Proc. IEEE*, **63**, 250–90, 1975.

INDEX

Printed and bound in Great Britain by
Morrison & Gibb Ltd., London and Edinburgh